INTEGRATED SERVICES DIGITAL NETWORKS

The Artech House Telecom Library

Telecommunications: An Interdisciplinary Text, Leonard Lewin, ed.
Telecommunications in the U.S.: Trends and Policies, Leonard Lewin, ed.
The ITU in a Changing World by George A. Codding, Jr. and Anthony M. Rutkowski
Integrated Services Digital Networks by Anthony M. Rutkowski
The Deregulation of International Telecommunications by Ronald S. Eward
Machine Cryptography and Modern Cryptanalysis by Cipher A. Deavours and Louis Kruh
The Competition for Markets in International Telecommunications by Ronald S. Eward
Teleconferencing Technology and Applications by Christine H. Olgren and Lorne A. Parker
The Executive Guide to Video Teleconferencing by Ronald J. Bohm and Lee B. Templeton
World-Traded Services: The Challenge for the Eighties by Raymond J. Krommenacker
Microcomputer Tools for Communication Engineering by S.T. Li, J.C. Logan, J.W. Rockway, and D.W.S. Tam
World Atlas of Satellites, Donald M. Jansky, ed.
Communication Satellites in the Geostationary Orbit by Donald M. Jansky and Michael C. Jeruchim
Communication Satellites: Power Politics in Space by Larry Martinez
New Directions in Satellite Communications: Challenges for North and South by Heather E. Hudson
Television Programming Across National Boundaries: The EBU and OIRT Experience by Ernest Eugster
Evaluating Telecommunication Technology in Medicine by David Conrath, Earl Dunn, and Christopher Higgins
Measurements in Optical Fibers and Devices: Theory and Experiments by G. Cancellieri and U. Ravaioli
Fiber Optics Communications, Henry F. Taylor, ed.
Mathematical Methods of Information Transmission by Kurt Arbenz and Jean-Claude Martin
Telecommunications Systems by Pierre-Gerard Fontolliet
Techniques in Data Communications by Ralph Glasgal
The Public Manager's Telephone Book by Paul Daubitz
The Cable Television Technical Handbook by Bobby Harrell
Proceedings, Conference on Advanced Research in VLSI, 1982, MIT
Proceedings, Conference on Advanced Research in VLSI, 1984. MIT

INTEGRATED SERVICES DIGITAL NETWORKS

ANTHONY M. RUTKOWSKI

This Book is Dedicated to
Kathleen and Kelly
and
Those in
CCITT Study Group XVIII
and Other Organizations Around the World
Who Are Working to Bring About ISDNs

CONTENTS

APPENDICES

PREFACE

This book focuses on the most far-reaching development in the field of telecommunications today. In the late 1970s it became apparent to many telecommunication system planners that electronics technology at every level, from small components to large networks, was evolving toward a common end. They foresaw the complete interconnection and interoperability of nearly all computer and telecommunication systems through a common network model to provide universal and complete services for capturing, storing, processing, and transporting most of the information which society would retain or communicate. They expected such advanced information systems to be rapidly implemented throughout the world during the next two decades.

To bring it about, millions of dollars of resources were expended to bring together experts from around the world to develop sufficient basic details to allow equipment to be manufactured and the networks constructed. The model was described by the term "integrated services digital network," or ISDN.

This book portrays this bold vision by integrating and explaining a broad array of technical and policy material emanating from the principal international and domestic forums. It begins by describing the ISDN concept, explaining the significance of each word in the term. The forums in which the activity occurred are discussed, followed by an exploration in detail of the principal product — the current accepted international standards for ISDNs. The thousands of documents associated with this effort are listed for reference.

As it became obvious to telecommunications policy-makers that these pursuits would result in a concrete product, the Federal Communications Commission (FCC) instituted a formal proceeding. This resulted in comments filed from many companies and a *First Report* on ISDN. The details of this proceeding, as well as associated proceedings and actions by the FCC and other federal agencies are presented.

The book concludes with a look toward the future. This includes a review of the issues to be considered by the International Consultative Committee for Telephone and Telegraph (CCITT) during the 1985–1988 activity period and by the scheduled World Administrative Telegraph and Telephone Conference (WATTC) in 1988. At the domestic level, the published pursuits of several nations are noted and possible regulatory issues are raised.

Also included in the appendix is an extensive bibliographic listing of published articles and papers relating to ISDN.

A basic primer on ISDN necessarily contains considerable specialized and complex material. The material runs the gamut from international organization descriptions and US domestic policy considerations to the seemingly arcane world of digital communication protocols. The introduction as well as many chapter sections attempt to assist the reader with less familiar material.

It is difficult to estimate the ultimate significance of these ISDN developments. The state of the art is evolving exponentially, and it is increasingly difficult to make assumptions concerning the capability and costs of parts and equipment. ISDN planners have attempted to circumvent this difficulty by concentrating on basic general network characteristics and developed detailed specifications for only a few "reference points" in the network.

ISDN developments over the last few years certainly represent the most comprehensive and extensive development of an integrated telecommunication and information system model ever undertaken. The results will significantly shape the future direction of such integrated systems. Whether ISDN achieves universal proportions remains to be seen. In any case, ISDN-like networks are likely to constitute a significant aspect of the world that we and our children will enjoy.

INTRODUCTION

This introduction begins with the basics. It dissects the constituent parts of the term "integrated services digital network," describing what these words mean individually and collectively. This is followed by a discussion of ISDN as a concept.

In describing the ISDN concept, several different perspectives are included: an ISDN as a "black box," the user looking in at an ISDN, the network looking out at the user, interconnecting ISDNs with other ISDNs or other networks. These different views are necessary to completely describe all the many facets of the complex collection of facilities and software that constitute an ISDN.

Most of these descriptions rely on classical engineering approaches relating to networks, interfaces, *et cetera*. ISDNs are carefully structured into many carefully interrelated and well-defined components which are subdivided into even more minute parts. This attention to organization and detail is reflected in the CCITT's ISDN Recommendations.

Although these descriptions are relatively generic, there is a tendency to orient the details around existing telecommunication and information facilities. For example, the initial standards were fashioned around the capabilities of existing wire-pair local loops for telephone service. This is a practical consideration, necessitated by the hundreds of billions of dollars invested in existing systems around the globe. Entirely new networks simply cannot be implemented on a widespread basis without regard to what already exists and is in use.

Nonetheless, the entire effort has been marked with a certain air of excitement at looking toward the future. The infusion of new ideas and people in the ISDN effort is a phenomenon unmatched in the field of telecommunication standards development, particularly on the international level. Perhaps this atmosphere was best captured by one Bell system expert at a recent meeting, who remarked: "It took 100 years to design and build the existing telecommunication network; we're now designing and building a new network in twenty."

I.1 ISDN: The Term

The term ISDN *is* cumbersome. It arose, however, through a natural evolutionary process in the International Telecommunication Union's (ITU) International Consultative Committee for Telegraph and Telephone (CCITT). Each of the words in the term "integrated services digital network" has special significance. They are discussed below in the same way as they were originally assembled, in reverse order.

Network

Each of us has some familiarity with the term "network": the telephone network, television networks. The word conveys the image of a complex organization of paths.

Figure I-1

It is precisely this image that forms the basis for the definition of network in the ISDN lexicon. The lines in the Figure I-1 represent transmission paths and are referred to as "links." Links may be a copper wire pair, optical fiber, radio transmission path, or any other means of conveying information bearing signals from one location to another. The points of interconnection represent locations at which the signals are routed or switched to alternative links and are referred to as "nodes."

All networks, large or small, can be represented in this fashion. Thus, the term network is defined.

> **Network,** a set of nodes and links that provides connections between two or more defined points to facilitate telecommunication between them.[1]

Because networks are often large and complex, communications engineers deal with them in a very structured way. They attempt to reduce a large, complex organizational problem to many smaller, simpler problems. Thus, when the international systems designers first began to meet and discuss ISDN, they frequently represented it with nothing more than a simple cloud-like diagram. (See Figure I-2.)

Figure I-2

The diagram is still found in some of the more generalized CCITT ISDN standards. This simple "cloud" represents an enormous, complex "black box" network of links and nodes, capable of providing all the electronic information services a user could desire. From simple telephone calls to sophisticated data bank inquiries to bulk information transfers to broadcast entertainment — all would be available from the ISDN.

The edges of the cloud represent the boundary that separates the ISDN from the outside world. Somehow, users must be able to connect their terminal equipment — whether it be a telephone, data terminal, television set, or local information system — to the network. The ability to connect such external equipment is a regulatory policy matter that varies considerably among different countries. Nonetheless, provision must be made for users to connect to ISDN, and this becomes the basis for the most significant type of interface to the network: user-network interfaces.

Thus, a user-network interface must be added to the diagram. (See Figure I-3.)

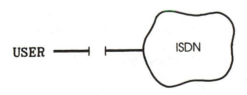

Figure I-3

Of course, countless numbers of such interfaces exist, one for every network user or, in the case of a shared interface, users. Since the beginning of the ISDN effort in the late 1970s, most of the work has been focused on this interface and the boundary between the user and the network.

The ability of ISDN to exist as a truly universal model is largely dependent on a well-defined, stable user-network interface. The definition consists of a complex set of "protocols" that describe the precise details of how a user accesses and communicates with the ISDN, from the level of the physical connector to the manner in which "intelligent" conversation occurs between user and network.

This enormously complicated endeavor is made even more difficult because of rapidly changing technological capabilities and costs, diverse national regulatory policies, and the impact on potential market opportunities.

The characteristics of the interface can be viewed two ways: from inside or from outside the network. The responsibilities and capabilities of both the user and the network must be defined from both perspectives. For example, at the outset of this section, ISDN capabilities were described in two very general terms: universality and intelligence. From the user's viewpoint at the user-network interface, universality means the ability to go anywhere in the world with any compatible electronic terminal and, if connected to an ISDN, obtain similar kinds of services through common protocols. From the network perspective at this interface, universality means a responsibility to support virtually any kind of user or user terminal.

Similarly, ISDN "intelligence" has a different meaning from user and network perspectives at the interface. For the user, it implies the ability to engage in an extremely sophisticated dialogue with the network to define the desired information services. It also implies the ability to obtain an extremely diverse range of information services in addition to mere transmission of information. From the network perspective, however, intelligence is an aggregate of resources which may be located in diverse locations and must be assembled to support each user service.

Some of those resources may only be accessible through another network. It is unlikely that a monolithic, all-encompassing ISDN will ever exist. The world consists of nation-states, and each would likely possess its own ISDN. Additionally, many different telecommunication networks will continue to exist and must be utilized by an ISDN to provide requested services. This results in additional internetwork interfaces to our cloud diagram. (See Figure I-4.)

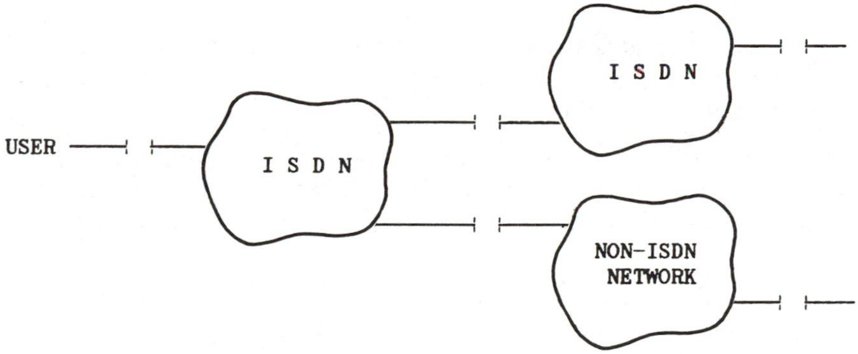

Figure I-4

It is obvious that a vast array of clouds could be appended to those in the diagram. This ability to interconnect ISDNs in a modular fashion is one of their more attractive features, and leads to the widespread, global extent of their application.

Digital

In order for information to be conveyed over a telecommunication network, it must be converted into an electronic representation, i.e., a signal, and then converted back again to a useful form.

For example, when we speak into a telephone, a device in the handset senses the varying sound pressure and produces an electronic representation of the instantaneous changes in pressure. After coursing the telephone network in electronic form, the signal enters a device at the other end that reverses the process. Such conversion devices are frequently called "transducers," Latin for "leading across."

There are many diverse kinds of information: voice, picture, text, physical measurement, commands, *et cetera*. For each, there are transducers capable of producing an electrical signal or converting it back to a form capable of being understood by humans.

Two fundamentally different kinds of signals may be produced. The older kind of representation, still in extensive use today, is referred to as an "analog signal" (also spelled *analogue*). This kind of signal consists of electrical energy levels that *continuously* vary to represent the information.

Analogue signal, a signal, one of whose characteristic quantities follows continuously the variations of another physical quantity representing information.[2]

The newer kind of representation that is quickly replacing the analogue technique is referred to as a "digital signal." This kind of signal has "well-defined discrete levels for discrete lengths of time" to represent the information.

Digital signal, a discretely-timed signal in which information is represented by a number of well-defined values that one of its characteristic quantities may take in time.[3]

This means that the information is coded to produce signals at only fixed levels. The simplest and most widely used are various binary coding that represent, for example, an alphabetical character as a string of eight successive time intervals during which the signal is only permitted to vary between two levels.

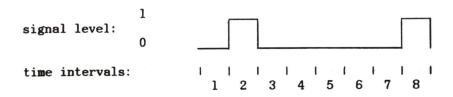

ASCII Representation of the Letter A

Figure I-5

In Figure I-5, assuming that the time intervals are one microsecond, the letter A is represented by a signal that exists at signal level 0 during the first microsecond; level 1 during the second; level 0 during the third through seventh; and level 1 during the eighth. When the letter A is depressed on a computer keyboard, the above signal is automatically produced.

More transient phenomena such as audio and visual information are generally converted to an analog signal, then "sampled," i.e., measured, at a sufficiently rapid rate to allow satisfactory reconstruction of the analog signal. Most of the entire electronics industry, including telecommunications, is rapidly converting to digital signal representation.

The significant benefits include the ability of computer systems to manipulate the signals to provide a myriad of additional related services, highly efficient use of telecommunication facilities for most types of signals, and essentially perfect reproducibility. This last attribute can be supported by anyone who has listened to a Compact Disc digital audio recording.

This conversion to digital is furthered by the availability of integrated semiconductor circuits to perform all the digital functions at increasingly more favorable cost/performance ratios. For all the above reasons, the digital conversion began occurring, and continues to occur, irrespective of ISDN developments.

For example, in the United States, the American Telephone and Telegraph (AT&T) Company began to set the conversion process in motion for the telephone network many years prior to the initiation of ISDN discussions in the CCITT. Similarly, Satellite Business Systems (SBS) introduced an entirely new, satellite-based, totally digital network for domestic communications.

Services

"Service" is a relatively vague term, simply referring to that which is provided to the user. It gives rise, however, to some of the major national and international controversies associated with the merging of information and telecommunication systems.

In the past, services were rather clear. Such offerings as telephony, telegraphy, facsimile, telex, *et cetera*, are good examples. Their provision was generally relegated to a monopoly run or regulated by the national government.

However, in recent years, when additional options began to be added to such discrete offerings, such as call forwarding, speed dialing, and voice mail, the distinctions began to lose their significance.

The same occurred when so-called value-added entrepreneurs began to lease traditional service capabilities from the monopolies and add new features. In an advanced digital network environment, numerous resources both inside and outside the network can be individually aggregated for each user request. Service distinctions tend to become technically meaningless, although there may be an operational and economic rationale for devising standard service packages.

Thus, the ISDN Recommendations focus more upon "service attributes" than on services *per se*. This is discussed at length in Chapter 4.

The subject, however, rises to an enhanced level of importance in an ISDN environment because of the ability for such a network to provide all services. Questions relating to who will provide what services or portions of services, how they will be provided, to whom they will be provided, and for how much, become highly significant matters. This is patent in the comments filed with the FCC in the *ISDN Notice of Inquiry*, which is considered in Chapter 8.

In the ISDN environment, an already difficult task of lending some order to the provision of services is exacerbated by the desire to superimpose regulatory policy frameworks, or create exclusive market opportunities. This promises to make the elaboration of service definitions a source of perennial difficulty.

At the international level, these difficulties are even reflected in the recently adopted definition of the term:

> **Service,** that which is offered by an administration or RPOA [Recognized Private Operating Agency] to its customers in order to satisfy a specific telecommunication requirement.[4]

A phrase in this definition relating to who will provide the service is obviously not necessary. Entities other than administrations and RPOAs are also capable of offering telecommunication services.

Because of the importance of defining and structuring services, the associated terms deserve careful examination and use. For example, the term "telecommunication," devolves to an almost incidental part of a whole range of information services that can be often conveniently and efficiently provided by the network. The ISDN CCITT Recommendations tend to avoid the use of the word "telecommunication" by dividing services into two categories: "bearer services" and "teleservices."

The former service represents "information transport," a synonym also used in the Recommendations, while the latter represents all services including transport. This fundamental ISDN dichotomy is often confused with another dichotomy used in the United States for national regulatory purposes, the "basic/enhanced dichotomy." These two different categorical distinctions have entirely different purposes and definitions. They will be discussed in greater detail in Chapters 4 and 7 dealing with service definitions and the Federal Communications Commission's ISDN-related proceedings.

Integrated

The term "integrated" has been used to express two different digital network attributes. The earlier use of the term had a kind of physical connotation of being able to connect digital networks in such a manner that they functioned as one network, i.e., they were operationally integrated. This situation arose when digital networks began to interconnect.

More recently, during early ISDN discussions, the term "integrated" began to be used to describe the ability of one network to provide a multiplicity of services such as telephony, data, *et cetera*. The newly adopted I-Series Recommendations resolves the ambiguity by setting forth definitions for both connotations.

Digital network, integrated digital network, a set of digital nodes and digital links that uses integrated transmission and switching to provide digital connections between two or more defined points to facilitate telecommunication between them.[5]

Integrated services network, a network that provides or supports a range of different telecommunication services.[6]

Thus, the word "integrated" as it is used in ISDN, implies both of these meanings.

Integrated Services Digital Network

The formal meaning of the term ISDN is a composite of the individual words discussed above. In addition, the new CCITT definition for ISDN adopted at the VIIIth CCITT Plenary in October 1984 makes explicit reference to user-network interfaces.[7]

Integrated services digital network (ISDN) [F: reseau numerique avec integration de services (RNIS); S: red digital de servicios integrados (RDSI)], an integrated services network that provides digital connections between user-network interfaces.[8]

The reference to user-network interfaces lends additional emphasis to the importance of these interfaces and is the vestige of more lengthly and emphatic versions of this phrase that appeared during the 1981-84 activity period of the CCITT. For example, in 1981, the draft definition was:

Integrated Services Digital Network (ISDN), a network evolved from the telephony IDN that provides end-to-end digital connectivity to support a wide range of services, including voice and non-voice services, to which users have access by a limited set of standard multipurpose customer interfaces.[9]

I.2 The ISDN Concept

The terms discussed above are the current formal CCITT definitions for ISDN and its constituent works. The phrase ISDN is, however, used in a variety of different ways in non-CCITT settings. The most generic is what might be called the "ISDN concept."

Conceptually, the term ISDN represents a technical and operational model for a universal, intelligent, and modular information system that includes as a prominent feature the transport of information on a global scale. In its ultimate form it would be even more ubiquitous than our electrical power system. It would provide anyone, anywhere, with any kind of electronic information service desired. What we now visualize as separate telecommunication and information systems would be completely integrated.

ISDN facility resources (processing, storage, transmission links, and imbedded software in the form of programs and information), whether they be the network's, user's or outside vendor's, would be dynamically aggregated by the network. This means that an ISDN will call upon these resources and allow them to operate in concert.

If specific resources are not specified by the user, the network would be free to decide for itself which would be utilized. It may also substitute similar resources from microsecond to microsecond to achieve maximum network efficiency. This "dynamic aggregation" process creates the ISDN functional elements (virtual transport paths, intelligence, information, and storage), which in turn provide the user with any desired communication or information services. It also allows services to be custom tailored for the user. The user would even have the capability to alter the parameters of the service during the course of its provision by the network.

Specific applications of the ISDN concept differ among the many national administrations, network operators, and individuals who are active in the field. The Appendix A bibliography lists scores of articles, papers, and documents describing different ISDN variations.

One of the leading figures in the development of ISDN in the United States is Irwin Dorros of Bell Research. His view is a mixture of vision and pragmatism and perhaps as succinct a statement on ISDN as exists anywhere.

[W]hat is the ISDN? It is a public end-to-end digital telecommunications network providing a wide range of user applications.

[The challenge of] network planners is to fulfill the ISDN's potential as much as possible. As usual when vision and reality meet, there is a crucial period of challenge when basic decisions must be made. Now is such a time, a time when standards are being set, large amounts of capital are being committed, and new industry structures are being mandated not just in Washington, D.C., but in other capitals around the world.

The main motivation for the ISDN are the economies and flexibilities which the integrated nature of the network would foster. The economies occur because many of the emerging new services are digital and can be combined with existing services to use an integrated transport capability at a significantly lower overall cost than it would take for each service to use a separate architecture. Where we may have different perspectives is in such issues as: first, the details under this scheme; second, interface specifications; third, how to go about making this happen; fourth, what should motivate the evolution; fifth, how rapidly it will evolve; and sixth, what will be the services driving the evolution process.[11]

REFERENCES

1. Rec. No. I.112, para. 305, CCITT Red Book (1985).
2. *Id.* para. 103.
3. *Id.* para. 105.
4. *Id.* para. 201.
5. *Id.* para. 306.
6. *Id.* para. 307.
7. The term "integrated services digital network," was first coined during the 1973-76 CCITT Study Period and appeared in Sixth Plenary Assembly (1976) Orange Book list of terms. The international standards for "digital networks" were developed in the CCITT in the 1960s, followed by further work on "integrated digital networks." As this work progressed and the state-of-the-art advanced, system planners foresaw the ability to provide a wide variety of services from these networks. This was reflected by adding the word "services." It was not until after the VIIth Plenary Assembly in November 1980, however, that work occurred on fleshing out anything beyond a definition.
8. Rec. No. I.112, para. 308, CCITT Red Book (1985).
9. Report of the Meeting of Working Party XVIII/1 (ISDN), CCITT Period 1981-1984, Doc. COM XVIII-No. R3 at 5 (July 1981). *Ref.* Definition of Integrated Services Digital Networks (ISDN), CCITT Doc. COM XVIII-No. 31 (April 1981) [contribution of AT&T].
10. Preamble, Final Report to the VIIIth CCITT Plenary Assembly (Part V), Document AP VIII-97-E (June 1984).
11. I. Dorros, Keynote Address to the IEEE Communications Society, Integrated Services Digital Networks Symposium (ISDN '81), Innisbrook, Florida (7 January 1981); published as Dorros, "Challenge and Opportunity of the 1980s: the ISDN," Vol. 200, No. 4, *Telephony* (26 January 1981) at 43, as amended *Telephony* (23 February 1981) at 28.

I Decision-Making Forums and their Work

Most of the developments related to ISDN are manifested within the many forums used by national administrations, network operators, government agencies, manufacturers, and users to reach a consensus on ISDN attributes so that they can begin its implementation. An integrated worldwide telecommunication and information network necessarily requires a consensus on basic attributes among all the parties.

These forums involve an extremely broad variety of international and domestic organizations and agencies. See Table I-1. The developments are all part of a process that starts with some individual drafting a document that is submitted to, and works its way through, a complex array of bodies — assemblies, study groups, committees, commissions, and working groups that meet to integrate and distill this material into a product, usually by consensus of the participants.

Part of understanding ISDN issues and developments is understanding these players and the processes utilized. These first two chapters are intended to provide a succinct overview of the international and domestic forums in which ISDN issues are considered.

Table I-1
Forums for the Consideration of
ISDN Issues and Planning

INTERNAT'L

```
                                              ITU
                                             CCITT
                                            PLENARY

  COM I    COM II   COM III   CCH IV    COM VII   CCH VIII   COM XI    COM XII   COM XV

  I/3      II/1     III/5     IV/2      VII/1     VIII/     XI/1      XII/3     XV/1
           II/2     III/6     IV/5      VII/2     VIII/     XI/2                XV/2
           II/3                         VII/3               XI/4                XV/3
           II/4                         VII/4               XI/5                XV/5
           II/5                         VII/5               XI/6                XV/6
           II/6                         3R ISDN


                          ITU
                          CCIR
                         PLENARY

             SG 4      SG 9      SG 11     CMTT

             WP 4C     WP 9A
             IWP4/2    WP 9C
```

REGIONAL

```
                 USA                                        USA
                CCITT                                      CCIR
                 NC                                         NC

      SG A    SG C    SG D    JWP                    USSG 4   USSG 9   USSG 11
                              ISDN
```

USA

```
                          NECA
                           T1

   T1C1     T1D1     T1M1     T1Q1     T1X1     T1Y1

   T1C1.2   T1D1.1   T1M1.1   T1Q1.3   T1X1.1   T1Y1.1
   T1C1.3   T1D1.2   T1M1.2   T1Q1.4   T1X1.2   T1Y1.2
            T1D1.3            T1Q1.5   T1X1.3   T1Y1.3
                                       T1X1.4
```

Table I-1
(Cont'd)

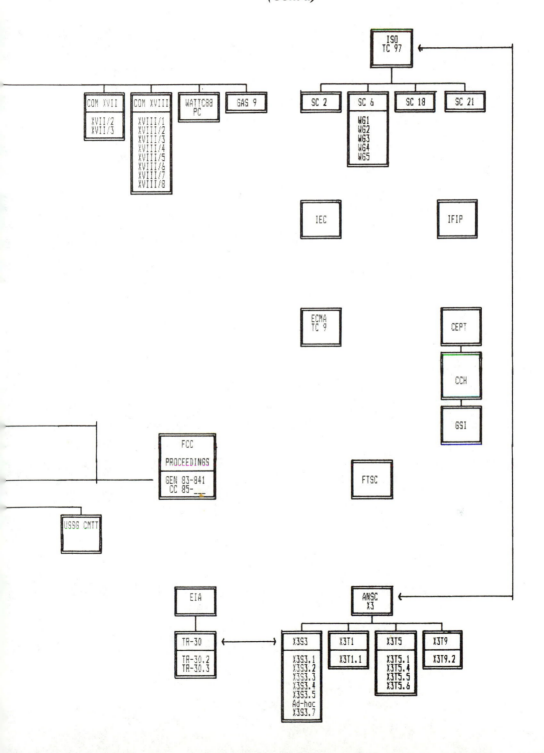

CHAPTER 1 — THE INTERNATIONAL TELECOMMUNICATION UNION AND OTHER INTERNATIONAL ORGANIZATIONS

At the global level, the two most active organizations in ISDN matters are the International Telecommunication Union (ITU) and the International Organization for Standardization (ISO).[1] At the regional level, the European Conference of Postal and Telecommunication Administrations (CEPT) is the only organization active in ISDN matters, although the European Computer Manufacturers Association (ECMA) does promulgate information systems standards that have some relevance to other ISDN forums. Additional international organizations are mentioned at the end of this chapter. Although most of the organizations participate in ISDN activities in the CCITT and ISO, most have not established their own ISDN forums.

1.1 The International Telecommunication Union

The ITU is the specialized international organization for telecommunication, at present comprised of 161 members.[2] The purpose of the ITU is to promote cooperation and development in the field of telecommunication, especially in the provision of worldwide services. The results of most ITU work are published as *Recommendations* of its consultative committees, although some provisions, largely relating to radio, are adopted as treaty agreements referred to as *Regulations*.

The scope of the ITU covers all aspects of telecommunication, including associated information systems. This results in activity increasingly overlapping with that of the International Organization for Standardization which has had primary jurisdiction over information systems.

The ITU principally brings together the interests of Administrations, i.e., the government agency in each country responsible for the provision of telecommunication services, typically the Ministry of Posts and Telecommunications (MPT) or Ministry of Posts, Telegraph and Telephone (PTT). In some countries, especially the United States, the "administration" is a complex mix of government agencies responsible for regulation (the Federal Communications Commission and the Department of Commerce), for international affairs (the Department of State), and for providing service to the public (a variety of Recognized Private Operating Agencies). The ITU work is largely carried out through some 175 technical bodies of widely varying size and formality, involving many thousands of experts. Currently, nearly 10,000 pages of provisions are adopted every four years. A relatively small proportion of work, relating almost entirely to radio, is carried out in several formal intergovernmental conferences.

The process of adopting a Recommendation normally occurs in the context of "questions," although those relating to radio are carried out in the context of "projects." They normally proceed from a draft status to an adopted status in the context of discrete four-year activity periods. At the end of each period, the provision is either adopted or passed on to the next four-year period. Adoption nearly always occurs by consensus.

Regulations are considered in the context of a single Administrative Conference at which adoption normally occurs by consensus. For all matters except those relating to radio, most of the substantive work actually occurs within Consultative Committee bodies. At present, there are no Regulations relating to ISDN.

Structurally, the ITU consists of a Plenipotentiary Conference, an Administrative Council, Administrative Conferences, the International Telegraph and Telephone Consultative Committee (CCITT),[3] the International Radio Consultative Committee (CCIR), the International Frequency Registration Board (IFRB), the General Secretariat, Secretary-General, Deputy Secretary-General, the CCITT Secretariat, the CCITT Director, the CCIR Secretariat, and the CCIR Director.[4]

Most of the ISDN related activity is confined to the CCITT, although some issues relating to radio are considered within the CCIR. In addition, a World Administrative Telegraph and Telephone Conference (WATTC), recently scheduled for 1988, may consider matters related to ISDN.[5]

1.1.1 The CCITT

General Infrastructure

The CCITT is comprised of a Plenary Assembly that meets every four years, and numerous study groups (SG) established by the Plenary Assembly.[6] The study groups in turn have their own plenary meetings and divide their work up among numerous working parties, working teams, and *rapporteurs*. The rapporteurs are individuals appointed to perform some specific drafting or liaison activity. This activity is assisted by a CCITT Secretariat staff located at ITU headquarters, Geneva. The principal staff are the CCITT Director, elected by the Plenary Assembly,[7] and the *conseillers*. The con-

seillers are technically knowledgeable consultants who are generally assigned
to a particular study group to facilitate the work of that group.

The dynamic nature of CCITT's work has resulted in constant reorganization during the last decade or two. The current study groups, as well as
the previous organization is shown in Table 1-1. The VIIIth CCITT Plenary
Assembly in October 1984 attempted to secure a more functional infrastructure to accomodate the ISDN environment. During the 1981–84 activity
period, Study Group XVIII[8] had jurisdiction over most ISDN matters, and
coordinated ISDN related work of other groups. That approach was changed
somewhat in the new organization which orients most of the CCITT study
groups around ISDN, and diffuses more of the responsibilities.

Table 1-1
Titles of CCITT Study Groups

Group	1981-1984	1985-1988
I	Definition and operational aspects of telegraph and telematic services	Definition, operation and quality of service aspects of telegraph, data transmission and telematic services
II	Telephone operation and quality of service	Operation of telephone network and ISDN
III	General tariff principles	General tariff principles including accounting
IV	Transmission maintenance of international lines/networks	Transmission maintenance of international lines, circuits and chains of circuits; maintenance of automatic and semi-automatic networks
V	Protection against dangers and disturbances of electromagnetic origin	Protection against dangers and disturbances of electromagnetic origin
VI	Protection and specifications of cable sheaths and poles	Outside plant
VII	New data communication networks	Data communication networks
VIII	Terminal equipment for telematic services	Terminal equipment for telematic services
IX	Telegraph networks and terminal equipment	Telegraph networks and terminal equipment

Table 1-1
(Cont'd)

X	[None]	Languages and methods for telecommunications applications
XI	Telephone switching and signalling	ISDN and telephone network switching and signalling
XII	Telephone transmission performance and local telephone networks	Transmission performance of telephone networks and terminals
XIII	[None]	[None]
XIV	[None]	[None]
XV	Transmission systems	Transmission systems
XVI	Telephone circuits	[None]
XVII	Data communication over the telephone network	Data transmission over the telephone network
XVIII	Digital networks	Digital networks including ISDN

This functional trend is likely to continue. Toward that end, a special Study Group S will meet during the 1985–88 activity period to consider an appropriate new infrastructure.

In addition to the groups shown in Table 1-1, there are a joint CCITT/CCIR Study Group, Special Autonomous Groups (referred to by their French acronym as the GAS groups), the Joint Plan Committees, and the CCITT Laboratory. The work of these groups occasionally addresses ISDN matters. For example, the CMV group on vocabulary defines ISDN related terms, and the GAS groups prepare handbooks describing various ISDN facets.

The Plenary Assembly also established a Preparatory Committee (PC) for the 1988 WATTC. In its attempt to devise *Regulations* for the new integrated telecommunication and information environment of which ISDN is representative, it is likely that ISDN concepts will filter their way into the work of the PC.

Study Group XVIII Infrastructure

At the international level, important ISDN related work has been done in many of the study groups, particularly VII, XI, and XVIII. The most

important of all these groups, however, is Study Group XVIII. This group
evolved out of former Special Study Group A in 1976, led by Theodor Irmer
of Germany until October 1984 when Mr. Irmer was rewarded for his
pioneering effort by election to the post of CCITT Director.

Table 1-2
Study Group XVIII Working Parties and Teams

1981-84 Activity Period

Working Parties	*Chairmen*
1. ISDN	H.K. Pfyffer (Switzerland)
2. Speech Processing	M. Decina (Italy)
3. Network Performance Objectives	V.I. Johannes (AT&T, USA)
4. Switching and Signalling	A. Roche (France)
5. Digital Equipments	K. Okimi (NTT, Japan)

Working Teams	*Chairmen*
WT1. Customer Access	W.S. Gifford (AT&T, USA)
WT2. Layer 1 Characteristics	V. DeJulio (SIP, Italy)
WT3. Network	J.C. Luetchford (BNR, Can)
WT4. Services	P. Kahl (FRG)
WT5. Signalling	B.N. Moore (BT, UK)
WT6. Switching	S. Kano (NTT, Japan)
WT7. Structure of the I-Series Recs.	H.K. Phyffer (Switzerland)
WTV. ISDN Terms	P.G. Clarke (BT, UK)

1985-88 Activity Period

Working Parties	*Chairmen*
1. Service Aspects	L. Ackzell (Sweden)
2. Network Aspects	J. Luetchford (BNR, Can)
3. User-network Interfaces, Layer 1	F. Lucas (France)
4. Architecture and Models	B.W. Moore (BT, UK)
5. Maintenance and General Aspects	T. Tomic (Yugoslavia)
6. Performance Aspects	V.I. Johannes (AT&T, USA)
7. Transmission Aspects	K. Okimi (NTT, Japan)
8. Speech Processing	M. Decina (Italy)

The intensive ISDN work of Study Group XVIII began after the 1980 Plenary Assembly and is reflected in Table 1-3. A detailed summary of activity is found in Part I of the study group's report to the Plenary Assembly,[9] and reflected in the bibliographic listing in Appendix A of this book.

During the 1980–84 activity period, the Vice-Chairmen of SG XVIII were M. Decina of Italy, V.I. Johannes of AT&T, K. Okimi of NTT, H.K. Phyffer of Switzerland, and A. Roche of France. Mr. Phyffer was made SG XVIII Chairman for 1985–88. Nearly all ISDN activities worldwide have been linked with the work of Study Group XVIII.

Table 1-3
Meetings of Study Group XVIII

1981-84 Activity Period

1981	1982
12–15 Jan 1981, Innisbrook	*11–15 Jan 1982, Darmstadt*
• Coordination	• Coordination
• ISDN Experts	*15–25 Feb 1982, Munich*
22 Jun — 1 Jul 1981, Geneva	• Coordination
• Plenary	• ISDN Experts
• Coordination	• Working Teams 1-6
• Working Parties 1-5	*10–22 Jun 1982, Geneva*
21–25 Aug 1981, Montreal	• Plenary
• Coordination	• Coordination
	• Working Parties 2-5
	• Vocabulary Party (non-ISDN)
	18–20 Oct 1982, Geneva
	• Drafting Group on Recs. I.xxw, I.xxx, I.xxy
	8–12 Nov 1982, Florence
	• Working Team 2

Table 1-3
(Cont'd)

1983	1984
10–25 Feb 1983, Kyoto	*9–24 Feb 1984, Brasilia*
• Coordination	• Coordination
• ISDN Experts	• ISDN Experts
• Working Teams 1-7	• Working Teams 1-5, 7
• Vocabulary Team (ISDN)	• Vocabulary Team (ISDN)
20 Jun–8 Jul 1983, Geneva	*24 May–1 Jun 1984, Geneva*
• Plenary	• Plenary
• Coordination	• Coordination
• Working Parties 2-5	• Working Parties 2-5
• Vocabulary Party (non-ISDN)	• Vocabulary Party (Non-ISDN)
• Working Teams 1-7	• Working Team 7
• Vocabulary Team (ISDN)	• Vocabulary Team (ISDN)
21 Nov–2 Dec 1983, Geneva	
• Coordination	
• Working Party 2	
• Working Teams 2-4	
12 Dec 1983, Geneva	
• Coordination with Study Groups III,VII,XI,XV,XVII	

1985-88 Activity Period

1985

17–25 Jan 1985, London
• Coordination (17-18 Jan)
• ISDN Experts (21-25 Jan)

17–27 Jun 1985, Geneva
• Plenary
• Coordination
• Working Parties 1-8

Dec 1985, Kyoto
• Coordination
• ISDN Experts

Product of the CCITT

The ultimate product of the CCITT is Recommendations. The entire field of telecommunication (except radio) has been codified by the CCITT with each major subdivision represented by a prefix letter. (See Table 1-4.)

Table 1-4
Outline of CCITT Recommendations

Series	Title
A	Organization and work of the CCITT
B	Means of expression (definitions, vocabulary, symbols, classification)
C	General telecommunication statistics
D	General tariff principles
E	Telephone operation, network management and traffic engineering
F	Telegraph operation and tariffs
G	Transmission: lines, radio-relay systems, radiotelephone circuits
H	Utilization of lines for telegraphy and phototelegraphy
I	Integrated services digital networks
J	Radio and television program transmissions
K	Protection against interference
L	Protection against corrosion
M	Maintenance of telephone circuits and carrier systems
N	Maintenance for sound-programme and television transmissions
O	Specification of measuring equipment
P	Telephone transmission quality. Telephone installations and local line networks
Q	Telephone switching and signalling
R	Telegraph channels
S	Alphabetical telegraph apparatus
T	Facsimile telegraph apparatus
U	Telegraph switching
V	Data transmission
X	New data networks
Z	Programming languages for SPC exchanges

These Recommendations are formally adopted at each Plenary Assembly, and known by the color of the outer covers of the published set of volumes and fasicles. For example, the CCITT Recommendations adopted by the Eighth Plenary Assembly in 1984 are referred to as the "Red Book." Table 1-5 not only depicts these colors and the associated Plenary Assemblies since 1956, but also traces the volumes containing digital standards and associated study groups over that period.

The work toward any Recommendation formally begins at a final study group plenary meeting preceding the CCITT Plenary Assembly. At this meeting, the questions to be considered during the next activity period are introduced and adopted by the study group. They become the first part of the study group's report to the Plenary Assembly at which the questions are routinely approved.

As the study group begins the next activity period, the list of questions becomes the first document of the period. At the first meeting of the study group during the period, the infrastructure of the study group is devised and the questions are apportioned among the working teams, parties, and rapporteurs.

During the remaining four years of the activity period, a variety of formal and informal meetings are held. Most tend to be in Geneva because of its central location, extensive meeting facilities, and ready availability of interpreters and support staff of the CCITT.

The work involves the consideration and production of four kinds of documents. The normal "submissions" to any meeting are referred to as "contributions" or "white documents." These are furnished to the CCITT Secretariat two to three months prior to the meeting, allowing their translation into the ITU's three official languages — French, English, and Spanish — and dissemination to all the participants in advance of their arrival at the meeting. During Study Group XVIII's 1981–84 activity period, 250 such contributions were submitted.

The activity has been occurring so rapidly, however, that such formal contributions are no longer the norm. Rather, the documents are simply brought to the meetings and distributed there. These are known as "delayed contributions," and 751 were submitted with SG XVIII during the same 1981–84 period. During the course of a meeting, a number of documents are typically submitted by rapporteurs or officers, prepared by drafting groups, and adopted by the meeting. These are known as "temporary documents." Several months later, the temporary documents comprising the report of the meeting are translated, typed, and distributed on buff color paper. For anyone attempting to influence or follow this activity, understanding these procedures and the documentation.[10]

Table 1-5
Chronology of CCITT Digital Standards Activity

CCITT Plenary Assembly	Color of Books	Digital Standards Adopted	Next Activity Period	Group
I 1956 Geneva	Red	—	1957–60	Working Party 43 (Data Transmission) [1st meeting — 1960]
II 1960 New Delhi	Red	—	1961–64	COM Sp. A Special Study Group A (Data Transmission)
III 1964 Geneva	Blue	Vol. VIII, V-Series	1965–68	COM Sp. A Special Study Group A (Data Transmission)
				COM XI (Telephone Switching & Signalling)
IV 1968 Mar del Plata	White	Vol. III, G-Series	1969–72	COM Sp. A Special Study Group A (Data Transmission)
		Vol. VI, G-Series		COM Sp. D Special Study Group D (Pulse Code Modulation)
		Vol. VIII, V-Series		COM XI (Telephone Switching & Signalling)
				GM NRD Joint Working Party (New Networks for Data Transmission)
V 1972 Geneva	Green	Vol. III, G-Series	1973–76	COM VII (New Networks for Data Transmission)

	Year/Location	Color	Period	Volume	Study Group
				Vol. VI, G-Series	COM XI (Telephone Switching & Signalling)
				Vol. VIII, V- & X-Series	COM Sp. A Special Study Group A (Data Transmission)
					COM Sp. D Special Study Group D (Pulse Code Modulation)
VI	1976 Geneva	Orange	1977-80	Vol. III, G-Series	COM VII (New Networks for Data Transmission)
				Vol. VI.1-4, G-Series	COM XI (Telephone Switching & Signalling)
				Vol. VIII.1, V-Series	COM XVII (Data Transmission)
				Vol. VIII.2, X-Series	COM XVIII (Digital Networks)
				Vol. X, Terms	
VII	1980 Geneva	Yellow	1981-84	Vol. III.3, G. 701-. 941	COM VII (Data Communication Networks)
				Vol. VI.1-8, G- & Z-Series	COM XI (Telephone Switching & Signalling)
				Vol. VIII.1, V-Series	COM XVII (Data Communication Over the Telephone Network)
				Vol. VIII.2, X.1-29	
				Vol. VIII.3, X.40-.180	COM XVIII (Digital Networks)
				Vol. X.1, Terms	
VIII	1984 Malaga-Torremolinos	Red	1985–88	—	[All except COM V and VI]

Unfortunately, the delayed contributions and temporary documents are only made available to meeting participants. Thus, any attempt to follow CCITT activity in a timely fashion is contingent upon either participating in the meetings or obtaining access to a participant's documents!

Most of the ISDN Recommendations are now found in the Red Book I-Series. Future work will modify these provisions and add to them — a subject covered in Chapter 9.

1.1.2 The CCIR

The International Radio Consultative Committee (CCIR) is an ITU organ similar to the CCITT. However, its methods of work are considerably different due to the nature of their subject matter and the relative isolation that has historically existed between the two groups. The CCIR work is narrowly confined to radio propagation and facilities, and has engaged in only a fraction of the activity as the CCITT. Another significant difference is the comparatively reduced status of CCIR Recommendations. The CCITT's Recommendations are generally regarded as mandatory by operators of international telecommunication networks. The CCIR's Recommendations on the other hand are generally just that — recommendations — with few exceptions.

Most of the CCIR work concerning ISDN involves satellite systems in ISDN circuits, a matter studied by a small Interim Working Party known as IWP4/2.

1.2 The International Organization for Standardization

The ISO is the specialized international agency for standardization, at present comprising the national standards bodies of countries.[11] The purpose of the ISO is to promote the development of standardization and related activities in the world with a view to facilitating international exchanges of goods and services, and to developing cooperation in the sphere of intellectual, scientific, technological, and economic activity. The results of ISO technical work are published as *International Standards*.

The scope of the ISO covers standards in all fields except electrical and electronic engineering, which for equipment are the responsibility of the International Electrotechnical Commission (IEC). For several decades, the ISO has been the major forum for devising international information systems standards, and telecommunication standards have generally been left to the International Telecommunication Union. However, with the integration of these systems, the activity of the ISO increasingly overlaps that of the ITU.

The ISO brings together the interests of producers, users (including consumers), governments, and the scientific community, in the preparation of International Standards. ISO work is carried out through some 2,200 technical bodies. More than 20,000 experts from all parts of the world participate each year in the ISO technical work which, to date, has resulted in the publication of 4,917 ISO standards.

The process of adopting a standard normally proceeds in the context of a "project formal description" (FD) that has four phases: WD (Working Draft); DP (Draft Proposal); DIS (Draft International Standard); and IS (International Standard). A ballot procedure is used to advance the standard to the next higher stage. The process typically takes two to three years.

Structurally, the ISO consists of a General Assembly which meets once every three years, a Council that meets at least once a year, a President, a Vice-President, a Treasurer, a Secretary-General, a Central Secretariat, technical committees and, if necessary, technical divisions.[12]

All of the ISDN related activity in the ISO is confined to one major technical committee, TC97. Extensive formal liaison activity occurs between all levels of the TC97 and CCITT infrastructures.

1.2.1 Technical Committee 97 — Information Processing Systems

TC97 is responsible for one of the most dynamic areas in international standardization. The secretariat for TC97 is not the ISO headquarters staff at Geneva, but rather the American National Standards Institute at New York City. The committee's work takes place in an environment which is constantly changing and expanding in scope and importance. The organization of its work has been altered recently in order to keep up with the dynamics of its responsibilities and maintain an efficiency and responsiveness which will parallel its environment.[13]

The new TC97 infrastructure consists of a general advisory group and three major groupings of subcommittees: application elements, equipment and media, and systems. The subcommittees most active in ISDN matters all belonging to the systems group: SC6 (Telecommunications and Information Exchange Between Systems) and SC21 (Information Retrieval, Transfer, and Management). However, three others engage in related work: SC2 (Information Coding); SC18 (Text and Office Systems); and SC20 (Information Processing Systems Security).

Sub-Committee 6 — Telecommunications and Information Exchange Between Systems

SC6 is responsible for more than fifty "projects" to develop standards for telecommunications and information transfer. This work is reflected in the subdivision of labor among five working groups: WG1 (Data Link Layer); WG2 (Network Layer); WG3 (Physical Layer); WG4 (Transport Layer); and WG5 (Architecture, Layers 1 through 4). Many of the working groups have broken their work down even further. The individual layer groups (WG1–4) are expected to enter into external liaisons on issues dealing exclusively with their layer.

The role of WG5 is to act as a liaison to represent SC6 in multi-layer issues. This includes: naming and addressing; connectionless data transmission; multipoint data transmission; service conventions; conformance; and management. Specific ISDN issues are typically found in WG5 in the project "Operation over ISDN." This involves: developing the concepts necessary to model the use of multiple sub-channels and relevant aspects of common channel signalling systems; understanding the relationship of particular facilities provided by ISDN to OSI; and harmonization in conjunction with CCITT of the architectures of OSI and ISDN.[14]

Sub-Committee 21 — Information Retrieval, Transfer and Management

SC21 is responsible for the Open Systems Interconnection (OSI) Reference Model, the OSI Management Framework, and their continuing development. This is the seven layer model serving as a nearly all-encompassing master standard for the integrate telecommunication-information systems environment. The CCITT now follows this model for ISDN work.

SC21 therefore stands at the center of all the work going on in the field, and it has numerous liaisons with dozens of other groups inside and outside the ISO structure. Its closest relationship is with SC6 as the work affects layers 1–4.

1.3 The European Conference of Post and Telecommunication Administrations

The European Conference of Postal and Telecommunication Administrations, more commonly known as CEPT, is the only regional international organization significantly involved in ISDN matters. CEPT, as the name implies, is a mechanism for coordinating the post and telecommunication policies of European governments. The organization has no permanent home, but entrusts the secretariat activities to the chairmen of its constituent bodies.

In the late 1970s, the Harmonization Coordination Committee (CCH) of CEPT created a Special Group on ISDN (GSI) that became a means of coordinating plans and strategies on ISDN, developing common contributions for submission and support within CCITT Study Groups, especially SG XVIII. In the context of this activity, one of the most cohesive and best prepared documents on ISDN, entitled "ISDN in Europe," was published in 1982.[15]

1.4 Other International Organizations

In addition to the ITU, ISO, and CEPT, there are other international organizations that have been or will be serving as forums for dealing with ISDN concerns.

The International Telecommunications Users Group (INTUG) is a private international association of associations. It is concerned with the representation of the user community, mainly the business user in international matters. The members consist of user groups from ten nations and one other international organization, plus a number of transnational corporations. INTUG not only participates in work of the CCITT as a recognized organization, but also hosts occasional meetings on ISDN and exchanges information among its members.[16]

The International Telecommunications Satellite Organization (Intelsat) also has a consultative committee and has international organization status to participate in CCITT activities. Intelsat's ISDN related activity has principally consisted of participation in CCITT and CCIR meetings relating to the use of satellite systems in hypothetical ISDN circuits.

To a varying extent, other international organizations such as the International Electrotechnical Commission (IEC), the European Computer Manufacturers Association (ECMA), the International Maritime Satellite Organization (Inmarsat), and the Society for Worldwide Interbank Financial Telecommunications (SWIFT) have similarly participated in CCITT ISDN forums and exchanged ISDN related information within their own organizations and among their membership.

REFERENCES

1. Note that the ISO changed its name in 1981 from "International Standards Organization" to "International Organization for Standardization," but retained the abbreviation ISO. This is a minor point, but failure to use the correct current name is rather endemic. Similarly, an "s" is often incorrectly placed after the word Telecommunication in the ITU's name. This latter tendency is generally isolated to the United States, in which it is customary to pluralize words like telecommunication or communication. The custom is not found outside the US.

2. Only Administrations, i.e., national governments, may be ITU members. However, Recognized Private Operating Agencies (RPOAs) [e.g., AT&T], Scientific and Industrial Organizations (SIOs) [e.g., IBM], and International Organizations can participate in most facets of ITU work, including all those related to ISDN.

3. It should be noted that although the terms "telegraph" and "telephone" constitute the CCITT's name, its formal jurisdiction is defined in terms of all telecommunications matters, except those specifically relating to radio. In fact, most of the CCITT's current work only indirectly relates to telegraph and telephone matters.

4. *See* International Telecommunication Convention, Nairobi, 1982.

5. The WATTC-88 is discussed in Chapter 9.

6. For a full discussion of the CCITT and its methods of work, reference Codding and Rutkowski, *The International Telecommunication Union in a Changing World,* Artech House, Dedham, MA, 1982.

7. This practice will cease in 1988, whereafter the Director will be elected by the Plenipotentiary Conference.

8. The CCITT designates its Study Groups using Roman numerals to help distinguish them from those of the CCIR which uses Arabic numerals.

9. *See* Final Report to the VIIIth CCITT Plenary Assembly (Parts I and II), Doc. No. COM XVIII-R29 [also the same as Doc. No. AP VIII-94] (July 1984).

10. All CCITT study groups use the same numbering scheme for their contributions (serial numbers) and reports (serial numbers prefixed with the letter R). (See Appendix A of this book.) A suffix (E, F, or S for English, French, or Spanish) is also generally employed. However, the numbering scheme for delayed and temporary documents is different in each study group.

11. A *member body* of ISO is the national body "most representative of standardization in its country." It follows that only one such body for each country is accepted for membership ISO. Member bodies are entitled to participate and exercise full voting rights on any technical committee of ISO, are eligible for Council membership and have seats in the General Assembly. By January 1983, the number of member bodies was 72. More than 70% of the ISO member bodies are governmental institutions or organizations incorporated by public law. The remainder have close links with the public administration in their own countries.

A *correspondent* member is normally an organization in a developing country which does not yet have its own national standards body. Correspondent members do not take an active part in the technical work, but are entitled to be kept fully informed about the work of interest to them. By January 1983, the number of correspondent members was 17.

12. *See* Arts. 5–7, ISO Constitution (1982).

13. ISO/TC97 Advisory Group, Draft Proposal for Restructuring ISO/ TC97, Doc. No. ISO/TC97/N1294 (21 Dec 1983) at 3.

14. *See* Initial Programme of Work for SC6/Working Group 5, Doc. No. ISO/TC97/SC6 3485.

15. *See* ISDN in Europe, Special Group ISDN (GSI) 1982 Report on Integrated Services Digital Network Studies, CEPT Doc. T/CCH (82)30, Doc. T/GSI (82)71, Stockholm, November 1982.

16. *See* The International Telecommunication Users Group, Workshop on ISDN (Cologne, 19 October 1984), Artech House, 1985.

CHAPTER 2 — UNITED STATES ORGANIZATIONS

A wide variety of organizational forums in the United States actively deal with ISDN matters. These forums can be grouped into four categories: government policy-making, international preparatory, domestic standards making, and professional colloquia. The boundaries of such a categorization are not always clear. The people, papers, and ideas regularly course their way through many of these forums in a continuing complex process of refinement and persuasion.

There are two dominant characteristics of these forums in the United States: most are non-governmental and the participation in all of them is overwhelmingly by the private sector. The activity typically brings together hundreds of experienced personnel from major telecommunications companies of the United States who use these forums to share their views and achieve a consensus on ISDN issues ranging from minute details of a connector to the broad policies of network interconnection and interoperation. Of these people, the staff of the American Telephone and Telegraph Company (pre-divestiture) and ATT Communications, ATT Information Systems, and Bell Communications Research (post-divestiture) have clearly played a leading role in all forums.

The sections below provide a brief description of major organizational forums, describing both their general role and their specific involvement in ISDN matters.

2.1 Federal Communications Commission Proceedings

The Federal Communications Commission (FCC) is the government agency in the United States responsible for the regulation of private sector communications. The FCC's regulatory scope is broadly subdivided into two major categories under its statutory charter, the Communications Act of 1934: "common carrier" telecommunication services[1] and the use of radio stations. These two categories are sometimes referenced to the major subdivisions of the Act that spell out the Commission's role: Title II and III, respectively. In addition, the FCC has a kind of general jurisdiction over all communication services, common carrier and otherwise, that emanates from Title I of the Act.

The FCC is generally described as an "independent regulatory agency" because it is a creature of the United States Congress and is not part of the Executive Branch headed by the President. The Executive Branch has its own agencies that regulate government use of telecommunications.

The FCC exercises its power in a variety of ways. It *authorizes* companies or individuals to provide common carrier services or use radio facilities or undersea cable facilities. It *prescribes* certain technical and operational criteria for telecommunication systems and equipment, and the rates that market dominant providers of common carrier services may charge. It *certifies* that equipment complies with certain technical standards. The FCC also, in cooperation with the Departments of State and Commerce, *determines* United States positions with respect to activities of international organizations and negotiations with foreign governments.

The FCC must exercise this authority through fairly formal processes that are almost entirely public, and are subject to judicial review. Most of its general policies and its specific rules are published in tentative form and public comment is received prior to adoption. The important documents adopting rules and policies are published as part of the Commission's permanent legal record, the FCC Reports, as well as in the Federal Register. The FCC's rules are contained in Title 47 of the Code of Federal Regulations. All the materials associated with policy- or rule-making proceeding are contained in a "docket" file at FCC headquarters.

The FCC's authorization processes vary in formality from the simple filing of a form to formal mechanisms similar to rule- and policy-making. This is particularly true where the authorization process invokes a request for a waiver of some general rule or policy.

The FCC clearly has a significant basis for involvement in ISDN matters. It is, however, a rather complex involvement because most of the ISDN work has been occurring entirely within the research and development efforts of private companies, or within private-sector organizations, or within the context of United States participation in international organizations. The FCC has a broad regulatory purview over the first two of these activities, and shares the third with Executive Branch agencies, especially the Department of State and the Department of Commerce.[2]

However, this relatively passive activity is beginning to change. In 1983 the FCC took the rather rare step of instituting a policy-making proceeding largely looking prospectively at ISDN issues. This proceeding is examined in detail in Chapter 8. In addition, the emergence of nascent ISDN-like services has resulted in a variety of ISDN issues being raised in increasingly frequent policy-making, rule-making, tariff and service authorization proceedings. These miscellaneous proceedings have become important ancillary ISDN forums, and are discussed in Chapter 7.

2.2 The Department of State Public Advisory Committees and Delegations for CCITT and CCIR

The Department of State is the government agency principally responsible for carrying out the President's constitutional duty of representing the United States before foreign governments. The Department of State gets indirectly involved in ISDN matters because of the many forums of the CCITT in which this activity occurs. The CCITT is a body of the International Telecommunication Union which was created by a treaty instrument among governments and has historically served as a meeting ground for government representatives.

The State Department has chosen to discharge its representational responsibility in two ways. The first is through two "public advisory committees," the United States Organization for the International Telegraph and Telephone Consultative Committee (CCITT) and a similar organization for the CCIR that "recommend" US policies and contributions.[3] These committees are often referred to as the USCCITT and USCCIR, and the State Department maintains approved charters defining the responsibilities and structures of both organizations. The second means by which the State Department effects the representation of the United States in these forums is through the formation, accreditation, and conduct of delegations to many of the CCIR and CCITT meetings, or otherwise bestow the title of "recognized private operating agency (RPOA)" or "scientific and industrial organization (SIO)" upon United States companies.[4] These designations allow companies and organizations, upon payment of a contribution to the ITU, to participate in their own name (rather than in the name of the United States) in CCITT or CCIR activities.

On substantive policy matters, the 1978 Executive Order on international telecommunications policy directs the Department of State to look to both the FCC and NTIA for advice in most telecommunications matters.[5] In the case of the CCITT, however, the Department of State has historically relied on the companies actually involved in the provision of telegraph and telephone service — Western Union, AT&T, RCA, and a few other international carriers — to perform most required policy-making and representational functions. During the last two decades, the number of companies involved in these activities has significantly increased, along with the scope and importance of the work. Nonetheless, this activity has remained largely a private sector function. In the case of the second important international organization heavily involved in ISDN matters, the ISO, the State Department has deferred entirely to the American National Standards Institute (ANSI), a private organization, to represent the United States in all of its activities.

The charter for the USCCITT specifies the following purposes for the advisory committees:

a. promote the best interests of the United States in CCITT activities;
b. provide advice on matters of policy and positions in preparation for CCITT Plenary Assemblies and meetings of the international CCITT Study Groups;
c. provide advice on the disposition of proposed contributions (documents) to the international CCITT;
d. assist in the resolution of administrative or procedural problems pertaining to United States CCITT activities.

The USCCITT infrastructure specified in its charter consists of a National Committee which constitutes a steering body having purview over the agendas and work of four study groups and a joint working party:

a. US Government Regulatory Policies;
b. Telegraph Operations;
c. World-wide Telephone Network;
d. Data Transmission; and
e. ISDN Joint Working Party.

In practice, however, the National Committee has largely concerned itself with the CCITT Plenary Assembly occurring every four years, and the study groups and working party have operated fairly autonomously. They determine *de facto* the disposition of proposed contributions to the CCITT.

Of these USCCITT groups, the ISDN Joint Working Party has assumed a lead role in approving US contributions to CCITT study groups and working parties. It typically has been convened several weeks in advance of a major CCITT meeting and reviews and approves the available US draft contributions. Notice of the meetings must be published at least 15 days in advance in the Federal Register. The role of the Joint Working Party in practice is, however, rather limited. The documents it considers are almost invariably made available only at the meetings. Typically hundreds of pages of complex and detailed material are disposed of in only a few hours, with little discussion of underlying policies or rationale. However, the use of preparatory committees of the National Exchange Carriers Association (NECA) (formerly the Exchange Carriers Standards Association (ECSA)) beginning in mid-1984 has improved this situation. The NECA Committee T1D1 on ISDN currently serves as a pre-clearance mechanism for most documents destined for CCITT major study group meetings.

The work of the CCIR in ISDN matters has been minimal. The USCCIR operates in a similar fashion to the USCCITT, except it generally has a domestic infrastructure that directly parallels that of the international groups. For example, there is a USCCIR Study Group 1 to prepare for the work of the international CCIR Study Group 1. Another significant difference is that the CCIR National Committee, and particularly the government officers of the Committee, maintain a close scrutiny over all documents emerging from the USCCIR study groups.

2.3 The National Exchange Carriers Association (NECA) Technical Subcommittee on ISDN

Prior to the AT&T divestiture, the massive Bell System Technical Standards provided the technical and operational specifications to allow the national telephone network to function in an integrated fashion. The only standards promulgated by the FCC were those for interconnecting simple telephone-type instruments to the network. AT&T *de facto* handled every other aspect of network operations.

It was realized that with the divestiture of the Bell Operating Company local exchange facilities, as well as the increasing number of alternative interexchange carriers, some kind of organization was necessary to carry out the national network integration functions formerly assumed by AT&T. Out of this need, the Exchange Carriers Standards Association (later to become the National Exchange Carriers Association) was born.

One of its major new committees dealt with technical standards (T1) and within it was established a subcommittee dealing with ISDN matters (T1D1). This subcommittee has also accredited itself with the American National Standards Institute (ANSI). As the awareness and extent of ISDN studies increased, T1D1 since its creation in early 1984 has become a major focal point for developing common ISDN standards and CCITT-related contributions in the US. It meets in many different locations in the United States to attract diverse participants, and schedules frequent gatherings to deal with the materials in a timely and thorough manner.

As of early 1985, T1D1 had three constituent working groups: T1D1.1 (Architecture and Services); T1D1.2 (Switching and Signalling Protocols); T1D1.3 (Physical Layer).

2.4 The American National Standards Committee (ANSC) Subcommittee on Information Processing Systems and Delegations to ISO

The American National Standards Institute (ANSI) was founded in 1918 as a nonprofit organization that coordinates voluntary standards activities in the United States. Its membership consists of approximately 220 nonprofit organizational members, and almost 1000 company members representing virtually every facet of commerce, trade, and industry. It is governed by a Board of Directors and most of its work is carried out under the direction of various councils. An extremely wide range of standards are developed and adopted on a consensus basis within the elaborate infrastructures of accredited committees. ANSI also represents the United States in two international telecommunication and information related organizations, the International Organization for Standardization (ISO) and the International Electrotechnical Commission (IEC).

Two accredited standards committees operate under the procedures of ANSI that are directly related to ISDN: X3 — Information Processing Systems, and T1 — Telecommunications. Committee T1 is a creature of the NECA, discussed above. Committee X3 is a large and complex organization dealing with a wide range of information processing systems matters, with secretarial support provided by the Computer and Business Equipment Manufacturers Association (CBEMA). (See Figure 2-1.) The focal point for ISDN activities in X3 is the subgroup on communications, Technical Committee X3S3, which generally meets concurrently with the Electronic Industries Association (EIA) Technical Committee on Data Transmission Systems and Equipment, TR-30. ANSC X3T5 (Open Systems Interconnection) and X3T9 (I/O Interface) also deal with ISDN related issues.

Committee X3 and its various task groups serve as clearinghouses for information brought to the meetings by liaisons from virtually all the other relevant international and domestic groups, as well as a mechanism for directly effecting US participation in ISO Technical Committee 97, and indirectly in the CCITT. Committee X3 performs this latter function through the preparation of contributions and position papers adopted by consensus, with extensive use of balloting by mail.

2.5 The Electronic Industries Association (EIA) Technical Committee on Data Transmission Systems and Equipment

The Electronic Industries Association was established in 1924 in Chicago and was originally called the Radio Manufacturers Association. With growing government involvement in industry affairs, it moved its headquarters to Washington, DC in 1933. Over the years, its name changed several times and finally reached its current EIA in 1957. It serves a number of common interests of electronic equipment and component manufacturers, including the adoption of technical standards. There are over 450 active member companies in the association.

In recent years, the telecommunication standards activity has been substantially entwined with ANSC committees. Indeed, EIA is an ANSI-accredited organization and all of EIA's standards may be considered for adoption as American national standards. ISDN matters are considered within the Information & Telecommunication Technologies Group (ITG) and the Engineering Committee on Data Transmission Systems and Equipment, TR-30. As noted above, this committee generally meets concurrently with ANSC X3C3 and functions similarly. EIA has adopted several of its own important and ubiquitous standards such as RS-232 that specify standard interfaces among information systems equipment.

In early 1985, TR-30 was subdivided into three subcommittees: TR-30.1 (Signal Quality and Electrical Characteristics); TR-30.2 (Digital Interface); and TR-30.3 (Telecommunication Network Interfaces).

2.6 Other Domestic Forums

Several additional organizations in the United States provide forums that are woven into the ISDN development process. Perhaps the most prominent and active of these is the Institute of Electrical and Electronic Engineers (IEEE). The IEEE and its various subdivisions disseminate information through their publications and meetings, and develop standards in a fashion similar to other standards groups described above.

The IEEE was founded as the Institute of Radio Engineers at the turn of the century, and merged in January 1963 with the American Institute of Electrical Engineers to form the IEEE. It is headquartered in New York City. Its major specialty subdivisions are known as societies, and operate somewhat autonomously.

The IEEE Communications Society is the most active in the ISDN area. This society's publication, the *Transactions on Communications* have contained ISDN material both randomly and aggregated in special issues. In addition, the Communications Society has held specialized symposia on ISDN, as well as panels at broader meetings such as the Globecoms, the International Conferences on Communication, and the International Switching Symposia. With the exception of the ISDN symposia which are off the record, the published proceedings of these meetings have been rich with ISDN material.

The IEEE's 802 Committee on Local Network Standards has been working

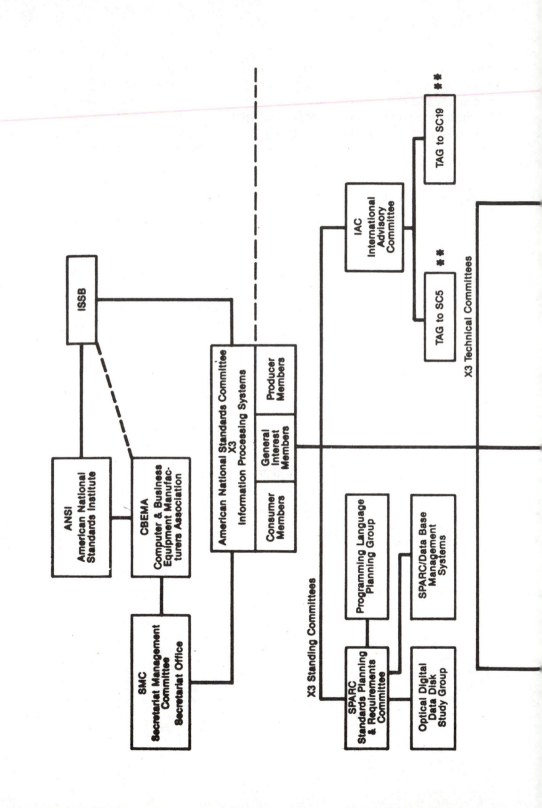

A—Recognition

X3A1	OCR
X3A1.1	Font Design
X3A1.2	OCR Supplies and Forms
X3A1.3	Image Def.
	Measurement
X3A7*	MICR

B—Media

X3B1	Magnetic Tape
X3B2*	Perforated Media
X3B3*	Punched Cards
X3B5	Mag. Tape Cassettes
X3B6	Instrumentation Tape
X3B7	Magnetic Disks
X3B8	Flexible Disks
X3B9	Paper Forms/Layouts
X3B10	Credit/ID Cards
X3B10.1	Integrated Circuit Cards

H & J—Languages

X3H1	OP Sys Cmd & Resp Language
X3H2	Database
X3H3	Computer Graphics
X3H3.1	Core Graphics System
X3H3.2	Reference Models
X3H3.3	Virtual Device Interface
X3H3.4	Conformance & Binding
X3H3.5	Min. Interface to Graphics
X3H4	Information Resource & Dictionary System
X3J1	PL/I
X3J1.2	PL/I Gen. Purpose Subset
X3J1.4	PL/I Real Time Subset
X3J2	BASIC
X3J3	FORTRAN
X3J4	COBOL
X3J4.2	COBOL Data Base
X3.4.3.	COBOL DML
X3J5	COMPACT/ACTION/SPLIT
X3J6	Text Processing
X3J6.1	Text Description
X3J7	APT
X3J9	PASCAL
X3J10	APL
X3J11	C

K—Documentation

X3K1*	Project Documentation
X3K2*	Flowchart Symbols
X3K5	Vocabulary
X3K7	Program Abstracts

L—Data Representation

X3L2	Codes & Character Sets
X3L2.1	Videotex/Teletext
X3L5	Labels & File Structure
X3L8	Data Representation
X3L8.3	Indiv. & Bus. ID
X3L8.4	Geographical Units

S—Communication

X3S3	Data Communication
X3S3.1	Comm. Stds. Planning
X3S3.2	Comm. Vocabulary
X3S3.3	Network Layer
X3S3.4	Control Procedures
X3S3.5	Comm. System Performance
X3S3.6	Transmission Speeds
X3S3.7	Public Data Networks

T & V—Systems Technology

X3T1	Data Encryption
X3T1.1	Data Link Encryption
X3T5	Open Systems Interconnection
X3T5.1	Architecture
X3T5.4	OSI Management Protocols
X3T5.5	Application & Pres. Layers
X3T5.6	Session & Trans. Layer
X3T9	I/O Interface
X3T9.2	Lower Level Interface
X3T9.3	Device Level Interfaces
X3T9.4	I/O Operational Specifications
X3T9.5	Loc. Dis. Data Interface
X3T9.6	Cartridge Tape Drives
X3V1	Office Systems
X3V1.1	User Requirements
X3V1.2	Symbols & Terminology
X3V1.3	Text Structure
X3V1.4	Procedure for Text Interchange
X3V1.5	Text Preparation & Presentation

** TECHNICAL ADVISORY GROUPS TO ISO TC97 SUBCOMMITTEES

* INACTIVE STATUS

Figure 2-1

for several years on a local area network standard. The standard may be used in conjunction with ISDNs in the provision of local services.

Within the United States government, there exists a Federal Telecommunication Standards Committee (FTSC) under the aegis of the National Communications System (NCS). The NCS is the government agency charged with providing integrated telecommunications among the separate facilities of the various US government agencies. Some ISDN issues have been considered within the NCS/FTSC, and information disseminated.

REFERENCES

1. "Common carrier" is a term frequently used by federal regulatory agencies that refers to any carrier offering its services to the public for interstate transportation of goods, persons, or information. In the case of telecommunication, the term is often contrasted with broadcasting and private services. The distinctions between these categories are, however, blurring, and in a fully implemented ISDN environment not capable of being distinguished.

2. The Department of Commerce has established a specialized division, the National Telecommunication and Information Administration (NTIA), for dealing with telecommunication and related matters. *See*, generally, Executive Order 12046 (regarding the respective roles of the FCC, Dept. of State and Dept. of Commerce on international telecommunication policy). In addition, the National Communications System (NCS) plays a significant role in coordinating national security related policies. *See* Executive Order 12472.

3. A "public advisory committee" is any committee established by the federal government to give advice. Such committees are closely regulated in accordance with the Federal Advisory Committee Act of 1972 which was enacted to stem a number of abuses that had occurred over the years. The most notable features of the act are that advisory committee meetings must have their agendas, times, and locations notified in the Federal Register, ordinarily be open to the public, keep records of their actions, and have a balanced membership. In addition, they must operate under charters approved by the sponsoring government agency and the Office of Management and Budget.

4. In an ISDN environment, the definition of a RPOA becomes rather vague. This has prompted a recent FCC policy making proceeding that may end in a finding that virtually any telecommunication or information services provider may fall within the ambit of the definition. *See Notice of Inquiry* in CC Doc. No. 83-1230, FCC83-516, 95 FCC2d 627 (1983).

5. *See* Executive Order 12046.

II ISDN Standards: The I-Series Recommendations

The source of the ISDN concept as well as the focal point of ISDN work is the ITU's International Telegraph and Telephone Consultative Committee (CCITT). In late 1981, this concept and work became directed toward the production of a set of international provisions known as the I-Series Recommendations.[1] At the CCITT's Eighth Plenary Assembly at Malaga-Torremolinos in October 1984, these Recommendations were formally adopted by the CCITT.

This series was cut almost entirely from whole cloth through an enormous effort by Study Group XVIII between November 1980 and October 1984. Several thousand documents were introduced into the study group over this period. All but the temporary documents are tabulated in Appendix A, Section 1 at the back of this book.

The speed of preparation and adoption of the I-Series by several separate working groups has produced a set of Recommendations that is far from perfect. There is redundancy and inconsistency, and occasional omissions. Some of the concepts have not been well considered, and much work remains for the 1985–1988 activity period.

Nonetheless, the I-Series remains a remarkably forward looking and comprehensive set of material generated by many exceptionally talented people working hard to achieve global consensus on a dream for the future. Additionally, it is the agreed model for ISDNs.

Chapters 3 through 6 portray and discuss most of these Recommendations, frequently referencing the work of Study Group XVIII and specific contributions that led to their development. The chapters are subdivided largely in the same manner in which the I-Series is organized: General Matters; Service Capabilities; Overall Network Aspects and Functions; and Interfaces. Not coincidently, this is an excellent general approach for any technical or issue analysis of integrated information networks.

REFERENCE

1.   The CCITT has for many years codified all its Recommendations into different telecommunication categories called "series", and each Recommendation in the category bears an identification consisting of the series prefix letter, followed by a period, followed by a unique identifying number, e.g., I.410.

CHAPTER 3 — GENERAL

This chapter describes the general aspects of the I-Series Recommendations. It encompasses such topics as the structure of the I-Series, relationships with Recommendations of other series, vocabulary, and general descriptions, including the principles and evolution of ISDNs.

3.1 STRUCTURE OF THE I-SERIES RECOMMENDATIONS

The first I-Series Recommendation, I.110, sets forth the general structure of the series. The decision to proceed with a possible new special series of Recommendations on ISDN was made during the course of small closed meetings of the Study Group XVIII leadership at Montreal (21–25 Sept 1981), Darmstadt (11–15 Jan 1982), and Munich (15–16 Feb 1982). At the Munich ISDN Experts meeting (17–25 Feb 1982), the first of the new I-Series Recommendations were introduced.

Several months later at the coordination meeting of Study Group XVIII on 23 June, Study Group Vice-Chairman Phyffer was asked to chair a Drafting Group on the Structure of the I-Series Recommendations. Contributions were principally received from NTT, Canada, and the Chairman of the Group, and the first draft outline was disseminated in Doc. COM XVIII No. 134 (Oct 1982). This structure was substantially revised at the Kyoto ISDN Experts Meeting (14–25 Feb 1983), but subsequently remained almost unchanged.[1] The structure adopted by the CCITT Plenary in October 1984 is shown below.

PART I — GENERAL

Section 1 — Framework of I-Series Recommendations; Terminology

      I.110   General Structure of the I-Series Recommendations

      I.111   Relationship with Other Recommendations Relevant to ISDNs

      I.112   Vocabulary of Terms for ISDNs

PART V — INTERNETWORK INTERFACES

(For further study, see 1985–88 Study Period Questions 6 & 7/ XVIII)

PART VI — MAINTENANCE PRINCIPLES

Section 1 — General Maintenance Principles
(For further study, see 1985–88 Study Period Question 18/XVIII)

Section 2 — User Related Testing and Maintenance Principles
(For further study, see 1985–88 Study Period Question 18/XVIII)

3.2 RELATIONSHIP OF THE I-SERIES RECOMMENDATIONS WITH OTHER RELEVANT CCITT RECOMMENDATIONS

Once the decision was made to develop a separate I-Series, it became necessary to create a short description of the relationship of this series to other CCITT Recommendations. The I-Series was never intended to stand entirely alone, nor could it, given the overlapping nature of the subject matter of the various Series.

Thus, Recommendation I.111 points out that the I-Series of Recommendations applies to the general concept and to the network capabilities of an ISDN mainly insofar as they appear at user-network interfaces and internetwork interfaces. The detailed specifications of ISDN interfaces are contained in the I-Series of Recommendations. The specific aspects within the network, and ancillary features that are necessary to support these specific network aspects, continue to be covered wholly, or in parts, by Series E, F, G, M, Q, S, V, and X, among others. Such aspects may include:

- technical characteristics of component parts and their performance objectives (i.e., transmission systems, switching systems, interexchange signalling systems)
- network synchronization
- maintenance and operation
- services
- tariffs and charging

Some of the existing Recommendations for telephony and other dedicated service networks are also directly applicable to ISDNs. However, other Recommendations in those series may need to be developed in order to cover applications in an ISDN.

3.3 VOCABULARY

At the outset of the 1981–84 Study Group XVIII effort, it was realized that the work would require a definitive understanding of terminology. New terms would be createdd, others would be altered or given new connotations. Toward that end, Question 6 was framed, and P. Clarke of British Telecom subsequently was appointed Special Rapporteur.

At the Kyoto ISDN Experts Meeting in February 1983, Mr. Clarke headed and Ad Hoc Group on Vocabulary, drawing upon his previous work as Question 6 Rapporteur and contributions from Sweden, ISO, France, USA, AT&T, and Australia. Out of this meeting, draft Recommendation I.112 was prepared. Subsequent work on several terms and continued liaison with other Study Groups yielded additional changes, and the Recommendation was adopted as part of the I-Series by the CCITT Eighth Plenary Assembly. All the terms from Recommendation I.112, together with additional terms in its annex, are contained in Appendix B at the end of this book.

Recommendation I.112 consists primarily of those terms and definitions that are considered essential to the understanding and application of the principles of ISDNs. Some terms are included that are already defined in other CCITT Recommendations. However, the definitions given in Recommendation I.112 embrace only the essential concepts, and on that basis it is considered that they are not inconsistent with the more specialized definitions that appear in those other CCITT Recommendations.

A few fine points are worth noting. Whenever the relationship between the user and network is described in a term, a (-) as opposed to a (/) is always used, e.g., "user-network." This demonstrates the degree of precision often found in the work of the vocabulary group. The terms are organized as common groups in a manner particularly relevant to ISDN: General, Services, Networks, Access, and Signalling. Throughout the I-Series Recommendations, where terms are used with their first letter(s) capitalized, it is a reference to the term as defined in Recommendation I.112.

Because the vocabulary is entwined with other ISDN concepts and Recommendations, its development was rather dependent on the resolution of issues considered by other Study Group XVIII working teams. Some of these matters were not substantially resolved until the end of the activity period in 1984, with the result that some inconsistencies exist between the definitions of terms in Recommendation I.112, and the way they are employed in other I-Series Recommendations, as well as some less than ideal definitions or lack thereof.[2] Nonetheless, the work represents one of the most cohesive and comprehensive sets of definitions, and certainly the most important, in this rapidly emerging field.

Of particular importance are the definitions dealing with "service" and service types, as well as what constitutes a "user." These definitions and the surrounding issues are extensively discussed in following chapters.

3.4 GENERAL DESCRIPTIONS

Part I, Section 2, of the I-Series contains but a single Recommendation (I.120) entitled Integrated Services Digital Networks. The Recommendation is devoted to two subjects: principles and evolution of ISDN. These are the general cannons of CCITT ISDN work and are worthy of detailed examination.

The provisions in this Recommendation have their origin in work done by Study Group XVIII during previous activity periods. The first conceptual principles appeared in Recommendation G.705 adopted at the 1980 CCITT VIIth Plenary.

Recommendation G.705

INTEGRATED SERVICES DIGITAL NETWORK (ISDN)

The CCITT,

considering

(a) the measure of agreement that has so far been reached in the studies of Integrated Digital Networks (IDNs) dedicated to specific services such as telephony, data and also of an Integrated Services Digital Network (ISDN),

(b) the need for a common basis for the future studies necessary for the evolution towards an ISDN,

recommends

that the ISDN should be based on the following conceptual principles:

(1) The ISDN will be based on and evolve from the telephony IDN by progressively incorporating additional functions and network features including those of any other dedicated networks so as to provide for existing and new services.

(2) New services introduced into the ISDN should be arranged to be compatible with 64-kbit/s switched digital connections.

(3) The transition from the existing networks to a comprehensive ISDN may require a period of time extending over one or two decades.

(4) During the transition period arrangements must be developed for the interworking of services on ISDNs and services on other networks.

(5) The ISDN will contain intelligence for the purposes of providing service features, maintenance and network management functions. This intelligence may not be sufficient for some new services and may have to be supplemented by either additional intelligence within the network, or possibly compatible intelligence in the customer terminals.

(6) A layered functional set of protocols appear desirable for the various access arrangements to the ISDN. Access from the customer to ISDN resources may vary depending upon the service required and on the status of evolution of national ISDNs.

Note — Existing relevant Recommendations for some of the constituent elements of the ISDN are contained in Series G, O, Q, and X Recommendations and also in relevant volumes of the CCIR.

At the first ISDN Experts Meeting at the beginning of SG XVIII's fast-track 1981–1984 period, there was considerable interest in reaching agreement on a new set of principles to guide the subsequent work. AT&T, in particular, introduced papers describing a new definition and set of principles that the Experts Meeting found useful.[3] The focus was not only integration of services, but, perhaps even more important, on limiting and standardizing interfaces. During the following months, additional contributions were submitted by AT&T and NTT. At the June 1981 meeting of Working Party XVIII/1 (ISDN), AT&T's key point was recommended for addition to Recommendation G.705:

> The main feature of the ISDN is the support of voice and non-voice services in the same network. A key element of service integration for the ISDN is to provide a limited set of standard multipurpose user interface arrangements.[4]

During the next 18 months, G.705 remained on the back burner as other matters absorbed the attention of Study Group XVIII. Finally at the Kyoto ISDN Experts Meeting in February 1983, Working Team 7 considered it in the context of their other I-Series, Part I work, and produced a draft that with minor subsequent changes became Recommendation I.120 that was adopted by the Eighth CCITT Plenary Assembly in October 1984.

Recommendation I.120

INTEGRATED SERVICES DIGITAL NETWORKs (ISDNs)

1. **Principles of ISDN**

1.1 The main feature of the ISDN concept is the support of a wide range of voice and non-voice applications in the same network. A key element of service integration for an ISDN is the provision of a range of services (see Part II of the I-Series of Recommendations) using a limited set of connection types and multipurpose user-network interface arrangements (see Parts III and IV of the I-Series of Recommendations).

1.2 ISDNs support a variety of applications including both switched and non-switched connections. Switched connections in an ISDN include both circuit-switched and packet-switched connections and their concatenations.

1.3 As far as practicable, new services introduced into an ISDN should be arranged to be compatible with 64 kbit/s switched digital connections. [G.705(2)]

1.4 An ISDN will contain intelligence for the purpose of providing service features, maintenance and network management functions. This intelligence may not be sufficient for some new services and may have to be supplemented by either additional intelligence within the network, or possible compatible intelligence in the user terminals. [G.705(5)]

1.6 It is recognized that ISDNs may be implemented in a variety of configurations according to specific national situations.

2. Evolution of ISDNs

2.1 ISDNs will be based on the concepts developed for telephone IDNs and may evolve by progressively incorporating additional functions and network features including those of any other dedicated networks such as circuit-switching and packet-switching for data so as to provide for existing and new services. [G.705(1)]

2.2 The transition from an existing network to a comprehensive ISDN may require a period of time extending over one or more decades. During this period arrangements must be developed for the interworking of services on ISDNs and services on other networks (see Part I, section 4 of the I-Series). [G.705(3)&(4)]

2.3 In the evolution towards an ISDN, digital end-to-end connectivity will be obtained via plant and equipment used in existing networks, such as digital transmission, time-division multiplex switching and/or space-division multiplex switching. Existing relevant Recommendations for these constituent elements of an ISDN are contained in the appropriate series of Recommendations of CCITT and of CCIR. [G.705(Note), in part]

2.4 In the early stages of the evolution of ISDNs, some interim user-network arrangements may need to be adopted in certain countries to facilitate early penetration of digital service capabilities.

i) Some of those interim arrangements are recommended by CCITT, such as hybrid access arrangements.

ii) Other arrangements corresponding to national variants may comply partly or wholly with I-Series Recommendations. However, the intention is that they are not specifically included in the I-Series.

2.5 An evolving ISDN may also include at later stages switched connections at bit rates higher and lower than 64 kbit/s.

A simple comparison of the old Recommendation G.705 and the new Recommendation I.120 reveals the changes that have occurred. Some are subtle, but significant. For example, the simple pluralization of the title, effected at the Kyoto meeting, was a recognition that there will be multiple ISDNs. The addition of paragraph 1.6 also complemented this change. Although not really necessary, the changes were a move to eliminate the monolithic connotation conveyed by the singular, "ISDN."

An allied change involved the reference to the facilities from which the ISDN will evolve. The old Recommendation G.705 indicated that "the ISDN will be based on and evolve from the telephony IDN," whereas the new Recommendation I.120 says that "ISDNs will be based on the concepts developed for telephone IDNs..."

The addition of paragraph 1.2 recognizes the potential availability of non-switched (i.e., leased line) services. This was a rather heated topic in the US at the time the change was made.[5]

The addition of paragraph 2.4 is a recognition that hybrid access arrangements may be appropriate in many situations, and in developing countries in particular.

There is now an apparent consensus that enough has been said on the subject of ISDN evolution. The study of this subject was removed from the repertoire of ISDN questions for the 1985–1988 activity period.

REFERENCES

1. *See* Document COM XVIII No. R15 at 212-216.
2. *See, e.g.,* para. 201 "services" and para. 203 "teleservice" where the delimiter "by an administration or RPOA" was added; and the frequently used and conceptually important terms "customer," or "subscriber" have not been included.
3. *See* Study Group XVIII Report on the Inter-Regnum meeting of Experts on ISDN matters (Innisbrook, 12-15 January 1981), Doc. COM XVIII-No. R1 (1981).
4. Report of the Meeting of Working Party XVIII/1 (ISDN), Doc. COM XVIII-No. R3 (1981) at 5.
5. *See* Chapter 8, below.

CHAPTER 4 — SERVICE CAPABILITIES

One of the most important and interesting aspects of ISDN work falls into the category of "service capabilities." A service is that which is provided by the network to the user (also called a customer or subscriber) at one point or between points in the network.[1] The matter gets confusing because of the possibility for non-transport information services being provided to a user solely by the network, in addition to the more conventional situation where a user transports information through the network to one or more other users.

Because discrete services are generally the basis for tariffs and the collection of revenue from the user by the network, service-related issues receive substantial attention by network operators and the international regulatory community. The participants in this process generally fall into two camps. One is monopoly oriented, and seeks to devise discrete, complete, fixed service packages for which there is an associated rigid tariff structure. The other camp is competition oriented, and generally seeks more flexible, more generic service and tariff structures, particularly at the higher OSI levels that typify information services, rather than telecommunication services.

In existing, "dedicated" telecommunication networks, the subject of "service" is almost trivial. For example, telephone networks provide and charge for telephone service. Today, however, many new services are being grafted onto traditional dedicated networks. These new services are so diverse and amorphous that the attempts to define or describe them are becoming difficult exercises.

In the ISDN environment, services can be almost instantaneously defined and varied by either the provider or the user. Realizing this, the ISDN experts sought to lend some organization to the subject during the 1981–1984 activity period. After considering scores of contributions during the course of more than a half dozen meetings, the CCITT adopted several Recommendations on services.

The experts used a kind of generic approach by identifying a laundry list of service "attributes" that would be configured by the user or the network through an electronic dialogue between the two, which might also include third parties.

In the rush to prepare a product at the end of the activity period, these Recommendations became somewhat redundant and confusing. Nonetheless, they represent the first worldwide dialogue on a subject fraught with economic, national, and technical controversies, and concerning which users and providers sometimes have very significant and sometimes divergent interests. For example, users generally have an interest in maximizing their service options, while providers (particularly telecommunication network providers) have an interest in limiting those options to maximize operating efficiencies and minimize losses to competitive providers.

This subject is also important for reasons external to ISDN. The 1988 World Administrative Telegraph and Telephone Conference (WATTC) will produce a new treaty instrument for the integrated services environment. Just as Study Group XVIII was required to face the meaning of "services," so that the Conference will be faced with the same task. Similar issues can be expected to arise, and the preparatory activity for the Conference may well borrow the service concepts embodied in the I-Series Recommendations, and given them the status of public international law. This matter is covered in greater detail in Chapter 9.

This chapter is divided into two parts. The first (section 4.1) describes how the work on the service concept began and evolved during the four years of Study Group XVIII meetings, resulting finally in four Recommendations: I.130 (Characterization of Services by Attributes), I.210 (Service Principles), I.211 (Bearer Services), and I.212 (Teleservices). The second part (section 4.2) describes those Recommendations.

4.1 EXPLORING THE SERVICE QUESTION

Seventh CCITT Plenary, Geneva 1980. The Study of ISDN services during its 1981–1984 activity period largely emanated from Question 1/XVIII, Point A, adopted by the Seventh CCITT Plenary, meeting at Geneva in November 1980. The question reads as follows:

1. Which services should be taken into account in the establishment of network features of the ISDN?
2. What are the network features needed to support these services? Which network features should be regarded as general throughout the ISDN, and which should be classed as service dependent for particular service application?
   Note: Among other network features, attention should be paid to charging so that adequate information could be made available for charging purposes.

3. For which services, if any, should a change of service on an established connection be envisaged? What are the implications and requirements of such a feature?

4. What kinds of leased paths will be required in the ISDN when it is in widespread operation?
   Note 1: Services should be identified which will supplant existing leased lines services.
   Note 2: Consideration should be given to the use of semi-permanent connections, closed user group and hot-line features, remote switching units, etc.

The nexus between the definition of services and pricing is obvious in the framing of Question 1. In addition, the emphasis on studying leased line services and their alternatives is an issue that remained controversial during much of the subsequent activity of the Study Group, and rose to prominence in the FCC's ISDN proceeding.

Innisbrook, January 1981. When Study Group XVIII convened its first meeting of the new activity period at Innisbrook, Florida, January 1981, one of the three major working groups was devoted to "services and general aspects in ISDN."[2] Delegates were described as "well aware of the importance of studying the service and general network aspects of ISDN."[3]

Initial contributions were largely exploratory, discussing in somewhat vague terms the subjects of "services" and "network features and capabilities." The work became focused on the categorization of services and relating them to network features and capabilities.[4] It was agreed that the analysis of ISDN services and network capabilities might be simplified by the development of a matrix table showing the various service requirements against the network capabilities. Annex B to the report of the working group, taken from a German (FRG) contribution, portrayed ISDN features in five major categories:

- General network features
- Performance requirements
- Transaction routing and control functions
- Features relating to service integration
- Features concerning information handling

Annex C, taken from a British Telecom contribution, discussed service and general aspects of ISDN, and argued that "since . . . the ISDN will evolve from progressive development of telephony equipment, it seems reasonable to develop the service concepts in a similar fashion."[5]

Geneva, July 1981. Study Group XVIII met as a plenary body and established its five permanent working parties at ITU headquarters in Geneva, in late June through early July, 1981. Working Party 1, entitled simply "ISDN," was assigned Question 1/XVIII. It met for three days with an objective to consolidate the preliminary results from the Innisbrook meeting, to amend or modify these results, and to give guidance "in such key areas as network and service aspects, which so far have only been covered in broad and general terms."[6]

The nine submitted contributions and four temporary documents on the question continued to be rather vague and general.[7] The Working Group, continuing to pursue the service matrix concept, devised a work plan for the "definition of information types," and the "identification of representative services." The latter was to encompass "national intentions and policy, economic considerations, existing or planned dedicated networks, trends in technology, etc."[8] All of this was to produce the details of a "service analysis matrix."

The ISDN features listing from Innisbrook was further embellished and portrayed in two annexes. The matrix sought to describe each service by a unique combination of service description and network features shown in the two columns below.

SERVICE DESCRIPTION

- Traffic-character
- Info-rate
- Info-type
- Example
- Reference service category

NETWORK FEATURES

Path Criteria
- General network features
- Performance requirements

Intelligence Requirements
- Transaction routing and control
- Customer related features
- Network related features
- Information handling

Due to a lack of time, further discussions were postponed. The Rapporteur for Question 1/XVIII, Point A (P. Kahl of the FRG), was instructed to carry on further work. In addition, each interested Administration was asked to elaborate upon the service analysis matrix.

Munich, February 1982. The CCITT ISDN Experts Meeting reconvened at Munich in February 1982. Prior to the meeting, the Study Group XVIII leadership had met in Montreal, 21–25 September 1981, and in Darmstadt, 11–15 January 1982, to discuss a number of important issues, including those related to services. The Munich meeting established an ad-hoc group on services under P. Kahl.

Nine contributions and six temporary documents were directed to the Group.[9] At this point in the ISDN activity, some significant new concepts begin to emerge, and old ones alter, as a result of the brainstorming at Montreal and Darmstadt and the new contributions.

The output of the ad-hoc group contained an "approach to a general ISDN services definition." Services were "seen from the customer's point of view" and "described as a set of functional requirements at the ISDN user-network interfaces, which can be organized in a hierarchical structure."[10] This structure marked the beginning of the application of the OSI model to characterize services. In addition, services were broadly divided into two classes: "transport oriented" and "application oriented." A distinction was also made between "services" and "supplementary services." The latter was regarded as a set of functional elements that could only exist ancillary to a service.

The material on services generated prior to Munich, such as the service analysis matrix, was reflected in the Group Report, but assumed a diminished importance. By the next ISDN Experts Meeting, it would disappear completely. The development of details for the new concepts introduced at Munich were, however, deferred.

Kyoto, February 1983. After Munich, no CCITT activity on the services question occurred until the ISDN Experts meeting at Kyoto, 14–25 February 1983. The Kyoto meeting was seminal in developing all the I-Series Recommendations, particularly those related to ISDN services. The Kyoto meeting established Working Team 4, under P. Kahl's leadership, to deal with services.

Thirty-three contributions and five temporary documents were directed to the team.[11] One of the most important of these was the Swedish contribution — Terms and Definitions for Services and Choice of Bearer Services in ISDN, CCITT Doc. COM XVIII-No. 151. The document reflected the results of considerable study and consensus among the European PTTs active in the special CEPT group on ISDN, under the leadership of L. Ackzell of Sweden.[12] Indeed, as the result of the work of a small Working Team 4 drafting group led by Ackzell at Kyoto, draft Recommendation I.200 on "Services Supported by an ISDN" was prepared. The Kyoto (February 1983) draft of Recommendation I.200 was a concise and well-organized description of Study Group XVIII views on ISDN services. In subsequent meetings, although improved in many respects, the provisions began to be divided up to eventually produce the I.130, I.210, I.211, and I.212 set of Recommendations. In this process, the organization and consistency of some of the material suffered.

Two significant new conceptual developments marked the Kyoto draft Recommendation I.200. The first was a largely European view that had some striking parallels to the computer basic/enhanced dichotomy in the United States. This "conceptual framework" characterized all services on the basis of connection types, network provided lower- and higher-layer functions, and terminal functions, and categorized all services on the basis of these types and functions into three groups (Bearer, Alpha, or Telecommunication).

Bearer Service. A service which uses the connection types defined for an ISDN and, optionally, Additional Lower Layer Functions (ALLF). It should be noted that ALLF cannot be offered as an independent service, but only in conjunction with a connection type. The customer may choose any set of high layer (4-7) protocols for his communication, and the ISDN does not ascertain compatibility at high layers (4-7) between customers. An example of a Bearer Service is a 64 kbit/s circuit-switched, transparent service.

Alpha Service. A service which uses the connection types defined for an ISDN, Additional Low Layer Functions (ALLF) as necessary, and High Layer Functions (HLF) supported by an ISDN. The customer must utilize all protocol layers 1-7 relevant both to the connection types and the High Layer Functions. An example of an Alpha Service is the access to and interaction with an information storage and processing facility.

Telecommunication Service. A service which is fully specified (protocol layers 1-7) including functions performed by the terminals. A Telecommunication Service will use connection types defined for an ISDN, and optionally ALLF and/or HLF supported by an ISDN. The checking of high layer compatibility is part of this service. Examples of Telecommunication Services are Telephony and Telex.[13]

The second conceptual development was one devised by AT&T. It proposed:

> ... a framework and nomenclature designed to describe ISDN services consistently and unambiguously in a way that captures all the network aspects, for each service, which are perceived by the users. It builds on Study Group VII Recs. X.1 and X.2, as well as some concepts introduced in earlier contributions by the FRG and Italy. It is a quantative approach that allows a precise statement of user needs, for the benefit of network planners, architects and engineers. Simultaneously, it provides users with relevant information for matching network services with specific applications.[14]

The specific attributes adopted by Kyoto to describe different kinds of bearer services were placed in the second section of draft Recommendation I.200. These included:

- Mode of connection
- Bit rate/maximum throughput
- Establishment of connection
- Channel type
- Access protocol
- Symmetry
- Connection configuration
- Bit transparency
- Additional low layer functions
- Quality of service

In a third section of draft Recommendation I.200, a number of bearer services were described in terms of specific attribute combinations.

In subsequent meetings, the attribute approach would attract additional adherents, and become the dominant method for describing ISDN services.

Geneva, July 1983. Four months after Kyoto, Working Team 4 reconvened in Geneva, 20 June to 8 July 1983. Sixteen contributions and three temporary documents were submitted relevant to the services question.[15]

This meeting witnessed some controversy concerning what had been drafted in Kyoto, particularly the subdivision of services into Bearer, Alpha, and Telecommunication. The SG XVIII report of the meeting, under the heading "principles of definition of services," contains an unusually detailed account of the discussions on this subject.

> The concept of alpha services was not clear. Some administrations saw alpha services as a sub-element of Telecommunication services where the terminals are not provided by the Administrations/ RPOAs, but could be privately owned. Other Administrations saw no need at all to have alpha services. Still again, others wanted the provision of HLF in the network, which can be common to several other services (e.g., message handling) to be considered as alpha services. In the end, it was agreed that alpha services would not be mentioned in I.200 for the time being. It will, however, be indicated that future work may well show the need to define more classes of services beside Bearer and Telecommunication Services.
>
> Furthermore, the discussion on alpha services made clear that a concept of clarifying services should be applicable to all countries in a sense that national situations and national regulations, e.g., the

provision of terminals or HLF by the Administration or other suppliers should not lead to different interpretations of the service definitions. Therefore, [SG XVIII] decided that the service concept should be independent from the question "who is providing terminals or HLF".

In addition to dropping the Alpha Service category, the definitions of Bearer Service and Telecommunication Service were significantly amended. The name of the "Telecommunication Service" category itself was also almost amended because of frequent use of the term in other CCITT Recommendations, where the term had a different meaning than it did in the Study Group XVIII provisions. (The change from "telecommunication" to "tele" would indeed be effected at the next meeting.)

However, the section dealing with "definition of ISDN services" based on "attributes" contained to be refined and find more widespread application.

Geneva, November 1983. Working Team 4 met again from 28 November to 1 December 1983 at Geneva. Twenty-three contributions and seven temporary documents were submitted to Working Team 4.[16]

Following up on a Recommendation made at Kyoto, the team split off much of the material in Recommendation I.200 dealing with Bearer Services into a second Recommendation, I.2xx. Recommendation I.200 now bore the title "Principles for defining services supported by an ISDN," while I.200 was titled "Bearer services supported by an ISDN." It was agreed that a similar separate Recommendation would be prepared at a subsequent meeting for Tele(communication) Services.

Continuing the trend, the service attribute concept began to find widening application. Services were now spoken of as "characterized and described by service attributes."[17]

The French, famous for their perseverance in developing new terms, finally succeeded in convincing the team that "Telecommunication Service" should be replaced by "Tele Service."[18]

A number of minor changes were introduced. These included such matters as the introduction of a "priority list" for bearer services, further additions to the list of attributes, and further additions to the list of bearer services — particularly primary rate bearer services. Now back into the list of attributes were "supplementary services," after having been dropped by the Kyoto meeting.

Brasilia, February 1984. Working Team 4 continued its work again at the ISDN Experts Meeting at Brasilia, 13–24 February 1984. This was to be the last of the major working meetings for the 1980–1984 activity period, so there was a rush to make many final changes to the draft Recommendations. Twenty-six contributions were relevant to the work of the Team.[19]

Major changes involved up the splitting general principles Recommendation I.200 into Recommendations I.130 (Method for characterization of telecommunication services supported by an ISDN and network capabilities of an ISDN) and I.210 (Principles of telecommunication services supported by an ISDN). Bearer Services Recommendation I.2xx became I.211, and a short Recommendation I.212 (Teleservices supported by an ISDN) was spun off the old draft Recommendation I.200.

In the process of this reorganization of material, the attribute concept became the dominant method for characterizing services. This was reflected quite dramatically in Recommendation I.130, which was placed "up front" in the I-Series to serve as a general model for the entire series.

In addition to essentially finalizing the I-Series Recommendations as ISDN services, Working Team 4 also produced answers to Question 1, Point A, as follows:

1. For the description of services supported by an ISDN, Study Group XVIII has defined principles which are laid down in draft Rec. I.210. Two general classes of services have been identified:

    i) Bearer services, which provide the capability for the transmission of signals between user-network interfaces, and

    ii) Teleservices, which provide the complete capability for communication between users for specified user terminals.

    Bearer services supported by an ISDN are described in draft Rec. I.211. The description makes use of a number of attributes, which are intended to be largely independent. Principles for the description of Teleservices supported by an ISDN are given in Rec. I.212.

2. Initial indications of network feature requirements are included under the description of attributes in draft Recs. I.210 and I.211. These have been input to the network Recommendations which take account of bearer service features (see also reply to Question IB/XVIII).

    Further development of network features required, was not considered to be useful during study period 1981–1984 until services have been identified and defined. Further study is needed during the next study period to identify Teleservices and network features.

3. The change of service on an established connection is an inherent feature of an ISDN. Study Group XVIII has taken into account this feature during the course of specification of Bearer Service attributes in draft Rec. I.211. The necessary signalling elements

have been considered in the relevant draft Recommendations by Study Group XI (draft Rec. I.451/Q.930, Specification of ISDN User-Network Interface Layer 3 Protocol and Q.761 to Q.766, ISDN User part). The network implications of change of service on an established connection have been considered in draft Rec. I.340 (see also the reply to Question 1B/XVIII).

4. A leased line service is seen by Study Group XVIII as one method to supply customers with a bearer service that complies with user's requirements. Leased line services are covered in terms of a service attribute in the draft Rec. on Bearer Services (I.211). The service attribute "Establishment of Communication" represents with its attribute values "reserved" and "permanent" the leased line service.

5. It is proposed to continue the study of Question 1A/XVIII during the next study period. (See Question 2/XVIII for the 1985–1988 activity period).[20]

Geneva, June 1984. Study Group XVIII met as a plenary body at Geneva, 24 May to 1 June 1984. At that meeting, I.130, I.210, I.211, I.212, and the Reply to Question 1B/XVIII, as drafted at the Brasilia meeting and subsequently editorially amended by the CCITT Secretariat, were adopted and forwarded to CCITT Eighth Plenary Assembly.[21]

4.2 The Adopted Recommendations

This part of Chapter 4 sets forth three of the four I-Series Recommendations on Services, as adopted by the CCITT in 1984. Because Recommendation I.211 on Bearer Services is long and largely an application of the more general principles found in Recommendations I.130 and I.210, only an outline is provided.

The first of these is found in Part I (General) of the I-Series, in a section titled "General Modelling Methods."

Recommendation I.130

METHOD FOR THE CHARACTERIZATION OF TELECOMMUNICATION SERVICES SUPPORTED BY AN ISDN AND NETWORK CAPABILITIES OF AN ISDN

1. **General Considerations**

1.1 The concept and the principles of ISDNs are described in Recommendation I.120. The Recommendations in the I.200 series cover the aspects of the Telecommunication services supported by ISDNs. The I.300 series of Recommendations deals with the aspects relating to the overall network and to network functional entities.

1.2 The purpose of this Recommendation is to provide a method for the characterization of Telecommunication services and Network Capabilities in an ISDN.

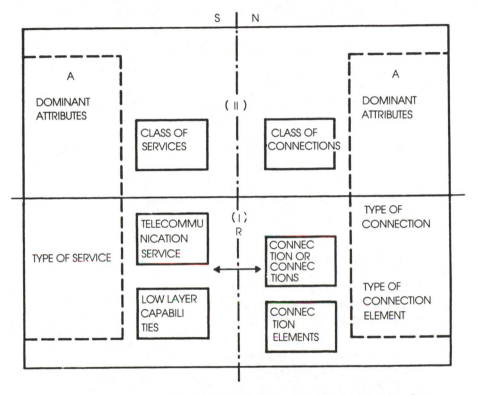

Figure 4-1   Concepts Used to Characterize Telecommunication Services and Connections

Area A   =   *Description using the attribute method*
Area I   =   *Elements to be described*
Area II =   *Classification*
Area N   =   *Network (Connection)*
Area S   =   *Services*
R   =   *Relation between services and connections*

Source: Rec. I.130, Fig. 1/I.130.

2.   Attribute Method

2.1 **Outline of the Method.** This characterization should be made by using a set of attributes [see Figure 4-1]. An attribute is defined as a specified characteristic of an object or element whose values distinguish that object, element from others. Particular values are assigned to each attribute when a given Telecommunication Service or Network Capability is described and specified. Characterization by attributes should be used in the ISDN series of Recommendations when appropriate.

2.2 **Basic Rules.**

- Each attribute is assigned a name and definition.
- A given attribute should have the same name and definition in all Recommendations.
- Some attribute may apply to only one object, others may be applicable to several objects. In this case the same attribute name is to be used.
- A given value should have the same name and the same definition in all the Recommendations.
- Depending on the nature of the object described, a particular attribute may need to be used more than once.

2.3 **Generic List of Attributes.** The list of attributes is not exhaustive. Further attributes will be identified as the studies progress.

- Information transfer mode
- Information transfer rate
- Information transfer capability
- Establishment of communication
- Establishment of connection
- Symmetry
- Communication configuration
- Connection configuration
- Topology
- Uniformity
- Dynamics
- Structure
- Access channel and rate
- Access protocol
- Signalling access protocol
- Information access coding/protocol
- Supplementary service provided
- Quality of service
- Performances

Note 1: Attributes concerning interworking, operational, commercial and maintenance aspects are for further study.

Note 2: Attributes concerning ISDN Higher Layer capabilities should be introduced according to progress on the Teleservice specification.

2.4 Attribute Definition. A provisional list of definitions of attributes and values is contained in the Appendix to this Recommendation.

3.   Application to the I-Series of Recommendations

3.1 This method has been applied in Recs. I.211 and I.212 for the specification of the Telecommunication Services supported by an ISDN and in Rec. I.340 for the characterization of ISDN Connection types and connection elements. The application of the attribute method can be envisaged for supplementary services or for other Network elements (e.g., exchange connections). The application of the attribute method for the characterization of multi-media services is for further study.

Recommendation I.130 has an associated Annex that lists the definitions of attributes and their values. Because of the importance of this model, these attributes and values are listed below.

Annex to Recommendation I.130

LIST OF DEFINITIONS OF ATTRIBUTES AND VALUES

Information transfer mode. The operational mode for transferring transportation and switching user information through the ISDN. It can be used to characterize a Telecommunication Service or a connection in the Network.

Values: Circuit.
Packet.

Information transfer rate. Either the bit rate (circuit mode) or the throughput (packet mode). It refers to the transfer of digital information between two access points or reference points. It can be used to characterize a Telecommunication Service or a connection.

Values: Bit rate.
Throughput rate.

Information transfer capability. The capability associated with the transfer of different types of information through the ISDN. It can be used to characterize a Telecommunication Service or a connection.

Values: Unrestricted digital information. Transfer of information sequence of bits at its specified bit rate without alteration. This implies: bit sequence independence, digital sequence integrity, and bit integrity.

Speech. Digital representation of speech coded according to a specified encoding rule, e.g., A-Law or μ-Law.

3.1 kHz audio. Digital representation of audio information such as voice band data and speech with a bandwidth of 3.1 kHz according to a specified encoding rule.

7 kHz audio. Digital representation of audio information with a bandwidth of 7 kHz according to a specified encoding rule.

15 kHz audio. Digital representation of audio information with a bandwidth of 15 kHz according to a specified encoding rule.

Video. Digital representation of video image information according to a specified encoding rule.

Establishment of communication. A mode, associated with a Telecommunication Service, used to establish and release a given communication.

Values: Demand. The communication can be started as soon as possible after the request is made. Communication and connection release occurs as soon as possible in response to the request of any of the users, calling or called.

Reserved communication. The communication can be started at the time instant at which connection and communication is established, which is explicitly specified at the time instant of communication and connection request. Communication and connection release occurs at the time instant at which communication and connection is cleared, also explicitly specified at the time of the initial request for communication and connection. Communication and connection duration is predetermined, i.e., the communication and connection is set up for a specified period of time. As an option, connection release occurs at the time instant at which communication and connection is cleared, following a release request made at the time instant at which request for release is made during the communication. This option corresponds to an unspecified duration of the communication and connection, or to a possibility of unanticipated release.

Permanent. The communication can be started after the connection is set up at the time instant at which connection and communication is established in response to a subscription request for the service at the time instant at which the request for communication and connection is made. The duration may be unspecified. The communication and connection is released at the time instant at which communication and connection is cleared corresponding to the end of the subscription.

Establishment of connection. The mode of establishment used to establish and release the connections in an ISDN.

Values: Switched. ISDN circuit switched connection/connection elements are set up at any time on demand via a bit channel in response to signalling information received from subscribers, other exchanges or other networks on a per call basis. Message/packet switched connections/connection elements provided by an ISDN may be set up on demand via circuit-mode channels, e.g., B-channels, and special packet switching units, or via the D-channel subject to any D-channel priority/flow control restrictions that may be applicable.

Semi-permanent. Semi-permanent connections/connection elements pass through a switching network. Semi-permanent connections/connection elements between agreed points may be provided for an indefinite period of time after subscription, for a fixed period, or for agreed periods during a day, week or other interval.

Permanent. Permanent connections/connection elements are described by the following characteristics: permanent connections/connection elements installed in the ISDN will not pass through a switching network. They will use the transmission network of ISDN and by-pass the exchanges. Permanent connections/connection elements are available to the connected subscriber at any time during the period of subscription between fixed network destination points requested by the subscribers.

Symmetry. The relationship of information flow between two or more access points or reference points involved in a communication. It characterizes the structure associated with a Telecommunication Service or a connection.

Values: Unidirectional. This value applies when the information flow of messages is provided only in one direction.
Bidirectional symmetric. This value applies when the same information flow characteristics provided by the service are the same between two or more access points or reference points in forward and backward direction.
Bidrectional asymmetric. This value applies when the information flow characteristics provided by the service are different in the two directions.

Communication configuration. The spatial arrangement for transferring information between two or more access points. It completes the structure associated with a Telecommunication Service as it associated the relationship between the access points involved and the flow of information between these access points.

Values: Point-to-point communication. This value applies when there are only two access points.
Multipoint communication. This value applies when more than two access points are provided by the service. The exact characteristics of the information flows must be specified separately based on functions provided by the ISDN. The number of access points can be undefined.
Broadcast communication. This value applies when more than two access points are provided by the service. The information flows from a unique point (source) to the others (destination) in only one direction. The number of destination access points is undefined.

Connection configuration. The spatial arrangements for transferring information on a given connection. It consists of three sub-attributes. Therefore no value is affected.

Values: Point-to-point connection. This value applies when only two end points are provided by the connection.
Multipoint connection. This value applies when more than two end points are provided by the connection, and thus many different information flows are possible.
Broadcast connection. [To be defined.]

Topology. The arrangements of connection elements to form the ISDN connection in addition to the connection configuration.

Values: Simple connection. A connection consisting of only one connection element.

Tandem connection. Two or more connection elements in series form a connection.

Parallel connection. Two or more connection elements in parallel form a connection.

Multipoint connection. Star or mesh [to be defined].

Uniformity. The commonality or differences of the attributes of the individual connection elements involved in a given connection.

Values: Uniform. This value applies when all connection elements have the same attribute value.

Non-uniform. This value applies in all other cases.

Dynamics. The way the connection elements are established, and the release time.

Values: Concurrent. The configuration of a connection is described as concurrent when all of the connection elements involved are established simultaneously and released simultaneously.

Sequential. A connection has a sequential configuration when its connection elements are established and released sequentially, i.e., only one of several connection elements or chains of connection elements exists at any given time.

Add/remove. When connection elements can be established and released while other connection elements of the same connections still exist, the configuration of this connection is described as add/remove.

Structure. The capability of the ISDN to deliver information to the destination access point or reference point in a structure (e.g., time interval for circuit mode, service data unit for packet mode), that was presented in a corresponding signal structured at the origin access point or reference point.

Values: 8 kHz integrity. This value applies when: (i) at each user-network interface, intervals of 125 μs are implicitly or explicitly demarcated, and (ii) all bits submitted within a single demarcated 125 μs interval are delivered within a corresponding single demarcated 125 μs interval.

Service data unit integrity. This value applies when: (i) at each user-network interface, protocols provide a mechanism for identifying the boundaries of service data units (e.g., X.25 complete packet sequence), and (ii) all bits submitted within a single service data unit are delivered in a corresponding service data unit.

Unstructured. This value is applicable when the Telecommunication Service or connection neither provides structural boundaries nor preserves structural integrity.

Access channel and rate. The channels and their bit rate used to transfer the user information and/or signalling information at a given access point or reference point. This attribute can be used several times for connection characterization.

Values: Letter identification of the channel and the corresponding bit rate.

Supplementary services provided. The supplementary services associated with a given Telecommunication Service.

Values: [To be determined.]

Quality of service. A group of specific sub-attributes, such as service reliability and service availability.

Values: [To be determined.]

Performances. The network performances that relate to an ISDN connection, such as error performance and slip performance.

Values: Error performance. The values are given in the appropriate CCITT Recommendations.
Slip performance. The values are given in the appropriate CCITT Recommendations.

Part II of the I-Series Recommendations deals specifically with ISDN Service Capabilities. At present it contains these Recommendations: I.210 (Principles), I.211 (Bearer Services), and I.212 (Teleservices).

Recommendation I.210

PRINCIPLES OF TELECOMMUNICATION SERVICES SUPPORTED BY AN ISDN

1. General

1.1 An ISDN will support at wide range of services as described generally in Rec. I.120. The purpose of this Recommendation is to provide a classification and a method of description of such services as well as giving a basis for the definition of the network capabilities required by ISDN. These network capabilities are defined in the I.300 series of Recommendations.

2. Service Concept

2.1 Services supported by an ISDN are the communication capabilities made available to customers by telecommunication service providers. An ISDN provides a set of Network Capabilities which are defined by standardized protocols and functions and enable Telecommunication services to be offered to Customers. A service provision by the network provider to a Customer connected to an ISDN may cover the whole or only part of the means required to fully support the services. The operational and commercial features associated with provision of the service are included in the service concept. The service classification and descriptions which follow are independent of different possible arrangements for ownership and provision to the customer of the means required to support a service.

2.2 Telecommunication services are described by attributes that define service characteristics as they apply at a given reference point where the customer accesses the service. Rec. I.130 describes the use of attributes for this purpose.

2.3 A Telecommunication service is composed of:

- technical attributes as seen by the customer; and
- other attributes associated with the service provision,
- e.g., operational and commercial attributes.

Realization of the technical attributes of a Telecommunication Service requires a combination of network and terminal capabilities and other service providing systems.

2.4 Telecommunication services are divided into two broad categories, i.e., Bearer Services and Teleservices, as defined in Rec. I.112. These services are described in Recs. I.211 and I.212.

2.5 A supplementary service modifies or supplements a basic Telecommunication Service. Consequently, it cannot be offered to a customer as a stand alone service. It must be offered together with or in association with a basic Telecommunication Service. The same supplementary service must be common to a number of Telecommunication Services. Supplementary services correspond to the concept of user facilities in the X series of Recommendations. A supplementary service is characterized by appropriate attributes. Their characterization requires further study.

2.6 The concepts introduced in this Recommendation are illustrated in [Table 4-1].

Table 4-1
Categorization of Telecommunication Services

Telecommunication Service			
Bearer Service		*Teleservice*	
Basic Bearer Service	Basic Bearer Service + Supplementary Services	Basic Teleservice	Basic Tele- service + Supplementary Services

Source: Rec. I.210, Table 1/I.210.

3. Customer access to Telecommunication Services supported by an ISDN

3.1 Considering the reference configurations defined in Rec. I.411, customers can access various Telecommunication Services at different access points. [Figure 4-2] shows these access points. This figure takes into account that the service provision by the network provider to a customer connected to an ISDN may cover the whole or only part of the means required to fully support the service.

3.2 The definitions of the access points introduced in [Figure 4-2] are as follows:

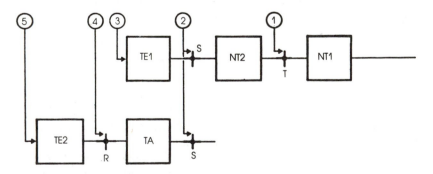

Figure 4-2   Customer Access to Service Supported by an ISDN
Source: Rec. I.210, Fig. 1/I.210.

i)   Access points 1 (reference point T) and 2 (reference point S) are the access points for Bearer Services supported by an ISDN. The choice between access point 1 (T) and 2 (S) depends on the ownership and form of provision (to the customer) of the communications equipment at the customer premises. The service classification and description in the following are independent of different possible arrangements for such provision.

ii) At access point 4 (reference point R), depending on the type of Terminal Adaptors provided, other CCITT standardized services may be accessed, e.g., according to the X and V series of Recommendations.

iii) At access points 3 and 5 (user to terminal interface), Teleservices are accessed — The Teleservice concept includes the terminal capabilities.

3.3 The following customer entities may be connected at access points 1 and 2:

- Customer terminals;
- Customer systems, e.g., PABXs, LANs Service Vendor Systems;
- Private Networks.

Note: Customer terminals and systems may be private or provided by Administrations or RPOAs.

All customer equipment connected to an ISDN interface at one of these access points must meet the specifications of the protocols at that interface for all the layers that are included in the definition of the Telecommunication Service used. For some Telecommunication Services the service definition also covers some terminal functions and characteristics in addition to those specified by the protocols at the interface.

4.   Capabilities to support a Telecommunication Service

4.1 The Capabilities required to fully support a Telecommunication Service for a customer connected to an ISDN include:

- Network Capabilities;
- Terminal Capabilities, when required;
- Other service providing capabilities, when required;
- Operational and commercial features associated with the service provision (i.e., sales or marketing aspects).

4.2 Network Capabilities are described in detail in Recommendation I.310. Two different levels of ISDN network capabilities are introduced:

- Lower Layer Capabilities, which relate to Bearer Services;
- Higher Layer Capabilities, which together with Low Layer Capabilities relate to Teleservices.

The Low Layer Capabilities are defined as a set of Low Layer Functions (LLF) (relating to layers 1-3 in X.200) which provide capability for the carriage of user information over an ISDN Connection.

These functions include:

- Basic Low Layer Functions (BLLF) supporting the necessary Layer 1-3 requirements;
- Additional Low Layer Functions (ALLF) supporting, in addition to BLLFs, Lower Layer requirements of supplementary services.

Higher Layer Capabilities are defined as a set of High Layer Functions (HLF) generally associated with layers 4 to 7 in X.200.

High Layer Functions are subdivided into Basic High Layer Functions (BHLF) and additional High Layer Functions (AHLF).

Note: Dependent upon national regulations, ALLF, BHLF, and AHLF may be provided by administrations, RPOAs, or other suppliers.

4.3 The concept of describing network capabilities in terms of Low Layer Capabilities and High Layer Capabilities can equally be applied to describe terminal capabilities. In the description of Teleservices, the HLF and LLF are included in the service definition. In the case of Bearer Service definition, the terminal capabilities are not included in the service definition. In the case of Bearer Service definition, the terminal capabilities are not included, but the terminal must conform to the LLF of the Bearer Service.

Note: The relationships between service categories, network/terminal capabilities and functions are illustrated in [Table 4-2].

4.4 The operational service capabilities associated with a service offering may include capabilities for maintenance, charging, user control of service features, etc. The user of such capabilities may involve terminal-network communication and may therefore be viewed as specific applications. A more precise description of these capabilities and the relationship to X.200 needs further study.

Table 4-2
Relationship between Service Categories, Network/Terminal Capabilities and Functions

Telecommunication Service	Network Capabilities Specified				Terminal Capabilities Specified				Commercial Features/ Operational Capabilities
	LLF		HLF		LLF		HLF		
	BLLF	ALLF*	BHLF*	AHLF*	BLLF	ALLF	BHLF	AHLF	
Bearer	X	opt	opt	opt	—	—	—	—	X
Teleservice	X	opt	opt	opt	X	opt	X	opt	X

X: specified   opt: optional   —: not specified

Note (*) — Dependent upon national regulations, ALLF, BHLF, and AHLF may be provided by Administrations, RPOAs or other suppliers.

Source: Rec. I.210, Table 2/I.210.

5. Telecommunication Service characterization

5.1 A Telecommunication Service supported by an ISDN is characterized and described by service attributes. There are two groups of service attributes applicable to user information flow:

- low layer attributes;
- high layer attributes.

Bearer Services are characterized only by Low Layer Attributes. Teleservices are characterized by both Low Layer Attributes and High Layer Attributes. The basic characteristics of a Telecommunication Service are described by the basic service attributes. The relationship between Telecommunication Service attributes and low/high layer functions is illustrated in [Table 4-3].

5.2 Bearer Services supported by an ISDN

5.2.1 Bearer Services supported by an ISDN provide the capability for information transfer between ISDN access points 1 or 2 and involve only low layer functions. The customer may choose any set of high layer (at least 4-7) protocols for his communication, and the ISDN does not ascertain compatibility at these layers between customers. An example of a bearer service is a switched circuit-mode 64 kbit/s unrestricted digital information service.

5.2.2 Bearer Services are characterized by a set of low layer attributes in Rec. I.211. These attributes are classified into three categories:

- information transfer attributes;
- access attributes; and
- general attributes, including operational and commercial attributes.

The Bearer Capability defines the technical features of a Bearer Service as they appear to the user at the appropriate access point (1 or 2). For the time being, the Bearer Capability is characterized by information transfer and access attributes. A bearer Capability is associated with every Bearer Service.

Note: It is likely that some quality of service parameters (attributes corresponding to Rec. I.211) — such as error rate or call set-up delay — should be extracted in order to form a new attribute allocated to the information transfer category. Identification and definition of such parameters requires further consideration.

Table 4-3
Relationship between Service Attributes and Low/High Layer Functions

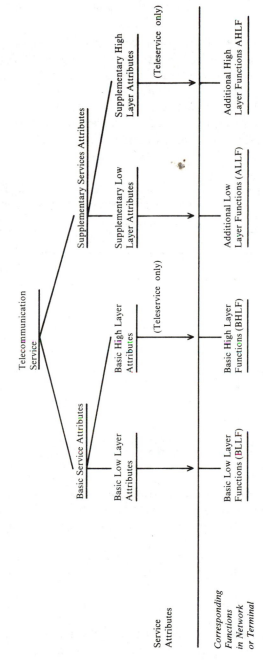

Source: Rec. I.210, Table 3/I.210.

5.2.3 A Bearer Service provides the user with the possibility of gaining access to various forms of communication, covering for example:

- information transfer between users employing the same access points (1 or 2) and access attributes [see Figure 4-3a];
- information transfer between users employing different access attributes at the access points (1 or 2) involved, [see Figure 4-3b]; and
- information transfer between a user and a separate resource providing high layer functions, [see Figure 4-3c].

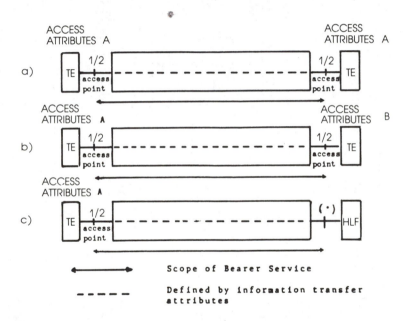

(*) Access point to be defined but not necessarily subject to CCITT Recommendations (see Recommendation I.310).

Note 1 - Further study is required on bearer services extending beyond the ISDN.

Note 2 - Further study is required on possible communications involving bearer services with different values allocated to information transfer attributes.

Figure 4-3   Examples of Bearer Service Operation

Source: Rec. I.210, Fig. 2/I.210.

5.3 Teleservices supported by an ISDN

5.3.1 Teleservices provide the full capacity for communication by means of terminals and network functions and possibly functions provided by dedicated services. A Teleservice supported by an ISDN should use only one (or a small number of) Bearer Capability recommended by CCITT. It should be noted that in the case where more than one of the recommended Bearer Capabilities is used for a given Teleservice, network interworking functions may be required under the responsibility of the Teleservice provider. However, a user operating a specific application is not prevented from using a terminal compatible with a given Teleservice in association with a Bearer Capability not recommended for this Teleservice. Examples of Teleservices are Telephony, Teletex, Videotex and message handling.

5.3.2 Teleservices are characterized by a set of low layer attributes, a set of high layer attributes and operational and commercial attributes.

Low layer attributes are those used to characterize the Bearer Capability (see section 5.2.2). High layer attributes are used in Recommendation I.212 to describe message (i.e., message on layer 7) related characteristics of a service (Basic high layer attributes) or of a supplementary service (supplementary high layer attributes). They refer to the functions and protocols of layers 4-7 in the X.200 which are concerned with the transfer, storage, and processing of user messages (provided by a subscriber's terminal, a retrieval Center on a Network Service Center).

Therefore not all these attributes can be applied directly at the user to terminal interface (access point 3 or 5) as they represent two kinds of features, the Bearer Capability and the Terminal features, that are not directly perceived by the user.

Note: The definition of appropriate attributes and the specifications of Teleservices at this access point from the user point of view (man-machine interface) is for further study.

5.3.3 A Teleservice provides the user with the possibility of gaining access to various forms of applications (or Teleservice applications) covering for example:

- Teleservice application involving two terminals providing the same Teleservice attributes at both access points (3 or 5) [see Figure 4-4a];

- Teleservice application involving a terminal at one access point (3 or 5) and HLF functions located within the ISDN [see Figure 4-4b];
- Teleservice application involving terminals based on different Teleservice attributes at each access point — in this case the use of HLF functions in the ISDN is necessary (interworking situation) [see Figure 4-4c];
- Teleservice application involving a terminal at one access point (3 or 5) and a system providing HLF functions [see Figure 4-4d].

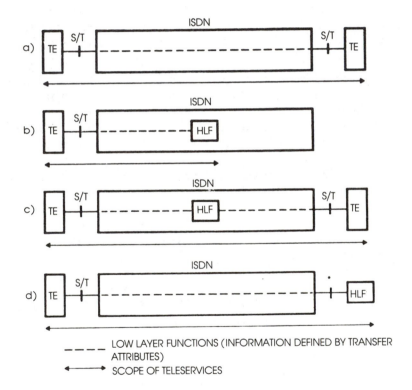

Note - Teleservices are accessed at access points 3 or 5 HLF
— High Layer functions
* Access point to be defined, but not necessary subject to CCITT Recommendations (see Recommendation I.310)

Figure 4-4   Examples of Teleservice Operation

Source: Rec. I.210, Fig. 3/I.210.

6.   Provision of Telecommunication Services

6.1 A Telecommunication Service is provided by an Administration, RPOA and/or other service providers. Customer terminals and systems may be privately owned or provided by Administrations or RPOAs. Depending on the nature of customer ownership within the customer premises (TE or TE-and-NT2), a Telecommunication Service is provided at different access-points.

6.2 The provision of Telecommunication Services implies:

- subscription ensuring the basic service and possibly subscription to supplementary services;
- registration into a service directory in the case where demand services are used;
- compatibility between terminals;
- interworking capabilities — (this point needs further study).

Recommendation I.211

BEARER SERVICES SUPPORTED BY AN ISDN

Outline

1.   **Framework for describing Bearer Services supported by an ISDN**

2.   **Description of Bearer Services**
2.1   **Circuit-mode Bearer Services**
2.1.1   Circuit-mode 64 kbit/s unrestricted, 8 kHz structured Bearer Service category
2.1.2   Circuit-mode 64 kit/s, 8 kHz structured Bearer Service category, usable for speech information transfer
2.1.3   Circuit-mode 64 kbit/s, 8 kHz structured Bearer Service category, usable for 3.1 kHz audio information transfer
2.1.4   Circuit-mode alternate speech/64 kbit/s non-speech, 8 kHz structured Bearer Service category
2.1.5   Circuit-mode alternative speech/3.1 kHz audio, 8 kHz structured Bearer Service category
2.1.6   Circuit-mode 384 kbit/s unrestricted, 8 kHz structured Bearer Service category
2.1.7   Circuit-mode 1536 kbit/s unrestricted, 8 kHz structured Bearer Service category
2.1.8   Circuit-mode 1920 kbit/s unrestricted, 8 kHz structured Bearer Service category

2.2   **Packet-mode Bearer Service**
2.2.1   Virtual call and permanent virtual circuit Bearer Service category
2.2.2   Connectionless packet Bearer Service category on a D channel.

3.   **Recommended provision of Bearer Services**
3.1   **Circuit-mode Bearer Services**
3.1.1   Circuit-mode 64 kbit/s, 8 kHz structured Bearer Service category
3.1.2   Circuit-mode 64 kbit/s, 8 kHz structured Bearer Service category, usable for speech information transfer
3.1.3   Circuit-mode 64 kbit/s, 8 kHz structured Bearer Service category, usable for 3.1 kHz audio information transfer
3.1.4   Circuit-mode alternate speech/64 kbit/s non-speech, 8 kHz structured Bearer Service category
3.1.5   Circuit-mode alternative speech/3.1 kHz audio, 8 kHz structured Bearer Service category
3.1.6   Circuit-mode 384 kbit/s unrestricted, 8 kHz structured Bearer Service category
3.1.7   Circuit-mode 1536 kbit/s unrestricted, 8 kHz structured Bearer Service category
3.1.8   Circuit-mode 1920 kbit/s unrestricted, 8 kHz structured Bearer Service category
3.2   **Packet-mode Bearer Service**
3.2.1   Virtual call and permanent virtual circuit Bearer Service category
3.2.2   Connectionless packet Bearer Service category on a D channel.

Recommendation I.212

TELESERVICES SUPPORTED BY AN ISDN

The purpose of the Recommendation is to provide an outline and allocation of attributes of Teleservices to be used as a basis for defining the network capabilities required by an ISDN and to give a framework for the standardization of Teleservices for guidance to other groups (i.e., the definition of values associated with the attributes.

1. **Framework for describing Teleservices supported by an ISDN.** Teleservices supported by an ISDN are described by a number of attributes which are intended to be largely independent.

They are grouped into three categories:

- Low Layer attributes, including information transfer attributes, and access attributes.
- High Layer attributes.
- General attributes.

Note: Teleservices generally make use of underlying lower layer capabilities of Bearer Services specified in Rec. I.211. However, where Teleservices are provided by a single Administration, RPOA or other service provider, the combination of values of lower layer attributes applicable to specific Teleservices may not necessarily be identical to any of those identified for the Bearer Services appearing in Rec. I.211.

[Figure 4-5] shows the relationship between the different categories of service attributes and their scope within a Teleservice.

Note: Sub-attributes are mentioned in order to give an example of a specific presentation description of characteristics such as coding of the user information, resolution and graphic mode. Sub-attributes for other presentation characteristics are for further study.

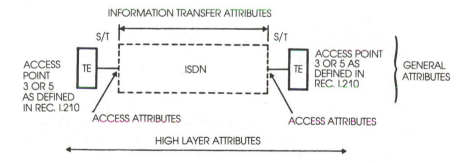

Figure 4-5 ***Relationship between the Categories of Service Attributes***
and their Scope within a Teleservice
Source: Rec. I.212, Fig. 1/I.212.

2. **List of the Teleservice attributes.**

2.1 **Low Layer attributes (see Rec. I.211).**
- information transfer attributes
- access attributes

2.2 **High Layer attributes.**
- type of user information
- Layer 4 protocol functions
- Layer 5 protocol functions
- Layer 6 protocol functions
  - — Resolution [if applicable]
  - — Graphic mode [if applicable]
- Layer 7 protocol functions

2.3 **General attributes.**

- Supplementary low and high layer attributes (supplementary services)
- User-oriented quality of service
  Interworking possibilities
- Operational and commercial

REFERENCES

1. Although Study Group XVIII was generally consistent in its use of the term "user" to describe a class of entities external to the network, it was not consistent in the application of the term or in refraining from using analogous undefined terms such as "customer" or "subscriber."

2. This meeting was called an "inter-regnum" meeting because Study Group XVIII, as a plenary body, did not convene until June 1981.

3. Report on the Inter-Regnum Meeting of Experts on ISDN Matters (Innisbrook 12-15 January 1981), CCITT Doc. COM XVIII-No. R1 at 19 (1981).

4. *See* CCITT Docs. COM XVIII-Nos. J and M, and Annex B, Innisbrook Report, *supra* at 22-23.

5. *Id.* at 24-25.

6. Report of the Meeting of Working Party XVIII/1 (ISDN), CCITT Doc. COM XVIII-No. R3 at 3 (1981).

7. *See* CCITT Docs. COM XVIII-Nos. 15, 25, 26, 30, 32, 33, AP, AQ, and AR.

8. *Id.* at 13.

9.   *See* CCITT Docs. COM XVIII-Nos. BM, BZ, CA, CD, CH, CQ, CR, DD, and DG.

10.   Report of the Meeting of the Group of Experts on ISDN Matters of Study Group XVIII (Munich, 17-25 February 1982), CCITT Doc. COM XVIII-No. R8 at 51 (1981).

11.   *See* CCITT Docs. COM XVIII-Nos. 69, 104, 115, 116, 125, 129, 140, 151, GY, HE, HF, HQ, HW, HX, HY, IE, IJ, IK, IL, IM, IN, IO, JB, BC, JF, JI, JL, JO, JR, JY, KA, KC and KT.

12.   *See* ISDN in Europe, Special Group ISDN (GSI) 1982 Report on Integrated Services Digital Network Studies, Conference Europeanne des Administrations des Postes et des Telecommunications, Doc. T/CCH(82)30, Doc. T/GSI (82)71 (Stockholm, November 1982).

13.   Report of the Meeting of the Group of Experts on ISDN Matters of Study Group XVIII (Kyoto, 14-25 February 1983), CCITT Doc. COM XVIII-No. R15 at 172 (1983).

14.   USA, Framework for Describing ISDN Services, CCITT Doc. COM XVIII-No. IJ (1983).

15.   *See* CCITT Docs. COM XVIII-Nos. LZ, MN, NM, MR, MS, MT, MU, NM, NO, NP, NT, NX, ON, PY, QD, and QE.

16.   *See* CCITT Docs. COM XVIII-Nos. 205, SG, SH, SI, SJ, SK, TI, TT, TX, TY, UD, US, UT, UX, UY, UZ, VA, VB, VC, VD, VE, VQ, and VL.

17.   Report of Working Term 4 (Services), CCITT Doc. COM XVIII-No. 211 at 11 (1983).

18.   *See* CCITT Doc. COM XVIII-No. UX.

19.   *See* CCITT Docs. COM XVIII-Nos. VW, WJ, WL, WS, WT, WV, WW, WY, WZ, XA, XQ, XR, YB, YD, YG, YM, YP, YQ, YR, YS, YV, YZ, ZB, ZC, ZD, and ZG.

20.   Report of the Meeting of the Group of Experts on ISDN Matters of Study Group XVIII (Brasilia, 13-24 February 1984), CCITT Doc. COM XVIII-No. 229 at 19-20 (1984).

21.   *See* Final Report to the VIIth CCITT Plenary Assembly (Parts I and II), CCITT Doc. COM XVIII-R29 [also Doc. AP VIII-94] (1984).

CHAPTER 5 — OVERALL NETWORK ASPECTS AND FUNCTIONS

In Chapter 4, ISDN services were discussed. The perspective was that of the user looking into the network. What the user "saw" was a large matrix of attributes called services. In this chapter, we take a look into the network itself, examining how the network goes about providing those services.

Just as with the services question, the beginning of the 1981–1984 activity period witnessed considerable searching for the best way to proceed in the matter. Unlike the services questions, however, the network questions were considerably more complex. The subject involved many considerations of how networks operate internally, as well as interoperate with other networks. Many of these matters may appear arcane, and often are. On the other hand, some of the most intriguing, complex, and important ISDN issues can be found entwined with these technical and operational considerations.

In addition, this subject is virgin policy-making territory. In the past, networks slowly evolved according to fairly immutable engineering and planning practices oriented around fixed economic and technical trade-offs. In the United States, network issues did not percolate into the public policy-making domain under the former *de facto* monopoly environment. AT&T simply made network policy decisions within their corporate domain, occasionally dealing with the government on national security matters, a few small carriers, and foreign administrations.

Today, however, the US environment is completely different. Every portion of the national telecommunication network is subject to competitive alternatives. Questions concerning network policy have been suddenly thrust into the public domain, with a host of market and public interest issues at stake in a multi-billion dollar game. ISDN has become the subject of this new public scrutiny. With ISDN, the networks are being redesigned *de novo* from the ground up, and many options are capable of being built-in at the inception of design and invoked in the future through software changes. These options sometimes enjoy significant social and economic implications.

This chapter portrays the study of *general* network issues by Working Team 3 (WT3) of Study Group XVIII. It was faced with conceptualizing and developing details for ISDN, internally. How would the services be provided? What kind of protocols would be used? How would information be addressed to or from users? What kind of network architecture would be defined? These and other matters were all under WT3's jurisdiction. Considerable work on these matters was accomplished by other working teams and working parties of Study Group XVIII, and other study groups as well, but the primary focus occurred in WT3.

This chapter is divided into several parts, beginning with a general discussion of ISDN network questions, followed by the subdivision of network topics generally used by Working Team 3 and manifested as I-Series Recommendations: ISDN architecture functional model, ISDN protocol reference model, ISDN hypothetical reference connection, network addressing, routing, connection types, internetworking interfaces, and maintenance philosophy. Because the subject of network tariffs was only raised very briefly at the Kyoto, February 1983 meeting, and the only action taken was to refer WT3 work to Study Group III, a special part on tariffs was not included in this chapter.

5.1 General

This part describes only the general activities of Study Group XVIII focusing on network aspects. This principally involved the initial framing of the questions, and how the subject was conceptually subdivided and administered.

Seventh CCITT Plenary, Geneva 1980. The study of ISDN overall network aspects and functions during its 1981–1984 activity period largely emanated from Question 1/XVIII, Points B and D, adopted by the Seventh CCITT Plenary, meeting at Geneva in November 1980. The questions read as follows:

Point B. Network Aspects
1. What are the principles in terms of network structure and systems architecture which define the ISDN and which form the basis for study of specific aspects?
2. Should layered protocols and functional layers be adopted for ISDN to form the basis of CCITT Recommendations? If so, what are the characteristics of this layering, and in which way is the concept of functional layers used with respect to sub-systems, such as, e.g., the signalling channels?
3. What are the implications of ISDN on numbering plans and service indicators for telephony and other services?
4. What methods of voice band encoding other than standard PCM (see also Question 7/XVIII) and what forms of digital speech interpolation can be considered in relation to the evolution of the ISDN?

Point D. Interworking

What are the principles which should form the basis for detailed study of the interfaces interconnections and interworking between ISDN and service dedicated networks?

Question 1, Point E, dealing with "evolution towards ISDN" was also considered by those working on overall network aspects. It did not, however, give rise to much work, and resulted in only four short paragraphs in Recommendation I.120, discussed in Chapter 3, above.

In addition to Points B and D of Question 1, there were many other questions dealing with detailed aspects of network operation. Indeed, nearly all the remaining Study Group XVIII Questions, 3 through 19, in whole or part deal with these kinds of detailed matters, that ultimately resulted in many changes and additions to the Q and G Series Recommendations.

Innisbrook, January 1981. At the first meeting within Study Group XVIII during the 1981–1984 activity period, most of the work focused on interface and service questions. Few internal network matters were considered, although the subject was subdivided into three areas for further study: "internal network interfaces, internetwork (international) interfaces, and ISDN performance characteristics."[1] The parenthetical characterization of internetwork interfaces as "international," reflected the tendency of the group at this time to envision only one ISDN per country. In addition, there was a brief discussion of "categorization of network capabilities," and "network provided resources" that dealt with some internal network considerations.[2]

Geneva, June 1981. Work on general network aspects did not really get organized until Study Group XVIII convened in June 1981 at Geneva. Working Party 1, which was assigned all the key ISDN questions, and ultimately produced most of the I-Series Recommendations, was created. Within this Working Party, an adhoc group on network aspects was created under the chairmanship of J.C. Luetchford of Canada's Bell Northern Research, who was also the Rapporteur for Points B and D.[3] Luetchford, throughout the activity period, continued to lead the study of this aspect of ISDN.

Eleven contributions were identified as relevant to the group's focus, and the work was subdivided into four areas: network functions, network addressing, network applications of technology, and ISDN architecture reference models.[4] All of these subjects, as they were dealt with at the meeting, are considered in the parts below except "network applications of technology." The subdivision was a curious short-lived artifact, since there were no contributions specifically on the subject at the meeting, and the subdivision was soon changed to "connection types."

Munich, February 1982. Luetchford's group was reconvened as Ad Hoc Group 4 at the Munich ISDN Experts meeting. As a result of the discussions of the Study Group XVIII leadership at Montreal in September 1981, the subdivision of work was significantly revised into five categories: connection types, network addressing, ISDN hypothetical reference connections, ISDN protocol reference models, and ISDN architecture functional models. This new subdivision became the basic conceptualization for general network issues, and ultimately each evolved into an individual I-300 Series Recommendation.[5]

In addition to dealing with these network issues, Ad Hoc Group 4 adopted a list of "critical issues ... on which contributions are urgently invited."[6]

1. Terminal addressing.
2. Service and application addressing.
3. Customer selection of routing.
4. Application of voice processing in the ISDN.
5. ISDN architecture reference models.
6. ISDN protocol reference models.
7. ISDN performance criteria for network designs: End-to-end performance requirements. Should performance dictate design? Should high performance requirements dictate performance for other channels?
8. Application of voice, visual and multimedia conferencing services.
9. Use of satellites in: (a) early ISDN implementation; (b) as ISDN evolves.
10. Signalling evolution in the ISDN: (a) Application of signalling in TDMA environment; (b) Application of CCITT No. 7 if connection is set up for multi-media applications, i.e., impact of ISDN on CCITT No. 7 user part strategy.
11. Which network interfaces should be subject of international standards?
12. Channel switching applications, e.g.: (a) switch out processing devices on data calls, e.g., echo control; (b) route only via channels having adequate bit rate capacity.
13. Allocation of performance criteria to network components.
14. Application of visual and wideband services in the network.
15. Application of ISDN to private networks. Interconnection between public and private ISDNs.
16. Location of the network boundary for multi-line customer equipment such as PBXs, concentrators, multiplexers, *et cetera.*
17. Operations and administration functions.
18. Routing control and routing restrictions.
19. Application of remote switching units to make the network more cost effective and more flexible for new services implementation.

20. ISDN network traffic characterization, e.g., distribution of traffic by type, by service, busy hour, *et cetera*.
21. Identify additional issues for the services/network features matrix developed under Question 1A.

Kyoto, February 1983. Luetchford's group met as Working Team 3 at the Kyoto ISDN Experts meeting. This was an identity it would continue to enjoy for the remainder of the activity period. In addition to the five Munich subdivisions of work, five more were added: routing, ISDN evolution, ISDN maintenance philosophy, internetworking interfaces, and tariff.[7] Four draft Recommendations were prepared: I.32x (Architecture Functional Model), I.311 (Protocol Reference Model), I.320 (Numbering and Addressing Principles), and I.340 (Connection Types).

Geneva, June 1983. At Geneva in June 1983, Working Team 3 consolidated the structure of its work into eight subdivisions: connection types, ISDN architecture functional model, ISDN protocol reference model, ISDN numbering and addressing principles, ISDN maintenance philosophy, evolution to an ISDN, ISDN inputs to HRX, and ISDN interworking.[8]

Geneva, November 1983. At Geneva in November 1983, Working Team 3 reconvened and continued to study the issues within the June 1983 framework. In addition, assignments were given to produce drafts of the questions for the next study period.[9]

Responding to a decision on the structural organization of the I-Series, WT3 borrowed material from several of the I-300 Series Recommendations it was developing, and produced a draft "principles" recommendation, initially identified as I.300 and later changed to I.310. As noted in Chapter 4, the working team on ISDN services took a similar action at this time.

Brasilia, February 1984. Working Team 3 met for the last time during the 1981–84 activity period at Brasilia in February 1984. It made final changes to the draft I.300-Series Recommendations and adopted draft questions for the next study period.[10]

In addition to essentially finalizing the I-Series Recommendations on ISDN network aspects, Working Team 3 also produced answers to Question 1, Points B and D, as follows:

Point B. Network Aspects

1. (a)   *Network functional principles.* Rec. I.310, Network functional principles, was developed as an introduction to the network series of ISDN Recommendations. Rec. I.310 develops functional principles and functional groups of network capabilities in an ISDN to provide a common understanding across ISDN Recommendations of network func-

tions. In addition, Rec. I.130, attributes for the characterization of telecommunication services supported by an ISDN and network capabilities of an ISDN, was prepared to define attributes used in ISDN services and network Recs. I.211 and I.390.

(b) *Network architecture model.* Work was initiated to develop an ISDN architecture model sufficiently detailed to be useful in directing other ISDN studies, but not so specific to restrict national network implementation arrangements. Draft Rec. I.32x, ISDN architecture functional model, was developed in two parts. Part A is a functional model independent of any architecture. Part B is an architecture example of how the functional requirements may be met. While there was substantial support for the work, it was not possible to obtain agreement in this study period to issue the model as a Recommendation. A question has been prepared for the next study period with draft Rec. I.32x attached as an annex to the Question. *See* Question 3/ XVIII.[11]

(c) *ISDN connection types.* Network connection types were identified as a key element in the ISDN functional architecture. Rec. I.340, ISDN connection types, was developed. Rec. I.340 describes the types, elements and characteristics of ISDN network connections to support the Bearer and Teleservices developed under Question 1, Point A, and Recs. of the I.200 series. A question has been prepared for the next study period to extend this work. *See* Question 5/ XVIII.

(d) *ISDN testing and maintenance principles.* Based on work in Study Group XI and the need to input ISDN information to Study Group IV, a number of ISDN maintenance principles were developed. It was not possible to obtain agreement on maintenance principles and a new Question covering access and network maintenance principles has been prepared for the next study period. Results from the current study period are included as annexes to Question 18/XVIII.

(e) *ISDN hypothetical reference connections (HRX).* Some preliminary work identified that ISDN HRX should take account of the network down to the T reference point, may require a number of models to cover mixed interworking between ISDN and dedicated networks, and should take account of Recs. I.340, X.110, G.104, X.92 and draft Rec. E. 17x. New questions have been proposed for the next study period. *See* Questions 13 thru 17/XVIII.

(f) *ISDN routing principles.* It was noted that interworking between ISDN and various dedicated networks will create a new range of network routing issues. It was agreed that ISDN routing principles were closely linked to ISDN numbering principles. It was further noted that ISDN numbering principles should be accorded higher priority. A new question was prepared for the next study period. *See* Question 10/XVIII. Work on the new question must be closely coordinated with Study Groups II and VII.

(g) *Connection supervision principles.* Preliminary work as carried out on the network implication of ISDN call connection supervision. It was agreed that there shall be consistency in connection supervision as perceived by the users of ISDN and dedicated networks. Such consistency shall apply within a class of connections, e.g., voice or data, but not necessarily across classes. Work on this topic should be included in the new question on connection types. *See* Question 5/XVIII.

2. Rec. I.320, ISDN protocol reference model was developed. Rec. I.320 describes the ISDN protocol reference model in relation to the OSI reference model (X.200). It provides a basis for the definition and structure of protocols and procedures for communication in an ISDN. Further work on ISDN protocol modelling needs to be carried out, particularly on the relationship between X.200 and I.320. A new question has been prepared for the next study period. *See* Question 4/XVIII.

3. Rec. I.330, ISDN numbering and addressing principles were developed. Rec. I.330 describes the addressing and numbering principles for addressing interfaces at reference points located at subscriber premises and other network functions for allowing communication with terminal equipment. It also identifies the requirements for applying a numbering plan to ISDN and provides a basis for studies of ISDN routing principles and routing plan in the next period. A question has been prepared to extend the studies in coor-

dination with Study Groups II and VII in the next study period. *See* Question 8/XVIII.

4.   Studies under other Questions resulted in draft Rec. G.7ZZ, 32 kbit/s coding. No further work was undertaken under Question 1, Point B.

Point D. Interworking

Where appropriate, studies of this Question were coordinated with the studies on Question 1B/XVIII. As a result of the concentration of work on services and work on network aspects, little progress was made on Question 1D. Some of the specific issues raised in Question 1D have been included in the reply to Question 1B.

The progress on ISDN network aspects established under Question 1B/XVIII will enable work to focus on interworking in the next study period. Two new Questions have been proposed: (a) internetworking interfaces between ISDN and dedicated networks. See Question 6/XVIII.[12]

5.2 ISDN Architecture Functional Model (I.310, I.32x)

The first step in discussing the subject of telecommunication networks generally involves the conceptualization of the basic functions the network is expected to perform and the manner in which it will be internally structured or organized. This is frequently referred to as the network architecture. It was, to be sure, one of the initial tasks of WT3.

Geneva, June 1981. Question 1, under which the work on general network aspects was occurring, contained two figures outlining functional network models. This was pointed out at the initial meeting of the working team at Geneva in June 1981, which considered architecture functional models together with protocol models under the topic of architecture reference models.[13] The development of architecture functional reference models was considered urgent to provide a basis for the development of transmission and switch connection models.

It was pointed out that the distributed nature of functions in an ISDN should be a feature of such models. By combining the results of core network models with the access reference models developed for the user-network interface, end-to-end architecture reference models could be developed. One contribution addressed the development of network models, suggesting the combination of existing access, switch and digital interface proposals into a single model.[14] Additional contributions for the next meeting were solicited.

Munich, February 1982. When the team reconvened at Munich, five new contributions were received, and architecture functional models were considered as a distinct subdivision of study.[15] The work focused on a relatively detailed document on architecture reference models developed at the Montreal Study Group XVIII meeting of chairman several months previous. Concern was expressed, however, that all the models considered to date were too specifically implementation oriented. It was agreed that a functional model without implementation implications was the desired objective, and that a "novel approach" was needed. To encourage studies towards development of a suitable functional model, several examples from the submitted contributions were included in the report of the meeting.[16]

The document on architecture reference models subsequently caused a considerable stir in the United States because the diagram depicting functional categories did not include non-switched "leased" circuit functions. (*See* the Chapter 8 material dealing with the leased circuit issue.) The diagram was subsequently amended.

Kyoto, February 1983. By the next time the working team reconvened at Kyoto, it was agreed that sufficient material was available to initiate a draft Recommendation on an ISDN architecture functional model.[17] Four contributions were submitted.[18] The objective was to provide a common understanding to assist the specification of characteristics that appear at user-network and interworking interfaces. In response to the only US government prepared contribution to Study Group XVIII during this activity period,[19] it was emphasized that "characteristics of the model should not preclude or inhibit any national implementation."[20]

The draft Recommendation was prepared in two parts, designated A and B. The first was to outline a conceptual view of "functional model" of ISDNs that would integrate the various Recommendations and identify their network relationship, based on two contributions.[21] The basic routing and interworking rules would also be included. The second part of the Recommendation would contain an example of how the needs of the functional model could be met, referred to as an "architectural model." The draft Recommendation was to be placed at the beginning of Recommendations dealing with protocol models and hypothetical reference circuits, and numbered I.310.

During the course of these discussions, the US contribution was extensively discussed. Working Team 3 noted that in some countries a customer network may be connected to more than one local network and possibly more than one transit network. However, Canada placed the following statement in the record:

An unrestricted capability for user selection could result in some end-to-end connections with 'round-about' routings not envisaged in network management arrangements and not necessarily meeting CCITT recommended service criteria. To avoid potential difficulties of this type, another general principle is needed as follows:

If a user is to be permitted selection of international routes, this selection must be restricted to the alternative combination of routes, services and characteristics between originating and terminating countries as bilaterally agreed between the concerned administrations (in consultation with their RPOAs).[22]

In response to the concern regarding leased circuits, the new figure on functional components was modified to contain "non-switched capabilities."

Geneva, June 1983. When WT3 met at Geneva in June 1983, there was little attention given draft Recommendation I.310.[23] Only one contribution concerning the subject was submitted, and minor adjustments were made.[24]

Geneva, November 1983. At the November 1983 meeting, the treatment of an architecture functional model becomes confused. Three contributions were submitted.[25] During the meeting, Recommendation I.310, Part A, was first redrafted and sections were placed in a new Recommendation I.311 dealing with protocol reference model issues. Then Recommendation I.311 was discarded and the Part A material was redrafted again to produce a new draft Recommendation dealing with "network functional principles," which was designated I.300, and the remainder of I.310 was left in limbo.[26]

Brasilia, February 1984. When activity was resumed at Brasilia in February 1984, several contributions were submitted in order to flesh out Recommendation I.300.[27] In the process of doing so, I.300 was designated I.310 (Functional Principles). Old I.310 was designated I.32x (Architecture Functional Model) and carried over to the next activity period with the statement "while there was substantial support for the work, it was not possible to obtain agreement in this study period to issue the model as a recommendation."[28]

Recommendation I.310, as adopted, is shown below.

Recommendation I.310

ISDN — NETWORK FUNCTIONAL PRINCIPLES

1.   **General.** This Recommendation outlines the functional principles of the network aspects of the ISDN as an introduction to the I.300 series of Recommendations on the ISDN. The objective of this Recommendation is to provide a common understanding of the ISDN network series of Recommendations by describing ISDN functional capabilities and their relationships.

2.   **Relationship with other I-Series Recommendations.** The concepts and the principles of an ISDN are described in Rec. I.120. The services supported by an ISDN are given in the I.200 series of Recommendations. The network capabilities to support those services are defined in the I.300 series of Recommendations and the relationship between them is shown in [Figure 5-1].

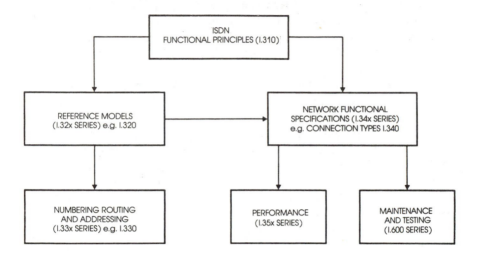

Figure 5-1   ISDN Network Series of Recommendation
Source: Rec. I.310, Fig. 1/I.310.

3.   **ISDN Functional Objectives.** As described in Rec. I.120, an Integrated Services Digital Network (ISDN) is a network providing end-to-end digital connectivity to support a wide range of telecommunications services. The standardization of ISDN by CCITT is centered on three main areas:

(a)   the standardization of services offered to subscribers, so as to enable services to be internationally compatible;

(b)   the standardization of user-network interfaces, so as to · enable terminal equipment to be portable and to assist in (a); and

(c)   the standardization of network capabilities to the degree necessary to allow user-network and network-network interworking, and so to achieve (a) and (b) above.

The I.200 series of Recommendations has identified the range of Telecommunication services to be offered in an ISDN, namely Bearer and Teleservices, and the attributes characterizing these services. The I.400 series of Recommendations describes both the functional and technical aspects of user-network interfaces. This Recommendation defines the network capabilities to support services via this interface in terms of Network *functions*. A network functional description enables a decoupling of services and network capabilities, and allows an implementation-independent approach.

The transition from an existing network to a comprehensive ISDN may require a period of time extending over one or more decades. Therefore the design of an ISDN will be evolutionary, adding capabilities in a flexible and modular form. An ISDN may therefore be expected to provide an open-ended set of functional capabilities able to accommodate new needs as they arise at acceptable cost.

During a long intermediate period, some functions may not be implemented within a given ISDN. Also specific arrangements should be used to ensure compatibility with existing networks and services. An ISDN should also give access to existing services and interwork with existing networks and terminals; in some countries this situation is likely to exist even in a very long term.

4.   **ISDN Functional Capabilities.** To achieve the functional objectives described in para. 3, the ISDN functional description has been designed to:

- define the overall characteristics of the ISDN;
- be implemented independent and place no constraints on national network architectures beyond the network and interface standards given in the I-Series of Recommendations;
- take full account of the constraints of existing dedicated networks;
- support the layering protocol concepts defined in Recommendations X.200 and I.320.

The ISDN functional description defines a set of network capabilities which enable Bearer and Teleservices to be offered to different levels of ISDN capabilities, viz.: the low-layer capabilities relate to the Bearer Services; and the high-layer capabilities together with the lower layer capabilities relate to the Teleservices.

In addition, operate and management capabilities are required to support both Bearer Services and Teleservices. These relationships between services and network capabilities are shown in [Figure 5-2].

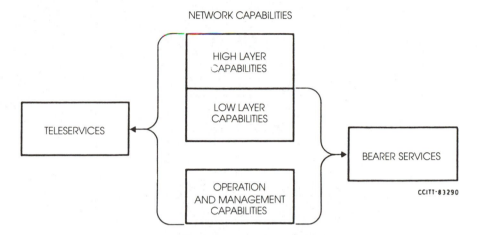

NETWORK CAPABILITIES

HIGH LAYER CAPABILITIES

LOW LAYER CAPABILITIES

TELESERVICES

BEARER SERVICES

CCITT-83290

OPERATION AND MANAGEMENT CAPABILITIES

Figure 5-2   Relationship between Services and ISDN Functional Capabilities

Source: Rec. I.310, Fig. 2/I.310.

ISDN functional capabilities can be further defined as follows:

(a) *Low-Layer Capabilities.* The set of low layer functions (LLF), pertaining to layers 1-3 of the OSI reference model in Rec. X.200, which provides the capability for the carriage of user information over an ISDN Connection. These functions include:

Basic Low Layer Functions (BLLF). These functions support the essential Layer 1-3 requirements of ISDN Connections. BLLF may be further subdivided into the two sub-types, namely:

Connection Control and Management Functions. These functions are needed for the control and management of connections in the network, e.g., signalling functions for the establishment and release of connections, maintenance functions performed during a connection;

Other Connection-Related Functions. These functions comprise all BLLF other than connection control and management functions necessary to provide the connection, e.g., switching and transmission functions.

Additional Low-Layer Functions (ALLF). These functions

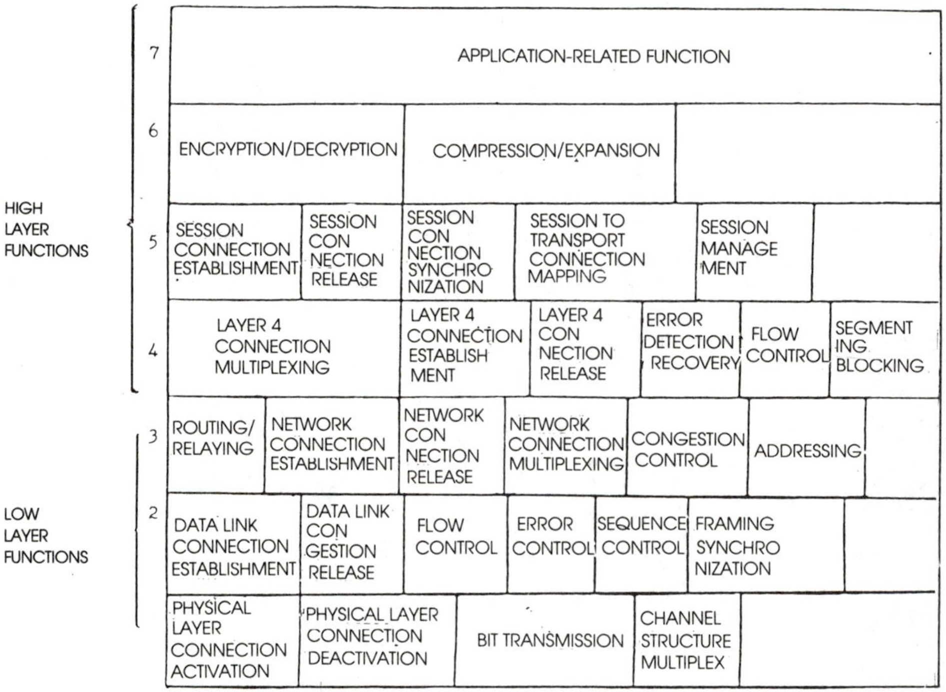

Layer	Functions					
7	APPLICATION-RELATED FUNCTION					
6	ENCRYPTION/DECRYPTION	COMPRESSION/EXPANSION				
5	SESSION CONNECTION ESTABLISHMENT	SESSION CONNECTION RELEASE	SESSION CONNECTION SYNCHRONIZATION	SESSION TO TRANSPORT CONNECTION MAPPING	SESSION MANAGEMENT	
4	LAYER 4 CONNECTION MULTIPLEXING	LAYER 4 CONNECTION ESTABLISHMENT	LAYER 4 CONNECTION RELEASE	ERROR DETECTION RECOVERY	FLOW CONTROL	SEGMENTING BLOCKING
3	ROUTING/RELAYING	NETWORK CONNECTION ESTABLISHMENT	NETWORK CONNECTION RELEASE	NETWORK CONNECTION MULTIPLEXING	CONGESTION CONTROL	ADDRESSING
2	DATA LINK CONNECTION ESTABLISHMENT	DATA LINK CONGESTION RELEASE	FLOW CONTROL	ERROR CONTROL	SEQUENCE CONTROL	FRAMING SYNCHRONIZATION
1	PHYSICAL LAYER CONNECTION ACTIVATION	PHYSICAL LAYER CONNECTION DEACTIVATION	BIT TRANSMISSION	CHANNEL STRUCTURE MULTIPLEX		

HIGH LAYER FUNCTIONS (7, 6, 5, 4)

LOW LAYER FUNCTIONS (3, 2, 1)

Figure 5-3   ISDN Functions Allocated to Layering Principles of Recommendation X.200

Note - The assignment of signal processing (e.g., speech processing) in the layered reference model is for further study.

Source: Rec. I.310, Fig. 3/I.310.

support, in addition to BLLF, low-layer requirements of supplementary services (e.g., call forwarding, abbreviated dialing). These functions are not always required in the provision of ISDN connections.

(b)*High Layer Capabilities.* The set of high layer functions (HLF), associated with layers 4 to 7, of the OSI model, described in Recommendation X.200. They may be implemented in nodes which are inside or outside an ISDN or in terminals. Dependent upon national regulations, HLF may be provided by Administrations, RPOAs, or other suppliers. These functions include: Basic High Layer Functions (BHLF); and Additional High Layer Functions (AHLF). The definition and identification of BHLF and AHLF is for further study. A general classification of high layer and low layer functions according to the layers defined in Rec. X.200 is shown in [Figure 5-3].

(c) *Network Operation and Management Capabilities.* These include functions required for network management and maintenance, but not necessarily performed in the course of a connection, e.g., link testing. The allocation of these functions according to the layering principles of Recommendation X.200 is for further study.

5. **Functional Realization of Service Requests.** From a functional point of view, the process involved in satisfying a service request in an ISDN can be described as follows:

(a)*Service request examination.* Given a service request, which is characterized by a set of attribute values, the appropriate connection type(s) to support it must be identified.

Input: Service request — set of service attribute values
Process: Examine service request and determine appropriate network connection type(s)
Output: Network connection type(s)

(b)*Connection element selection.* Once selected, the connection type (which has end-to-end significance) can further be broken down into one or more smaller functional components called "connection elements."

Input: Connection type
Process: Determine connection element(s) to implement connection type
Output: Connection element(s)

(c) *Function set determination.* Each connection element would require a set of network functions in order to be established.

Input: Connection element
Process: Select appropriate functions to establish connection element
Output: Set of functions

Note - Similar treatment for ALLF and HLF needs further study.

6. **Functional Description of Interworking.** A key element of service integration for an ISDN is the provision of a limited set of standard multi-purpose user-network interfaces.

The I.400 Series of Recommendations describes the characteristics of user-network interfaces for the following cases:

1. access of a single ISDN terminal;
2. access of a multiple ISDN terminal installation;
3. access of multiservice PBXs local area networks (LANs) or, more generally, private networks;
4. access of a non-ISDN terminal;
5. access of specialized storage and information processing centers.

In addition, considering that the evolution to a comprehensive ISDN will take place over a long period of time interworking with existing networks as well as other ISDNs will be necessary. These cases include:

1. access to existing telephony network and to dedicated networks (e.g., packet network, telex network);
2. access to another ISDN;
3. access to service providers outside the ISDN.

The ISDN user-network interfaces or internetwork interfaces may be used in the above cases. The definition of internetwork interfaces is necessary for these arrangements for interworking and administrative requirements.

Interworking with other networks or other ISDNs requires the provision of Interworking Functions (IWF); either within the ISDN or in the other network or in both. These functions would ensure interworking between different protocol and user procedures.

Within a country or geographical area, an ISDN connection may consist of an interconnection of several networks, each of which supports the attributes of one or more ISDN Connection Types (as defined in Recommendation I.340).

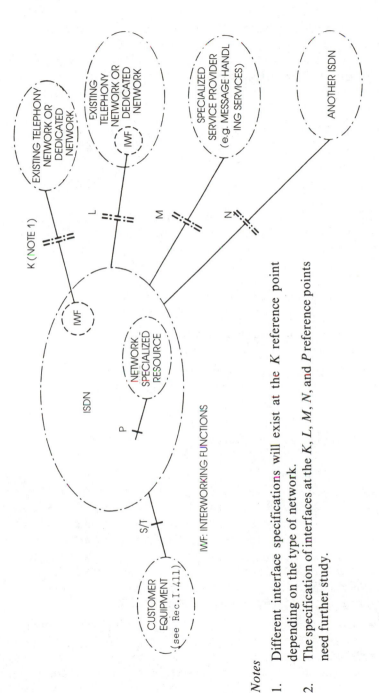

Figure 5-4 Reference Points Associated with the Interconnection of Customer Equipment and Other Networks to an ISDN

Source: Rec. I.310, Fig. 4/I.310.

Notes

1. Different interface specifications will exist at the *K* reference point depending on the type of network.

2. The specification of interfaces at the *K, L, M, N,* and *P* reference points need further study.

[Figure 5-4] depicts the ISDN user-network interfaces as defined in the I.400 Series of Recommendations, as well as reference points at which interwork interfaces between an ISDN and other networks (including other ISDNs) may exist. Whether these internetwork interfaces shall be defined by CCITT Recommendations is for further study.

7. **Basic Architecture Model.** A basic architectural model of an ISDN is shown in [Figure 5-5] that shows the seven main switching and signalling functional capabilities of ISDN:

- ISDN local functional capabilities, e.g., user-network signalling, charging,
- 64 kbit/s circuit switched functional capabilities,
- 64 kbit/s circuit non-switched functional capabilities,
- packet switching functional capabilities,
- common channel interexchange signalling functional capabilities,
- > 64 kbit/s switched functional capabilities,
- > 64 kbit/s non-switched functional capabilities.

Note - Circuit switched and non-switched functional capabilities at rates less than 64 kbit/s are for further study.

These capabilities need not be provided by distinct networks but may be combined as appropriate for a particular implementation. Further refinement of this model is for further study.

5.3 ISDN Protocol Reference Model (I.320)

Together with the basic functions and architecture of the network, it is necessary to develop a detailed methodology by which information and instructions are provided to or received from, or communicated within the network. These processes are referred to as protocol. They range from the most basic and simple, such as the matter in which physical connection is made to the network, to the sophisticated dialogue necessary to manipulate a remote data base. Protocols also enjoyed a high WT3 priority. Their efforts were assisted by the International Organization for Standardization's creation of the Open Systems Interconnection Model (OSI).

Geneva, June 1981. At the inception of the working team's effort, the subject of network protocol models was regarded as "important" and received explicit focus.[29] The discussion largely revolved around a document from Study Group VII describing the OSI Reference Model, and one contribu-

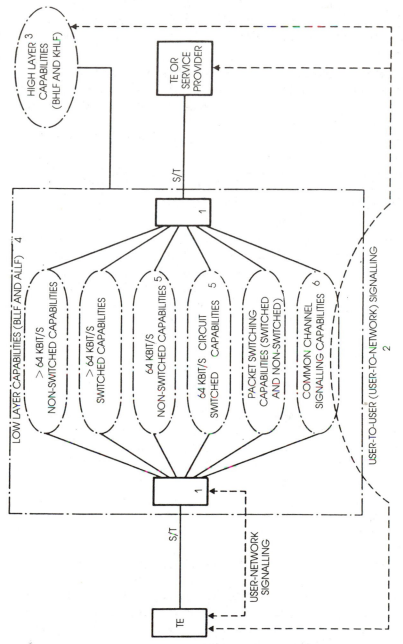

Figure 5-5 *Basic Architectural Model of an ISDN*
Source: Rec. I.310, Fig. 5/I.310.

tion.[30] The team agreed that it was likely that the OSI layered model will provide a basis for further study, and that protocol models will require the development of three kinds of ISDN protocols: access, internal network, and internetwork.

Munich, February 1982. The Montreal meeting of Study Group XVIII chairmen in September 1981 confirmed the suitability of a layered reference model and provided a good basis for the work in Munich. In addition, two contributions on network protocols were submitted.[31]

During the course of the meeting, a number of diagrams were developed that portrayed protocol models for: general user-network use; circuit switching; packet switching using the B-channel; and packet switching using the D-channel. These were believed to be useful in providing a basis for continued work.[32] Additionally, a nomenclature was suggested to clearly distinguish the access protocols (type A) from the network protocols (type B).

Kyoto, February 1983. At its February 1983 meeting, WT3 focused on the protocol reference model as one of its primary subdivisions of work. Fifteen contributions on the subject were submitted.[33] The need for a protocol reference model was confirmed as essential input to signalling design work, network control, signalling performance, address, *et cetera*. Discussion of the contributions proceeded in two stages: development of an overall protocol reference model, and testing it through iterations of network control functions.[34]

It was soon agreed to prepare a draft Recommendation of the overall protocol model based on Australian Doc. COM XVIII-No. KB, together with the work from the Munich meeting. The draft model had several desired features: integrity of layers 1 to 7 maintained across the network, signalling protocols that contained address information that routed through the signalling network, and transmission of information between users at each end of the network. The initial draft was given the designation I.311, which would be eventually changed to I.320.

Geneva, June 1983. At the June 1983 meeting of WT3, five new documents were submitted,[35] that together with feedback from Study Group XI, Working Party 6, provided the basis for a redraft of the protocol reference model Recommendation.[36]

A number of issues were considered: whether or not to include a separate management dimension; support of separate user and signalling dimensions; 3 layer or 7 layer signalling model; differences and similarities with X.200; points at which signalling control functions are invoked; and definitive layering of network and terminal entities. A list of mandatory model requirements was assembled, together with three essential components: functional component interface locations must be identified; network and terminal protocol functions to each layer of the model must be allocated; and the network control functions and signalling must be defined between each network interface. A revised draft recommendation for a protocol model was produced.

Geneva, November 1983. At the November 1983 meeting of WT3, considerable soul searching occurred. After a "lively discussion" of the two contributions[37] and the draft protocol Recommendation, an agreement was reached on several points. The current draft I.311 was not mature and required substantial work to bring it to Recommendation status. Key issues regarding inconsistencies between Q-Series Recommendations and current modelling principles existed. Urgent work was necessary to identify the issues where X.200 does not and cannot support ISDN protocols. To expedite the work, the drafting was turned over to a new chairman, who assisted in producing a new draft version of I.311.[38] Some of the issues were, however, carried over to the next meeting in February 1984.

Brasilia, February 1984. At the February 1984 meeting of WT3, several contributions were submitted that provided a basis for a number of final changes to the draft recommendation on a protocol reference model.[39] In addition, the identification was changed from I.311 to I.320.[40]

I.320, as adopted, is shown below.

Recommendation I.320

ISDN PROTOCOL REFERENCE MODEL

1. **Introduction**

1.1 **General.** The objective of the ISDN protocol reference model is to model information flows, including user information and control information flows, to and through an ISDN. It is based on the general principles of layering given in the X.200 Series of Recommendations, but it is recognized that many of the entities and information flows modelled here do not consist of Open Systems in the X.200 sense.

It is also recognized that the signalling protocols currently recommended by CCITT, e.g., Signalling System No. 7 (Q.700 series), and D-channel protocol (Q.900 series) are layered, and it is a matter for further study how these protocols and this model should correlate.

It is not intended as a definition of any specific implementation of an ISDN or of any systems or equipment in, or connected to, and ISDN.

Examples of applications of this model are included in this Recommendation.

1.2 **Need for a unified approach to ISDN protocol modelling.** A fundamental concept for protocol modelling is based on the principles of layered communication defined in Rec. X.200 (The Reference Model of Open Systems Interconnection (OSI) for CCITT Applications). The OSI Model was originally conceived for data communications, while the ISDN is conceived to support multiservice types of communications, including voice and video applications. The OSI Model therefore needs to be applied judiciously in order to effectively represent the ISDN-specific features not encountered in current data networks. With these features, a wide range of communication modes and capabilities can be achieved in the ISDN, including the following:

- circuit-switched connection under the control of common channel signalling;
- packet-switched communication over B-, D- and H- channels;
- signalling between users and network-based facilities, e.g., information retrieval systems such as Videotex;
- operations data bases such as directory;
- end-to-end signalling between users, e.g., to change mode of communication over an already-established connection;
- combinations of the above as in multi-media communication, whereby several simultaneous modes of communication can take place under common signalling control.

With such diversity of ISDN capabilities in terms of information flows and modes of communication beyond those of data networks, there is a need to model all these capabilities within a common framework, i.e., reference model. This would enable the critical protocol architectural issues to be readily identified and facilitate the development of ISDN protocols and associated features.

1.3 **Relationship with Recommendation X.200.** The protocol reference model, interface structures and protocol reference configurations are defined by layered structures based on and using the terminology of the reference model for Open Systems Interconnection (OSI) for CCITT Applications (Rec. X.200). The layer identification used in Rec. X.200 is limited in this Recommendation to the use of layer numbers.

Layer titled, e.g., network layer, as used in Rec. X.200 are sometimes misleading the ISDN context, and have not been used here.

The following ISDN needs have not at present been considered in the X.200 Series of Recommendations:

- information flows for out-of-band call control processes, or more generally, information flows among multiple related protocols;
- information flows for selection of connection characteristics;
- information flows for re-negotiation of connection characteristics of calls;
- information flows for suspension of connections;
- information flows for overlap sending;
- information flows for multi-media calls;
- information flows for asymmetric connections;
- information flows for network management, e.g., change over and change back, and for maintenance functions, e.g., test loops;
- information flows for power activation/deactivation;
- interworking;
- switching and information flows;
- new layer service definitions for non-data services;
- application to other than end-systems, e.g., signal transfer points (STPs) and inter-networking points;
- information flows for multi-point connections;
- information flows for applications such as: voice, including A/μ-law conversion; full motion video; transparent; telex.

Depending on examination and resolution of issues related to the modelling of the above, it is a matter for further study whether the ISDN protocol reference model remains a separate Recommendation or whether the concepts contained in this Recommendation should be incorporated in the X.200 series of Recommendations.

1.4 **Relationship with the Q-Series of Recommendations.** The functions and procedures described in the Q-Series of Recommendations for access and network signalling in general conform to the principles described in this Recommendation. Certain features, however, in particular facility procedures and user-user signalling, may require further study to determine the most appropriate method of modelling.

2. **Modelling concepts**

2.1 Information flows. The information flows identified in section 1.3 can be considered as information flows between:

- ISDN users and a functional entity within an ISDN, e.g., network control facilities;

- ISDN user and a functional entity inside or outside an ISDN, e.g., an information storage/processing/messaging facility;
- various functional entities in ISDN;
- an ISDN and other networks.

Modelling these information flows as well as information flows within an ISDN functional entity, e.g., an ISDN exchange or terminal, is required. These information flows can be classified into the following categories:

(i)   user information, e.g., digitized voice, data and information transmitted between users. This information may be transmitted transparently through an ISDN, or it may be processed or manipulated. Examples of the latter include data which is stored or encrypted within the network;

(ii)   control information — this is information which is acted upon, e.g., in: controlling a network connection, such as establishing and clearing down; controlling the use of an already established network connection, e.g., change of service characteristics during a call such as alternate voice/data; providing both above control functions, as in a multipoint conference call with service change.

2.2 **Protocols and associated interactions.** In order to construct the ISDN protocol reference model, a fundamental generic protocol block has been identified. Such a protocol block can be used to describe various elements in the ISDN user premises and the network, e.g., terminal equipment (TE), network termination (NT), exchange termination (ET), signalling point (SP), and signalling transfer point (STP), etc.

In some applications, some of the layers in a protocol may be null, i.e., contain no protocol functions. In such cases, the service provided to the layer above will be identical to the underlying service provided to the null layer and the primitives which cross the higher service boundary are mapped directly onto primitives which cross the lower service and vice versa.

The seven layers of the protocol structures represent even distinct ordered partitions. Each layer exhibits specific adjunct layers and with more general aspects of communications. Each layer offers a specific layer service or set of layer services to the layer above. The functions of each layer and the service offered by each layer are defined in general terms in the Recommendations of the X.200 series. Detailed specification of layer services and protocols are the subject of other Recommendations.

[Figure 5-7] illustrates the conceptual aspects of the protocol block. A three dimensional representation is used to depict: user (U) information and associated layered protocols; and control (C) information and associated layered protocols.

In addition, [Figure 5-7] represents generically all local, e.g., terminal, management (M) aspects associated with the transfer of user information and control information.

Examples of management functions include the control of the switching action within a circuit switch and selection of appropriate responses to connection failure and other exception conditions occurring over the communication facility. These functions also include "network management" and traffic control to optimize utilization of network resources.

Management aspects should be treated as purely local matters associated with a given entity, whether ISDN terminal equipment, or network equipment. In any given entity, these functions are necessary in: monitoring the activities in the user information and control information domains; and providing a mechanism for information interchange between U and C processes.

If at any stage, there is a need for local management to be exchanged between different entities, especially for Administrations/RPOAs to perform network management, this communication can be supported by either U, or C, or both protocols.

Interactions at the lower faces of the protocol block are illustrated in [Figure 5-7] and they represent the physical transfer of information, whether user or control, between one protocol block and another. This transfer takes place over the physical media associated with U and C information protocols. In some cases, e.g., ISDN basic access, a common physical medium may be shared by both U and C protocols.

Interactions at the lower faces of the protocol block are illustrated in [Figure 5-7] and they represent the physical transfer of information, whether user or control, between one protocol block and another. This transfer takes place over the physical media associated with U and C information protocols. In some cases, e.g., ISDN basic access, a common physical medium may be shared by both U and C protocols.

Interactions at the upper face of the protocol block represent the transfer of information to various application processes external to the block. These include user applications, control applications, and system management applications.

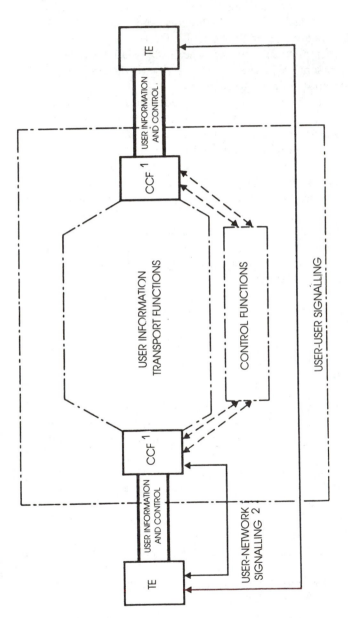

Figure 5-6   Information Flows
Source: Rec. I.320, Fig. 1/I.320.

Notes

1. CCF: Connection Control Function (see I.310)
2. Includes connection control and communication with, e.g., operations
    centers

Interactions between different protocol blocks or peer protocols take place in a layered fashion as defined by the OSI Reference Model. For clarity, however, these peer interactions are not shown in [Figure 5-7].

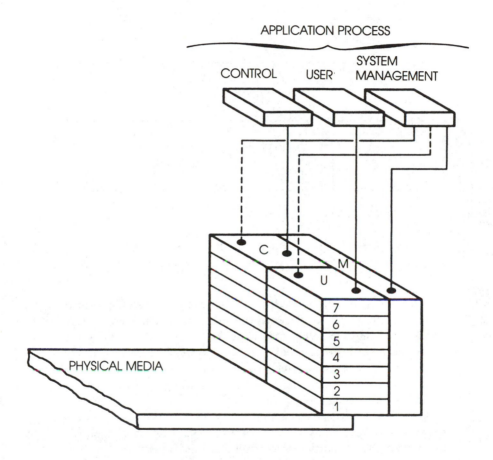

Note — Peer-to-peer protocols associated with *U* and *C* are not shown.

Figure 5-7   *Interactions Associated with a Protocol Block*

Source: Rec. I.320, Fig. 2/I.320.

2.3 Communication contexts. The allocation of information flows into the two above mentioned categories is communication context dependent. [Figure 5-8] illustrates some possible communication contexts, for which the end systems and the information flows

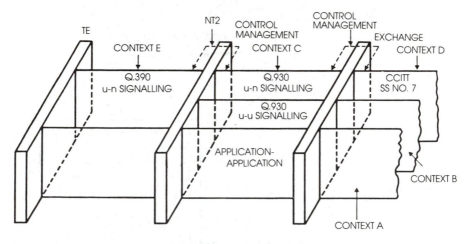

Figure 5-8   Examples of Communication Contexts
Source: Rec. I.320, Fig. 3/I.320.

between them may be modelled. [Figure 5-9] illustrates a generic communication context. Between end protocol blocks there may be one or more intermediate protocol blocks. The end protocol blocks do not necessarily correspond to the end systems as defined in the X.200 series of Recommendations. The end system protocol blocks may reside in subscriber's TE or network exchanges or other equipment related to an ISDN.

Any of the various elements in the ISDN user premises and the network may have many of these contexts operating simultaneously or sequentially. A particular communication context may involve two or more end protocol blocks, e.g., multipoint context. Communication contexts may be chained together simultaneously or sequentially in time, with information passing from one context to another through an application process or a management entity. Examples of using multiple communication contexts are contained in paragraph 4.

Having first set the context for modelling these information flows, they can then be modelled from the end system perspective as

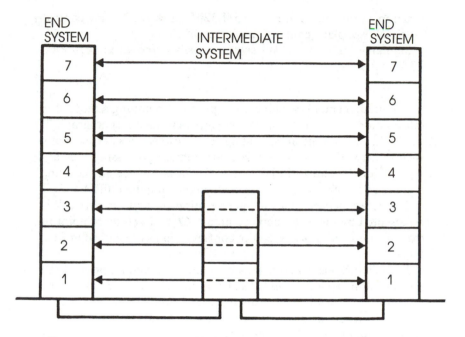

Note — The end system protocol blocks may reside in subscriber's TE or network exchanges or other equipment related to an ISDN.

Figure 5-9   A Generic Communication Context

Source: Rec. I.320, Fig. 4/I.320.

belonging to either a user in-context plane (U), or control out-of-context plane (C). The dialogue in each plane is independently described in terms of separate layer structures, corresponding to the structure of the U protocol block and C protocol block described in paragraph 4.

2.4 **Perspective.** Layering of ISDN protocols may be usefully modelled from two essentially independent perspectives: that of the user and that of the control system. The main rationale for protocols within the user perspective is the transfer of information among user applications. The main rationale for protocols from the control perspective is the transfer of information within the control system. One key "application" of the control system is the control of user plane connections.

One implication of this is that functions within the control plane may be "called" from the user plane. Such nesting of control functions is illustrated in Figure 5/I.320 [not shown] — the control of ISDN user plane connections using Q.930.

Similar nesting for packet switched calls is shown in Figure 6/ I.320 [not shown].

3. The Model

The fundamental modelling concepts for developing a model for information flows within an ISDN were described in paragraph 2. From the standpoint of modelling, the various network elements such as network control facilities, information processing/messaging facilities as shown in [Figure 5-2] can be treated in the same manner as a user system such as a terminal equipment (TE).

The access between the customer equipment and the network is represented by the S/T reference plane. *Cf.* S/T reference point in the ISDN user-network reference configuration as described in Rec. I.411.

For network elements such as exchanges, signalling points (SP) and signalling transfer points (STP), a mirror image version of the fundamental block is used. This representation allows peer-to-peer protocols inside the network as well as ISDN user-network access to be taken into account. Note however, that for clarity, these peer-to-peer protocols are not shown.

4. Examples of applications of the ISDN protocol reference model

From the fundamental modelling concepts described in paragraph 2, ISDN protocol configurations have been developed.

Figures 7/I.320 to 10/I.320 [not shown] illustrates examples of applications of the model for ISDN connections within various ISDN communication contexts.

4.1 Figure 7/I.320 [not shown] illustrates modelling principles for circuit-switched connections. Four communication contexts are illustrated. Context A is the realm of user-user information transfer over the circuit-switched connection. Context B is the realm of user-network signalling between the left TE and the ISDN. Context C is the realm of intra-network signalling. Context D in this example is the realm of user-network signalling between the right TE and the ISDN.

Within context A, the two TEs contain the two end protocol blocks for this context. Each NT1 performs those layer 1 functions necessary to transfer the channel bits between the T reference point and the digital subscriber line. The two network switches relay the bit stream of this connection with a layer 1 switch fabric. The layer

1 switch fabric is controlled by the management entities of the network switches. An application processes is present in each TE; this process generates and receives the information transmitted over the circuit-switched connection.

Within context B, an end protocol block for the user-network signalling is contained in the TE. Another end protocol block for this context is contained in the local network ET. Within the TE, a process initiates the transmission of signalling information to the ET. At the ET, this signalling information is delivered to a call management process. The call management process, through the management entity, can control the layer 1 switch fabric as necessary to establish the circuit switch path through the ET.

Context D is similar to context B in this example. Note that, within these contexts B and D, the signalling protocol layers are independent from the protocols used for user-user information transfer in context A at layers 2 to 7. A common protocol is shown at layer 1, where the signalling channel (D at the S/T interface) is multiplexed at layer 1 with the user-information channel (B at the S/T reference point). The multiplexed channels are transmitted over a common physical media between the TE and the NT1, and then from the NT1 to the ET.

Within the network, context C illustrates the inter-exchange signalling. The two ETs shown in this example each contain an end protocol block for this contest. Inter-exchange signalling is initiated by the call management processes in each ET, as required. The right ET shows that the layered signalling protocols are independent from context A for all seven layers. In this example, inter-exchange signalling information (context C) is not multiplexed with the user information (context A) at layer 1 for transmission between the two ETs. Two independent but parallel physical media between the ETs carry the information for each context (quasi-associated signalling).

4.2 Figures 8/I.320 to 10/I.320 [not shown] can be similarly interpreted as in the text for Figure 7 in section 4.1.

4.3 Figure 11/I.320 [not shown] illustrates a model for representing information flows and associated logical blocks for the communication process in terminal equipment (TE).

4.4 For network elements such as exchanges, signalling points (SP), signalling transfer points (STP), a mirror image version of the protocol modelling block is used. This representation allows peer-to-peer protocols inside the network as well as ISDN user access to be taken into account. An example of such a model is shown in Figure 12/I.320 [not shown].

4.5 Figure 13/I.320 [not shown] provides some additional details on the switching of information flows at various points in the model.

5.4 ISDN Hypothetical Reference Connections (I.32y)

Hypothetical reference connections have traditionally been a means for standardizing network transmission segments for operational purposes. It is also often used to establish certain basic performance requirements to assure that when networks are integrated with each other, the overall performance will be acceptable. For this reason, the ISDN work on hypothetical reference connections was associated with other "models" such as those for architecture and protocol.

Munich, February 1982. The subject of hypothetical reference connections (HRXs) did not arise until the February 1982 meeting of WT3. At that time, British Telecom (BT) introduced a contribution that proposed consideration of the subject.[41] From the outset, the focus was the problems associated with the use of satellites in ISDN circuits,[42] and was thus certain to remain a controversial topic. The working team took the BT contribution as the basis for their work.

The proposed HRXs were conceived for connections between ISDN users and based on those for digital telephone network in Recommendation G.104. They were primarily conceived for voice and data circuit-switched connections at 64 kbit/s. A need to specify also heterogeneous types of ISDN HRXs was also recognized. This last type of connection involved tandem linking of circuit-switched and packet-switched portions of the HRX. A typical configuration occurs when circuit switching is employed on local access and packet switching is used on the long distance sections.

It was noted that when end to end performance objectives for ISDN HRXs, such as transit delay, packet transport delay and call set-up time, were assigned, the performance offered by physical configurations at user premises, such as single terminals, multi-terminal installations, PABXs and LANs, should be appropriately taken into account. It was also noted that there was a need to consider ISDN HRXs for connections at bit rates greater than 64 kbit/s, such as 1544 and 2048 kbit/s.

Working Team 3 agreed that the 1250 km length assigned to the national terrestrial portions of the HRXs should be modified for very large countries.

It was proposed that circuits comprising satellite links could be incorporated in the local, national, and international portions of HRXs, but for voice services, not more than one geostationary satellite should be allowed in any connection between of excessive transmission delay, and for data services, not more than x geostationary satellites should be allowed in any connection, the overriding criterion being again excessive transmission delay. The value of x was a subject of further discussion. Interactive data and bulk data services will likely have different delay requirements, the bulk data services being more tolerant to delay than interactive data services.

The Team agreed that in order to establish an ISDN HRX Recommendation that includes satellite links, information on the maximum permissible delay must be obtained. For voice services, most delegates favored the one satellite hop restriction approach. However, it was observed that voice connections via two satellite hops may constitute a possible alternative in certain particular cases, such as connections to dispersed communities in the Pacific Islands.[43]

Kyoto, February 1983. At the meeting of WT3 in February 1983, the subject of HRXs was not given much consideration. The subject was also procedurally complicated by its overlap with Question 9/XVIII. However, satellite interests began to rally and introduced contributions.[44] Indeed, within the CCIR, a special group, Interim Working Party 4/2, was established under the chairmanship of a COMSAT representative to deal with the matter.

Geneva, June, November 1983. The June 1983 meeting of WT3 received one contribution on HRXs and continued to defer to other forums.[45] The subject was not considered at the November 1983 meeting.

Brasilia, February 1984. At the Brasilia meeting, provision was made in the structure of the I-Series for a Recommendation dealing with hypothetical reference connections, designated I.32y. However no draft had ever been prepared.

At the end of the activity period, the subject of hypothetical reference connections was considered in the context of other Recommendations such as I.340, X.110, X.92, E.17x, G.801, and G.821. Recommendation G.801 amended the method of specification of digital error in a manner more accommodating to satellite systems. However, the subject of multi-hop satellite links remained highly controversial. In the end, the current consensus limitation was that "two or more satellite circuits in one connection may be used when no other reliable means of communication is available."[46] Further debate on the issue was deferred to the 1985–1988 activity period.

5.5 Network Addressing (I.330)

Telecommunication networks exist for the purpose of providing information services. The dominant function is the movement of information from one point to another within the network or external to the network. In order to perform most transport functions, those points must be capable of being uniquely addressed. The only exception is broadcasting, where all points receive the same information. Addressing is fundamental to the operation of any non-broadcast telecommunication network.

In an ISDN environment, addressing can get very complicated in two different ways. First, the point to be addressed is not always at just the physical interface between the user and the network. The point could be literally anywhere, real or virtual, inside or outside the network. Second, the addressing can occur in more than one stage. That is, an addressed point could simply be a virtual location in look-up table that pointed to another address point.

Geneva, June 1981. The subject of ISDN addressing received substantial consideration by Study Group XVIII from the outset. At the June 1981 meeting of the Working Team, two contributions were submitted on addressing.[47] Several issues were considered.

An interim network addressing plan was recognized as a practical necessity and port and escape code schemes were agreed for interim use.

The use of Service Indicator Codes (SICs), which would be included in the signalling information, was preferred over the option of including service identification in the numbering scheme.

There was some confusion over the requirements for terminal and service addressing, the requirements for sub-addressing, and the requirements for direct inward dialing to PABX extensions.

A requirement was identified to provide capability for addressing by terminal and by information type in both directions. Two options were identified: provide one directory number and select the service, or provide separate directory numbers for each available service.

The need to establish ISDN country codes was identified. The possibility of using telephony country codes was mentioned.

In addition to the identification of a terminal within a customer's installation, the capability may also be required to identify services, information type, and processes at the terminal. The OSI layered reference model provided a good reference for study.

The need to accomodate portable terminals was recognized. Some were concerned that functions associated with automatic identification of terminals moved within a customer's premises not impose significant additional requirements on public exchanges.[48]

Munich, February 1982. At the February 1982 meeting of the Working Team, three new contributions were received.[49] The primary issues, continued from the last meeting, related to the numbering plan, terminal identity, and sub-addressing.

The matter of a special ISDN numbering plan caused some friction with Study Group II that was to remain through most of the activity period. Repeated attempts were made by Study Group XVIII to moderate the concern. At Munich, it was pointed out that fewer network problems would be incurred if the ISDN numbering plan was based on the telephony numbering plan produced by Study Group II and found in Recommendation E.163. However, additional numbering capacity was considered necessary. In addition, during the evolution to the ISDN, it was determined that interworking number plans of ISDN and dedicated networks would be required. Contributions were solicited concerning network problems which might occur by adoption of any existing numbering plan as a basis for the ISDN numbering plan.

It was agreed that the directory number for any terminal should ultimately be independent of the service. It was further agreed that service identification between the terminal and the network should be accomplished through a User Service Identity Code (SIC) at protocol level 3. This implied that the network must route this information. During the evolutionary period, it will be necessary to interwork between ISDN terminals and existing numbering arrangements. The resulting interworking problems must be identified. Caution was expressed on the network implications of making interim arrangements for terminal identification.

It was agreed that sub-addressing at level 3, such as to a terminal attached to a PABX, was a desirable requirement for the ISDN. However, it was expected that sub-addressing at level 3 would not accomodate all the sub-addressing requirements in the ISDN, such as for a local area network. Therefore, it was necessary to study sub-addressing at level 4.[50]

Kyoto, February 1983. At the February 1983 meeting of WT3, more contributions began to appear.[51] Several matters were identified as key issues. These included the kind of digit system used in the address, the routing of information separately from address information, the application and definition of service identification codes (SIC), access to services as well as terminal addressing, interworking with private networks, interworking with dedicated networks, definition of sub-addressing needs, addressing for multifunction terminals, and identification of the point in the address does the network begin charging for the transport of information.

It was agreed that a draft Recommendation addressing these issues was desirable. It would follow OSI layering principles where possible and would focus on layer 3 addressing and on terminal-network aspects rather than the user-terminal human interface. A drafting group was established that produced a draft Recommendation on numbering and addressing principles, and designated I.320.[52]

Geneva, June 1983. Interest in addressing principles at the June 1983 meeting of WT3 remained significant,[53] and the main objective was to refine the draft Recommendation on addressing. Study Group II had continued to assert its views on ISDN addressing, suggesting that its telephony numbering plan should be the basis for the ISDN numbering plan and that country codes be as those given in its Recommendation E.163. However, there were some doubts about the suitability of this Recommendation for ISDN purposes because of the limited number of digits comprising the codes. Interworking between the ISDN and other networks was proposed in both single stage and two stage methods.

Agreement was reached on several matters. Routing, including RPOA or carrier selection, was to be outside the numbering plan. The difference between the numbering plan and addressing capability would need definition. On interworking arrangements, a single-stage arrangement was preferred. However, a two stage method may be required as an interim arrangement.

It was also agreed that sub-addressing should not be included as part of the ISDN number. Determination of the presence of a sub-address remained a critical numbering issue. Options included a time out after receipt of a minimum number of digits, or dialing procedures which could include allocation of prefixes or examination of appropriate digits. The number of additional digits in the sub-address ranged from two to 32.

However, there was no agreement on whether the ISDN numbering plan should be based on, and should be an enhancement of Recommendation E.163 and that telephone country codes should be used in ISDNs. The decision was premature, pending results of studies on topics such as network identification, interworking and integration with dedicated bearer service networks, effect on non-zoned services supported through or by an ISDN, and effect on areas using integrated numbering areas for some services but not for others. Also, additional study was necessary on mobile systems, maritime satellites, *et cetera*, to determine the impact on ISDN numbering requirements. Working Team 3 noted that the prefix definition in Recommendation E.160 may require expansion to include use of a prefixes to identify if a NIC, for example, is included in the subsequent number.[54]

A new draft I.320 on addressing principles was prepared.

Geneva, November 1983. The November 1983 meeting witnessed additional contributions and further refinements to the draft Recommendation.[55] The work focused on identification of the presence of a NIC or sub-address, sub-addressing separation from the main address, use of the S or T reference point for addressing, application of prefixes, interworking with dedicated networks and the relationship of the OSI model. Most significantly, it was agreed that ISDN numbering will be based on a revised version of Recommendation E.163.[56]

Brasilia, February 1984. Several contributions to the February 1984 meeting suggested minor changes to the addressing Recommendation.[57] Only very minor changes were made, although the Recommendation identification was changed to I.330.

Recommendation I.330, as adopted, is shown below.

Recommendation I.330

ISDN NUMBERING AND ADDRESSING PRINCIPLES

1. **Introduction.** This Recommendation provides the general concepts, principles, and requirements for addressing reference points located at subscriber premises, for addressing other functions, and for allowing communications with TEs. Further study is required on the principle of describing how a call is routed to a user based on, e.g., address, service indication (see Rec. I.33x).

Recommendation E.164 (I.331) describes the numbering plan for the ISDN era. Alignment between I.330 and E.164 (I.331) needs to be maintained during the evolution of further studies.

The following understanding of relevant nomenclature is established:

(a) an ISDN number is one which relates to an ISDN network and ISDN numbering plan;

(b) an ISDN directory number is that which may be listed in public directories against the subscriber's name;

(c) an ISDN address comprises the ISDN number and the mandatory and/or optional additional addressing information;

(d) private communications facilities are communication capabilities confined to use by one or more particular subscribers, as opposed to facilities which are shared by subscribers of public networks. Examples of private communications facilities include LANs, PABXs, and other private network arrangements.

Depending on the different cases and stages identifiable within an addressing process, and ISDN number may be: (a) an international ISDN number; or (b) a national ISDN number; or (c) an ISDN subscriber number.

An ISDN address comprises: (i) the ISDN number; and (ii) mandatory and/or optional additional addressing information.

As an objective, all ISDNs should evolve towards a single numbering plan, namely the ISDN numbering plan. Considering the wide penetration of the telephone network in the world and its existing resources, the ISDN numbering plan should be developed by enhancing Rec. E. 163. Therefore, it is recommended that the telephone country code (TCC) be used to identify a particular country (or geographical area).

An existing numbering plan may inter-work and co-exist with the ISDN numbering plan. All interworking cases from ISDN to dedicated networks, and vice versa, have to be covered by the appropriate Study Groups. Preference should be given to single stage selection methods whenever possible.

It is recognized that some of the present data networks, for instance, could retain the X.121 numbering structure and inter-work with ISDNs. Necessary interworking arrangements should be studied for securing interconnectability between ISDNs employing the ISDN numbering plan and, e.g., multiple service network evolving from data networks using the X.121 numbering structure.

2. **Principles for relating an ISDN number to ISDN user-network reference configurations.** An ISDN number shall be able unambiguously to identify a particular:

(a) physical interface at reference point T [ref. Figure 1/I.330 not shown];

(b) virtual interface at reference point T; i.e., for a NT2 + NT1 configuration [ref. Figure 2/I.330 not shown];

(c) multiple interfaces (physical or virtual) at reference point T [ref. Figure 3/I.330 not shown];

(d) for point-to-point configurations, physical interface at reference point S [ref. Figure 4/I.330 not shown];

(e) for point-to-point configurations, virtual interface at reference point S [ref. Figure 5/I.330 not shown];

(f) for point-to-point configurations, multiple interfaces (physical or virtual) at reference point S [ref. Figure 6/I.330 not shown];

(g) for multi-point configurations (e.g., passive bus), all of the interfaces at reference point S [ref. Figure 7/I.330 not shown].

As a result, from the view point of the network side of the interface, an ISDN number is associated with one, or a multiple of, D channel used to single to the user.

Note — If the ability to selection the TE is a multi-point configuration (e.g., passive bus) solely by address information is a requirement, the TE may have to memorize some addressing information. The size of this memory and the associated procedures are for further study.

A particular interface, or multiple of interfaces, may be assigned more than one ISDN number. [Ref. Figure 8/I.330, not shown.]

All ISDNs shall be able to assign an ISDN number to an interface at reference point T or S. However, a particular ISDN number fulfills only one of the functions identified in paragraph 2.1 above.

For mobile services an ISDN number shall be capable of unambiguously identifying an interface in the mobile subscriber's premises, as defined in paragraph 2.1. [Ref. Figure 9/I.330, not shown.]

The ISDN number is not required to identify a particular connection where, on a particular interface, more than one connection may be present at a given instant.

The ISDN number is not required to identify directly a particular channel, where, within a particular interface, there may be more than one channel. Indirect identification of particular channels may occur, e.g., when the ISDN number identifies a particular interface and there is a one-to-one correspondence between that interface and particular channels.

3. **Relationships between ISDN number, transit network/RPOA selection (when permitted), service indication, and quality of service indication.** The establishment of an ISDN connection will require an ISDN address. In addition, separate non-address related information may be necessary for completing a connection.

Routing of ISDN connections shall take into account the following information, when supplied by the user:

(a) ISDN numbers, including destination network identification and digits for direct dialing in (DDI) where applicable.

(b) service identification, possibly including requested quality of service parameters such as transit delay throughout, and security.

(c) multiple transit RPOA/network selection, when permitted by the originating ISDN.

Note — The need for remote transit RPOA/network selection by the user of an ISDN which has no local transit RPOA/network selection is for further study.

In addition, transit RPOA/network selections by the originating ISDN, if provided, shall also be evaluated in the routing of a connection. In national networks on a particular connection, the user may choose to specify some or all of this information, at either subscription time or connection-establishment time.

The ISDN number does not identify the particular nature of the service, type of connection, or quality of service to be used, nor does it identify a transit RPOA/network.

In the case where an ISDN number identifies a mobile TE or a TE served by several interfaces or networks, an ISDN may need to map from the ISDN number on to a specific interface designation.

4. ISDN number design considerations. Numbering plan design information is covered by Rec. E.164 (I.331). The ISDN number shall include an unambiguous identification of a particular country (or geographic area). The ISDN number is allowed to include an unambiguous identification of a particular geographic area within a country (or geographic area).

As an objective, all ISDNs should evolve towards a single numbering plan. However, an existing numbering plan may interwork and this coexist with the ISDN numbering plan.

When a number of public or private ISDNs exist in a country (or geographic area), it shall not be mandatory to integrate the numbering plans of the ISDNs. Methods for interworking are for further study, with the objective that connections between the TEs and these various networks can be completed by using only the ISDN address.

The ISDN number shall be capable of containing an identification of the ISDN to which the called user is attached. For a private network which spans more than one country, the international ISDN number will cause delivery of a call to the particular private network in the country specified by the country code.

The ISDN number shall be capable of providing for interworking of TEs on ISDNs with "TEs" on other networks. As an objective, with respect to the ISDN number, the procedure for interworking should be the same for all cases. The single-stage method of interworking is the preferred approach.

5. Structure of the ISDN address. The structure of the ISDN address is illustrated in [Figure 5-10]. A function marking the end of the ISDN number shall always be provided if a subaddress is present. The end of number function may also be provided even if no subaddress is present. When there is no subaddress present, the end of number and end of address functions are coincident, when used.

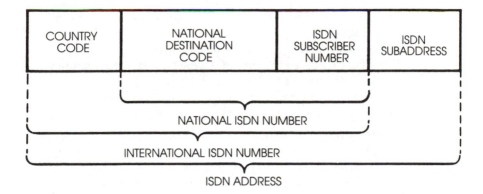

Figure 5-10 Structure of the ISDN Address

Source: Rec. I.330, Fig. 10/I.330.

The ISDN address may be of variable length.

International ISDN number.

- The structure of the international number and the maximum number length are as defined in Recommendation E.164 (I.331).
- In a particular international ISDN number, the exact number of digits shall be governed by national and international requirements.
- The ISDN numbering plan shall provide substantial spare capacity to accommodate future requirements.
- The ISDN number shall be a sequence of decimal digits.
- The ISDN number shall include the capability for direct dialing inward where this facility is offered.

ISDN subaddress.

- All ISDNs shall be capable of conveying the ISDN subaddress transparently.
- Special attention is drawn to the fact that subaddressing is not to be considered as part of the numbering plan, but constitutes an intrinsic part of the ISDN addressing capabilities.

- The subaddress shall be conveyed in a transparent way as a separate entity from both ISDN number and user-to-user information.
- A maximum length shall be 32 decimal digits.
- The subaddress is a sequence of decimal digits, the maximum length of which shall be 32 decimal digits.
- The future use of non-decimal digits in the subaddress, and the maximum number length in this case, is for further study.

6. **Representation of ISDN address.** At the person-machine interface, the objective is to establish one method of distinguishing between abbreviated and complete representations of an ISDN number. This method is for further study. International recommended methods will be chosen.

The method of distinguishing between and ISDN number and a number from another number plan shall be by separate identification of the applicable numbering plan. If such methods are required, international recommended procedures will be chosen.

5.6 Routing (I.33x)

The subject of routing is one of the few issues that has been contentious since the first meeting of the International Telegraph Union in 1865. The issues in those days primarily revolved around which national networks in Europe the message would transit as it coursed its way from one end of the continent to the other. In today's ISDN environment, the issues are analogous, only there are innumerable additional variables, especially in those countries that enjoy a multiplicity of competitive carriers. However, in the context of hundreds of CCITT meeting days on ISDN, the subject was raised only infrequently, and generally in the context of the amount of control that users should have over routing alternatives.

Geneva, June 1981. At the June 1981 initial working team meeting, the matter of routing was raised during discussion on the subject of international interworking. Preference was expressed by some Administrations that the configuration of interconnections between networks for a call originated in one country and destined for a different network in a distant country, should be under the control of the originating country network. In other words, the Administration within which the call was originated should select the routing through the network. The requirement for the customer to be able to influence selection of that routing was, however, recognized. Provision of the capability in the addressing plan allowing customers to select their own routing through the network was considered to incur significant problems for the network, and further study was necessary.[58]

Munich, February 1982 and Kyoto, February 1983. The subject received no attention at the February 1982 meeting, but did arise in February 1983 with the introduction of two contributions.[59] Attention was called to the revision of the telephony routing plan, Recommendations E.171 to E.17x by Study Group II, as well as Study Group VII's revision to Recommendation X.110.

It was agreed, however, that it was too early to provide definitive advice on ISDN routing principles. It was agreed to forward the draft Recommendations for the ISDN functional architecture model and numbering and addressing principles to Study Groups II and VII, to suggest that the current routing plan for telephony may not be sufficiently flexible for ISDN, and to indicate that numbering and addressing studies should have higher priority than routing.[60]

Geneva, June, November 1983 and Brasilia, February 1984. The subject of routing remained as decided at the February 1983 meeting of WT3. An I.33x identification has been assigned for a future Recommendation on ISDN routing principles.

5.7 Connection Types (I.340)

Although the concept of connection types had its roots in discussions on network functions at the beginning of the activity period, the subject did not explicitly arise until after the special meeting of Study Group XVIII leadership at Montreal in late 1981. Connection types rapidly became important as the means of conceptualizing how the network would provide services to the user.

Munich, February 1982. At the February 1982 meeting of the Working Team, eight contributions were submitted.[61] Connection types received the attention of those dealing with switching matters in other working teams as well in WT3. It was agreed that a limited number of connection types should exist in an ISDN, and two general categories were established: transport connection types (up to OSI level 3), and application connection types (above OSI level 3).

As a first step to demonstrate the approach to connection types, the following transport connection types were proposed: clear channel circuit switched 64 kbit/s connection to Recommendation G.821, packet-switched connections, and circuit-switched 64 kbit/s connections with bit manipulation. However, WT3 found a need to fully specify these connections and to identify if further connection types were needed. In any case, there was a strong desire to specify only a limited set of connections characterized by service needs.

Other connection types considered included "$n \times 64$ kbit/s." It was agreed, however, that there was no network requirement to maintain digit sequence integrity for an $n \times 64$ kbit/s switched connection for any value of n greater than 1. A switched connection digit sequence integrity for the aggregation of channels would be maintained, if necessary, by terminal equipment and the user would be aware that the full $n \times 64$ kbit/s capacity may not be available for user information. For semi-permanent connections, digit sequence integrity would be maintained by the network.

It was agreed that single sub 64 kbit/s information streams were permissible within a 64 kbit/s connection. In this case, the need should be recognized to specify the rate adaption method for suitable multiple of 8 kbit/s. Recommendation X.1 bit rate adaptions of 4.8 to 8, 9.6 to 16, and 48 to 64 kbit/s were possible.

Three additional connection types were identified in contributions: wideband voice, facsimile, and packet voice and variable bit rate voice. It was also noted that bit manipulation within a channel may result from service requirements, e.g., digital speech processing to provide voice service at a lower cost, or as a result of network requirements, e.g., echo control, digital pads, *et cetera.*[62]

Kyoto, February 1983. When WT3 reassembled in February 1983, the number of contributions on connection types increased significantly.[63] The subject was placed on the back burner, however, awaiting the resolution of some fundamental considerations concerning ISDN services, with which connection types were inextricably associated. The two subjects were considered together in a joint WT3/WT4. The work in the joint meeting resulted in the preparation of draft Recommendations on both ISDN services and network connection types. The draft on connection types was further reviewed by WT3 and designated I.3xx.[64]

That draft Recommendation stated the basic concept of connection types. "ISDN services are provided to the user and are the user's perception of the network capabilities. Network connections are provided by the ISDN network to support ISDN services."[65] The detail provided in the draft Recommendation amplified somewhat upon that discussed at the Munich meeting, and was subdivided into sections enumerating network connection types, and the application of network connections. The latter was a new section that spelled out simple, tandem, multiple, and multi-media connection configurations.

Geneva, June 1983. The focus on connection types intensified at the June 1983 meeting.[66] The key issues necessary to update the draft Recommendation I.3xx were agreed.

The first issue draft with the relationship of connection types with services. It was agreed that connection types would not have a 1:1 relationship with bearer services. Bearer services would be offered to the customer. Connection types would be the network implementation. Therefore, one connection type would support a number of bearer services which would be mapped on to connection types by the network provider in the most suitable manner. It was also agreed that selection of a connection type may require service information plus additional information to define end system needs. The service definition included quality of service parameters as seen by the user, whereas the connection type included network performance as provided by the implementation.

The second issue dealt with connection attributes. It was agreed that connection attributes should be based on the same structure developed for bearer service attributes. However, some typical differences between connection type and bearer service attributes would included performance specifications, network control functions, operation and maintenance functions, network protocols for connection, access protocols for bearer services, and network configuration. It was agreed that each connection type should be specified according to the range of attributes and parameters.

The third issue involved the subdivision of connections. It was agreed that connection types must be defined for customer-to-customer connections as well as for connections from customer to specific network nodes. It was also agreed that connection types should normally be first specified between two S/T reference points. Application of such specifications to the case of customer to network node connections needed a precise definition of a network node especially with regard to reference points. However, there may be advantages in subdivision of connections into local components in some instances. Customer premises equipment would not be included in connection type specification.

The third issue dealt with changing services during a call. Two methods for accomplishing this were discussed: the universal approach, where all service demands must use a 64 kbit/s connection; and the defined service on demand approach during the progress of a call. In either case, the network can respond in one of two ways: set up a connection whose attributes can be changed during the call, or set up the most economical connection for service needs at each request. Initially, both network options would be included. However, some administrations indicated that they would not like to implement a solution which required re-routing of calls.

The fourth issue dealt with possible additional connection types. A connection type at 382 kbit/s, non-switched, reserved was added. There was also considerable discussion on the need for a further wide band connection type. Possible standards at 1536 and 1920 kbit/s were proposed. A third alternative possibly using an $n \times 384$ kbit/s rate was considered. There was agreement that a single standard was desirable. However, no agreement on the rate could be reached.[67]

Geneva, November 1983. When WT3 met again in November 1983, it considered a number of refinements to the draft Recommendation.[68] Some of these refinements included a stronger assertion of network control over ISDN services. This was reflected in the addition of strong admonitions such as, "it should be noted that subscribers will not be able to select a particular connection type" in the Recommendation's statement of purpose.[69]

There was some discussion of the distinction between "connection types" and "connection elements." It was agreed that connection types should receive the prime focus, although they may be subdivided into connection elements for further analysis. Attribute and performance parameters relating to connection types would be similarly subdivided. The draft Recommendation was renumbered from I.3xx to I.325.

Brasilia, February 1984. At the Brasilia meeting, more refinements and additional connection types continued to be introduced.[70] Many of these changes were incorporated and the Recommendation was renumbered again from I.325 to I.340. In the course of drafting study questions for the next activity period, a separate question was framed for ISDN connection types, Question 5/XVIII.[71]

Recommendation I.340, as adopted, is shown below.

Recommendation I.340

ISDN CONNECTION TYPES

1.   **General.** The ISDN may be described by a limited set of user-network interfaces (refer to Rec. I.411) and a limited set of ISDN connection types to support the telecommunication services described in the I.200 series of Recommendations. This Recommendation identifies and defines these connection types insofar as they relate to the provision of particular network capabilities for an ISDN. The basic lower layer capabilities of an ISDN (refer to Rec. I.310) are represented by a set of ISDN connection types. This

Recommendation should be considered in conjunction with other Recommendations in the I-series, with particular reference to Recs. I.120, I.210, I.211, I.212, I.310, I.320, I.411, and I.413. For definitions of terms used in this Recommendation refer to Rec. I.112.

2. Basic concept of ISDN connection types

2.1 **Introduction.** An ISDN provides a set of network capabilities which enable telecommunication services to be offered to a user (refer to I.200 series Recommendations).

An ISDN connection type is a way of referring to and describing an ISDN connection. The attributes of connection types are defined in Rec. I.130, and a set of possible values of these attributes is given in section 2 of this Recommendation.

An ISDN connection is a connection established between ISDN reference points (see Recs. I.310, I.410, and I.411). Thus an ISDN connection is a physical or a logical realization of an ISDN connection type. Each ISDN connection can be categorized as belonging to a connection type, depending on its attribute values.

[Figure 5-11] shows a number of examples of ISDN connections having different configurations. Each of these different connections are of the same connection type and described by the same set of attribute values.

[Figure 5-12] shows a number of examples of ISDN connections with similar configurations, each of which, however, are of a different connection type and are described by a different set of attribute values.

2.2 **Purpose of ISDN connection types.** Definition of a set of ISDN connection types provides necessary input to identify the network capabilities of ISDNs. Other key requirements of an ISDN are contained in other I-series Recommendations, in particular, Recs. I.310, I.410, and I.411.

In addition to describing network capabilities of an ISDN, the identification of connection types facilitates the specification of network-to-network interfaces. It may also assist in the allocation of network performance parameters.

It should be noted that the user specifies only the service required while the network allocates resources to set up a connection of the specific type as necessary to support the requested service. It is further noted that for certain service offerings, additional network

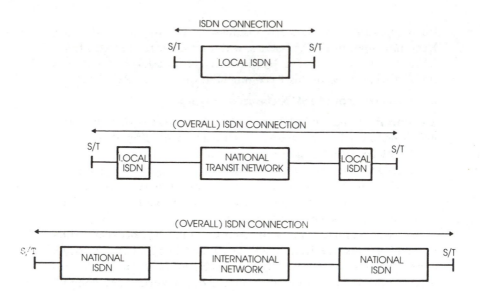

All connections are of the same connection type: e.g., speech

Note — (Overall) ISDN connections involving several networks are covered in section 2.5 [Rec. I.340].

Figure 5-11 *Examples of ISDN Connections with Different Configurations,*
All of Which Are of the Same Connection Type

Source: Rec. I.340, Fig. 1/I.340.

functions, e.g., additional lower layer functions and/or higher layer functions, may be required [ref. Figure 3/I.340 not shown]. For examples of such cases, refer to Rec. I.310.

2.3 Functions associated with ISDN connections. Any ISDN connection involves an association of functions to support telecommunication services [ref. Figure 4/I.340 not shown]. Three sets of functions are required:

    (i)   connection means — including transmission and switching;

    (ii) control functions and protocols — including signalling, flow/congestion control and routing functions;

    (iii) operations and management functions — including network operations, network management and maintenance functions.

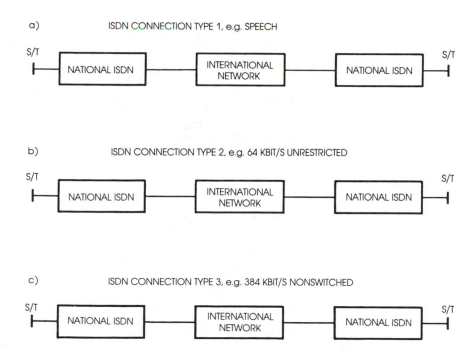

Note — (Overall) ISDN connections involving several networks are covered in section 2.5 [Rec. I.340].

Figure 5-12   Examples of ISDN Connections having Similar Configurations,
Each of a Different Connection Type

Source: Rec. I.340, Fig. 2/I.340

2.4 **Applications of ISDN connection types.** Four situations have been identified thus far to which ISDN connection types apply:

- between two ISDN user-network interfaces, i.e., between S/ T reference points [refer to Figure 5-13a] (Note — There may be a need in certain cases to differentiate between the S and T reference points. This is for further study.);
- between an ISDN user-network interface and an interface to a specialized resource [refer to Figure 5-13b];
- between an ISDN user-network interface and a network-to-network interface [refer to Figure 5-13c];
- between two ISDN-to-other network interfaces (refer to Figure 5-13d].

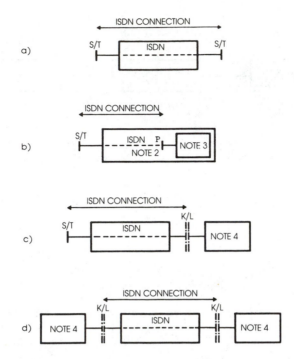

Note 1 — The location of reference points used in this figure is defined in Recommendation I.310 and I.411.

Note 2 — This reference point becomes reference point M if the network specialized resource is outside the ISDN.

Note 3 — This box represents a network specialized resource. The use of a network specialized resource originates from a service request or is for internal administrative purposes. Some examples are:

(1)   a network node incorporating additional lower layer functions (ALLFs) and/or higher layer functions (HLFs), (refer to Recommendation I.310);

(2)   a network provided database;

(3)   an operations or management centre;

(4)   a database or signal transfer point which serves as an end-point of a connection set up by the network to fulfil network functions (billing, signalling, control, etc.).

Note 4 — This box represents either an existing telephone network or a dedicated network.

Figure 5-13   Applications of ISDN Connection Types

Source: Rec. I.340, Fig. 5/I.340.

2.5 **ISDN connection involving several networks.** An ISDN connection may comprise a number of tandem network connections. [Figure 5-14] shows an example in which each end network is an ISDN. The intermediate networks may or may not be ISDNs, but they offer the appropriate network capabilities for the service supported by the overall ISDN connection. Other configurations are for further study.

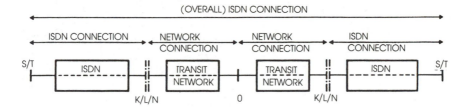

Note — Reference points are defined in Recommendations I.310 and I.411. Reference point 0 may or may not be an ISDN defined reference point.

Figure 5-14   Example of an ISDN Connection Involving Several Networks

Source: Rec. I.340, Fig. 6/I.340.

In overall ISDN connections involving several networks, each network provides a part of the connection and may be categorized by different attribute values. In such cases, the characterization of the performance for the overall ISDN connection is for further study.

3. **ISDN connection types and their attributes**

3.1 **Attributes and their values.** ISDN connection types are characterized by a set of attributes. Each attribute has a set of admissible values. The definitions of these attributes are given in Rec. I.130. Table 1 of this Recommendation [see Table 5-1] lists the set of attributes and their possible values in an ISDN.

The attributes which are associated with ISDN connection types have a similarity to those used to define telecommunication services in Recs. I.211 and I.212. However, the two sets of attributes differ in several important aspects. For example:

(a)   ISDN connection types represent the technical capabilities of the network and are a means to ensure defined performance and interworking between networks. Telecommunica-

Table 5-1
Attributes for ISDN Connection Types

Attributes	Possible Values of Attributes
1. Information transfer mode	circuit — packet — others for further study
2. Information transfer rate	64, 384, 1536, 1920, Others for further study — Throughput options for further study — further study
3. Information transfer capability	unrestricted digital info — speech — 3.1 kHz audio — video — others for further study
4. Establishment of connection	switched — semi-permanent — permanent
5. Symmetry	unidirectional — bidirectional asymmetric — bidirectional symmetric
6. Connection configuration	
6(a) Topology	point-to-point (simple, tandem, parallel) — multipoint — others for further study
6(b) Uniformity	uniform — non-uniform
6(c) Dynamics	concurrent — sequential — add/remove — others for further study

	8 kHz integrity	service data unit integrity						unstructured
	D (16)	D (64)	E (64)	B (64)	HO (384)	H11 (1536)	H12 (1920)	
7. Structure								
8. Access channel and rate. See Note 1 for both user and sig. information	others for further study							
9. Signalling access protocol (Note 1)	I.451/Q.930	I.440/Q.920			Q.710	I.462/X.31		others for further study
10. Information access coding/protocol (Note 1)	I.451/Q.930		G.711		I.460 -464		X.25	others for further study
11. Performance								
11(a) Error performance			G.821		others for further study			
11(b) Slip performance			G.822		others for further study			
11(c) Others for further study (Note 2)								
12. Interworking					Further study			
13. Operations and maintenance					Further study			

Source: Rec. I.340, Table 1/I.340.

tion services supported by the ISDN are the packages offered to customers and the definition of their attributes is the means to standardize the service offerings worldwide.

(b)   Quality of service and commercial attributes are relevant to telecommunication services, whereas network performance, network operations and maintenance attributes are relevant to connection types.

3.2 **Limited set of ISDN connection types.** From the given list of attributes and their possible values, a large number of connection types can be identified. However, some of these attributes are of a general or dominant nature and an initial set of ISDN connection types can be based on these dominant attributes.

Table 2 [not shown] enumerates a limited set of connection types based on the following dominant attributes: information transfer mode, information transfer rate, establishment of connection, information transfer capability, and symmetry. These connection types are intended to be sufficient to support the telecommunication services identified in Recs. I.211 and I.212. Additional connection types are for further study.

3.3 **Change of an attribute during a call.** It is possible for some attributes to vary during a call, for example in a response to a change of service request. The relationship between service request and the ISDN connection type is described in section 5.

4.   **Connection elements.** An ISDN connection is composed of connection elements. This concept is illustrated in Figure 7/I.340 [not shown] in which, as an example, a 64 kbit/s circuit switched connection within a national ISDN is shown as composed of two access connection elements and a transit connection element.

The connection element analysis may assist in the description of a complex and asymmetric ISDN connection. This is illustrated in Figure 8/I.340 [not shown], in which the configuration attributes topology, uniformity and dynamics for a connection type are described using the concept of connection elements.

Different connection elements which constitute an ISDN connection may have different sets of attributes. In this case, the attributes across the connection are not homogeneous, and the available attributes of the connection are limited by the most restrictive set of attributes of all the connection elements in the connection.

The development of the concept of connection elements and the analysis of the reference end points of connection elements are for further study.

5. Relationship between services and ISDN connection types

5.1 General relationship. Given a user request for a telecommunication service at the initiation of a call, the network must choose a connection of a connection type that supports the attributes of the service requested. This selection of a connection is effected at the time of call set-up as a routing function based on a table of options derived during the planning and implementation of the network. The options a network implements will be based on the capabilities needed to support the services the network intends to offer.

5.2 Network capability to support a change of service during a call. Recommendation I.211 identifies a particular need for an ISDN to support a change in service during a call, namely that of alternative speech and 64 kbit/s non-speech.

When the capability for this change of service is desired by a user, this requirement and the initial service desired should be identified in the signalling messages during call set-up. During the call, the user will also use signalling messages to request the change in service when it is actually desired; and the network will confirm the response to the request for change.

Unless the change of service capability is requested by the user (and agreed to by the network) at the time of call establishment, a change in service request during the call may or may not be granted by the network. The user always has, of course, the option of terminating the call and establishing a new call with different service characteristics.

The capability for change of service during a call can be implemented by several methods. For service and operational reasons, a rapid and reliable changeover is required and this should be considered in implementing this capability. One possible method requires the disabling, bypassing or introduction of particular network functions, e.g., A-μ-law conversion equipment, which relate to the support of specific service. Another method involves re-switching, possibly including re-routing of the connection or of particular connection elements. However, re-switching, possibly including re-routing, of the international portion of an ISDN connection is not considered appropriate for the present.

The implementation of the network capability to support a change of service during a call is for further study.

5.8 Internetworking/Interworking Interfaces

It is plain that there is never likely to be a single, monolithic, worldwide ISDN. Many ISDN or ISDN-like networks are likely to exist that are national or regional in size. In the near term, many so-called "dedicated" networks, especially the existing telephone network, will also be operating.

It is possible to conceptually treat these multiplicity of networks as simply another kind of "user." Indeed, some of the ISDN Recommendations actually indicate this alternative. At the same time, there has been a tendency to place networks in class by themselves, and discussed under the topics of "interworking" or "internetworking," with no apparent distinction between the terms.

However, this was not a priority topic in Study Group XVIII. The subject arose only sporadically, late in 1981–1984 activity period.

Kyoto, February 1983. At the February 1983 meeting at Kyoto, one contribution was submitted on internetworking interfaces, and the work in Study Group VII and XI reported.[72] WT3 agreed that internetworking interfaces were likely to become one of the more urgent issues during the next few years. Major emphasis has focused to date on the user-network interface. There was growing recognition that network-to-network and network-to-vendor (which may also be a network) interfaces will become equally important. Administrations were urged to submit further contributions, in particular to identify which interworking interfaces, if any, should be subject to CCITT Recommendations.[73]

Geneva, June 1983. In response to the solicitation at Kyoto, several contributions were submitted to the June 1983 meeting that discussed interworking with existing dedicated service networks.[74] It was agreed that Study Group XVIII needed to identify and prioritize the interworking issues for voice and data service in an ISDN environment.[75]

Geneva, November 1983. At the November 1983 meeting, several more contributions were considered on interworking with existing networks.[76] Again, internetworking was recognized as important, but the only response was to defer the matter to the next study period through the preparation of special new draft study Question 6 (ISDN-ISDN internetwork interfaces) and Question 7 (Internetworking of ISDNs and other networks).[77] These were edited and adopted at subsequent meetings.

5.9 Maintenance Philosophy

The subject of network maintenance was another of the second order topics sporadically considered during the 1981–1984 activity period. It did not enjoy a high priority and was entwined with work occurring under multiple study questions and groups.

Kyoto, February 1983. At the Kyoto ISDN Experts meeting in February 1983 several contributions were submitted that addressed network maintenance issues.[78] The objective in considering maintenance under Question 1 by Working Team 3 was to prepare some early maintenance philosophy on ISDN as preliminary input to study under Question 12, where ongoing study would be carried out.

Working Team 3 adopted a number of maintenance objectives: to make the network highly reliable, to incorporate techniques that minimize the effect of failures on service, to rapidly detect failures that affect service, and to indicate them to the maintenance staff by incorporation features in the facilities to enable the failure to be approximately located. It was assumed that no intelligence would be located at the NT interface.

One of the more contentious maintenance issues was that of remote testing of ISDN customer terminal equipment. After a lively discussion on the topic, preliminary agreement was reached. Test loop back arrangements at the network side of the user-network interface should be a mandatory requirement for ISDN termination equipment. Activation of the test loop back arrangements at the network side of the user-network interface would be a layer 1 function. The possible activation of the test loop-back feature on the network side of the user-network interface by a user remotely via the network should be studied. However, any such activation should only be permitted under supervision of the network. Security aspects of remote activation of the test loop back features on both sides of the interface by users should be taken fully into account.[79]

Geneva, June 1983. The issues raised at Kyoto were revisited several months later in June 1983.[80] Agreement on several points was achieved.

Fault localization is a necessary requirement for the ISDN. Fault localization procedures should indicate the minimum set of requirements, for example to localize to the S/T interface only or to a preferred set which may include localization to specific wiring or to NT2, TA or terminals. The destination network should retain control of network remote test functions for only the network side of the user-network interface. The same maintenance philosophy should apply to all access systems, e.g., basic, primary, et cetera. Automatic supervision of access systems was agreed, with specification recommended for the functional information crossing the interface to the local exchange and definition of information to cross the user-network interface. Localization across internetwork interfaces of excessive performance impairments must be taken into account in the ongoing work.

Draft Recommendation Q.950 was proposed to be included into the I-Series as I.4xx with joint Study Group XI and XVIII responsibility.[81]

Brasilia, February, Geneva, June 1984. When the questions for the next study period were drafted at the February and June 1984 meetings, several were adopted on the subject of ISDN maintenance, and secondary responsibility assigned to a number of other CCITT and CCIR study groups. These included new Questions 13 through 18/XVIII.

REFERENCES

1. Report on the Inter-Regnum Meeting of Experts on ISDN Matters (Innisbrook, 12-15 January 1981), CCITT Doc. COM XVIII-No. 1 at 19.
2. *Id.* at 20-21.
3. *See* Report of the Meeting of Working Party XVIII/1 (ISDN), CCITT Doc. COM XVIII-No. R3 at 19 (1981).
4. *See* CCITT Docs. COM XVIII-Nos. 14, 38, 41, 48, S, AH, AP, AQ, BB, BE, and BG.
5. *See* Report of the Meeting of the Group of Experts on ISDN Matters of Study Group XVIII (Munich, 17-25 February 1982) at 60 (1982).
6. *Id.* at 70.
7. *See* Report of the Meeting of the Group of Experts on ISDN Matters of Study Group XVIII (Kyoto, 14-25 February 1983), CCITT Doc. COM XVIII-No. R15 at 93-94 (1983).
8. *See* Report of Working Team 3 (ISDN Network Aspects), CCITT Doc. No. COM XVIII-No. R19 at 2-3 (1983).
9. *See* Report of the Meeting of Working Team 3 (ISDN-Network Aspects), CCITT Doc. COM XVIII-No. 210 at 1-3 (1983).
10. *See* Report of the Meeting of the Group of Experts on ISDN Matters of Study Group XVIII (Brasilia, 13-24 February 1984), CCITT Doc. XVIII-No. 229 (1984).
11. All the new CCITT questions relating to ISDN are listed in Chapter 9.
12. Final Report of the VIIIth CCITT Plenary Assembly (Parts I and II), CCITT Doc. No. COM XVIII-No. R29 [also Doc. AP VIII-No. 94] (1984).
13. *See* Report of the Meeting of Working Party XVIII/1 (ISDN), CCITT Doc. COM XVIII-No. R3 at 25-26 (1981).
14. *See* CCITT Doc. COM XVIII-No. BG (1981).
15. *See* CCITT Docs. COM XVIII-No. BI, BV, CQ, CU, and DB (1982).

16. *See* Report of the Meeting of the Group of Experts on ISDN Matters of Study Group XVIII (Munich, 17-25 February 1982), CCITT Doc. COM XVIII-No. R8 at 70 (1982).

17. *See* Report of the Meeting of the Group of Experts on ISDN Matters of Study Group XVIII (Kyoto, 14-25 February 1983), CCITT Doc. COM XVIII-No. R15 at 95 (1983).

18. *See* CCITT Docs. COM XVIII-Nos. 130, IA, JJ, AND JF (1983).

19. *See* CCITT Doc. COM XVIII-No. 130 (1983).

20. *Ibid.*

21. *See* CCITT Docs. COM XVIII-Nos. JJ and IA (1983).

22. Report of the Meeting of the Group of Experts on ISDN Matters of Study Group XVIII (Kyoto, 14-25 February 1983), CCITT Doc. COM XVIII-No. R15 at 96.

23. *See* Report of Working Team 3 (ISDN Network Aspects), CCITT Doc. No. COM XVIII-No. R19 at 5 (1983).

24. *See* CCITT Doc. COM XVIII-No. NT (1983).

25. *See* CCITT Doc. COM XVIII-Nos. TS, UV, and UW (1983).

26. *See* Report of the Meeting of Working Team 3 (ISDN-Network Aspects), CCITT Doc. COM XVIII-No. 210 at 3-4 91983).

27. *See* CCITT Docs. COM XVIII-Nos. VU, YK, and YN (1983).

28. *See* Report of the Meeting of the Group of Experts on ISDN Matters of Study Group XVIII (Brasilia, 13-24 February 1984), CCITT Doc. COM XVIII-No. 229 at 21 (1984).

29. *See* Report of the Meeting of Working Party XVIII/1 (ISDN), CCITT Doc. COM XVIII-No. R3 at 25 (1981).

30. *See* CCITT Doc. COM XVIII-No. BE.

31. *See* CCITT Docs. COM XVIII-Nos. DE and CS (1982).

32. *See* Report of the Meeting of the Group of Experts on ISDN Matters of Study Group XVIII (Munich, 17-25 February 1982) at 69 (1982).

33. *See* CCITT Docs. COM XVIII-Nos. 138, 149, HG, HI, HQ, HR, IH, IO, IT, JB, JC, JP, JY, KB, and KT.

34. *See* Report of the Meeting of the Group of Experts on ISDN Matters of Study Group XVIII (Kyoto, 14-25 February 1983), CCITT Doc. COM XVIII-No. R15 at 97-98 (1983).

35. *See* CCITT Docs. COM XVIII-Nos. MM, MU, NS, NT and OY.

36. *See* Report of Working Team 3 (ISDN-Network Aspects), CCITT Doc. No. COM XVIII-No. R19 at 3 (1983).

37. *See* CCITT Docs. COM XVIII-Nos. UB and UD.

38. *See* Report of the Meeting of Working Team 3 (ISDN-Network Aspects), CCITT Doc. COM XVIII-No. 210 at 3 (1983).

39. *See* CCITT Docs. COM XVIII-Nos. WK and YJ.

40.   *See* Report of the Meeting Group of Experts on ISDN Matters of Study Group XVIII (Brasilia, 13-24 February 1984), CCITT Doc. COM XVIII-No. 229 (1984).

41.   *See* British Telecom, Hypothetical Reference Connexions for ISDN, CCITT Doc. COM XVIII-No. DA (Feb. 1982).

42.   *Ibid.*

43.   *See* Report of the Meeting of the Group of Experts on ISDN Matters of Study Group XVIII (Munich, 17-25 February 1982) at 67-68 (1982).

44.   *See* CCITT Doc. COM XVIII-No. IX (COMSAT) and Temp. Doc. 10 (CCIR).

45.   *See* CCITT Doc. COM XVIII-No. MH; Report of Working Team 3 (ISDN-Network Aspects), CCITT Doc. No. COM XVIII-No. R19 at 11 (1983).

46.   Final Report to the VIIIth CCITT Plenary Assembly (Parts I and II), CCITT Doc. COM XVIII-No. R29 at 29 (1984).

47.   *See* CCITT Docs. COM XVIII-Nos. 38 and S.

48.   *See* Report of the Meeting of Working Party XVIII/1 (ISDN), CCITT Doc. COM XVIII-No. R3 at 23-24 (1981).

49.   *See* CCITT Docs. COM XVIII-Nos. BX, CC, and DB.

50.   *See* Report of the Meeting of the Group of Experts on ISDN Matters of Study Group XVIII (Munich, 17-25 February 1982) at 66-67 (1982).

51.   *See* CCITT Docs. COM XVIII-Nos. ID, IF, IH, JA, JE, and JL.

52.   *See* Report of the Meeting of the Group of Experts on ISDN Matters of Study Group XVIII (Kyoto, 14-25 February 1983), CCITT Doc. COM XVIII-No. R15 at 96-97 (1983).

53.   *See* CCITT Docs. COM XVIII-Nos. LP, MV, NL, QC, QH, and QI.

54.   *See* Report of Working Team 3 (ISDN Network Aspects), CCITT Doc. No. COM XVIII-No. R19 at 8-11 (1983).

55.   *See* CCITT Docs. COM XVIII-Nos. SL, SM, TB, TC, TJ, and VF.

56.   *See* Report of the Meeting of Working Team 3 (ISDN-Network Aspects), CCITT Doc. COM XVIII-No. 210 at 25-26 (1983).

57.   *See* CCITT Docs. COM XVIII-Nos. VP, WB, YO, and ZJ.

58.   *See* Report of the Meeting of Working Party XVIII/1 (ISDN), CCITT Doc. COM XVIII-No. R3 at 24 (1981).

59.   *See* CCITT Docs. COM XVIII-Nos. 135 and 136.

60.   *See* Report of the Meeting of the Group of Experts on ISDN Matters of Study Group XVIII (Kyoto, 14-25 February 1983), CCITT Doc. COM XVIII-No. R15 at 98 (1983).

61.   *See* CCITT Docs. COM XVIII-Nos. BK, BN, BQ, BX, BZ, CB, CL, and DG.

62.   *See* Report of the Meeting of the Group of Experts on ISDN Matters of Study Group XVIII (Munich, 17-25 February 1982) at 64-66 (1982).

63. *See* CCITT Docs. CCITT COM XVIII-Nos. 140, 149, 151, GZ, HA, HG, HH, IH, IK, IL, IM, and JO.
64. *See* Report of the Meeting of the Group of Experts on ISDN Matters of Study Group XVIII (Kyoto, 14-25 February 1983), CCITT Doc. COM XVIII-No. R15 at 94 (1983).
65. *Id.* at 103.
66. *See* CCITT Docs. COM XVIII-Nos. MP, MU, NB, NJ, NK, NN, NO, NP, NQ, NR, NX, OY, OZ, PC, and PU.
67. *See* Report of Working Team 3 (ISDN Network Aspects), CCITT Doc. No. COM XVIII-No. R19 at 3-5 (1983).
68. *See* CCITT Docs. COM XVIII-Nos. SG, SH, SI, SJ, SK, TI, TS, TX, TY, UA, UD, UH, UQ, and UZ.
69. *See* Report of the Meeting of Working Team 3 (ISDN-Network Aspects), CCITT Doc. COM XVIII-No. 210 at 11 (1983).
70. *See* CCITT Docs. COM XVIII-No. VS, VW, WA, WR, WT, WW, WY, YB, YD, YL, YZ, ZB, ZC, and ZE.
71. *See* Report of the Meeting of the Group of Experts on ISDN Matters of Study Group XVIII (Brasilia, 13-24 February 1984), CCITT Doc. COM XVIII-No. 229 at 21 (1984).
72. *See* CCITT Doc. COM XVIII-No. JR.
73. *See* Report of the Meeting of the Group of Experts on ISDN Matters of Study Group XVIII (Kyoto, 14-25 February 1983), CCITT Doc. COM XVIII-No. R15 at 102 (1983).
74. *See* CCITT Docs. COM XVIII-Nos. MO, PY and MR.
75. *See* Report of Working Team 3 (ISDN Network Aspects), CCITT Doc. No. COM XVIII-No. R19 at 11-12 (1983).
76. *See* CCITT Docs. COM XVIII-Nos. TG, TS, and UD.
77. *See* Report of the Meeting of Working Team 3 (ISDN-Network Aspects), CCITT Doc. COM XVIII-No. 210 at 4 (1983).
78. *See* CCITT Docs. COM XVIII-Nos. 148, HD, HK, HU, and JS.
79. *See* Report of the Meeting of the Group of Experts on ISDN Matters of Study Group XVIII (Kyoto, 14-25 February 1983), CCITT Doc. COM XVIII-No. R15 at 99-102 (1983).
80. *See* CCITT Doc. COM XVIII-Nos. 162, 180, LX, MC, and OQ.
81. *See* Report of Working Team 3 (ISDN Network Aspects), CCITT Doc. No. COM XVIII-No. R19 at 7 (1983).

CHAPTER 6 — USER-NETWORK INTERFACES

In Chapters 4 and 5 we examined ISDN from the outside and the inside, respectively. In this chapter, ISDN is discussed at the most prevalent points of demarcation between outside and inside — the user-network interfaces. Considerable creative energy was consumed during the 1981–1984 activity period of Study Group XVIII to describe in great detail every important aspect of these interfaces. Details to allow manufacturers to design and fabricate very large scale integrated circuits, and networks to implement prototype ISDN terminal equipment.

The issues entwined with this subject are not as broad and complex as those associated with services and networks. The great level of detail describing these interfaces also tends to mask those issues that are more than simple engineering design trade-offs. Nonetheless, there are significant issues that will have a considerable effect on the nature and extent of the terminal equipment market for manufacturers, and the availability of equipment and features to customers.

The study of user-network interfaces was largely carried out by Working Teams 1 and 2 of Study Group XVIII. They were faced with conceptualizing and developing all the physical, electrical, functional, and protocol details that comprise the I-400 Series Recommendations.

This chapter is divided into two parts. The first describes the manner in which Working Teams 1 and 2, as well as Working Party 1, went about their work during the 1981–1984 activity. The second part sets forth several of the I-400 Series Recommendations.

6.1 Exploring the User-Network Interface Questions

Work on the User-Network Interfaces largely emanated from two Questions adopted by the VIIth CCITT Plenary Assembly in 1980.

Question 1, Point C. Customer Access

> What are the principles in terms of network structure and systems architecture which define customer access to ISDN and which should form the basis of studies of related transmission, switching, signalling and interface aspects?

Question 2. User-Network Interface

1.   What are the principles which should form the basis for detailed study of the customer/network [this term was subsequently changed to "user-network"] interface to ISDN, taking into account existing and new, analogue and digital, voice and non-voice, service dedicated and multi-purpose terminals? (To include single access, multi-line access, multi-service access, and PABXs.)

2.   *Considering*
2.1   that the functional requirements for the interface between dedicated-service customer terminals and the ISDN will be identified by [other listed Study Groups];
2.2   that some customers will have multi-service terminals using one or more access paths to the ISDN;
2.3   that there will be a need to connect multiplexed groups of digital PABX groups of digital PABX lines to local digital exchanges in the ISDN;
2.4   that the multiplex arrangements in 2.3 may be applicable to remote multiplexers used to connect several direct lines to the local digital exchange;
2.5   that the principles relating to the customer/network interface, and the associated customer network signalling, will be studied by Study Group XVIII (Question 9/XVIII).

What are the preferred characteristics to be recommended for the interface between customer terminals and the ISDN?[1]

Both of these questions had received some study during the 1977–1980 activity period, and a basic decision had been made to split the interface on the user side into two separate terminations. The Customer Terminal (*CT*) would connect to a Network Termination (*NT*) that would connect to a Line Termination (*LT*) that would connect to the network transmission line, as shown in Figure 6-1.[2]

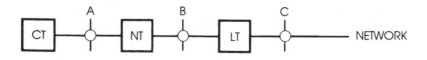

Figure 6-1

This approach was an important recognition of the national regulatory situation in some countries, most notably the United States, where the network would not necessarily be providing all the equipment. This was rather fortuitous. As a result of regulatory decisions that were subsequently made in the United States, the dominant networks, e.g., AT&T and the Bell Operating Companies, were to be the providers of only some of this equipment, and none of it on an exclusive basis.

Innisbrook, January 1981. When Study Group XVIII participants met for the first time after the VIIth Plenary Assembly, at Innisbrook, Florida, the user-network interfaces received considerable attention. Two of the three working parties at the meeting dealt with customer access and customer reference configurations, and most contributions were on these subjects.[3]

The working parties reached some important preliminary agreements, oriented around the kind of integrated digital services capable of being furnished on an existing wire pair. The kind of bit rates necessary to support PABXs, local area networks, or video information was excluded.[4]

Customer access types were to be characterized by subsidiary information and channel types. Information types and their associated designations included: analog telephone (v), 64 kbit/s digital voice (f), "standard" data (d), slow speed data (d'), customer signalling (s), $n \times 64$ kbit/s digital information (w), and very low rate telemetry (t). Channel types and their associated designations included: 64 kbit/s for f and d type information (b-channel), $\times 8$ kbit/s for type information (b'-channel), $n \times 8$ kbit/s for s and optionally t and d' information (Δ channel), analog for v type information (a-channel), and hybrid access for t, d' and possibly s information (δ channel).

Some work was also done toward describing a possible Δ channel protocol. The stated objectives was to define a uniform flexible network control signalling protocol for different services.

Interfaces A and B, shown in Figure 6-1 above, were described as "functional and optionally physical." This meant that the hardware and software necessary to implement the interface could be placed in the same piece of equipment — something that might well occur in a PTT monopoly environment. Interface C is functional and physical, with the physical characteristics to be defined by Study Group XV.

Work was accomplished in defining some reference configurations at customer premises. Only a single access arrangement, 2 b-channels plus a Δ channel, was considered. The reference diagram was altered to subdivide the ST box as shown in Figure 6-2. ST' represented a terminal adaptor, in case the terminal (ST) was not an ISDN terminal.

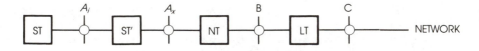

Figure 6-2

Several general principles were adopted concerning this reference config-uration. A_X should be a "universal interface," as simple as possible, and able to support as many services and terminals as possible. New ISDN terminals should interface directly with A_X. The network exchange should not be required to take account of the physical arrangement of customer premises equipment. This implied that subscriber equipment can be physically moved from one A_X interface to another on the same access line without any changes at the exchange. Four different generic reference configurations — single, star, bus, and ring — were identified.[5]

Geneva, June 1981. At the first organizational meeting of Study Group XVIII for the 1981–1984 activity period, separate ad-hoc groups were established: the group on Question 1, Point C (Customer Access) under V. DeJulio of Italy, and the group on Question 2 (Customer/Network Interface) under W. S. Gifford of AT&T.

The Customer Access Group considered 13 new contributions.[6] The char-acterization of access types by subsidiary information and channel types was altered to primarily focus on channel types alone. Six channel types were identified: the b-channel, Δ channel, b'-channel, a-channel, δ channel, and F-channel. These remained as described at Innisbrook, except for the ad-dition of the F-channel, which was characterized as a digital channel that can be used in conjunction with an a-channel to provide a digital circuit switched capability as part of hybrid access. Channels at 1544 and 2048 kbit/s rates were discussed. It was decided, however, to describe these as $n \times b$-channels. These access types were identified: "basic access," which consisted of one or two b-channels and one Δ channel; "broadband access," which consisted of $n \times b$-channels and one Δ channel; "PABX access," which consisted of an a-channel and either a δ channel or a F-channel.[7]

The Customer/Network Interface Group considered 13 new contribu-tions.[8] Much of the work accomplished at Innisbrook was used and amended. The reference model was modified as shown in Figure 6-3. Additional sub-figures were provided that depicted combined ST and ST' boxes or combined NT_Y and NT_X boxes to account for the various implementation options. Somewhat more precise use of terms was also effected. The points P, S, and

S' were referred to as "physical interfaces," while the boxes were referred to as "functions."

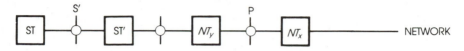

Figure 6-3

The functions performed by each box were also described in somewhat greater detail. NT_X consisted of test looping, power feeding, timing, line transmission termination, time division multiplexing. NT_Y consisted of protocol handling, switching, statistical multiplexing, and physical distribution/ concentration. PABXs, terminal controllers and local area network gateways were portrayed as examples of NT_Y functions. ST consisted of those functions typically performed by a digital telephone or digital termination equipment. ST' consisted of such functions as the provision of a X.21 or X.25 interface.[9]

Without explanation, the C interface was dropped from the reference model. As discussed in Chapters 7 and 8, this interface became a source of considerable controversy, and ultimately the focus of a special Federal Communications Commission finding called the *NCTE Decision*.

Munich, February 1982. The ISDN Experts convened at Munich in February 1982 following meetings by the Study Group XVIII leadership at Montreal and Darmstadt. Those meetings had given user-network interface issues a very high priority, and produced some new ideas and organization as well. The work at Munich was now subdivided into two ad-hoc groups: 1) (User Access) under Gifford, and 2) (Basic Access Level 1 [later changed to Layer 1] Characteristics) under DeJulio. These groups would subsequently be known as Working Teams 1 and 2.

The User Access Group, which received a great many contributions,[10] focused on three interrelated subjects: reference configurations, channel types, and channel structures. The work was undertaken with such earnest that three new draft I-Series Recommendations were produced: I.xxx on reference configurations; I.xxy on channel structures and access capabilities; and I.xxw on general matters relating to user/network interfaces.[11]

Still again, the reference configuration designations were changed! In addition, the points R, S, and T were now referred to as "reference points." However, the basic concepts of the functions described above were not significantly changed.

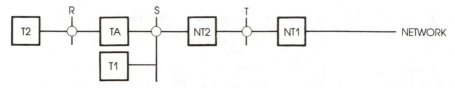

Figure 6-4

Figure 6-4 became the pictorial representation at the core of Recommendation I.xxx. In addition to discussing the purpose and application of the reference configuration, each functional box was described in detail.

Rather interestingly, the missing reference point at the end of the transmission line was now explained in a note that read "there are no reference points assigned to the transmission line, since an ISDN user/network interface is not envisaged at this location." Notwithstanding this bold assertion that was never subsequently removed,[12] the FCC in its *NCTE Decision*, as well as the *First Report* in its ISDN proceeding, made it quite clear that ISDNs in the United States will very much have this interface present. There is probably no better example of how a seemingly minor technical detail translates into a domestic and international controversy of significant proportion, and the availability of an equipment market worth many millions of dollars.

The various channel types, their structure, and the access arrangements are all described in draft Recommendation I.xxy. The various channel types were altered *vis-a-vis* previous versions. The old *b*-channel was designated the *B*-channel, but not substantively altered. The old Δ channel became the *D*-channel, and also was not substantively altered. The old *F*-channel, used with hybrid access, became the *C*-channel, and was expanded in scope to include packet switched information with a bit rate of either 8 or 16 kbit/s. No other channel types were defined, although reference was made to analogue channels in the provision of hybrid access, to broadband channels, and "other" channels.

Eight channel structures were identified in Recommendation I.xxy: a "basic channel structure" $2B + D$, with a *D*-channel bit rate of 16 kbit/s; a "*C*-channel structure" using one *C*-channel plus a conventional analogue channel; an undefined "intermediate channel structure;" a "primary rate channel structure" corresponding to 1544 and 2048 kbit/s but otherwise undefined; a "multiplexed channel structure" at 1544 and 2048 kbit/s plus associated *D*-channels of either 4 or 64 kbit/s; and undefined "broadband," "higher rate," and "other" channel structures. The different primary rates resulted from different equipment standards followed by AT&T *vis-a-vis* European PTTs, the former using 1544 and the latter using 2048 kbit/s. It was important to agree on a channel rate definition that accomodated both rates in a related fashion, i.e., different multiples of 64 kbit/s.

Draft Recommendation I.xxw, although intended to precede I.xxx or I.xxy, was not finished, and thus was placed in an annex to the group's report. It collected many of the general principles and bases for work in Study Group XVIII and the groups working on the user-network interface. It would surface near the end of the 1981–1984 activity period as the general principles recommendation introducing the I-400 Series.

The Group on Basic Access Layer 1 Characteristics began to focus in considerable detail on all the most primitive requirements to initiate connection with an information system — requirements fall within the scope of OSI layer 1. These include many really detailed design specifications such as the physical definition of the connectors, pin assignments for various functions, power feeding, activation/deactivation of terminals, the length and configuration of distribution system wiring, terminal identification, contention resolution among multiple terminals, rate adaption, and maintenance.[13] A number of contributions were submitted on the subject.[14]

Some of the issues that were more than design engineering trade-offs included the subject of power feeding. Some felt that ISDN, like telephone networks, should be able to provide power to the terminals from the exchange to allow continued operation in the event of a general electrical power failure in the community. Others felt that an implementation option should exist that might allow for use of backup batteries in ISDN terminals. The latter view prevailed.

Another subtle but important issue before the Basic Access Group dealt with the "passive-bus." Again using an analogy to contemporary telephone networks, some felt that the user-network interface should allow for customer premises wiring, i.e., a passive-bus, that allowed users to move terminals freely from one location to another. Others argued that ISDN should be based on a strict, point-to-point approach. The former view prevailed with the compromise that such internal wiring will not exceed 300 meters in length, although some considerations relating to contention resolution, timing, and synchronization were also affected.

Geneva, June 1982. In June 1982, the full Study Group XVIII Plenary met. Working Team 1 and 2 did not meet, and therefore no substantive changes were made with respect to the user-network material. The meeting was notable, however, because of a submission by all the CEPT countries noting the "very significant progress...and good results achieved particularly in the area of the definition of the ISDN user/network interfaces."[15] The document went on to cite Recs. I.xxx, I.xxy, and I.xxw, and called for the Study Group Plenary to invoke a special procedure that would establish these Recommendations as provisionally adopted.

The delegates of the United States and France, while strongly supporting the draft Recommendations, argued that the provisions were "editorially inadequate at present and open to possible differences of opinion; thus they could not endorse the proposal [by the CEPT countries]."[16] Because the procedure for provisional adoption requires unanimity, the proposal failed. The Chairman of Study Group XVIII indicated, however, that there was "unanimous agreement on the technical content of these draft Recommendations," and will thus "form the basis for future work to be performed on the establishment of ISDN Recommendations."[17]

Florence, November 1982. Mr. DeJulio, acting in his capacity of special rapporteur for Question 1, Point C, called a special meeting experts on Level 1 Characteristics at Florence in November 1982. In light of the strong support given the existing draft user-network interfaces at the Geneva meeting in June 1982, this group sought to reach agreement on more of the layer 1 details. A large number of contributions were submitted.[18]

The focus of the meeting was on introducing and harmonizing the related work done in Study Groups VII, XI, and XVII, reaching agreement on a contention resolution mechanism, consolidating the physical and electrical parameters, and developing preliminary proposals on other design details. Considerable work was accomplished, but the drafting of any I-Series Recommendations was deferred.[19]

Kyoto, February 1983. Working Teams 1 and 2 reassembled at Kyoto, one year after Munich. In light of the general approval of WT1's draft Recommendations, most of the submitted contributions were largely editorial in nature.[20] Recommendations I.xxx and I.xxy were designated I.411 and I.412, respectively. Most of the work focused on those channels and access structures left undefined — those related to high speed channels, and to a lesser extent, channels at rates less than 64 kbit/s. I.xxw was not discussed at this or any Working Team 1 meeting until February 1984.

In Recommendation I.411, the basic reference configuration diagram shown in Figure 6-4, above, was not modified except for the very minor change of the "T1" and "T2" functional boxes to "TE1" and "TE2." In Recommendation I.412, an additional channel type, the E-channel was defined as a 64 kbit/s signalling channel to support primary rate multiplexed channel structures, and Signalling System No. 7 procedures would be used. In addition, new speeds for rate adaption, requirements for the D-channel to accomodate the hybrid access arrangement, and redefinition structure and use were incorporated.[21]

Working Team 2, dealing with basic access layer 1 details, continued to receive a very large number of contributions.[22] Most of the work focused on the most difficult and important design considerations relating to multi-terminal configurations, activation/deactivation, power feeding, and maintenance.[23] After intensive work, it finally was able to agree on a draft Recommendation, designated I.431. The Recommendation was subdivided into seven major parts: a general introduction, enumeration of point-to-point and point-to-multipoint configurations, description of functional characteristics, interface procedures, electrical characteristics, power feeding, and mechanical characteristics.

Geneva, June 1983. Working Teams 1 and 2 both met at Geneva, June 1983. The focus was again on Recommendations I.411 and I.412, and the issues remained the same: subrate channels and adaptation; high speed channels and their structure; and a sub-set of the D-channel protocol to support low cost terminals. Twenty-five contributions were considered during the course of WT1's meeting.[24]

Considerable progress was made on all three of the issues by Working Team 1. The D-channel protocol issues were largely referred to the team dealing with signalling. A few minor editorial changes were made to Recommendation I.411. A report on sub-group rate adaption was prepared, together with a draft Recommendation I.www. The principal additions to draft Recommendation I.412 were the definition of H-channels of two varieties. The $H0$ channel would have a rate of 384 kbit/s, and $H1$ channels, rates of either 1536 or 1920 kbit/s. H-channels were envisioned for a variety of user information streams, particularly for PABXs. In addition, the broadband channel characterization for any channels was dropped.[25]

Working Team 2 continued its work on the layer 1 details, reviewing and considering forty-seven contributions.[26] As a result, many additional details, and a new section dealing with the apportionment of functions between layers 1 and 2 were added to draft Recommendation I.431 on the Basic Interface, and new draft Recommendation I.432 was prepared for the primary rate (H) user-network interface. Several useful reports on related subjects were also prepared. These include the electrical characteristics of the basic interface, activation/deactivation, and power in emergency situations.[27]

Geneva, November 1983. Working Team 2 met at Geneva, November 1983 to deal with the continuing interest in reaching agreement on layer 1 details.[28] The work was apportioned among three groups: mechanical characteristics, interface procedures and frame structure, and power feeding. Each of these groups prepared reports on their areas of study and additional changes to draft Recommendations I.431 and I.432 were made.[29]

Brasilia, February 1983. Working Team 1 and 2 both reconvened at Brasilia in February to make consider the last changes to their work and to prepare questions for the next activity period.

Working Team 1 tasks were largely complete by February 1983, a fact reflected in the reduced number of contributions.[30] Old draft Recommendation I.xxw on general principles, originally drafted at Munich in 1982, was resurrected, a few editorial changes made, and designated Recommendation I.410. Draft Recommendation I.411 was essentially unchanged. Additional work occurred, however, on Recommendation I.412. The *C*-channel was dropped, having been opposed for some time by several participants who argued that variants of the *D*-channel could serve the same purpose. The channel interface structures for primary rate channels *H*1 and *H*0 were also added. Several short Recommendations, I.420, and I.421 were added by the team to explain the general relationships among other Recommendations with respect to both the Basic and Primary Rate User-Network interfaces. The Recommendation on rate adaption formerly designated I.www was amended and designated I.460. Lastly, a short Recommendation related to rate adaption, support of 56 kbit/s information streams in an ISDN, was adopted in part, with the work to be finished by mail.[31]

Working Team 2 continued to receive a very large number of contributions.[32] As a result of these, some additional changes were made to the Recommendations for Basic and Primary Rate Layer 1 Specification, which were designated from I.431, I.432 to I.430, and I.431.[33]

Some of the unfinished tasks of both Working Teams 1 and 2 were continued by mail and discussed at the Study Group XVIII plenary meeting at Geneva in May 1983. In addition to finalizing their I-400 Series Recommendations, both teams also drafted the replies to the Questions under their respective jurisdictions.

Question 1, Point C. Customer Access

1. Under Question 1c, Study Group XVIII studied the customer access to ISDN — in particular, referring to the interface aspects, Study Group XVIII has defined Layer 1 characteristics of the various ISDN user-network interfaces (at reference points S and T) and has produced two draft Recommendations:

    i) *Recommendation I.430*: Layer 1 characteristics of the basic user-network interface, that defines the functional (frame structure, activation/deactivation, etc.) and electrical characteristics of the basic interface, at the rate of 192 kbit/s.

    ii) *Recommendation I.431*: Layer 1 characteristics of the primary rate user-network interface, that defines the functional and electrical characteristics of the primary interface at the rates of 1544 and 2048 kbit/s.

2. It is proposed to continue the study of this question during the next period (see Question 1/XVIII).

Question 2. User-Network Interface

1. This Question defines the principles which should be used as the basis for detailed study of user-network interfaces for ISDNs. The basic principles have been established and are contained in Recommendations I.410, I.411, and I.412. These principles form the basis for the specifications of the user-network interfaces described in I.420 (Basic Interface) and I.421 (Primary Rate Interface). Recommendations for permitting other interfaces to work with the ISDN interfaces are contained in I.460, I.461, I.462, I.463, and I.464.

Recommendation I.410: General aspects and principles relating to Recommendations on ISDN user-network interfaces. Describes the basic concepts and importance of interfaces in characterizing ISDN. These are essential due to the wide variations expected in the internal implementations of ISDNs around the world. Thus the user-network interfaces are the key to both successful characterization of the ISDN and to providing services which are useful to customers around the world. Of particular importance is the commonality of interface characteristics for a wide range of applications through the use of a limited set of different user-network interface, corresponding to widely different bet rate requirements.

Recommendation I.411: ISDN user-network interfaces — Reference Configurations. Describes the different types of arrangements at user-network interfaces, non-exhaustively based on functions which may be performed. It established that even though many different physical and functional configurations are possible, the interface Recommendations should be able to be applied to many different situations — in particular, there should not be any additional interfaces required based solely on differences in these configurations.

Recommendation I.412: ISDN user-network interfaces — Interface structures and access capabilities. Defines the channels which will be carried across the ISDN user-network interfaces and the expected combinations of these channels which form the interfaces defined: basic interface and primary rate interface. Each interface can be used for a variety of different channels and combinations of channels in keeping with the overall requirements for the use of each interface for many different applications.

Recommendation I.420: Basic User-Network Interface. Refers to the other Recommendations which provide the detailed specifications.

Recommendation I.421: Primary Rate User-Network Interface. Provides the references to the specific Recommendations which define the Primary Rate User-Network interface.

Recommendation I.460: Multiplexing, Rate Adaption and Support of Existing Interfaces. Describes the techniques for adapting among the various ISDN rates, multiplexing these rates together and also refers to the specific Recommendations containing the detailed specifications for adapting existing interfaces to the ISDN interfaces. Adaption between 8, 16, and 32 kbit/s and 64 kbit/s is described along with techniques for multiplexing these channels together. The same mechanism is used for adapting between 56 and 64 kbit/s.

Recommendation I.461: Support of X.21 and X.21bis Based DTEs on an ISDN (X.30). Describes the techniques for adapting these existing terminal interfaces to the ISDN interface Recommendations. A two stage process is used with the second stage being that described in I.460 from 8, 16, 32 kbit/s to 64 kbit/s   .

Recommendation I.462: For the Support of Packet Mode Terminal Equipments on an ISDN (X.31). Describes two techniques for adapting from the packet mode terminal interfaces to ISDN interfaces. One method uses the two stage approach, as described in I.460. The other method uses flag stuffing to go directly to 64 kbit/s.

Recommendation I.463: Support of DTEs with V-series Type Interfaces on and ISDN. Describes the techniques for adapting from the V-series interfaces to the ISDN interfaces, using the two stage rate adaption described in I.460.

Recommendation I.464: Rate adaption, multiplexing and support of existing interfaces for restricted 64 kbit/s transfer capability. Refers to the other Recommendations which provide detailed specifications for rate adaption and multiplexing. Also describes limitations to the above.

2. Resulting from discussion of these topics, guidelines for the detailed studies in Study Group XI have been produced.[34]

6.2 The I-400 Series Recommendations

The Recommendations developed by Working Teams 1 and 2, after the four years of work described in section 6.1 above, were adopted by the CCITT VIIIth Plenary Assembly, and appear in the CCITT Red Book (1985). Recs. I.410, I.411, and I.412 are fundamental to describing the basic characteristics and configurations of the user-network interfaces. These are set forth below. The remaining I-400 series recommendations are so detailed that they are unsuitable for inclusion here.

Recommendation I.410

GENERAL ASPECTS AND PRINCIPLES RELATING TO RECOMMENDATIONS ON ISDN USER-NETWORK INTER-FACES

1. General

1.1 Rec. I.120 gives the conceptual principles on which an ISDN should be based. The main feature of an ISDN is the support of a wide range of service capabilities, including voice and non-voice applications, in the same network by offering end-to-end digital connectivity.

1.2 A key element of service integration for an ISDN is the provision of a limited set of standard multipurpose user-network interfaces. These interfaces represent a focal point both for the development of ISDN network components and configurations and for the development of ISDN terminal equipment and applications.

1.3 An ISDN is recognized by the service characteristics available through user-network interfaces, rather than by its internal architecture, configuration, or technology. This concept plays a key role in permitting user and network technologies and configurations to evolve separately.

2. Interface applications

[Figure 6-5] shows some examples of ISDN user-network interfaces. The following cases are identified corresponding to:

(1)   access of a single ISDN terminal;
(2)   access of a multiple ISDN terminal installation;
(3)   access of multi-service PBXs, or local area networks, or, more generally, or private networks;
(4)   access of specialized storage and information processing centres.

In addition, depending on the particular national regulatory arrangements, either ISDN user-network interfaces or internetwork interfaces may be used for access of:

(1) different types of terminals and applications to use the same interface;

(2) portability of terminals from one location to another (office, home, public access points) within one country and from one country to another country;

(3) separate evolution of both terminal and network equipment, technologies and configurations;

(4) efficient connection with specialized storage and information processing centres and other networks.

User-network interfaces should be designed to provide an appropriate balance between service capabilities and cost/tariffs, in order to meet service demand easily.

4. **Interface characteristics.** User-network interfaces are specified by a comprehensive set of characteristics, including:

(1) physical and electromagnetic, including optical, characteristics;

(2) channel structures and access capabilities;

(3) user-network protocols;

(4) maintenance and operation characteristics;

(5) performance characteristics;

(6) service characteristics.

A layered approach has been adopted for the definition of ISDN user-network interfaces according to the ISDN protocol reference model, Rec. I.320.

5. **Interface capabilities.** In addition to the multi-service capability, an ISDN user-network interface may allow for capabilities such as the following:

(1) multi-drop and other multiple terminal arrangements;

(2) choice of information bit rate, switching mode, coding method, etc., on a call-by-call or other, e.g., semi-permanent or subscription time option, basis, over the same interface according to the user's need;

(3) capability for compatibility checking in order to check whether calling and called terminals can communicate with each other.

6. **Other I-Series Recommendations**

6.1 The reference configurations for ISDN user-network interfaces define the terminology for various reference points and the types of functions that can be provided between reference points. Rec. I.411 contains the reference configurations and shows significant applications.

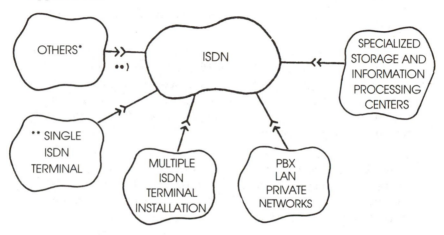

*) *See* paragraph 2
**) Alternatively internetwork interface may apply

Figure 6-5   ISDN User-Network Interface Examples

Source: Rec. I.410, Fig. 1/I.410.

6.2 The number of different interfaces is kept to a minimum. Rec. I.412 defines a limited set of channel structures, and possible access capabilities for the ISDN user-network interfaces. A distinction is necessary between the channel structure supported by the interface and the access capability supported by the particular network access arrangement.

6.3 The user-network interfaces, as defined in Rec. I.420 and I.421, are applicable to a wide range of situations without information, e.g., to both reference points S and T, as defined in I.411.

Recommendation I.411

ISDN USER-NETWORK INTERFACES

REFERENCE CONFIGURATIONS

1. General

1.1 This Recommendation provides the reference configurations for ISDN user-network interfaces.

1.2 From the user's perspective, an ISDN is completely described by the attributes that can be observed at an ISDN user-network interface, including physical, electromagnetic, protocol, service, capability, maintenance, operation, and performance characteristics. The key to defining, and even recognizing, an ISDN is the specification of these characteristics.

1.3 An objective of ISDN is that a small set of compatible user-network interfaces can economically support a wide range of user applications, equipment and configurations. The number of different user-network interfaces is minimized to maximize user flexibility through terminal compatibility, from one application to another, one location to another, and one service to another, and to reduce costs through economics in production of equipment and operation of both ISDN and user equipment. However, different interfaces are required for applications with widely different information rates, complexity, or other characteristics, as well as for applications in the evolutionary stages. In this way, simple applications need not be burdened with the cost of accomodating features employed by complex applications.

1.4 Another objective is to have the same interfaces used even though there are different configurations, e.g., single terminal versus multiple terminal connections, connections to a PABX versus direct connections into the network, etc., or different national regulations.

2. Definitions

2.1 **Reference configurations** are conceptual configurations useful in identifying various possible physical user access arrangements to an ISDN. Two concepts are used in defining reference configurations: reference points and functional groupings. Layout and application examples of reference configurations are given in para. 3.

2.2 **Functional groupings** are sets of functions which may be needed in ISDN user access arrangements. In a particular access arrangement, specific functions in a functional grouping may or may not be present. Note that specific functions in a functional grouping may be performed in one or more pieces of equipment.

2.3 **Reference points** are the conceptual points dividing functional groupings. In a specific access arrangement, a reference point may correspond to a physical interface between pieces of equipment, or there may not be any physical interface between pieces of equipment, or there may not be any physical interface corresponding to the reference point. Physical interfaces that do not correspond to a reference point, e.g., transmission line interfaces, will not be the subject of ISDN user-network interface Recommendations.

3.   Reference configuration

3.1 The reference configurations for ISDN user-network interfaces define reference points and types of functions that can be provided between reference points. [Figure 6-6] shows the reference configurations, while [Figures 6-7, 6-8, and 6-9] show examples of such configurations.

3.2 The ISDN user-network interface Recommendations in the I-series apply to physical interfaces at reference points S and T, using the recommended channel structures according to Recommendation I.412. At reference point R, physical interfaces in accordance with other CCITT Recommendations, e.g., the X-series interface Recommendations, may be used.

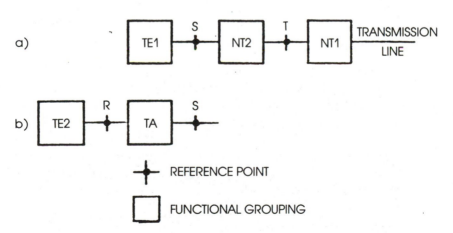

Figure 6-6 Reference Configurations for the ISDN User-Network Interfaces

Source: Rec. I.411, Fig. 1/I.411.

Note 1 - Physical interfaces not included in CCITT Recommendations may appear at reference point R.

Note 2 - There is no reference point assigned to the transmission line, since an ISDN user-network interface is not envisaged at this location.

3.3 [Figure 6-6a] defines the reference configuration of functional grouping NT1, NT2 and TE1. [Figure 6-6b] illustrates that TE1 may be replaced by the combination of TE2 and TA.

3.4 Lists of functions for each functional group are given below. Each particular function is not necessarily restricted to a single functional grouping. For example, "interface termination" functions are included in the function lists of NT1, NT2, and TE. The function lists for NT2, TE and TA are not exhaustive. For a particular access arrangement, specific functions in a functional group are either present or absent.

The functional groupings are described in relation to the ISDN protocol reference model in Rec. I.320.

3.4.1 **NT1, network termination 1,** includes functions broadly equivalent to Layer 1 (Physical of the OSI Reference Model). These functions are associated with the proper physical and electromagnetic termination of the network. NT1 functions are:

- line transmission termination;
- layer 1 line maintenance functions and performance monitoring;
- timing;
- power transfer;
- interface termination, including multi-drop termination employing Layer 1 contention resolution.

3.4.2 **NT2, network termination 2,** includes functions broadly equivalent to layer 1 and higher layers of the X.200 Reference Model. PABXs, local area networks, and terminal controllers are examples of equipment or combinations of equipment that provide NT2 functions. NT2 functions include:

- layers 2 and 3 protocol handling;
- layers 2 and 3 multiplexing;
- switching;
- concentration;
- maintenance functions; and
- interface termination and other layer 1 functions.

For example, a simple PABX can provide NT2 functions at layers 1, 2 and 3. A simple terminal controller can provide NT2 functions at only layers 1 and 2. A simple time division multiplexer can provide NT2 functions at only layer 1. In a specific access arrangements, the NT2 functional grouping may consist of only physical connections.

3.4.3 **TE, terminal equipment,** includes functions broadly belonging to layer 1 and higher layers of the X.200 Reference Model. Digital telephones, data terminal equipment, and integrated work stations are examples of equipment or combinations of equipment that provide the functions. The TE functions are:

- protocol handling;
- maintenance functions;
- interface functions;
- connection functions to other equipments.

3.4.3.1 **TE1, terminal equipment type 1,** includes functions belonging to the functional grouping TE, and with an interface that complies with the ISDN user-network interface Recommendations.

3.4.3.2 **TE2, terminal equipment type 2,** includes functions belonging to the functional group TE but with an interface that complies with interface Recommendations other than the ISDN interface Recommendation, e.g., the X-series interface Recommendations, or interfaces not included in CCITT Recommendations.

3.4.4 **TA, terminal adaptor,** includes functions broadly belonging to layer 1 and higher layers of the X.200 Reference Model that allows a TE2 terminal to be served by an ISDN user-network interface. Adaptors between physical interfaces at reference points R and S or R and T are examples of equipment or combinations of equipment that provide TA functions.

4.   Physical realizations of reference configurations

4.1 [Figure 6-7] gives examples of configurations illustrating combinations of physical interfaces at reference points R, S, and T. [Figures 6-7a and 6-7b] show separate interfaces at S and T. [Figures 6-7c and 6-7d] show an interface at S but not T. [Figures 6-7e and 6-7f] show an interface at T but not S. [Figures 6-7g and 6-7h] show an interface at S and T where they coincide. Additionally, [Figures 6-7b, 6-7d, 6-7f and 6-7h] show an interface at reference point R.

4.2 [Figures 6-8 and 6-9] show examples of physical implementations. The examples given in [Figure 6-8] show physical realizations of functional groupings TE, NT1, NT2, based on physical interfaces

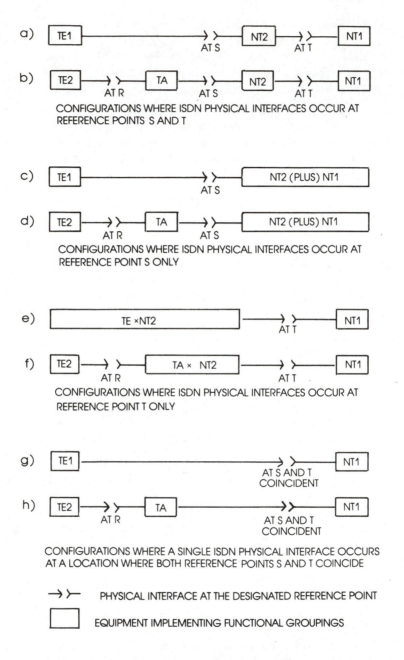

Figure 6-7   Examples of Physical Configurations

Source: Rec. I.411, Fig. 2/I.411.

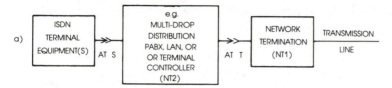

a) ISDN TERMINAL EQUIPMENT(S) — AT S — e.g. MULTI-DROP DISTRIBUTION PABX, LAN, OR OR TERMINAL CONTROLLER (NT2) — AT T — NETWORK TERMINATION (NT1) — TRANSMISSION LINE

AN IMPLEMENTATION (SEE FIGURE 6-7) WHERE ISDN PHYSICAL INTERFACES OCCUR AT REFERENCE POINTS S AND T

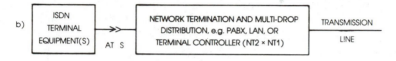

b) ISDN TERMINAL EQUIPMENT(S) — AT S — NETWORK TERMINATION AND MULTI-DROP DISTRIBUTION, e.g. PABX, LAN, OR TERMINAL CONTROLLER (NT2 × NT1) — TRANSMISSION LINE

AN IMPLEMENTATION (SEE FIGURE 6-7) WHERE AN ISDN PHYSICAL INTERFACE OCCURS AT REFERENCE POINT S BUT NOT T

c) NON-ISDN TERMINAL EQUIPMENT(S) — AT R — e.g. PABX, LAN, OR TERMINAL CONTROLLER (NT2 ×TA) — AT T — NETWORK TERMINATION (NT1) — TRANSMISSION LINE

AN IMPLEMENTATION (SEE FIGURE 6-7) WHERE AN ISDN PHYSICAL INTERFACE OCCURS AT REFERENCE POINT T BUT NOT S

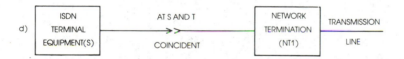

d) ISDN TERMINAL EQUIPMENT(S) — AT S AND T COINCIDENT — NETWORK TERMINATION (NT1) — TRANSMISSION LINE

AN IMPLEMENTATION (SEE FIGURE 6-7) WHERE A SINGLE ISDN PHYSICAL INTERFACE OCCURS AT A LOCATION WHERE BOTH REFERENCE POINTS S AND T COINCIDE

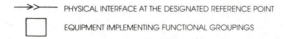

PHYSICAL INTERFACE AT THE DESIGNATED REFERENCE POINT

EQUIPMENT IMPLEMENTING FUNCTIONAL GROUPINGS

Figure 6-8   Examples of Implementation of NT1 and NT2 Functions

Source: Rec. I.411, Fig. 3/I.411.

occurring at reference points R, S and T. The examples given in [Figure 6-9] show applications of the reference configurations to physical configurations when multiple physical interfaces occur at a reference point.

The examples given in [Figure 6-9] are not intended to be either exhaustive or mandatory. Square blocks in [Figures 6-8 and 6-9] represent equipment implementing functional groupings.

Note - TE1 or TE2 + TA may be used interchangeably in [Figure 6-9].

4.2.1 [Figures 6-9a and 6-9b] show applications of the reference configurations in the cases where NT2 functions consist of only physical connections. [Figure 6-9a] describes the direct physical connection of multiple TEs (TE1s or TE2s + TAs) to NT1 using a multidrop arrangement, i.e., a bus. [Figure 6-9b] illustrates the separate connection of a number of TEs to NT1.

In these cases, all of the characteristics of the physical interfaces applied at reference points S and T must be identical.

4.2.2 [Figure 6-9c] shows the provision of multiple connections between NT2 and TEs. NT2 may include various types of distribution arrangements, such as star, bus or ring configurations included within the equipment. [Figure 6-9d] shows a case where a bus distribution is used between TEs and NT2 equipment.

4.2.3 [Figures 6-9e and 6-9f] show arrangements where multiple connections are used between NT2 and NT1 equipment. In particular, [Figure 6-9e] illustrates the case of multiple NT1 equipment, while [Figure 6-9f] refers to the case where NT1 provides Layer 1 upward multiplexing of the multiple connections.

4.2.4 [Figure 6-9g] illustrates the case where NT1 and NT2 functions are merged in the same equipment; the corresponding merging of NT1 and NT2 functions for other configurations in [Figure 6-9] may also occur.

4.2.5 [Figure 6-9h] illustrates the case where TA and NT2 functions are merged in the same equipment. The corresponding merging of TA and NT2 functions for other configurations in [Figure 6-9] may also occur.

4.2.6 In addition to the examples of physical implementation shown in [Figures 6-8 and 6-9], a possible combination of NT1, NT2, and TA into one physical entity could be considered, in which both reference points S and T exist, but are not realized as physical interfaces. Such an implementation is to be considered an interim

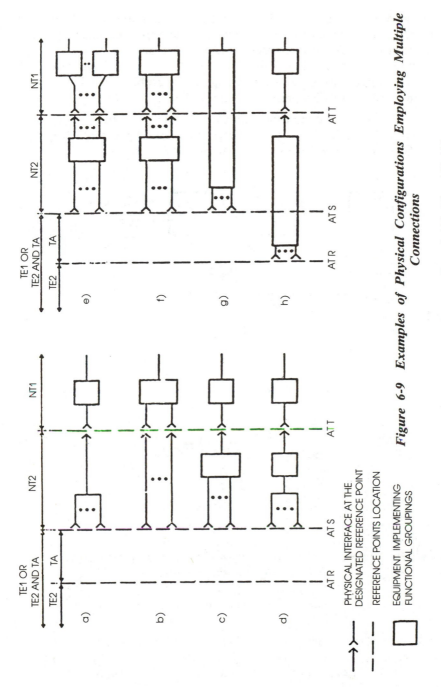

Figure 6-9 Examples of Physical Configurations Employing Multiple Connections

Source: Rec. I.411, Fig. 4/I.411.

means of providing connection to an ISDN and might be used to complement the recommended means of connecting terminals via physical interfaces at reference points S and T in the early states of ISDN implementation. This should not be considered as a reference configuration because it poses significant problems in relation to the models of ISDN presently being studied.

4.2.7 These physical implementations are limited in their arrangements and combinations by the electrical and other characteristics of the interface specifications and equipment.

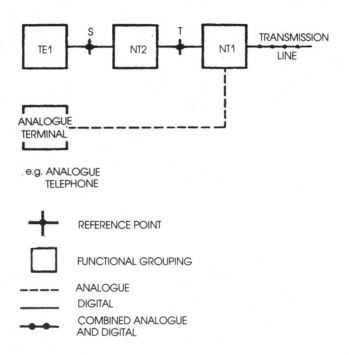

Figure 6-10   Reference Configuration for Hybrid Access Arrangements for ISDN User-Network Interfaces

Source: Rec. I.411, Fig. 5/I.411.

4.3 The reference configurations given in [Figure 6-6] apply for the specification of the channel structures and access arrangements given in Rec. I.412 with the exception of channel structures for the hybrid access arrangement. For this arrangement, the reference configuration given in [Figure 6-10] applies. This reference configuration includes the analogue telephone. TE1 may be replaced by TE2 and TA as illustrated in [Figure 6-6b]. Examples of physical implementation shown in [Figure 6-8 and 6-9] may also apply to hybrid access arrangements.

Recommendation I.412

ISDN USER-NETWORK INTERFACES

INTERFACE STRUCTURES AND ACCESS CAPABILITIES

1. **General.** This Recommendation defines limited sets of both channel types and interface structures for ISDN user-network physical interfaces.

2. **Definitions**

2.1 A **channel** represents a specified portion of the information carrying capacity of an interface.

2.1 Channels are classified by **channel types**, which have common characteristics. Channel types are specified in para. 3.

2.3 The channels are combined into **interface structures**, specified in para. 4. An interface structure defines the maximum digital information-carrying capacity across a physical interface.

2.4 In an actual access arrangement, some of the channels available across an ISDN user-network physical interface, as defined by the applicable interface structure, may not be supported by the network. Some ISDN services will not require the full capacity of a B channel; in those cases in which users require only such services, the access capability might be further reduced. The capability provided by those channels that are actually available for communication purposes, is referred to as the **access capability** provided through the interface.

3. **Channel types and their use**

3.1 **B channel**

3.1.1 A B channel is a 64 kbit/s channel accompanied by timing. The method for providing this timing is a subject of the individual interface Recommendations. A B channel is intended to carry a wide variety of user information streams. A distinguishing characteristic is that a B channel does not carry signalling information for circuit switching by the ISDN. Signalling information used for circuit switching by the ISDN is carried over other types of channels, e.g., a D channel.

3.1.2 User information streams may be carried on a B channel on a dedicated, alternate (within one call or as separate calls), or simultaneous basis, consistent with the B channel bit rate. The following are examples of user information streams:

(i)   voice encoded at 64 kbit/s according to Rec. G.711;
(ii)   data information corresponding to circuit or packet-switching user classes of service at bit rates less than or equal to 64 kbit/s, according to Rec. X.1;
(iii) wideband voice encoded at 64 kbit/s (under consideration); and
(iv)   voice encoded at bit rates lower than 64 kbit/s alone, or combined with other digital information streams.

It is recognized that a B channel may also be used to carry user information streams not covered by CCITT Recommendations.

3.1.3 B channels may be used to provide access to a variety of communication modes within the ISDN. Examples of these modes are:

(i)   circuit switching;
(ii)   packet switching, supporting packet mode terminals; and
(iii) semi-permanent connections.

In case i, the ISDN can provide either a transparent end-to-end 64 kbit/s connection or a connection specifically suited to a particular service, such as telephony, in which case a transparent 64 kbit/s connection may not be provided. In case ii, the B channel will carry protocols at layers 2 and 3 according to Rec. X.25 which have to be handled by the network. The application of D channel protocols for this case is for further study. In case iii, the semi-permanent connection can be provided, for example, by using circuit or packet switching modes.

3.1.4 Single information streams at bit rates less than 64 kbit/s should be rate adapted to be carried on the B channel as described in Rec. I.460.

3.1.5 Multiple information streams from a given user may be multiplexed together in the same B channel, but for circuit switching, an entire B channel will be switched to a single user-network interface. This multiplexing should be in accordance with Rec. I.460.

Note - Independent routing of subrate channels circuit switched to different destinations is for further study.

3.2 D channel

3.2.1 A D channel may have different bit rates as specified in para. 4. A D channel is primarily intended to carry signalling information for circuit switching by the ISDN. A D channel uses a layered protocol according to Recs. I.440, I.441, I.450, and I.451. In particular, the link access procedure is frame oriented.

3.2.2 In addition to signalling information for circuit switching, a D channel may also be used to carry teleaction information and packet-switched data. In certain cases where such signalling is not being utilized, the D channel may support only teleaction information or packet-switched data. In a hybrid access arrangement, the D channel will also carry none, some or all of the signalling information for the analogue channel. See para. 5.2.

3.3 E channel.
An E channel is a 64 kbit/s channel. It is primarily used to carry signalling information for circuit switching by the ISDN. At the user-network interface, it is used only in the primary rate multiplexed channel structures as an alternate arrangement for multiple access interface configurations. An E channel uses a layered protocol to provide the means to establish, maintain and terminate network connections. The grouping of functions by layers is described in Rec. I.450. The control procedures for control of circuit switched connections (layer 3-upper) are those used on a D channel in the primary rate B channel interface structure, and are described in Rec. I.451. Link layer and layer 3-lower services and protocols are based on the Message Transfer Part of CCITT Signalling System No. 7. See Rec. Q.710.

3.4 H channels

3.4.1 H channels have the following bit rates, accompanied by timing: **H0 channel** (384 kbit/s); **H1 channels** (1536 kbit/s ($H1_1$) and 1920 kbit/s ($H1_2$). Higher rate H channels are for further study. The method for providing this timing is a subject of the individual interface Recommendation. An H channel is intended to carry a variety of user information streams. A distinguishing characteristic is that an H channel does not carry signalling information for circuit-switching by the ISDN.

3.4.2 User information streams may be carried on an H channel on a dedicated, alternative (within one call or as separate calls), or simultaneous basis, consistent with the H channel bit rates. The following are examples of user information streams:

(i)   fast facsimile;
(ii) video, e.g., for teleconferencing;
(iii) high speed data;
(iv) high quality audio or sound programme material;
(v)   information streams, each at rates lower than the respective H channel bit rate, e.g., voice at 64 kbit/s, which have been rate adapted or multiplexed together;
(vi) packet-switched information.

3.5 **Other channels.** For further study

4.   **Interface structures.** ISDN user-network physical interfaces at ISDN reference points S and T shall comply with one of the interface structures defined below.

4.1 **B channel interface structures**

4.1.1 **Basic interface structure**

4.1.1.1 The basic interface structure is composed of two B channels and one D channel. The bit rate of the D channel in this interface structure is 16 kbit/s.

4.1.1.2 The B channels may be used independently, i.e., in different connections at the same time.

4.1.1.3 With the basic interface structure, two B channels and one D channel are always present at the ISDN user-network physical interface. One or both B channels, however, may not be supported by the network. See Appendix.

Note - The basic interface structure may also be used in association with a conventional analogue channel in a hybrid access arrangement. See para. 5.2.

4.1.2 **Primary rate B channel interface structures.** These structures correspond to the primary rates of 1544 kbit/s and 2048 kbit/s.

4.1.2.1 The primary rate B channel interface structures are composed of B channels and one D channel. The bit rate of this D channel is 64 kbit/s.

4.1.2.2 At the 1544 kbit/s primary rate, the interface structure is 23B + D.

4.1.2.3 At the 2048 kbit/s primary rate, the interface structure is 30B + D.

4.1.2.4 With the primary rate B channel interface structures, the designated number of B channels are always present at the ISDN user-network physical interface. One or more of the B channels may not be supported by the network.

4.1.2.5 In the case of a user-network access arrangement containing multiple interfaces, it is possible for the D channel in one structure to carry the signalling for B channels in another primary rate structure without an activated D channel. When a D channel is not activated, the designated time slot may or may not be used to provide an additional B channel, depending on the situation, e.g., 24B for a 1544 kbit/s interface.

4.1.3 Alternative primary rate B channel interface structure

4.1.3.1 In the case of a type of NT2 which would typically be connected to the ISDN by more than one primary rate B channel access interface, it might be desirable in certain situations to employ the signalling network capabilities of CCITT Signalling System No. 7. In such a case, the alternative primary rate B channel interface structures described below could be used, although the primary rate B channel interface structures defined in para. 4.1.2 are preferred.

4.1.3.2 The alternative primary rate B channel interface structures are composed of B channels and one E channel.

4.1.3.3 At the 1544 kbit/s primary rate, the interface structure is 23B + E.

4.1.3.4 At the 2048 kbit/s primary rate, the interface structure is 30B + E.

4.1.3.5 With the alternative primary rate B channel interface structures, the designated number of B channels are always present at the ISDN user-network physical interface. One or more of the B channels may not be supported by the network.

4.1.3.6 It is possible for the E channel of one alternative primary rate interface structure to carry the signalling for B channels in another alternative primary rate B channel interface structure without an activated E channel. When an E channel is not activated, the designated time slot may or may not be used to provide an additional B channel, e.g., 24B for a 1544 kbit/s interface.

4.2 H channel interface structure

4.2.1 Primary rate H0 channel interface structures

4.2.1.1 The primary rate H0 channel interface structures are composed of H0 channels with or without a D channel, as indicated below. When present in the same interface structure, the bit rate of the D channel is 64 kbit/s. Additional H0 channel interface structures are for further study.

4.2.1.2 At the 1544 kbit/s primary rate, the H0 channel interface structures are 4H0 and 3H0 + D. The use of the additional capacity across the interface is for further study. When the D channel is not provided, signalling for the H0 channels is provided by the D channel in another interface.

4.2.1.3 At the 2048 kbit/s primary rate, the H0 channel interface structure is 5H0 + D. In the case of a user-network access arrangement containing multiple interfaces, it is possible for the D channel in one structure to carry the signalling for H0 channels are in another primary rate interface without a D channel in use.

4.2.1.4 With the primary rate H0 channel interface structures, the designated number of H0 channels are always present at the user-network physical interface. One or more of the H0 channels may not be supported by the network.

4.2.1.5 In the case of a user-network access arrangement containing multiple interfaces, it is possible for the D channel of one structure to carry the signalling for H0 channels in another primary rate interface structure without an activated D channel. When a D channel is not required in a 1544 kbit/s interface, the 4H0 channel structure may be used.

4.2.2 Primary rate H1 channel interface structures

4.2.2.1 **1536 kbit/s $H1_1$ channel interface structure.** The 1536 kbit/s $H1_1$ channel. The bit rate of the D channel is 64 kbit/s. Signalling for the $H1_2$ channel, if required, is carried in this D channel or the D channel of another interface structure within the same user-network access arrangement.

4.3 Primary rate interface structures for mixtures of B and H0 channels. A primary rate interface may have a structure consisting of a single D channel and any mixture of B and H0 channels. The bit rate of the D channel is 64 kbit/s. In the case of a user-network access arrangement containing multiple interfaces, a D channel in one interface structure may also carry signalling for channels in another interface structure. When a D channel is not activated, its 64 kbit/s capacity may or may not be used for the mixture of B and H0 channels, depending on the situation, e.g., 3H0 + 6B for a 1544 kbit/s interface.

4.4 **Other interface structure(s).** For further study.

5.   **Examples of application of interface structures**

5.1 **Access arrangement for PABX, terminal controller, local area network, etc.** [Figure 6-11] illustrates a typical PABX, or LAN access arrangement. For this particular configuration, it is not necessary to apply the same interface structure at both S and T reference points. For example, basic interface structures may be used for interfaces located at reference point S. Either basic or primary rate or other interface structures may be used at interfaces located at reference point T.

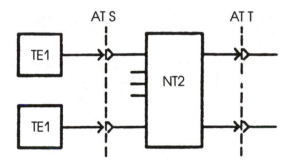

Figure 6-11   Example of the Reference Configurations for ISDN User-Network Interface Applied to Physical Configuration Employing Multiple Connections

Source: Rec. I.412, Fig. 1/I.412.

5.2 **Hybrid access arrangement.** [Figure 6-12] illustrates a possible configuration for a variety of hybrid access arrangements. A hybrid access arrangement consists of a digital interface structure used in conjunction with an analogue channel. A physical interface is shown at reference points S and T, where the basic interface structure may be used. In addition to the analogue channel, the hybrid access arrangement includes one of the following digital access capabilities:

(i)   D;

(ii)   B + D; or

(iii) 2B + D.

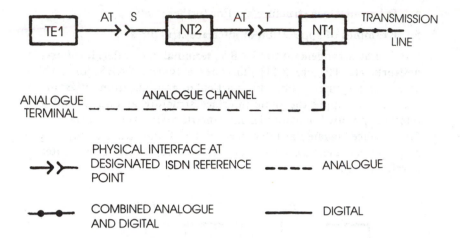

Figure 6-12   *Reference Configuration for Hybrid Access Arrangements for ISDN User-Network Interface*

Source: Rec. I.412, Fig. 2/I.412.

Appendix to Rec. I.412

Access capabilities. As stated in section 2.4, not all of the channels present in an ISDN user-network physical interface are necessarily supported by the network. The resulting capability provided in an ISDN user-network access arrangement is defined as the **access capability**. To assist in guiding the implementations of ISDN equipment and services around the world, several preferred access capabilities are identified here. While these preferred arrangements do not preclude the implementation of other access capabilities, they are intended to assist in the world wide commonality which is a key objective of ISDN.

Preferred basic access capabilities

- 2B + D
- B + D
- D

Primary rate B channel access capabilities

- nB + D
- n ≤ 23 for 1544 kbit/s primary rate, unless signalling is provided in another physical interface, then n = 24 may be allowed. See para. 4.1.2.5

- n $\leq$ 30 for 2048 kbit/s primary rate, unless signalling is provided in another physical interface, then n = 31 may be allowed. See para. 4.1.2.5.

REFERENCES

1. *See* Questions allocated to Study Group XVIII for the Period 1981-1984, CCITT Doc. COM XVIII-No. 1 at 8 and 47 (1981).
2. *See Id.* at 11.
3. *See* CCITT Docs. COM XVIII-Nos. 2, 3, A, B, C, E, E, F, I, K, L, N, and O.
4. *See* Report on the Inter-Regnum Meeting of Experts on ISDN matters (Innisbrook, 12-15 January 1981), CCITT Doc. COM XVIII-No. R1 (1981).
5. *Id.* at 12-13.
6. *See* CCITT Docs. COM XVIII-Nos. 25, 32, 34, 38, 39, 40, 46, AG, AN, AO, AU, AV, and AY.
7. *See* Report of the Meeting of Working Party XVIII/1 (ISDN), Doc. COM XVIII-No. R3 at 33-38 (1981).
8. *See* CCITT Docs. COM XVIII-Nos. 5, 25, 32, 38, 39, 40, AN, AU, AV, AX, AY, BC and BE.
9. *See* Report of the Meeting of Working Party XVIII/1 (ISDN), Doc. COM XVIII-No. R3 at 42-46 (1981).
10. *See* Docs. COM XVIII-Nos. 56, BL, BO, BP, BU, BV, BZ, CD, CF, CG, CH, CK, CM, CO, CP, CR, CT, CU, CV, CW, CX, CY, DG, DE, DF, DH, DI, and DJ.
11. *See* Report on the meeting of the group of experts on ISDN matters of Study Group XVIII (Munich, 17-25 February 1982), CCITT Doc. COM XVIII-No. R8 at 11-37.
12. *See* Rec. I.411, Para. 3.2, Note 2 (1985). Notwithstanding this note, Study Group XVIII did adopt Question 20/XVIII for the 1985–1988 activity period that calls for "definition of parameters at the network side of *NT* equipment."
13. *See* Report on the meeting of the group of experts on ISDN matters of Study Group XVIII (Munich, 17-25 February 1982), CCITT Doc. COM XVIII-No. R8 at 38-47.
14. *See* CCITT Docs. COM XVIII-Nos. 67, BR, BS, BT, BU, CE, CI, CJ, CO, CX, CZ, and DH.
15. British Telecom and Administrations of Belgium, *et. al.*, Comments on the Results of the ISDN Experts Meeting, Munich 17-25 February 1982, Doc. COM XVIII-No. 101 (1982).

16.   Report of the Geneva meeting (10-22 June 1982), CCITT Doc. COM XVIII-No. R9 (1982).

17.   *Ibid.*

18.   *See* Docs. COM XVIII-No. 117, 126, 127, FU, FV, FW, FX, FY, FZ, GA, GB, GC, GC, GE, GF, GG, GH, GI, GJ, GK, GL, GM, GN, GO, GP, GQ, GR, GS, GT, GU, GV, and GW.

19.   *See* Report on the meeting of experts on level 1 characteristics of the basic ISDN user-network interface (Question 1/XVIII, Point C), CCITT Doc. COM XVIII-No. R14 (1982).

20.   *See* CCITT Docs. COM XVIII-Nos. GX, GY, HB, HS, HX, HZ, JK, JU, JX, KD, KH, KJ, KK, KL, KM, KN, KS, KT, KX, and LC.

21.   *See* Report of the Meeting of the Group of Experts on ISDN matters of Study Group XVIII (Kyoto, 14-25 February 1983), CCITT Doc. COM XVIII-No. R15 at 13-46 (1983).

22.   *See* CCITT Docs. COM XVIII-Nos. 89, 134, 142, 147, 148, HJ, HK, HL, HM, HN, HO, HP, NT, HU, HV, IG, IP, IQ, IR, IU, IV, IW, IY, JM, JN, JQ, JT, JU, JV, KD, KE, KF, KH, KI, KM, KN, KO, KP, KQ, KV, KW, KY, KZ, LA, LB, and LD.

23.   *See* Report of the meeting of the group of experts on ISDN matters of Study Group XVIII (Kyoto, 14-25 February 1983), CCITT Doc. COM XVIII-No. R15 at 47-92 (1983).

24.   *See* CCITT Docs. COM XVIII-Nos. LY, LZ, MA, MD, MG, NA, NC, NJ, NV, OC, OD, OP, OS, OT, OZ, PA, PB, PC, PE, PF, PS, PV, QS, QW, and RA.

25.   *See* Report of Working Team 1 (Customer Access), CCITT Doc. COM XVIII-No. R17 (1983).

26.   *See* CCITT Docs. COM XVIII-Nos. 180, 181, 183, LJ, LQ, LS, LT, LU, LV, LW, LX, MA, MC, MQ, MW, MX, MY, MZ, NF, NG, NU, NW, OA, OB, OJ, OO, OQ, OR, PD, PG, PM, PN, PO, PQ, PR, PV, PW, PX, PZ, QA, QF, QX, QY, QZ, RE, RF, and RK.

27.   *See* Report of Working Team 2 (Layer 1 Characteristics), CCITT Doc. COM XVIII-No. R18 (1983).

28.   *See* CCITT Docs. COM XVIII-Nos. SC, SO, SS, ST, SU, SV, SW, SX, SY, SZ, TL, TM, TN, TO, TP, TQ, TR, TU, TV, TW, UC, UE, UF, UG, UI, UJ, UK, UL, UM, UN, UO, UP, UR, UU, VG, and VH.

29.   *See* Report of Working Team 2 (Layer 1 Characteristics), CCITT Doc. COM XVIII-No. 209 (1983).

30.   *See* CCITT Docs. COM XVIII-Nos. WO, WU, XO, YB, TC, YC, YE, and ZC.

31.   *See* I-Series of Recommendations (Brasilia Meeting, 13-24 February 1984) — Part III of the report, CCITT Doc. COM XVIII-No. 228 at 137-161, 218-222 (1984).

32.   *See* CCITT Docs. COM XVIII-Nos. VQ, VR, VV, VY, VZ, WA, WC, WD, WE, WL, WM, WN, WP, XB, XC, XD, XE, XF, XG, XH, XI, XJ, XK, XL, XM, XN, XP, XS, ST, XU, XV, XW, XX, XY, XZ, YA, YF, YI, YT, ZA, ZK, and ZM.

33.   *See* I-Series of Recommendations (Brasilia Meeting, 13-24 February 1984) — Part III of the report, CCITT Doc. COM XVIII-No. 228 at 161-217 (1984).

III UNITED STATES DOMESTIC POLICY-MAKING

Many of the ISDN developments described in Part II have occurred against a backdrop of numerous policy developments related to telecommunication and information in the United States. These developments have both affected and been affected by the ISDN work occurring in international forums. This relationship varies from the subtle to the profound, and the effect is generally long-term.

The CCITT develops its provisions to accommodate all national regulatory policies, to the extent feasible. In the case of the United States, this accommodation is more than just international comity. Most of the telecommunications in the world are to and from the United States. In addition, telecommunication equipment manufacturers around the world are interested in markets which extend beyond their own country or region.

This section describes the US policy developments that are directly and indirectly relevant to integrated networks. Some are very broad and establish the overall framework for regulation of networks in the US. Others are more narrowly focused, addressing specific subjects or applications of the broader policies. Nearly all these policies emanate from the Federal Communications Commission which has broad and nearly exclusive statutory authority to regulate domestic and international communications networks of the United States.

CHAPTER 7 — ISDN RELATED POLICIES

ISDN developments have occurred within a larger context of policy making by the United States Government. For the most part, policy has been effected by the Federal Communications Commission (FCC), which has broad statutory authority to regulate domestic and international communications and has been doing so since the agency was established in 1934.

The FCC is not, however, the only government entity in the United States that has significantly affected telecommunications policy. The Department of Justice and the United States Judicial System have also had a significant impact by obtaining and implementing the AT&T Consent Decree and Modified Final Judgment (MFJ). These actions have profoundly affected the national network architecture by separating the local Bell Operating Company (BOC) networks from the AT&T long haul network, and controlling the nature of the services each may offer. In addition, the US Congress in oversight hearings and in legislation has supported and furthered policies that encourage competitive conduct in the provision of telecommunication and inforamtion services.

For the last twenty years, as pre-ISDN digital or integrated services began to be offered, a variety of related issues were considered in numerous proceedings of the Federal Communications Commission. These proceedings have shaped what is now ISDN policy in the United States. One of these proceedings focused explicitly on ISDN, to which Chapter 8 is entirely devoted. All the other proceedings, covered in this chapter, both precede *and succeed* the ISDN Inquiry. In addition, most of these other proceedings resulted in FCC findings, orders, or authorizations that had direct impact on the parties involved. The ISDN proceeding, on the other hand, had no such impact.

Most of the actions emanated from fairly lengthy, formal *policy making proceedings*. However, policy can also emerge from other kinds of proceedings, such as requests for *authorization of service* or for *waiver of a rule or policy*. For example, after the formal Computer II policy proceeding was terminated, the FCC increasingly tended to decide Computer II related issues through waiver proceedings.

The following table lists most of the proceedings of the FCC that are currently relevant to ISDN, their identifying number, and the ISDN aspect affected, i.e., services, network functions, or user-network interfaces.

TABLE 7-1

Policy Making Proceeding	Docket No.	Services	Network	I/F
• Computer II	20828	X	X	X
• Protocols	GEN 80-756	X	X	X
• ISDN	GEN 83-841	X	X	X
• Pt. 68 Connection to the Network	CC 80-216			X
• Int'l Resale [undecided]	CC 80-176		X	
• AT&T:Computer II Implementation	CC 81-893			X
• BOCs:Computer II Structural Separation	CC 83-115	X	X	
• RPOAs, IRUs, and DNIC's	CC 83-1230		X	
• AT&T: Computer II Structural Separation	CC 85-26			X
• Competitive Carrier	CC 79-252		X	
• Int'l Competitive Carrier	CC 85-107		X	

Authorization of Service Proceedings	File No.	Services	Network	I/F
• BPSS	WPC 4841	X		
• Telenet/Tymnet	ITC 81-274 et al.	X		

Waiver Proceedings	File No.	Services	Network	I/F
• Disclosure	ENF 82-5		X	
• Protocols	ENF 84-15 et al.	X		
• Centrex	ENF 84-2	X		
• LADT Service	ENF 83-34	X		X

All of these proceedings are related to each other, in some cases portraying different aspects of a problem; in others, fleshing out details of an earlier policy. In still other cases, the initial policies have been altered to reflect new circumstances.

In order to examine the relationship of these proceedings to ISDN developments in a coherent way, the proceedings are grouped and discussed in the generic ISDN structure: Service Capabilities, Overall Network Aspects and Functions, and User-Network Interfaces. The most significant overlap occurs with *Computer II*, which because of its two major dichotomies, deals with all these areas.

The documents in each of these proceedings contain lengthy discussions and findings on matters of FCC jurisdiction, authority, and rationale. Because the focus here is on the determinations directly related to ISDN, such legal and policy issues will not be extensively described.

7.1 Proceedings Related to Service Capabilities

Because service capabilities involve that which is actually marketed and provided to the customer, as well as the basis for payment, service-related issues have perennially been important. In addition, in the United States, service capabilities are frequently part of schemes by which the government regulates private businesses. The classic functions of regulation include granting authorizations to companies to provide telecommunication services, approving tariffs for those services, and adopting standards which the service must meet. For years, a vast regulatory bureaucracy, both inside and outside the government, has churned away as it initiated, maintained, altered, and terminated these functions.

In the ISDN environment, however, widely distributed telecommunication and information system resources can be dynamically aggregated for each individual user. Traditional discrete service packages such as telephony, telex, broadcasting, *et cetera*, need no longer exist. The quandary is: What do providers market, how are costs attributed and charged, and what is regulated by the government? The last of these questions is reached in a kind of negative way by the most fundamental telecommunication regulatory decision of the FCC — *Computer II*. It decided *what will not be regulated*.

The subsections below describe the evolution of *Computer II* from its origin, through five years of interpretation and amendment, to the point of transition to a new emerging perspective — *Computer III*.

7.1.1 Fundamental Categorizations: *Computer II*

In the United States, the regulation of information services has generally been minimal. Part of this is due to historical reasons reaching back to the founding of the country and the creation of the First Amendment to the Constitution, which severely restricts the government's role in many areas related to information gathering, processing, and dissemination. It is also grounded on a pragmatic realization that information-related activities are evolving very rapidly, that this is very beneficial to society, and continued progress and innovation requires minimal intervention by the government.

The provision of telecommunication service, on the other hand, has been traditionally subject to considerable government regulation. In the mid-1960s, however, the problem inherent in the merging of telecommunication and information systems was recognized and resulted in a set of 1969–71 decisions in what became known as the "First Computer Inquiry."[3] The FCC distinguished between unregulated data processing and permissible regulated telecommunication common carrier utilization of computers by establishing a defined dichotomy between data processing and message- or circuit-switching.

However, the deficiencies of the *Computer I* definitional distinctions became apparent over several years as new integrated services began to arise. This resulted in the initiation of a new proceeding, culminating in several decision-making documents known collectively as the "Computer II Decision."[4] This decision is now the starting point for any discussion on US policy in the field of integrated communication and information systems.

Although there are several aspects of the *Computer II* policy, the most fundamental one, and of direct relevance to ISDN services, is the categorization of all telecommunication and information services into either "basic" or "enhanced."

> [B]asic service is limited to the common carrier offering of transmission capacity for the movement of information, whereas enhanced service combines basic service with computer processing applications that act on the format, content, code, protocol or similar aspects of the subscriber's transmitted information, or provide the subscriber additional, different, or restructured information, or involve subscriber interaction with stored information.[5]

In the adopted Rule, enhanced services are defined as:

> ... services, offered over common carrier transmission facilities used in interstate communications, which employ computer processing applications that act on the format, content, code, protocol or similar aspects of the subscribers transmitted information, provide the subscriber additional, different, or restructured information, or involve subscriber interaction with stored information.[4]

The FCC, in several paragraphs of the *Final Decision* and the *Memorandum Opinion and Order on Reconsideration*, described in different ways, and in somewhat greater detail, the distinctions between basic and enhanced services.

[A] basic transmission service should be limited to the offering of transmission capacity between two or more points suitable for a user's transmission needs and subject only to the technical parameters of fidelity or distortion criteria, or other conditioning.[6]

In providing [basic] services a carrier offers to the public channel(s) of communications with associated network switching and routing. In this sense, a basic service is the offering of a "transmission pipeline"...[7]

Use internal to the carrier's facility of companding techniques, bandwidth compression techniques, circuit switching, message or packet switching, error control techniques, etc. that facilitate economical, reliable movement of information does not alter the nature of the basic service.[8]

In the provision of a basic service transmission service, memory or storage within the network is used only to facilitate the transmission of the information from the origination to its destination, and the carrier's basic transmission network is not used as an information storage system. Thus, in a basic service, once information is given to the communication facility, its progress towards the destination is subject to only those delays caused by congestion within the network or transmission priorities given by the originator.[9]

In offering a basic transmission service, ... a carrier essentially offers a pure transmission capability over a communications path that is virtually transparent in terms of its interaction with customer supplied information.[10]

In an enhanced service ... computer processing applications are used to act on the content, code, protocol, and other aspects of the subscriber's information. [I]n an enhanced service the content of the information need not be changed and may simply involve subscriber interaction with stored information.[11]

With the nonregulation of all enhanced services, FCC regulations will not directly or indirectly inhibit the offering of these services, nor will our administrative processes be interjected between technology and its marketplace applications.[12]

Drawing the boundary with respect to protocol conversion was, however, a close decision, and a matter in which a respected FCC Commissioner had strong dissenting views.[13] A separate paragraph and a footnote addressed the matter in the *Final Decision*, and the matter was revisited in the *Memorandum Opinion and Order Reconsideration*. It quickly became the subject of a separate proceeding which is discussed in section 7.1.4 below.

> While we have concluded that code and protocol conversion are enhancements to a basic service, we recognize that they also increase the utility of the communications channel by allowing disparate terminals to communicate with one another.[13]

> [T]he question arises as to whether some flexibility should be afforded a basic service provider . . . It may be that certain low level protocol conversions should be allowed as part of a basic service. In the near future we will consider a Notice of Inquiry to examine in detail the implications of forbidding all protocol translation in such instances . . .[14]

> [T]he *Final Decision* is not intended to restrict protocol conversion capabilities a carrier may employ internal to its own network. [T]he Commission has discretion to determine the terms and conditions under which code and protocol conversion may be incorporated into the underlying network. Thus, we have not prejudged further consideration in a separate proceeding of the limits of permissible protocol conversion.[15]

These distinctions, however, were soon to evolve.

7.1.2 The "Information Service" Categorization in the *Modified Final Judgement*

On January 8, 1982, following the adoption of the *Computer II* rules, AT&T entered an agreement with the Department of Justice to terminate antitrust proceedings. The agreement called for AT&T to divest itself of the BOCs. The United States District Court approved the spin-off of 22 wholly-owned operating companies and their consolidation into seven regional BOCs.[16]

The MFJ removed the line-of-business restrictions which were imposed on AT&T as a result of the Consent Decree entered in 1956 between AT&T and the Justice Department. The only exception was a prohibition on "electronic publishing services" through its own facilities for a period of seven years from divestiture.[17]

On the other hand, the MFJ imposed line-of-business restrictions of the new regional BOCs in order to prevent them from utilizing their control of monopoly telecommunication facilities to provide an unfair advantage in competitive markets. The divested BOCs are limited to providing exchange telecommunications, exchange access information service access, Yellow Pages directory services, and customer premises equipment (CPE).

The MFJ entered the services definitional area by prohibiting the BOCs from offering "information services." Of course, because information transport is an "information service," the MFJ phrase, absent a restrictive interpretation, is rendered meaningless. Although the FCC declined to expressly resolve this question, it has assumed that "information services" under the MFJ are fairly high level information functions. This allows the BOCs to offer enhanced services which are exchange telecommunication services, exchange access services, or information access services, under the MFJ.[18]

7.1.3 The Scope of the Computer II Decision: The *Telenet/Tymnet* Decision

Not long after the *Computer II Decision*, two US carriers, Telenet and Tymnet, sought to extend the provision of their services to the United Kingdom and Western Europe, and filed for Sec. 214 authorization with the FCC. The Commission's Common Carrier Bureau, acting on delegated authority, applied the *Computer II Decision* to the Telenet/Tymnet authorization requests, found the services to be "enhanced" and indicated that Sec. 214 authorization was not needed. The matter was appealed to the FCC and decided in what became known as the *International Computer II Decision*.[19]

The circumstances of the decision were somewhat confusing because the FCC not only authorized provision of the service but also held that such service was enhanced, and the two carriers needed no authorization to provide it.[20] The seeming contradiction arose because the *Computer II Decision* had not yet become effective.

The *International Computer II Decision* was short and straightforward, affecting the scope of applicability of the original *Computer II Decision*. It pointed to a footnote in the *Computer II Decision* that stated "[t]he basic/enhanced dichotomy is applicable to both domestic and international services provided over common carrier facilities,"[21] and applied it to the Telenet/Tymnet authorization petitions. The FCC further emphasized that it "... explicitly rejected the notion of distinguishing among various types of enhanced services or otherwise treating some enhanced services differently than others."[22]

The immediate effects of this decision will probably be minimal. The FCC itself pointed out that the:

> [a]pplication of the basic/enhanced dichotomy to the international arena will not alter existing operational relationships between enhanced service providers and their foreign correspondents. Enhanced service providers will have to adhere to established practices with respect to offering international services. Where operating agreements are required by foreign telecommunications entities, enhanced service providers will have to negotiate such agreements to govern the terms and conditions of service.[23]

The long range effects, however, may be substantial.

A number of parties filed for reconsideration of the decision, and some sought an immediate judicial appeal. One party in a petition for reconsideration went so far as to assert that "... the adverse consequences of the extension of *Computer II* internationally are of cosmic proportions."[24] For ISDN purposes, the most significant point raised in the *Petition* was the assertion that "[a]bandonment of jurisdiction over international enhanced services ... could well lead to the unfettered infiltration into the unregulated US domestic market of foreign entities who could easily gain dominance over US international telecommunications in concert with overseas affiliates."[25] The same point was alluded to in Commissioner Fogarty's Dissent to the *International Computer II Decision*.

In early 1985, the FCC issued a decision exhaustively reviewing all the arguments. It found that "it is clear that our Computer II basic/enhanced dichotomy applies to services provided internationally and that petitioner's arguments to the contrary are without merit."[26] In reaching the decision, the FCC rather pragmatically noted that "the same computer and transmission facilities user in interstate communications can be used in conjunction with interstate or international communications.[27] On the matter of basic underlying policy, the FCC stated that "so long as this Commission has jurisdiction over domestic transmission facilities and the US segment of international facilities, we maintain the ability to ensure that entities operating in the US do so in a manner consistent with our policies. The Commission stands ready to ensure that our policies are not circumvented by foreign entities through their use of US controlled transmission facilities in an anticompetitive manner."[28]

The ISDN implications of the *Telenet/Tymnet Decision* are important. In an ISDN environment, interoperation with a foreign network could be technically achieved at will. It may become difficult to control use of the network in the ISDN world. However, this is one of several similar interworking matters which the CCITT will address in coming years, and the solution it adopts may effectively remedy the situation.

7.1.4 The Signalling Amendment to the Services Dichotomy: The **Protocols Decision.**

One of the major substantive defects of the original *Computer II* services dichotomy was its failure to consider the entire special "services" category of network signalling, maintenance, and operational functions. In the ISDN environment, this is the *D*-channel. In order for the network to provide transport service between users, a variety of information must be exchanged with, stored, and processed by the network and users. But these kinds of functions fell within the ambit of the enhanced service definition, and thus could not be provided. It was obviously a Catch-22. Effecting a correction, although not the original intention, was a major contribution of the *Protocols Decision.*

In large part because of Commissioner Fogarty's vehement dissent over the FCC's failure to categorize code and protocol conversion as basic, within a few weeks after the *Computer II Decision* was adopted, the Commission issued a *Notice of Inquiry* in the matter of Digital Communications Protocols.[29] It posed six specific questions seeking to define the kinds of code and protocol conversions that should fall within the scope of "basic service."

However, the proceeding languished for three years before a *Protocols Decision* was adopted.[30] In the end, the decision took a more technically and functionally accurate — as well as a more candid — look at the basic/enhanced dichotomy. It noted at the outset that:

> In essence, there is a continuum of possible transmission capabilities which encompasses transmission with no changes in these electrical signals (clearly, a basic service offering) and transmission involving creation, deletion, and alteration of information (clearly, a service traditionally thought of as "data processing", and within the enhanced service definition). Changes of a less clear nature involve changes to control information, including code and protocol changes (the focus of this proceeding).[31]

This new sophistication in looking at the problem is also reflected in the major finding of the decision.

> [A] basic switched service may properly include those forms of protocol processing which are necessary for a switched service to be offered. Specifically, the network may accept and utilize premises equipment-generated signals which alert the network that the terminal is ready to generate or to receive a call ... signals which tell the network the destination of the call ..., and signals which alert the network that a call has ended.[32]

In ISDN terms, this was a recognition by the FCC of the D-channel functions as an intrinsic part of bearer service provision. The original *Computer II* distinction simply ignored this, addressing only B-channel functions. It would appear that any signalling or operationally related functions associated with D channel, no matter what their level, are likely to be found "basic."

The decision also included what appear to be Level 1 (Physical Layer) protocol conversions within the ambit of "basic," indicating:

> in circumstances involving no change in an existing service, but merely a change in electrical interface characteristics to facilitate transitional introduction of new technology, we are prepared to act favorably and expeditiously on petitions for waiver of the *Computer II* ... [3]

Lastly, the decision addressed the matter of inter-network protocol conversions, suggesting that such conversions would likely be regarded as "basic."

> [A] waiver request to permit association with basic service of protocol conversion to an intermediate internetworking protocol (e.g., similar in principle to conversion to X.75 for network-to-network interconnection of packet-switched networks otherwise operating on the X.25 protocol) will be treated more favorably than other waiver requests seeking broader association of protocol conversion with basic service. [34]

7.1.5 The Packet Switching Amendment to the Services Dichotomy: The BPSS Decisions and the LADT Decision

In late 1982, AT&T sought authorization to install and operate packet facilities at locations throughout the United States, a service known as Basic Packet Switching Service (BPSS). Several years earlier, AT&T had sought to offer an integrated end-to-end service that included packet transport, known as Advanced Communications Service (ACS). AT&T withdrew its application for that service to redevelop it into separate basic and enhanced offerings in accordance with the *Computer II Decision*, and sought Sec. 214 authorization of the basic packet switched portion in 1981. The FCC rejected that offering, largely because of its limited availability. [35] AT&T subsequently revised the offering, adding the work "Basic," allowing shared use of BPSS facilities by unrelated users through all ports, and making available 9.6 kbit/s ports in addition to 56 kbit/s.

The BPSS applications thus squarely raised the question of whether packet switched services could be provided as a basic service. Some of the opposing parties argued, *inter alia*, that because packet switching involved momentary "storage of data," it was impermissible under *Computer II*. In the second *BPSS Decision*, the FCC flatly stated that packet switching transmission can clearly be provided as a "basic service."[36] In reviewing the characteristics of BPSS, the Commission added another clarification to its basic/enhanced dichotomy. A footnote in the decision states:

> *Computer II* did not preclude a basic network from converting to different transmission speeds. Speed conversion alone, unaccompanied by changes in the format, content, code, and protocol, is implemented in principle by the use of ... intermediate network storage [during the course of transmission, to facilitate transmission], and does not involve subscriber "interaction" with stored information.[37]

In late 1983, the subject matter of the *BPSS Decision* was revisited when IBM requested the FCC issue a declaratory ruling alleging, *inter alia*, that Southern Bell's Local Area Data Transport (LADT) offering was an enhanced service. LADT was a packet network available both on a direct or full-time private line basis and on a dial-up basis, using a X.25 interface. The FCC, in the *LADT Decision*, simply referenced the *BPSS Decision*, and denied this aspect of IBM's petition.[38]

7.1.6 Implementing the Services Dichotomy: The *BOC Separation Order*

After the divestiture of the Bell Operating Companies (BOCs) from AT&T under the Modified Final Judgement, the FCC was faced with the question of whether the new Regional BOCs were required to establish a separate subsidiary to provide enhanced services under the *Computer II Decision*. In early 1983, the FCC adopted a Notice of Proposed Rulemaking to consider the matter.[39]

From an ISDN policy perspective, the matter was very important because of its impact on ISDN architecture. A separate subsidiary requirement to provide enhanced services was necessarily reflected back into the network so that all storage, processing, and application programs functions for enhanced services would be provided through a separate node in the ISDN, with all the inefficiencies associated with creating existing connection elements for each user service request.

In late 1983, the FCC adopted a Report and Order that became known as the *BOC Separation Order*.[40] The order discussed the ambiguity between the MFJ's definition of "information services" and the FCC's definition of "enhanced services" in the context of considering the kinds of enhanced services the BOCs might offer. As noted above, however, the FCC declined to resolve the question and assumed that the BOCs may offer some enhanced services.[41]

After considering the costs and benefits of requiring the BOCs to establish
a separate subsidiary, the FCC determined "that following the planned
divestiture, the separate structure approach is the most cost-effective regulatory tool to protect ratepayers from bearing the costs of providing
competitive products and services and to promote competition."[42] However,
a somewhat different, separate subsidiary requirement than that effected for
AT&T was adopted.

In a somewhat candid admission, however, the FCC did address the
efficiency issue, stating "we recognize that not permitting enhanced services
to be provided as part of the basic network creates inefficiencies."
"[B]ut ... these inefficiencies should be tolerated in light of the public interest
benefits which could be derived from compliance with separation conditions."[43]

7.1.7 The Protocol Conversion Amendment to the Services Dichotomy: The *Protocol Waivers*

In early 1984, after the *Protocols Decision* and the *BOC Separation Order*,
the FCC was faced with eight petitions by the Bell Operating Companies
for waivers seeking to provide certain types of protocol conversions to
customers within their basic telephone networks. The resulting actions taken
by the FCC represented a significant *de facto* amendment to the *Computer
II* services dichotomy. More importantly, as will be discussed further in
Chapter 9, the second waiver item suggested the use of a new decision-making
standard, and pointed the way to a new comprehensive rule-making on the
entire services dichotomy issue — *Computer III*.

The first waiver authorization was granted by the FCC in late 1984. The
BOCs sought, *inter alia*, to provide interconnection with X.25 packet networks using the X.75 network access protocol. As a consequence, information transiting networks using the X.75 interface protocol would result in
a net protocol conversion when the information originated or was received
at a BOC network subscriber terminal in a X.25 format. The FCC reviewed
the *Computer II Decision* and, in particular, the *Protocols Decision*, and
found "that it is in the public interest that the subject petitions be granted,"
contingent on the filing of satisfactory interstate access tariffs.[44]

The second waiver authorization, dealing with conversion from asynchronous protocols to standard X.25 packet-switched network protocols using
facilities in the BOCs' central offices, was far more significant. The BOCs
argued that grant of the waiver request would enable them to provide an
inexpensive local data transport service. More importantly, they argued that
they could provide this service in an intrinsically more efficient fashion, to

the benefit of the millions of terminals and terminal-emulating personal computers in the United States which communicate only in the asynchronous format.

In a lengthy and meticulously analytical Memorandum Opinion and Order, the FCC concluded "that allowing the BOCs to provide local packet switched services, under the conditions we are adopting to ensure equality of treatment in the pricing of the inter-office channels and of access by end-users to such services, will create incentives for the BOCs to make available new, less expensive inter-office channel offerings and new subscriber loop service offerings that will foster the growth of data communications generally and information age data communications services specifically."[45]

Of particular note is reference to what appears to be a new decision making emphasis. At the outset of its discussion of the issues, the FCC noted "that flexibility could be required in the treatment of protocol conversion by carriers subject to structural separation to ensure that the efficiency of communications — a primary objective under the Communications Act — is not unacceptably impeded."[46] After making its finding, the Commission concluded with the statement that by "our action herein, we believe that we are striking an appropriate public interest balance. Subscribers will have the benefits of efficiencies promised by the petitioners, . . . while mere pricing disparities and other forms of unreasonably discriminatory and anticompetitive conduct will be foreclosed.[47] To add emphasis to this perspective, Commissioner Patrick, both during the public FCC discussion at adoption, and in his statement attached to the item, concluded with almost identical remarks.[48]

7.1.8 Amending the Services Dichotomy: The Centrex Decision

In late 1984, the North American Telecommunication Association (NATA) petitioned the FCC to rule that certain Centrex features and certain residential telephone services based on provision of the calling party's telephone number were enhanced services. "Centrex" is a term in general use to describe a variety of switching and control features locally provided by the network, but under the control of the user, through a variety of signalling techniques. The petition brought into question the definition and application of the services dichotomy of the Computer II Decision. NATA sought, inter alia, to define an enhanced service to "include any service capable of being provided by CPE."

The FCC responded in early 1985, stating that "we cannot conclude that any of the features described by the parties go beyond providing a basic transmission channel and facilitating the customer's use of that transmission channel."[49] The FCC added "that the calling party number, like the other signalling information discussed above, is not additional information in the sense intended by [the enhanced services definition], and that even if it might be so considered, it should not be so treated."[50]

The *Centrex Decision* thus complements the *Protocols Decision*, and appears to impart an additional gloss to the services dichotomy, stating that services that "facilitate the customer's use of a transmission channel" will be regarded as basic.

7.2 Proceedings Related to Overall Network Aspects and Functions

The world telecommunication network is a diverse composite of many national networks and information service providers, linked together at various points. The location of these links, and the matter in which networks, information service providers, and users interoperate, give rise to complex and difficult issues. Many of these issues were dealt with in considering the work of CCITT Study Group XVIII and the I-300 Series Recommendations in Chapter 5.

The Federal Communications Commission has, in many of its proceedings, dealt with related issues that establish US policies applying generally to overall network aspects and functions. Some of the most important of these proceedings that relate to ISDN developments are described in the subsections below.

7.2.1 Establishing Overall Network Aspects and Functions: The *Computer II Decision* and the *BOC Separation Order*

The focus on the services dichotomy and the network/CPM dichotomy of *Computer II* often tends to obscure the concomitant effect on the network itself, and network architecture in particular. The most profound of these effects, brought about by the combined requirements of the services dichotomy and the separation requirements, was the creation of a separate node at countless thousands of existing nodes for the provision of any higher level information services in the overall network.

During the Computer II proceeding, there was little direct focus on network architecture issues. In the 1980 *Final Decision*, some of the network effects were indirectly referenced, usually couched in terms of efficiency. For example, in discussing the basic/enhanced dichotomy, the FCC stated that "[n]o compelling evidence has been submitted in this proceeding that this [structural] separation will impose significant efficiency losses on the carrier or the public it serves." In an associated footnote, it is added that "the question arises as to whether some flexibility should be afforded a basic service provider that is subject to the separation requirement, in view of the structure we are setting forth. It may be that certain low level protocol conversions should be allowed as part of a basic service."[51]

Six months later, on Reconsideration, when applying its *Final Decision* to some potential new AT&T services, the FCC began to acknowledged its uncertainty about the effects on the network.

> [W]e recognize that strict adherence to such structural separation may foreclose the availability to consumers of certain enhanced services, if, for example, state of the art technology dictates that only through the use of network facilities could the carrier provide a given enhanced service, or if complying with the separate subsidiary requirement results in the imposition of unreasonable costs upon consumers. Should such situations arise we are prepared to assess the merits of granting a waiver of our separation requirement for a specific service after notice and opportunity to comment ...[52]

By the time the BOC Separation Proceeding was initiated late in 1983, there was already considerable concern about the necessity for structural separation. Commissioner Fogarty strongly objected because the impending divestiture of the BOCs had so changed the entire regulatory environment. Although a structural separation was adopted in the *BOC Separation Order*, it was qualified with the remark that "[w]e may revise our balancing in the future based on the market developments."[53]

As described in section 7.1, above, as time progressed, considerably greater attention began to be given to the effects on the network, manifested in concerns for intrinsic efficiencies associated with network architectures that do not require separate nodes to perform transport related, albeit enhanced, functions.

7.2.2 *International Dimensions of Virtual Networks: The Resale Proceeding*

In April 1980, the FCC adopted a *Notice of Proposed Rulemaking* concerning the resale and shared use of common carrier international communication services.[54] This NPRM immediately raised a furor around the world, as foreign administrations thought that the FCC had unilaterally abrogated agreements between US carriers and these administrations. As of mid-1985, the proceeding remained open, with no further action taken.

The NPRM is worthy of mention here because of its association with the *Telenet/Tymnet Decision*. The proposals in the *Resale Proceeding* were broad and ambitious.

This rulemaking proceeding encompasses the entire spectrum of services offered by international carriers to the US public. The tariff restrictions for each of these services prohibit or substantially restrict resale and shared use by third parties.

We propose to order the elimination of all restrictions against resale and shared use as part of our policy of promoting the public interest by allowing the production and pricing of services to be determined through market rather than regulatory activities to the greatest extent possible.[55]

For ISDN purposes, this proceeding has probably been superseded by the *Telenet/Tymnet Decision*. However, because it still remains open, further action could be taken that might have an ISDN impact.

7.2.3 Network Recognition and Interworking: The *RPOA, IRU, DNIC Proceeding*

In 1983, the FCC issued a *Notice of Inquiry* to look at three interrelated matters: designation of Recognized Private Operating Agencies (RPOAs), grants of Indefeasible Rights of Users (IRUs) in international facilities, and assignment of Data Network Identification Codes (DNICs).[56] All three involved the status of enhanced services providers in the context of certain representational and administrative activities. Its ISDN implications lie in the raising of status of such service providers above that of a mere user. At present, the CCITT only dealt with this subject in the context of network addressing questions and specialized interfaces.

With respect to the RPOA designation, the FCC noted "at the outset that the RPOA concept has significance under the ITU Convention and in relations among ITU members; it has, however, had no particular significance under our internal United States law or practice."[57] However, the petitioner of the proceeding, the Association of Data Processing Service Organizations (ADAPSO), suggested that RPOA status "may provide an appropriate mechanism for participation by non-carrier, enhanced-service vendors in international telecommunications and the ITU regardless of whether the administration at the foreign end does, or does not, observe similar service distinctions in its own nation.[58]

The IRU question raised a familiar philosophical/regulatory question.

A policy allowing non-carrier IRUs would alter those current customer/carrier relations by opening a new class of ownership and operation. If enhanced-service providers avail themselves of such a policy they will be transformed from users to owners of facilities. While this might allow such service providers to reduce their costs, and presumably their charges to their customers, it might remove our control of the underlying basic services.[59]

The primary purpose of the DNIC is to allow overseas customers or carriers to route traffic to a particular data network. The first three digits of the DNIC constitute the Data Country Code which identifies the country or geographical area in which the network to be identified is located. In the NOI, the FCC noted that:

> ...because the DNIC permits automatic switching directly to a particular network, assignment of a DNIC would obviously simplify any networks' provision of an international service, whether or not it maintains its own overseas lines. [I]t does not, however, appear that the absence of a DNIC would make it impossible in every case for a given U.S. entity to operate internationally or to receive inbound calls. However, reliance upon such arrangements would likely make operation of a network more difficult.[60]

As of June 1985, the FCC had not made any policy determinations in this proceeding.

7.2.4 Implementing Network Access: The **Disclosure Order**

After AT&T began to implement the separate subsidiary requirements of the *Computer II Decision*, questions arose concerning the disclosure of information by AT&T concerning their transmission networks to promote equal access by all enhanced service and CPE vendors. In 1982, CBEMA requested the FCC clarify the matter. In response, the FCC adopted what is commonly referred to as the *Disclosure Order*.[61]

The *Disclosure Order* does not have a direct substantive effect on ISDN related policy, but does affirmatively state a position with respect to network access. The FCC indicated in the order that "AT&T must publicly disclose information disclosed to or for the benefit of American Bell [now AT&T Information Systems] concerning network design, technical standards, interfaces or generally the manner in which interconnected CPE or enhanced services will interoperate with AT&T's network.[Footnote omitted] The disclosure requirement encompasses the information necessary to enable all users to gain access to and use common carrier facilities, services and capabilities in the same manner and on a non-discriminatory basis.[62]

7.2.5 Encouraging Multiple Networks: **Competitive Carrier** *and* **International Competitive Carrier**

In the United States, a great many decisions have been made by the FCC that effect a fundamental regulatory policy of permitting entry into telecommunication markets by new service providers. The Competitive Carrier Proceeding, and its more recent progeny, International Competitive Carrier, epitomize this policy.

Competitive Carrier began the process of eliminating unnecessary regulatory burdens applicable to service providers operating in the domestic interstate service market. Its foundation was a finding that, in a competitive environment, market forces could provide the public the statutory mandated protection against unreasonably high rates and undue discrimination. That is, marketplace forces could replace regulation and make unnecessary burdensome regulatory requirements for both carriers and the FCC. Over a six year period, more and more steps were taken to implement this result.[63]

As a result of the confidence gained in effecting a domestic competitive environment, the FCC in early 1985 began an analogous proceeding aimed at the international telecommunication environment by defining relevant markets and examining their dimensions.[64] The FCC in its *Notice* "tentatively concluded that there is now sufficient competition in the international telecommunications market to allow implementation of competitive carrier policies."[65] Additional tentative decisions included dividing markets into International Measured Telecommunication Service (IMTS) and non-IMTS.

While neither of the above Competitive Carrier proceedings presently have a direct bearing on ISDN developments, their indirect influence is significant.

7.3 Proceedings Related to User-Network Interfaces

The last of the three major policy areas relevant to ISDN developments is the matter of user-network interfaces. In the United States, the unraveling of network monopoly control over terminal devices began with the FCC's 1968 *Carterfone* decision.[66] Since that time there has been a conscious policy of promoting competition in the terminal equipment market.[67] This policy had had a direct impact on both domestic and international ISDN developments. The latter because of the necessity for the CCITT to accomodate the US environment in CCITT Recommendations.

7.3.1 Establishing the User-Network Basic Interface: The Computer II Decision

As discussed above in Section 7.1, the FCC in its *Computer II Decision* drew a distinction between enhanced and basic services. For similar reasons, it also drew a distinction between the network and customer premises equipment (CPE).[68]

In reaching the decision, the FCC considered the nature of the terminal equipment market and the effects of advances in technology on equipment and use, the benefits of competition, and its statutory responsibility to insure the reasonableness of rates charged. It noted the FCC's continuing policy during the preceding fifteen years of encouraging competition in the market, and the resulting innovation in types of CPE introduced into the market place by an increasing large number of manufacturers, at lower cost.[69] Moreover, this policy afforded consumers more options in obtaining equipment that best suited their communication or information processing needs. Benefits of this competitive policy were found in such areas as improved maintenance and reliability, improved installation features including ease of making changes, competitive sources of supply, the option of leasing or owning equipment, and competitive pricing and payment options.

As a result of all the above considerations, the FCC found that CPE must be unbundled from network service offerings, detariffed, and allowed to evolve on a competitive basis. "There is nothing inherent in any carrier-provided CPE, including the basic telephone, that necessitates its provision as an integrated part of a carrier's regulated transmission service."[70] For dominant carriers such as AT&T, this also meant that CPE could only be offered through a fully separated subsidiary. Carrying out this complex process was left to the *AT&T Implementation Order*, mentioned below.

The *Computer II Decision* also established that there was to be no FCC regulation of such equipment — other than requiring it to meet certain minimal FCC technical standards — and a registration process.[71]

7.3.2 Implementing the Network/CPE Dichotomy: The AT&T Implementation Order

After the adoption of the *Computer II Decision*, the FCC was faced with the ardorous task of developing the criteria and procedures for the removal of embedded customer premises equipment and transferral to the fully separated subsidiary, which as a result of the MFJ, was AT&T Information Systems. This task was instituted through a proceeding begun in April 1982.[72]

The *AT&T Implementation Order* did not have, however, any substantive effect on ISDN related policy.[73]

7.3.3 AT&T Structural Separation for CPE Revisited: The AT&T Separation Proceeding

In 1984, AT&T filed a petition with the FCC seeking relief from structural separation requirements imposed upon it as a result of the *Computer II Decision* with respect to its provision of CPE and enhanced services.

The FCC, in acting on the petition, established a proceeding addressing whether there may be some means other than structural separation to effect its policies of promoting cost-based pricing for regulated offerings, protecting ratepayers from adverse consequences of carrier provision of competitive CPE, and promoting an environment in which all vendors of CPE may compete without unfair advantage.[74]

The FCC, noting that there had been fundamental changes in circumstances of both AT&T and the telecommunications industry since structural separation was imposed on AT&T, and tentatively concluded "that the costs of continuing to require structural separation for AT&T provision of CPE outweighs the benefits."[75] Some immediate relief was afforded in the form of sharing certain administrative functions and the development of software.

As of June 1985, a decision on the issue of structural separation for the provision of CPE had not been reached.

7.3.4 Refining the User-Network Basic Interface: The NCTE Decision and the LADT Decision

This proceeding was initiated by a number of petitions requesting amendment of Part 68 of the Rules to permit registration and direct electrical connection of various customer provided equipment to the telephone network. Part 68 of the FCC rules provides the technical and procedural standards under which direct electrical connection of customer provided telephone equipment, systems, and protective apparatus may be made to the nationwide network without causing harm and without a requirement for the interposition of telephone company provided protective circuit arrangements.

One of these petitions dealt with a new AT&T service called Dataphone Digital Service (DDS). It involved the interconnection of Channel Service Units (CSU) [analogous to the ISDN NT2 function] to the Network Connection Terminating Equipment (NCTE) [the analog of the ISDN NT1 function].[76]

In the Third Notice of Inquiry, which became known as the *Interconnection Order*, the FCC not only concluded that customers could provide and interconnect CSUs, but NCTE as well, and proposed technical rules to effect the decision.[77]

In reaching the conclusion, the FCC stated:

[W]e find no technical, legal, or policy justification for restricting independent manufacturers from providing CSUs or digital NCTE to digital service subscribers.

We find that there exist no reasons to further delay development of appropriate standards under Part 68 [of the Commission's Rules] to permit registration and direct connection of terminal equipment to DDS (and other digital services, circuits and facilities utilizing digital NCTE or digital NCTE-like devices).[78]

A number of network service providers subsequently petitioned the FCC to reconsider the decision on several grounds, including the Study Group XVIII work discussed in Chapter 6, Section 6.1, that placed the established S reference point as the interface with an ISDN.[79] The FCC rejected the argument, emphasizing that by "permitting the carrier to unilaterally define the termination point of its transmission network located on the customer's premises could preclude subscribers from providing their own equipment which is privately beneficial and not otherwise harmful."[80]

In the FCC's Second Report and Order in this proceeding, it adopted the proposed rules.[81] Other actions dealt with customer premises wiring issues unrelated to ISDN.[82]

In the *LADT Decision* in early 1985, the FCC reinforced and clarified the *NCTE Decision* in a case involving Southern Bell's Local Area Data Transport (LADT) service, already mentioned in Section 7.1. LADT made use of a customer premises termination unit called the data subscriber line carrier (DSLC) which provided the interface between the subscriber's data terminal/telephone and the local loop. In finding that this unit was NCTE, and therefore must be unbundled and provided through a separate subsidiary, the FCC based its decision on the provision of modem-like functions by the DSLC, as well as equalization, and remote loopback.[83]

REFERENCES

1. *See Notice of Inquiry* [in Docket No. 16979], FCC 66-1004, 31 Fed.
    Reg. 14752 (1966); *Report and Further Notice of Inquiry*, FCC 69-
    468, 17 FCC 2d 587 (1969); *Tentative Decision of the Commission*,
    FCC 70-338, 28 FCC 2d 291 (1970); *Final Decision and Order*, FCC
    71-255, 28 FCC 2d 267 (1971); *aff'd sub. nom.* GTE Service Corp. v.
    FCC, 474 F.2d 724 (2d Cir. 1973); *Order* [on remand], FCC 73-342,
    40 FCC 2d 293 (1973).

2. *See Notice of Inquiry and Proposed Rulemaking* [in Docket No.
    20828], FCC 76-745, 61 FCC 2d 103 (1976); *Supplemental Notice of
    Inquiry and Enlargement of Proposed Rulemaking*, FCC 77-151, 64
    FCC 2d 771 (1977); *Tentative Decision and Further Notice of Inquiry
    and Rulemaking*, FCC 79-307, 72 FCC 2d 358 (1979); *Final Decision*,
    FCC 80-189, 77 FCC 2d 384 (1980); *Memorandum Opinion and
    Order*, FCC 80-628, 84 FCC 2d 50 (1980); *Memorandum Opinion and
    Order on Further Reconsideration*, FCC 81-481, 88 FCC 2d 512
    (1981), *aff'd sub. nom.* CCIA v. FCC 693 F.2d 198 (D.C. Cir. 1982);
    cert. denied sub. nom., Louisiana Public Service Comm'n. v. FCC,
    461 U.S. 938 (1983). *See also, Memorandum Opinion and Order* [in
    the matter of American Telephone and Telegraph Co. Revisions to
    Tariffs FCC No. 260 and 267 Relating to Dataspeed 40/4], FCC 76-
    1199, 62 FCC 2d 21 (1976), *aff'd sub. nom.* International Business
    Machines Corporation v. FCC, 570 F.2d 452 (2d Cir. 1978).

3. *Final Decision, supra*, at 387 [summary para. 5], 419, 420 [paras. 93,
    97].

4. 47 C.F.R. Sec. 64.702(a).

5. *Id.* at 419-420, para. 95.

6. *Memorandum Opinion and Order, supra*, at 53-54, para. 10.

7. *Final Decision, supra*, at 420 para. 95.

8. *Ibid.*

9. *Id.* at 420, para. 96.

10. *Id.* at 420-21, para. 97.

11. *Id.* at 429, para. 116.

12. "I think that this provision somewhat arbitrarily removes protocol and
    code conversion from the ambit of basic service. It is difficult for me
    to see why protocol or code conversion is an *enhancement* to a
    communications service. It is, rather as much a necessity to the
    provision of any communications service at all, for customers who
    happen to have disparate terminals, as in the presence of a local loop."
    Statement of Commissioner Joseph R. Fogarty Dissenting in Part, *Id.*
    at 512.

13. *Id.* at 421-22, para. 99.
14. *Id.* at 421, note 37.
15. *Memorandum Opinion and Order, supra,* at 60-61, paras. 26, 27.
16. *See* United States v. American Telephone & Telegraph Co., 552 F. Supp. 131 (D.D.C. 1982), *aff'd sub. nom.* Maryland v. United States, 460 U.S. 1001 (1983).
17. *See Id.* at 225.
18. *See Report and Order* [in CC Doc. No. 83-115], 95 FCC 2d 1117, 1126-28.
19. *See Memorandum Opinion and Order* [in File Nos. I-T-C-81-274, I-T-C-82-210], FCC 82-377, 91 FCC 2d 232 (1982).
20. *See Id.* at 322, para. 2.
21. *Memorandum Opinion and Order* [in Doc. No. 20828], 84 FCC 2d at 53, note 4.
22. *Memorandum Opinion and Order* [in File Nos. I-T-C-81-274 and I-T-C-82-210], 91 FCC 2d at 236, para. 11.
23. *Id.* at 238, note 8.
24. *Western Union International, Petition for Reconsideration,* [in File Nos. I-T-C-81-274 and I-T-C-82-210] at 2.
25. *Id.* at 3.
26. *Memorandum Opinion and Order,* FCC 85-29, __ FCC 2d __, (adopted 18 Jan. 1985).
27. *Id.* at 23, para. 55.
28. *Id.* at 28, para. 72.
29. *See Notice of Inquiry* [in General Docket 80-756], FCC 80-702, 83 FCC 2d 318 (1980).
30. *See Memorandum Opinion, Order, and Statement of Principles,* FCC 83-510, 95 FCC 2d 584 (1983).
31. *Id.* at 591, para. 15.
32. *Ibid.*
33. *Id.* at 592, para. 17.
34. *Id.* at 594, para. 22.
35. *See Memorandum Opinion and Order,* 91 FCC 2d 1 (1982).
36. *See Memorandum Opinion, Order, and Authorization,* [in File No. W-P-C-4841], FCC 83-221, 94 FCC 2d 48 (1983). This was the second of two decisions on AT&T's offering of BPSS. *See American Telephone and Telegraph Company, Bell Packet Switching Service,* 91 FCC 2d 1 (1982).
37. *Id.* at 56, note 17.
38. *See Memorandum Opinion and Order* [in File No. ENF 83-34], FCC 85-292, __ FCC 2d __ (adopted 31 May 1985).
39. *See Notice of Proposed Rulemaking* [in CC Doc. No. 83-115], FCC 83-71, 93 FCC 2d 722 (1983).

40. *Report and Order*, FCC 83-552, 95 FCC 2d 1117 (1983), *aff'd sub. nom.*, Illinois Bell Tel. Co. v. FCC, 740 F.2d 465 (7th Cir. 1984).

41. *Id.* at 1127.

42. *Id.* at 1139.

43. *Id.* at 1130.

44. *See Memorandum Opinion and Order* [in File Nos. ENF-84-15 *et. al.*], FCC 84-561, __ FCC 2d __ (adopted 21 Nov. 1984) at 6.

45. *Memorandum Opinion and Order* [in File Nos. ENF-84-15 *et al.*], FCC 85-101, __ FCC 2d __ (adopted 1 Mar. 1985) at 53, para. 105.

46. *Id.* at 38, para. 73.

47. *Id.* at 68, para. 138.

48. *See* Separate Statement of Commissioner Dennis R. Patrick, appended to *Memorandum Opinion and Order, supra.*

49. *Memorandum Opinion and Order* [in File No. ENF-84-2], FCC 85-248, __ FCC 2d __ (adopted 9 May 1985) at 22, para. 53.

50. *Id.* at 21, para. 52.

51. *Final Decision, supra*, at 77 FCC 2d 422, para. 99, note 37.

52. *Memorandum Opinion and Order, supra*, at 84 FCC 2d 57, para. 19.

53. *Report and Order, supra*, at 95 FCC 2d 1121.

54. *See Notice of Proposed Rulemaking* [in CC Docket No. 80-176], FCC 80-220, 77 FCC 2d 831 (1980).

55. *Id.* at 832-835, paras. 3, 9.

56. *See Notice of Inquiry* [in CC Docket No. 83-1230], FCC 83-516, 95 FCC 2d 627 (1983).

57. *Id.* at 635, para. 22.

58. *Id.* at 636, para. 25.

59. *Id.* at 648-49, paras. 56-57.

60. *Id.* at 651, para. 63.

61. *See Report and Order* [in ENF-82-5], FCC 83-182, 93 FCC 2d 1226 (1983).

62. *Id.* at 1238.

63. *See Notice of Inquiry and Proposed Rulemaking* [in CC Doc. No. 79-252], 77 FCC 2d 308 (1979); *First Report and Order*, 85 FCC 2d 1 (1980); *Further Notice of Proposed Rulemaking*, 84 FCC 2d 445 (1981); *Second Report and Order*, 91 FCC 2d 59 (1982), *recon.* FCC 83-69 (1983); *Second Further Notice of Proposed Rulemaking*, FCC 82-187, (1982); *Third Further Notice of Proposed Rulemaking*, mimeo No. 33547, 48 Fed. Reg. 28292 (1983); *Third Report and Order*, mimeo No. 012, 48 Fed. Reg. 46791 (1983); *Fourth Report and Order*, 95 FCC 2d 554 (1983); *Fourth Further Notice of Proposed Rulemaking*, FCC 84-82, __ FCC 2d __ (1984); *Fifth Report and Order*, FCC 84-394, __ FCC 2d __ (adopted 4 Sep. 1984); *Sixth Report and Order*, FCC 84-566, __ FCC 2d __ (adopted 10 Jan. 1985).

64. *See Notice of Proposed Rulemaking* [in CC Doc. No. 85-107], FCC 85-177, __ FCC 2d __ (adopted 11 Apr. 1985).

65. *Id.* at 21, para. 49.

66. *Carterfone*, 13 FCC 2d 420, *recon. den.* 14 FCC 2d 571 (1968).

67. *See Final Decision, supra*, at 77 FCC 2d 439, para. 141, and citations listed.

68. *See Final Decision, supra*, 77 FCC 2d at 438, para. 139.

69. *See Id.* at 439, para. 141.

70. *Id.* at 441, para. 144.

71. *See Id.* at 440, para. 142.

72. *See Notice of Inquiry* [in CC Doc. No. 81-893], FCC 81-576, 89 FCC 2d 694 (1982).

73. *See Report and Order*, FCC 83-551, 95 FCC 2d 1276 (1983); *Memorandum Opinion and Order* [on Reconsideration], FCC 85-118, __ FCC 2d __ (adopted 15 Mar. 1985).

74. *See Memorandum Opinion and Order and Notice of Proposed Rulemaking* [in CC Doc. No. 85-26, and ENF-84-17 *et al.*], FCC 85-56, __ FCC 2d __ (adopted 31 Jan. 1985).

75. *Id.* at 12, para. 17.

76. *See Notice of Proposed Rulemaking and Notice of Inquiry* [in CC Doc. No. 81-216], FCC 81-130, 85 FCC 2d 868 (1981).

77. *See Third Notice of Proposed Rulemaking*, FCC 83-268, 94 FCC 2d 5 (1983).

78. *Id.* at 22.

79. *See Memorandum Opinion and Order*, FCC 84-145, __ (1984).

80. *Id.* at para. 14.

81. *See Second Report and Order*, FCC 84-522, __ FCC 2d __ (1984).

82. *See Second Notice of Proposed Rulemaking and Order*, 92 FCC 2d 1 (1982); *First Report and Order*, FCC 84-182, 97 FCC 2d 527 (1984).

83. *See Memorandum Opinion and Order* [in File No. ENF-83-34], FCC 85-292, __ FCC 2d __ (adopted 31 May 1985) at para. 12.

CHAPTER 8 — THE FEDERAL COMMUNICATIONS COMMISSION INQUIRY ON ISDN

In August 1983 the Federal Communications Commission issued the first significant policy-related document on ISDN in the United States. This *Notice of Inquiry* (NOI) described ISDN developments leading up to its issuance, carefully set forth the FCC's jurisdiction and authority, noted major policies that seemed to be affected, and solicited public comment within a docket established to accumulate a formal record. Thirty parties filed comments and twenty filed reply comments. A *First Report*, subsequently issued in March 1984, contained a number of conclusions and left the docket open for further action.

The inquiry produced a watershed of sometimes divergent views on a broad range of ISDN-related issues. It is a unique resource that is examined at length in this chapter.

8.1 Prelude to the Inquiry

After the CCITT Seventh Plenary Assembly in November 1980, it was clear that the international community was serious about ISDN work. The CCITT infrastructure had started to organize the ISDN effort, and numerous substantial issues had been assigned to Study Group XVIII.

FCC staff had been observing the activity and attended the first study Group XVIII meeting of the 1980–84 period, jointly held with the IEEE's ISDN'81 Symposium in January 1981 near Tampa, Florida. During the course of the next two and a half years, an ever-increasing schedule of meetings and submission of documents served to focus more people's attention on ISDN work domestically and internationally. Within the FCC, this resulted in the creation of an intra-agency committee on ISDN, referenced in the NOI, that brought together divisions in the Common Carrier Bureau and the Office of Science and Technology.

In addition to this internal activity, FCC officials sought to make a larger circle of the public and the telecommunication and information industry aware of the ISDN work. Much of this material is listed in the Bibliography, Appendix A. Perhaps the most visible example occurred shortly after the FCC's former Chief Scientist, Dr. Steven J. Lukasik, stated in his last press

conference that ISDN developments were the most important in the telecommunications field. The comment was widely quoted.

Also instrumental in bringing about a formal proceeding were various
industry officials who briefed FCC officials during this period. By mid-1983,
a notice of inquiry was an idea whose time had come.

8.2 The Notice of Inquiry

Whenever a federal government agency intends to adopt policies or rules
affecting the public, it must follow the provisions of the Administrative
Procedure Act.[1] Although these provisions are somewhat cumbersome, they
are intended to ensure that both the government and the public are informed
and aware of what is about to be adopted. Generally, this entails the issuance
of a "notice" informing the public of the contemplated action, and the
solicitation of comments and reply comments within a certain specific period
of time (generally 60 or 90 days). In so doing, a "docket," i.e., a document
file, is established for administrative convenience. After reviewing the submissions of the public, the government agency is then free to adopt the
policies or rules.

The FCC generally subdivides these proceedings into two varieties, depending on whether the end results are rules or general policies. Thus, there
are Notices of Proposed Rule Making, or NPRMs, and Notices of Inquiry,
or NOIs.[2] NOIs also serve the additional roles of making the public aware
of important issues and soliciting general comment.

On 4 August 1983 the FCC adopted the ISDN *Notice of Inquiry*, creating
General Docket No. 83-841. The document was released on 10 August. This
delay is normal, and allows the staff to make last minute editorial changes,
alter text at the behest of Commissioners, and to reproduce the several
hundred copies for the press office and the various bureaus and offices of
the FCC. Because both the Common Carrier Bureau and the Office of
Science and Technology were formally responsible for the proceeding, a
"general" docket was established.

8.2.1 The Introduction

There have been few subjects as forward-looking as ISDN policy. Considerable care was taken in drafting the *ISDN NOI*, covering all the issues
that had been repeatedly raised by private-sector representatives. The dimensions of the proceeding were stated at the outset.

The purpose of this *Notice of Inquiry* (NOI) is to provide back-ground on ISDN developments to date, and on related telecommunications policy, and to discuss various issues raised by the potential implementation of ISDNs. We shall seek comment on the appropriate role for the FCC to play in the ongoing ISDN standards development effort. In particular, we solicit comment on how the FCC should best continue to promote its pro-competitive policies as ISDN evolves. Furthermore, this NOI is intended as a clearing-house for comments of U.S. telecommunications service providers, equipment manufacturers, users, and the public.[3]

There was concern, however, that the inquiry might impair CCITT work currently underway. The matter was squarely addressed.

[W]e are cognizant that international and domestic standardiza-tion efforts involving the U.S. government, telecommunications providers, large users, and foreign entities are presently underway. We do not intend that this proceeding hinder or conflict with these ongoing efforts, rather, this *NOI* seeks to complement existing efforts.[4]

Nonetheless, the growing importance of ISDN activities compelled an in-creased FCC involvement in ISDN forums.

In addition to the FCC's involvement in the [US CCITT National Committee], and the Joint Working Party, the Commission estab-lished, in 1981, an intra-agency ISDN Coordinating Committee to monitor ISDN developments. During the last year and a half, observing that international ISDN planning efforts have accelerated rapidly, this Committee stepped up its own efforts to remain abreast of developments by participating more actively in international and domestic meetings.[5]

8.2.2 Commission Jurisdiction

In order to make it clear that the FCC had a substantial legal basis for its interest in ISDN, the appropriate provisions in the FCC's statutory authority were cited and the nexus to ISDN developments was stated.

The Commission maintains jurisdiction over U.S. domestic and international common carrier facilities and service providers pur-suant to Title I and Title II of the Communications Act of 1934 as amended. [Title III of the Act, 47 U.S.C. 301 (1976), *et. seq.*, extends the Commission's jurisdiction to radio and satellite facilities, covering common carriers to the extent that they hold radio licenses.] Under 47 U.S.C. § 214 (1976), the FCC authorizes service providers to extend, acquire, and operate facilities, and evaluates Section 214 applications to insure against excessive plant additions which unduly expand the rate base, thus causing higher revenue requirements. In the last decade, the Commission has initiated international facilities planning processes to examine U.S. carrier traffic forecasts and facility requests prior to the Section 214 authorization process. It has done so to provide overall policy guidance on the complex issues raised by large scale facilities investments, finding this approach preferable to reliance on *ad hoc* Section 214 oversight alone. In addition, the facilities planning process gives service providers the ability to develop long-term plans and removes the uncertainty inherent in *ad hoc* authorizations.[6]

A further basis for institution of this inquiry is the potential that our equipment registration rules (47 C.F.R. Part 68) may require amendment to accomodate digital interconnection with the telephone network in an ISDN environment. Since 1976, when the registration program initially became effective, most terminal equipment connected with the network has been registered as conforming with technical specifications to prevent harm, or as conforming with technical specifications to prevent harm, or has been used with registered protective apparatus. In some cases, we have considered use of tariff alternatives to registration of equipment under our rules [citation omitted]. While we do not decide here whether rule or tariff procedures would be appropriate for ISDN, it is fair to inquire in this proceeding, at least initially, whether such procedures may prove necessary or useful.[7]

The Commission's jurisdiction over networks and service providers will remain unchanged by the evolution of ISDN. ISDN will require additional construction of facilities and service offerings. Thus, the Commission will continue to address policy issues and authorize facilities in an ISDN environment. While we do not seek to plan ISDN facilities, we here seek to review the large policy issues raised by ISDN at an early stage in the facilities planning cycle, rather than only acting on an *ad hoc* basis.[8]

8.2.3 Current Regulatory Policy

Following this extensive statement of its legal basis for instituting the inquiry, the current thrust of FCC regulatory policies was stated.

In response to dramatic technological change, the Commission has, over the last fifteen years, increasingly relied on the forces of the marketplace to complement traditional common carrier regulation, and to ensure that such regulation is not inappropriately or unnecessarily extended. The Commission, therefore, has promulgated pro-competitive policies and has begun to deregulate competitive telecommunications services. In a series of decisions the FCC has fostered competition in the provision of customer premises equipment, promulgated policies fostering new common carrier entrants, permitted domestic resale and shared use, and authorized COMSAT to provide end-to-end service. Although each of these decisions related to a different aspect of common carrier operations, a single regulatory philosophy is common to them — a desire to foster competition while reducing governmental involvement.[9]

8.2.4 Domestic Impact of CCITT Activities

After the relatively long introduction and background section, the NOI approached some of the central issues. It focused on the basic user-network interface, and described how setting various specifications can impact service providers, manufacturers, and users.

[T]hese [CCITT] Recommendations will outline performance specifications and will apportion telecommunications functions between the ISDN network and the user. For example, performance standards such as bit speed and bit error rates will have to be specified so that information can be efficiently sent from a terminal through the ISDN and to a designated terminal. In addition, CCITT's ISDN planning efforts will include the adoption of a protocol model and the apportionment of protocol handling between the network and the user. The CCITT may also recommend the degree of control the network users have to select and use network and non-network services according to a consensus on what functions the ISDN network should be allowed to perform and which are best left outside the network.

The Recommendations CCITT formulates will directly affect U.S. ISDNs, service providers, equipment manufacturers and users. In order to interface with the ISDNs of other nations, a nation's ISDN(s) must be compatible with them at the point of interface. ISDNs will have to be designed to transmit data through interfaces with other nation's ISDNs in formats which are compatible with, or convertible to, internationally agreed upon specifications, to permit interworking. If the technical specifications of one nation's ISDN(s) vary from those of other nations, it might require translation in order to interface with other ISDNs. Absent such translation, non-conforming ISDNs would probably be unable to interface with other ISDNs.

CCITT ISDN planning efforts are designed to produce a uniform set of technical specifications which extend from the network down to customer premises equipment. However, in the U.S., competitive market forces could result in some deviation from these standards. If in the U.S., customer premises equipment were to operate at standards which were technically incompatible with or inferior to CCITT adopted standards, it could result in traffic being restricted to domestic termination points, unless an additional layer of hardware and/or software could be added. Some CCITT schematics recognize this possibility by including a terminal adapter for this purpose. We invite comment on the relationship between the CCITT's ISDN planning efforts and the design of U.S. ISDNs. In addition, we solicit comment on whether this hardware and/or software is technically and economically feasible. Further, we request comment on whether specifications of this adapter, if done through voluntary standard setting activities, would as a practical matter be adhered to absent governmental involvement and/or whether Commission involvement in this area is necessary.[10]

8.2.5 Impact on Computer II

The *Computer II* decision (reviewed in Chapter 7) was until very recently a fixed cornerstone of FCC policy. It was not surprising, therefore, to find the FCC looking at ISDN developments from a *Computer II* perspective, as the following paragraph illustrates.

Computer II divided telecommunications services into two categories, basic and enhanced services. CCITT Study Group XVIII [at its June 1983 meeting] created two categories of service that ISDNs would perform or support: (1) bearer services; and (2) telecommunication services. Bearer services may generally be described as those services that provide the capability for information transfer between ISDN interfaces (transport services) and defined in protocol layers 1-3. Telecommunication services are those that provide the capability for communications between users of specific user terminals. Both types of services may be provided within or outside an ISDN.

We solicit comment on whether the bearer/telecommunication services approach can readily accomodate our market structure (which is comprised of multiple service providers offering regulated and unregulated services in an unbundled manner)-and telecommunications policies.[11]

8.2.6 Impact on US Competition and the Availability of Leased Lines

In the main body of the NOI, the FCC dealt in a general way with the impact of ISDN on the US competitive environment and on users, and specifically on the perennial favorite — private leased lines. Of particular interest is the extent to which the unique operational and regulatory environment in the United States might affect its ability to deviate from ISDN specifications.

The most practical approach to planning an ISDN model would seem to be one that accomodates the interests of U.S. telecommunications service providers, equipment manufacturers and users during the international planning phase. In particular, it would appear important to U.S. telecommunications service providers and users that CCITT's technical ISDN standards not preclude or restrict service providers ability to interface with the other nations' ISDNs nor adversely affect users' ability to select among numerous service providers. Unless an ISDN model is designed with sufficient flexibility, both U.S. and foreign users could be precluded from, or limited in, their ability to specify the service providers and services they wished to utilize.

The United States, with our diversity of service providers, might not be able to conform to technical specifications that nations with a centralized telephone network could meet. For example, in the United States, the users' ability to utilize numerous service providers and the geographic span of the U.S. network often result in calls being routed over a higher number of connections than in other countries. Each connection adds to the time which it takes to complete a call. Thus a specification, such as timing, which could be conformed to over a limited number of connections might prove impossible to conform to in our country. In addition, satellite common carriers could be precluded from relaying traffic from national satellite systems if restrictive time specifications were adopted which would have the effect of prohibiting "double hop" situations. Thus, if CCITT were to adopt a standard that might be too restictive, and if U.S. service providers were to bound by such a standard, they could be limited in the number of services they could provide, and users could be restricted in the routing and number of service providers they might utilize.

Also, users might register concern over whether ISDN will be designed to technically and economically accomodate private leased lines. If ISDNs cannot or are not designed to meet the needs of private leased line users, the question then becomes whether a circuit and/or packet switched network could provide suitable alternatives. For instance, would the substitution of permanent virtual circuits for private lines, satisfy current private line users? Is there some reason for the U.S. to seek, as a policy objective, the continued availability of dedicated leased channels in an ISDN environment?

In addition, are there any ISDN developments which the Commission should be aware of that have, or could, raise issues of U.S. national security? We request comment on these issues.

In addition, we solicit comment identifying other possible areas of U.S. concern; how U.S. interfaces can be affected by international ISDN standards, and how our interests can best be accommodated.[12]

In a wide variety of settings, the issue of private leased lines has vexed US transnational corporations in the communication business and US international telecommunication policy-makers over a number of years, but particularly during the last five. This issue, more than any other, seemed to spur interest in ISDN developments by non-carriers. The issue evoked copious discussion in the comments filed. As a result, the matter was extensively treated in the *First Report*.[13] Eventually, Study Group XVIII responded by adding an array of different connection attributes, including switched, semi-permanent, and permanent. The last is one which "...will not pass through the network...and by-pass the exchanges."[14]

As ISDNs evolve, the entire U.S. telecommunications market — service providers, equipment manufacturers and users — will be affected. We solicit comment on the potential impact of ISDN, as discussed [above], and request comment on additional ways in which ISDN could affect U.S. service providers, equipment manufacturers and users. These comments will help clarify various U.S. interests, which is essential if our interests and policies are to be effectively communicated internationally.[15]

8.2.7 Role of the FCC

All of the above issues dealt with substantive ISDN issues. An additional institutional issue also existed: what should the FCC's role be in all this?

As discussed in Chapter 2, the US government has historically played a very minor role in CCITT matters. Most of the individuals involved in these activities from the United States have been in the private-sector.

During the 1976–84 time period however, a number of major changes began to occur in domestic and international telecommunication infrastructures. First, the CCITT itself began to change by assuming responsibility for the entire field of integrated telecommunication and information systems. In addition, the CCITT in its ISDN activities included not only the traditional international interface matters, but also the intimate details of model *national* systems. It began designing systems from the ground up. At the same time, in the United States, AT&T was losing its monopoly foothold, and radically different domestic regulatory policies were emerging.

It was clear in this new environment of integrated communications and competition that the FCC would no longer be able to ignore what was occurring in CCITT forums. This was particularly true of ISDN developments.

One of the purposes of this NOI is to discuss the appropriate role of the FCC in ISDN matters. The Communications Act of 1934 charges the FCC with the responsibility for ensuring that construction of new facilities and the provision of regulated sevices are in the public interest. Pursuant to the Act, the Commission has adopted pro-competitive communications policies which mandate that marketplace forces be allowed to determine, to the maximum extent possible, the best methods of providing service to users. Thus, we believe that any FCC involvement in ISDN specification activities should be designed to complement existing planning efforts, with the objective of fostering our domestic and international United States telecommunications policies, and not directed to the design considerations involved in the ISDN specification process as such. For example, it is not our intention to hinder the progress of international activities or unilaterally impose standards in lieu of CCITT's efforts. Rather it is our tentative view that the public interest would best be serviced by assuring that U.S. policy is understood by all participants in the ISDN specification process, to the end that it will be accommodated in this process.

In order for the Commission effectively to continue to foster its pro-competitive policies, it appears necessary for us more actively to monitor and participate in international and domestic ISDN specification activities, with the focus noted above. Correspondingly, it would also be necessary for the Commission to become increasingly aware of the views of U.S. service providers, equipment manufacturers, users and the public on this matter. Therefore, we solicit comment on how the FCC can best ensure that ISDNs are structured to foster competition and serve the public interest. We request comment on how the competitive nature and structure of U.S. telecommunications can best be maintained without unnecessarily diminishing any alleged efficiencies which may be inherent in uniform ISDN specifications. In addition, we more specifically solicit comment on how the specification of ISDNs may best conform to the regulatory scheme adopted in *Computer II*. Furthermore, we request comment on how the Commission best can continue to promulgate pro-competitive policies as ISDN develops and how we can best represent divergent interests of U.S. service providers, equipment manufacturers, users and the public at international forums. We also expect that this NOI will generate comment on what short and long term ISDN goals the FCC should set for itself.[16]

8.3 Comments of the Parties

The response to the *Notice of Inquiry* was substantial. Thirty parties, representing most of the major telecommunication and information service providers in the United States, filed comments or reply comments. Even one foreign manufacturer, L.M. Ericsson of Sweden, filed. These parties are listed in the table below, together with the mnemonic used to identify them.

Table 8-1
Parties Submitting Comments or Replies[17]

Aeronautical Radio, Incorporated	ARINC
Aerospace Industries Association of America	AIAA
American Petroleum Institute	API
American Satellite Company	ASC
American Telephone and Telegraph Company	AT&T
Association of American Railroads	AAR
Association of Data Communications Users	ADCU
Association of Data Processing Service Organizations	ADAPSO
Bell Operating Companies	BOCs
Communications Satellite Corporation	COMSAT
Computer and Business Equipment Manufacturers Association	CBEMA
Continental Telecom Incorporated	CONTEL
Ericsson Communications	ERICSSON
Exchange Carriers Standards Association, Incorporated	ECSA

Table 8-1
(Cont'd)

GTE Service Corporation .... GTE
Harris Corporation, Farinon Division .... HARRIS
Independent Data Communications Manufacturers Association .. IDCMA
International Business Machines Corporation .... IBM
International Communications Association .... ICA
M/A-COM, Incorporated .... M/A-COM
MCI Communications Corporation .... MCI
MarTech Strategies, Incorporated .... MARTECH
Motorola, Incorporated .... MOTOROLA
Mountain States Telephone and Telegraph Company, Northwestern Bell
  Telephone Company, Pacific Northwest Bell Telephone Company MN&P
National Telecommunications and Information Administration ...... NTIA
Northern Telecom, Incorporated .... NORTHERN TELCOM
RCA Communications, Incorporated .... RCA
Satellite Business Systems .... SBS
Tymnet, Incorporated .... TYMNET
United Telephone System, Incorporated .... UTS

The following docket record lists all the events associated with the ISDN proceeding. The number of pages of comments is often a useful gross indicator of the party's interest. Those comments containing only a few pages generally just stated their support for FCC initiation of the inquiry and for continued FCC involvement.

At the outset of the proceeding, several parties petitioned the FCC to extend the due date for comments. They argued that the complexity of the issues addressed, as well as CCITT meetings occurring at that time which were relevant to their comments, merited more than the normal 60-day comment period. Extensions of three weeks for the comments and six weeks for the replies were granted.

The comments represented a broad range of views.[19] At one end of this range were large organizations of equipment manufacturers, service providers, and users (ADAPSO, CBEMA, and IDCMA are representative) who were concerned about ISDN developments and the associated US policy-making process. At the other end were the carriers who played a dominant role in shaping those developments (AT&T and the BOCs are representative). In between, there were a collection of carriers and vendors who were concerned about a variety of issues (IBM, GTE, and SBS are representative). In addition, there were two parties who nominally represented independent viewpoints (NTIA and MarTech), and the ECSA.

Many of the comments contained both general statements as well as replies to specific questions posed in the *ISDN Notice.* Because many of these replies are subsequently described and discussed in the *First Report* found later in this chapter, only the general statements are presented below.

Table 8-2
General Docket No. 83-841 Record

Date	Document	Party	Pages[18]
4 Aug 1983	*Notice of Inquiry* adopted		
10 Aug	*Notice of Inquiry* released [Comments due: 3 Oct, Replies due: 18 Oct]		
9 Sep	Motion for Extension of Time	GTE	
16 Sep	Comments Concerning Motion	CBEMA	
16 Sep	Response to Motion	IBM	
16 Sep	Comments in Support of Motion	TYMNET	
21 Sep	Comments in Support of Motion	ADAPSO	
23 Sep	Motion for Extension	RCA	
27 Sep	Comments on Motion	M/A-COM	
30 Sep	*Order* [Comments due: 24 Oct, Replies due: 28 Nov]		
3 Oct	Comments	APA	8
3 Oct	Comments	ADCU	11
24 Oct	Comments	AAR	5
24 Oct	Comments	ADAPSO	41
24 Oct	Comments	ARINC	6
24 Oct	Comments	ASC	5
24 Oct	Comments	AT&T	19+23
24 Oct	Comments	BOCs	31+12
24 Oct	Comments	CBEMA	22+10
24 Oct	Comments	COMSAT	7
24 Oct	Comments	CONTEL	7
24 Oct	Notice of Intent to File	DOD	2
24 Oct	Comments	ECSA	7
24 Oct	Comments	ERICSSON	2
24 Oct	Comments	GTE	54
24 Oct	Comments	HARRIS	3

Table 8-2
(Cont'd)

Date	Document	Party	Pages
24 Oct	Comments	IBM	31
24 Oct	Comments	ICA	12
24 Oct	Comments	IDCMA	14
24 Oct	Comments	M/A-COM	23
24 Oct	Comments	MARTECH	81
24 Oct	Comments	MCI	3
24 Oct	Comments	MOTOROLA	2+3
24 Oct	Comments	MN&P	13
24 Oct	Comments	NTIA	31
24 Oct	Comments	NORTHERN TELCOM	19
24 Oct	Comments	RCA	8
24 Oct	Comments	SBS	12
24 Oct	Comments	UTS	4
21 Nov	Motion for Extension	GTE	
25 Nov	*Order* [Replies due: 5 Dec]		
28 Nov	Reply Comments	RCA	7
5 Dec	Reply Comments	ADAPSO	28
5 Dec	Reply Comments	AIA	10
5 Dec	Reply Comments	ARINC	14
5 Dec	Reply Comments	AT&T	21
5 Dec	Reply Comments	BOCs	15
5 Dec	Reply Comments	CBEMA	15
5 Dec	Reply Comments	ECSA	9
5 Dec	Reply Comments	ERICSSON	5
5 Dec	Reply Comments	GTE	23
5 Dec	Reply Comments	IBM	29
5 Dec	Reply Comments	ICA	12
5 Dec	Reply Comments	IDCMA	21
5 Dec	Reply Comments	M/A-COM	9
5 Dec	Reply Comments	MARTECH	4
5 Dec	Reply Comments	MCI	5
5 Dec	Reply Comments	MN&P	10
5 Dec	Reply Comments	NORTHERN TELCOM	11
5 Dec	Reply Comments	NTIA	5
5 Dec	Reply Comments	SBS	7
5 Dec	Reply Comments	TYMNET	12
30 Mar 1984	*First Report* adopted		
2 Apr	*First Report* released		

8.3.1 ADAPSO Comments

In traditional fashion, ADAPSO began by telling the FCC something about itself and what its interests were in this proceeding.

ADAPSO is the principal trade association of the nation's data processing services industry. Its member companies provide the public with a wide variety of computer services, such as local batch processing, software design and support, and remote access data processing services. These latter services enable customers around the world to access and use the centralized computers of ADAPSO's member companies for both batch and interactive data processing purposes. The connection between user and computer is achieved through the use of domestic and international common carrier communications services. Usually, these are private line circuits provided by domestic common carriers, international record carriers ("IRCs"), and foreign telecommunications administrations.

ADAPSO's interest in ISDN is thus a function of its members' dependence upon domestic and international communications facilities to provide their data processing services to the public. As an association of major users of international communications services, ADAPSO has an interest in maintaining the continued availability of basic transmission facilities and, in particular, private line circuits at reasonable rates, terms and conditions. As vendors of enhanced services, ADAPSO's members also have an interest in ensuring that all competitors are afforded equal access to ISDN services and that any carrier implementation of ISDN in the United States is consistent with the Commission's procompetitive telecommunications policies. ADAPSO is also participating in this proceeding to assist the Commission in understanding the needs and views of users who have, as a class, been underrepresented in forums addressing ISDN issues.[20]

The body of ADAPSO's comments contained numerous points that were either responsive to the questions posed in the NOI, or were matters considered important by ADAPSO. The first point made a rather extreme and not entirely accurate argument against the entire ISDN concept.

The Commission Should Consider, and Should Urge Other Administrations to Consider, Whether ISDN Will Promote the Development of Efficient and Economical Communications Services.[16]

The source of ADAPSO's concern about ISDN lies in the fact that it has never been demonstrated that ISDN will promote user options and flexibility or replace existing networks with an equally or more cost-effective alternative. Rather, it appears that the technical and economic advantages associated with the evolution of analog networks into digital networks — the so-called Integrated Digital Network — have been used in an unquestioning manner to justify the creation of ISDN. As the Commission is aware, however, ISDN represents more than the application of digital technology to provide new and existing services. ISDN is a network, which happens to use digital technology, that combines in a single transmission facility the ability to offer, on an integrated basis, many disparate service offerings ranging from traditional voice to sophisticated information services. As such, ISDN is necessarily a technological compromise. Instead of being designed to do a limited number of things well, ISDN is designed to do everything. As a consequence, ISDN may not be able to provide users with all of the services that are currently available, such as full-period private line circuits and circuit switched message services.[21]

ADAPSO also made the following points:

The manner in which the regulatory issues presented by ISDN are resolved will have a far-reaching impact on enhanced service providers and the Commission's domestic telecommunications policies.

The Commission, along with other interested parties, should take an active role in representing U.S. policy before the CCITT.

"Virtual" circuits are not acceptable substitute for full-period, flat-rate private line circuits.

Consideration of user costs should be an essential element of ISDN standards-setting activities.

The Commission should pursue ISDN standards that: a) accommodate the basic-enhanced dichotomy of the Second Computer Inquiry, b) allow multiple vendors to offer basic services and allow users to enhance those services, and c) ensure the continued availability of transparent, full-period, flat-rate private line service.

The issues raised by ISDN concerning the Second Computer Inquiry require the Commission's prompt consideration of the pending code and protocol inquiry and ADAPSO's petition for rulemaking [concerning RPOA accreditation of enhanced service providers].[22]

8.3.2 CBEMA Comments

The Computer and Business Equipment Manufacturers Association (CBE-MA) is one of the major trade organizations of the information industry. Not unexpectedly, its concerns paralleled those voiced by its sister organization in the industry, ADAPSO.

The specification of international standards for [ISDN] raises issues and concerns of profound significance for the future of American and worldwide telecommunications services. If properly established, ISDN presents the promise of dramatic progress in telecommunications capabilities, efficiencies and costs. If improperly established, ISDN could retard or reverse the Commission's *Computer II* and other pro-competitive policies which have served this nation so well.

There is no reason why international ISDN standards cannot accommodate the Commission's policies governing the provision of basic transmission services, enhanced services and customer premises equipment in this country. On the other hand, there are serious reasons to be concerned that the international forums for addressing ISDN specifications may tend to view standards questions in terms of the monopoly conditions prevalent elsewhere in the world.

Countries in which Postal Telephone and Telegraph (PTT) entities provide all services and equipment on an exclusive end-to-end basis can hardly be expected to be proponents for accommodating the competitive conditions existing in this country. Moreover, notwithstanding the best efforts of our State Department, there are additional reasons to be concerned that the interests of manufacturers and users are not being adequately articulated or represented in the U.S. planning process preparing for international ISDN conferences.

In this context, the Commission's Notice of Inquiry presents a welcome recognition of the high stakes at issue in the ISDN proceedings as well as the important role the Commission can play in crystallizing the U.S. position in preparation for these meetings. Such participation is essential to the effective representation of all U.S. interests in the international meetings.

Aside from the foregoing points of concern...CBEMA's concerns...may be briefly summarized as follows:

- A single set of internationally recognized ISDN standards is needed to permit woldwide compatibility.
- The international standards must be sufficiently flexible to accommodate the *Computer II* and other pro-competitive policies of the U.S.
- A separation of competitive functions from basic transmission services should not be precluded by ISDN standards.
- Users should have the option of interconnecting their own equipment at each of the ISDN reference points.
- A simple basic and user interface should be defined.
- Users should not be precluded from obtaining transparent, basic transmission services in ISDN.
- ISDN standards should not restrict users in their ability to manage their communications systems in which ISDN is an element.
- There will be a continued need for leased channel services. Such services must not be limited or eliminated by ISDN standards.
- The implementation of ISDN requires a carefully conceived transition plan to minimize disruptions and to avoid the stranding of investments by carriers, enhances service providers, manufacturers or users.[23]

8.3.3 IDCMA Comments

The Independent Data Communications Manufacturers Association (IDCMA) is an industry group similar to CBEMA. It also was strongly supportive of the FCC's *ISDN NOI* and "concerned" over current ISDN activities. IDCMA's comments focus fairly narrowly on the basic user-network interface, as well as a perceived domination of US forums by AT&T.

In considering ISDN issues, it is important to keep in mind that other countries' participation in CCITT reflects the views of their national postal telephone and telegraph authorities (PTTs), which operate according to different national policies and which tend to take an expansive view of their telecommunications monopolies. Moreover, U.S. contributions to international ISDN planning are heavily influenced by AT&T and its subsidiaries. AT&T and the other carriers which participate in ISDN planning share, at least to some extent, the PTTs' interest in sweeping additional functions into the telephone network.

What concerns IDCMA is that CCITT planning efforts have largely focused on two possible interfaces between the user and the network (interfaces at the "S" and "T" reference points). Current draft ISDN recommendations presuppose that the carrier, not the customer, will control certain equipment located at the customer's premises. But this is precisely the type of equipment which IDCMA members manufacture and which the Commission has recently determined should be classified as customer-premises equipment (CPE) for purposes of U.S. regulatory policies.

Despite the Commission's decision to permit customer control of functions up to the transmission wires themselves (which dictates a need to define the "U" interface), CCITT activities have focused solely on the "S" and "T" interfaces. As a result, the interface specifications needed to permit ISDN to be implemented consistently with U.S. policies have yet to be addressed.

Specifically, IDCMA suggests that the Commission seek to persuade CCITT participants to define specifications for the "U" interface, for use in those countries which choose to permit full CPE competition.[24]

8.3.4 AT&T Comments

AT&T, at the outset of its introduction, characterized the proceeding as "unnecessary in that it would: (1) duplicate the work of the USCCITT, and (2) detract from USCCITT's efforts to secure an international ISDN model which is compatible with US policies." "In such a fluid atmosphere it is important that the USCCITT be able to obtain expeditious policy guidance from the FCC, which would not be possible should an ISDN rule-making be employed to develop US ISDN positions."[25]

AT&T then proceeded to comment generally on the CCITT ISDN standards, their impact on the US, and the appropriate role of the FCC. A terse conclusion made the point:

AT&T submits that current CCITT ISDN standards proposals are consistent with U.S. telecommunications policies, and that existing forums are adequate to ensure that U.S. policies will continue to be properly advanced in international forums. Accordingly, AT&T submits that the Instant Notice of Inquiry should be terminated, and that the Commission should continue to work in the existing USCCITT process to ensure that U.S. ISDN proposals will remain consistent with U.S. policies.[26]

AT&T's rather detailed appendix to their comments attempted to address each question posed by the FCC in the *ISDN NOI*. In nearly every answer, AT&T suggested that procedurally and substantively few significant problems had arisen. The following two responses are illustrative.

The significance of the interrelationship between CCITT's bearer/ telecommunications dichotomy and basic/enhanced service dichotomy of *Computer Inquiry II* is that, if adopted, it will theoretically facilitate the ability of U.S. carriers to provide a bearer service in compliance with the Commissioner's definition of a basic service. While the importance of this correlation between the CCITT system architecture and the Commission's basic/enhanced dichotomy cannot be judged completely at this early stage in ISDN development, it would appear that CCITT recommendations based upon such constructs are more likely to be consistent with U.S. policy than if they were based on a system architecture completely at odds with such policy. For example, it would appear that standards formulated in conformance with the analogy between basic and bearer services would facilitate their interconnection.

Even if the CCITT ultimately adopts a bearer/telecommunications services dichotomy that is not wholly consistent with the basic/ enhanced services dichotomy of *Computer Inquiry II*, there may well be sufficient flexibility in CCITT standards to allow U.S. carriers to provide basic services consistent with the CCITT's definition of a bearer service. However, because the ISDN model is still evolving, it is possible that the international standards ultimately adopted will prevent or impair the ability of U.S. carriers to provide a basic service via an ISDN. This is the type of potential adverse effect that the Commission and other USCCITT participants should work to avoid.[27]

U.S. users, service providers and equipment manufacturers should benefit from ISDN. ...ISDN will offer users increased operational flexibility at potentially lower costs. For example, ISDN will allow the user to access, through a limited number of standard interfaces, a multiplicity of service providers, offering basic transmission capabilities as well as enhanced applications, locally, nationally, and internationally. In addition, because ISDNs will rely on a limited number of standard interfaces, terminal equipment is expected to be "portable," i.e., it will be able to be bought, sold, and used worldwide. Thus, the user will be able to move from one service provider to another without having to incur the expense of obtaining new equipment. The portability of terminal equipment should result in increased competition among service providers; also, because ISDNs will rely on relatively few standard interfaces, competition among terminal equipment vendors can be expected to increase. As a direct result, the users of ISDNs will have the freedom to choose from among multiple sources of network services and terminal equipment at competitive prices, in concert with the overall cost efficiencies of digital transmission.

Equipment and service providers would also benefit from ISDN. Because an ISDN interface is designed to support many network services, the same network or terminal equipment can be manufactured for a variety of applications (e.g., circuit switched or leased 64 kb/s services). These factors allow the equipment provider the market opportunity to expand production and increase revenues. Also, ISDN ensures that the network service provider has access to a large body of end users, similarly enlarging his market opportunity and revenues.[28]

8.3.5 The BOCs' Comments

The newly divested Bell Operating Companies filed extensive comments that were similar in character to those of AT&T. Both procedurally and substantively, they saw no significant problem with the existing ISDN work. However, the BOCs devoted considerably more attention to the basic user-network interface. This is not surprising because it is the BOCs that will largely be providing this interface. The importance of a stable, uniform standard for this interface was emphasized. The BOCs then raised what they believed were erroneous FCC decisions in the *NCTE* and *Digital Protocol* proceedings. The following comments are illustrative.

Thus, interface standards play a significant role in the overall architecture of ISDNs. From a *user's perspective*, they permit selection of terminal equipment, transport and other services from a range of competitors without changes in equipment or use of special adapters, and pave the way for universal, Information Age telecommunications services. From a *manufacturer's perspective*, interface standards permit high volume, low cost production of terminal and network components which are focused on user oriented features and which can be made with assurance that they will be compatible with the equipment across the interface. From a *transport provider's perspective*, ISDN interface standards permit flexibility in selection of suppliers, consistent OA&M procedures, technical innovation and evolution within its network without customer involvement and a wide variety of customer applications which will use ISDNs. From a *service provider's perspective*, ISDN standards will simplify access since end users would not be required to buy special arrangements or terminal devices in order to gain access to particular services.[29]

The [NCTE decision] in its particular realization, seriously limits the CCITT ISDN principle which specifies that the interface on customer premises between the user's equipment and the network be one of the small family of standard interfaces. This principle is seen as essential to worldwide availability for network and customer equipment compatibility and the interoperability of ISDNs and thus is supportive of the Commission's pro-competitive policies. Under the approach taken in the recent digital NCTE decision, the interface on the customer's premises between the user's equipment and the network would be technology dependent (e.g., copper wire, fiber optics, digital radio). Network providers would tend to use the technology which minimizes network costs. However, they may be constrained by user reaction when the user's equipment is not compatible with a change in network technology. This reaction would slow or possibly prevent the deployment of ISDNs in the U.S. — a result which could lead to erosion of the leadership position the U.S. has enjoyed in the telecommunications field. In any event, portability of terminal equipment would certainly suffer in a situation where interfaces were technology dependent. Further, as discussed in the digital NCTE proceeding, effective maintenance would require joint customer/network procedures.

As to the protocol conversion of network signalling, CCITT-ISDN standards neither prescribe nor preclude protocol conversion as a network function and therefore they are not in conflict with FCC decisions in this matter. However, a basic principle of ISDN architecture is that users (i.e., customers) access the network by means of a digital message-oriented signalling procedure (or protocol) which supports a wide variety of services, such as telephone, telex, videotex, and access to existing (e.g., the GTE Telenet and Tymnet packet networks) and planned networks supporting dedicated services, such as packet data transport. The ISDN principle further suggests that while each of the services accessed may be implemented either within, or external to the ISDN, those implementations themselves could be optimized, using unique protocols internal to the ISDN and optionally selected access protocols. In fact there may be differences in the network signalling protocols employed by various users. From a user's perspective, it would be more efficient to allow a variety of devices/networks to use ISDN and to have it provide the necessary compatibility. The ability for ISDN to provide for various devices/networks may be required both during transition to and in a mature ISDN network. The latter is due to the differences in the communications needs of various users who will want to exchange information with each other and due to innovations in both the connecting terminal equipment and networks.[30]

8.3.6 IBM Comments

Because ISDN represents the integration of telecommunication and information systems, the interests of the major information systems manufacturer, IBM, were certainly implicated. IBM never characterized its precise interests as a party to the proceeding, but three general goals and nine specific points were set forth.

I.   The CCITT Draft Recommendations should be modified to accommodate U.S. pro-competitive telecommunications regulatory policies.
   A.   The CCITT Draft Recommendations should be modified to accommodate U.S. policy requiring competitive provision of CPE.
   B.   The CCITT Draft Recommendations should be modified to accommodate U.S. policy requiring separation of basic and enhanced service offerings.
   C.   The CCITT Draft Recommendations should be modified to accommodate the unbundled offering of services provided over the signalling channel.
   D.   ISDN tariffs should accommodate U.S. policy incorporating cost-based pricing of basic transmission services.
   E.   The CCITT Draft Recommendations for ascertaining interoperability should be modified to accommodate the U.S. equipment registration program.
   F.   CCITT Recommendations should accommodate the competitive provision of basic transmission services.
II. ISDNs should be designed to expand rather than constrain user choices.
   A.   The CCITT Draft Recommendations should be revised to ensure the continued availability of leased circuits.
   B.   The CCITT Draft Recommendations should be revised to provide for a simpler user interface.

C.   The CCITT Draft Recommendations should be revised to ensure continued user system management capability.

III. The Commission should actively seek to ensure that ISDNs accommodate U.S. regulatory policies.[31]

The issue dealing with use of the *D*-channel, a matter of substantial long-range importance, was uniquely addressed by IBM. In addition, the issue of user system management, perhaps *the* most important long-range issue, was well articulated. Both are set forth below.

[I]t appears that the CCITT draft Recommendations could inhibit the offering of packet-switched services over the signalling channel except by carriers on a bundled basis. The draft Recommendations currently provide for the transport of user information over two "B channels," and for exclusive carrier use of a "D channel" for network signalling. But the Recommendations also envisage the offering by carriers of packet-switched services over the D channel, because that channel would not be used to full capacity for signalling purposes.

The fact that the proposed ISDN model provides for a possibly underutilized channel does not justify bestowing on carriers the competitive advantage of exclusive access to a channel for provision of packet-switched services. The D channel, like the current local loop, will be a bottleneck facility whose availability for other than signalling purposes on reasonable, unbundled, nondiscriminatory terms must be assured. Making that facility available for exclusive carrier use would severely handicap the ability of other service vendors to offer for local distribution competitive packet-switched service over a D channel may have an efficiency appeal, that "efficiency" should not be gained at the cost of excluding or greatly inhibiting competitive provision of packet-switched services.[32]

Current technology permits users effectively to manage and improve the overall efficiency of their networks. System faults can be diagnosed and corrected. Yet CCITT deliberations to date have devoted little attention to the need for users to be able to manage their own networks through use of performance optimization and fault isolation techniques, and such matters have been left for further study. Any failure of CCITT Recommendations to accommodate users' ability to manage their own networks would retard the effectiveness of user and manufacturer efforts to improve efficiency and to locate and resolve operational problems. In addition, a failure to accommodate user system management capability will increase the burdens on carriers who will be required to devote greater efforts to communicating with customers to diagnose and solve operational difficulties.[33]

8.3.7 GTE Comments

GTE Service Corporation activities encompass common carrier operations, equipment manufacturing, and the provision of information services. It had been significantly involved in shaping ISDN Recommendations for several years, second only to pre-divestiture AT&T. GTE's "position" appeared similar to, but less strident than, AT&T's.

GTE agrees with the Commission that there could be many versions of digital networks and that a lack of uniformity in technical standards would require equipment manufacturers to construct, and some users to buy, equipment tailored to meet each differing standard. ISDN efforts are aimed at preventing this situation. GTE supports the goals of the ISDN planning process which are "to permit national ISDNs to interconnect and form a worldwide system or systems and... [to] promote ubiquity of terminal equipment used therein."

GTE urges that the Commission — and the U.S. interests which could be affected by the ISDN specifications — continue to play an active role in the CCITT process to help ensure that U.S. pro-competitive policies are reflected in the final CCITT ISDN Recommendations. With the proper guidance, GTE believes the implementation of ISDNs will have a beneficial effect on users, service providers and manufacturers, in addition to enhancing national security interests. In its review of the CCITT ISDN recommendations, the Commission should keep an open mind on the ISDN's customer interface point and appropriate regulatory demarcation points. The implementation of ISDNs in this country should be left to the competitive U.S. interest involved, with any detailed technical problems decided in an open forum such as the ANSI committee process. Finally, the Commission should realize that significant resources have been invested in the implementation of ISDNs, and if the Commission finds it necessary to provide additional policy direction to this implementation, it should do so quickly.[34]

8.3.8 SBS Comments

Satellite Business Systems (SBS) voiced concerns that were representative of satellite system operators.

> [E]xcessively restrictive interface requirements and allowances for link or circuit impairments could effectively block or severely inhibit satellite communication providers. Commission expressions of interest in this area, cooperatively explored with other CCITT participants both domestically and internationally, would be one step in ensuring that ISDNs are designed to accommodate the U.S. competitive scheme.[35]

8.3.9 NTIA Comments

The National Telecommunications and Information Administration (NTI-A), an agency within the Department of Commerce, has a mandate to formulate and advocate Executive Branch views on both domestic and international telecommunication and information policy. For a number of years, one of its technical staff in the Institute for Telecommunication Sciences (ITS) subdivision at Boulder, Colorado, was very active in CCITT groups dealing with digital systems, and chaired the USCCITT ISDN joint Working Party since its inception in 1981. Several months prior to the FCC's issuance of the *ISDN NOI*, NTIA had also included a contractor produced section in its Report to the Congress on Long-Range Goals in International Telecommunications and Information. NTIA had an institutional incentive to file comments in the FCC's proceeding.

NTIA divided the issues into five major categories: integration of voice and data — who benefits and who pays; network interconnection; *Computer II*, the AT&T divestiture, and ISDN; the effect of the standards process in U.S. policy interests; the role of satellites in ISDN; and private leased lines.[36] NTIA did not address domestic policy making issues in its comments, except obliquely in its conclusions.

> Our representatives at the CCITT and other forums have worked hard to advance U.S. communications policies, to the extent developed and known.[37]

However, the comments filed by many other parties in the *ISDN NOI* made it rather evident that one of the major domestic ISDN problems

involved the failure of USCCITT forums to adequately develop and make
known those U.S. communications policies in an ISDN context. Indeed,
NTIA in its reply comments admitted:

> Other commentors cited [NTIA addressed issues] and a variety
> of other policy concerns which have not been, and perhaps cannot
> be, adequately addressed within the technically oriented mechanism
> of the USCCITT Joint Working Party and its technical working
> group.[38]

8.3.10 MarTech Comments

MarTech Strategies is the company name used by Ronald S. Eward of
Indialantic, Florida. For some years, Mr. Eward has done contract reports
on emerging telecommunication and information issues for diverse entities,
including for purposes of this subject, NTIA.* Although not a participant
in ISDN forums, he proffered nominally independent observations on ISDN
issues. His executive summary is reproduced below.

The ISDN — A Technological Restructuring of Telecommunication
Networks, Services, and Markets

The ISDN may be viewed as tantamount to a technological
restructuring...of telecommunication facilities, networks and services. These changes...will have important effects, direct and indirect.

Both of these changes — the technology and the collateral market
restructuring — are [at present] evolving largely independent of
formal regulatory oversight and certainly not incorporated into
legislative rewrite efforts nor have they been considered in conjunction with the AT&T Consent Decree Modification. However, the
Federal Communications Commission has finally released its long-
awaited Notice of Inquiry on ISDN. Thus, it is conceivable that
formal regulatory oversight over these matters will improve.

ISDN's Elements — Restructuring Forces

Essentially, the technological restructuring...implied by the
ISDN era arises from three basic elements, each subject to definition
and change.

---

*See, e.g., R.S. Eward, *The Competition for Markets in International Telecommunications*
(Artech House, Dedham, MA, 1984) and *The Deregulation of International Telecommunications* (Artech House, Dedham, MA, 1985).

The transition to integrated services digital networks depends upon three basic changes, which are both the subject of discussions within the CCITT and the result of independent events occurring in several countries:

Element 1:   The use of *common* digital pathways for transmission *switching* and *signalling* of voice, data and images which travel from end-user to end-user wholly in digital form.

Element 2:   The incorporation into network nodes of digital storage and processing equipment which allows for a range of enhanced information and communication services.

Element 3:   The re-ordering of functions and protocols (between nodes and customer-premises equipment) within a system whose architecture prescribes terms and conditions of user access and interface, performance and of multiple carrier/service provider interconnection.

Broad international agreement has been reached regarding the first set of changes (common digital transmission, switching, and signalling), although the particulars will take many years to negotiate. Notwithstanding, there are still conflicts that need to be resolved such as the incompatibility of using two signalling methods — CCITT Signalling System No. 7 and LAP-D.

There is no such broad agreement on approaches to the second set of changes (incorporated storage and processing). Nations will differ on where the functions should be provided and who will provide them. Fortunately, it is at least recognized now that appropriate interfaces may need to be defined to higher layer functional (HLF) entities.

eDuring 1983, much work has been done toward a consensus on the third set (structuring of the network). Draft Recommendations have been prepared; for user/network interfaces; architectural functional models; protocol reference models; hypothetical reference connections and others. There are still important differences among Administrations and substantial issues not yet sufficiently addressed such as service and network interworking interfaces and policies.

ISDN's Implications

The issues involved in ISDNs are extremely broad; the definition of services and their terms of delivery; the organization and structure of telecommunications (and its relationship to data processing); the terms of customer and third-party access; terms of interconnection for multiple carriers or service providers; national and global tariff structures; national and global equipment and service markets. This list is not inclusive of all issues or concerns. One general example illustrates the gravity of the problems spawned by ISDN technology. There is a tendency in international discussions to view and speak of the ISDN as just that — *the* ISDN to which users and *others* will access via standard interfaces.

Access and interconnection issues will be critical aspects of pro-competitive policies in the ISDN environment, both domestically and internationally. An environment of multiple ISDNs, mutually compatible and interoperable, must be a prime concern to U.S. policy makers and industry. Interconnection to foreign country ISDNs — where there will be just one ISDN per country for many countries — is a related aspect of this concern.

Most importantly, tariff policies and principles for the ISDNs have not been formulated (though studied on a limited basis) during this plenary period. Consequently we have a situation where service standards may be adopted and actual services initiated without development of ISDN tariff principles.

Consequently, tariff principles and issues would be decided, *de facto*, by the first organization offering ISDN services (or expedient ISDN-like services).

In summary, the FCC is faced with the reality that equipment and service standards and services will be readied for implementation in 1984 yet important areas *critical* to pro-competitive policies are left for discussion in the *next* plenary period (1985–1988). These include the *vital* area of network interworking and interconnection, and tariff principles. In the U.S. context, the FCC faces an additional major dilemma in reconciling the ISDN service structure with the FCC-defined market structure.[39]

8.3.11 NECA Comments

The National Exchange Carriers Association (formerly the Exchange Carriers Standards Association (ECSA)) described how it was formed and the important role it will play in United States ISDN matters.

The Exchange Carriers Standards Association (ECSA) is an association voluntarily established by members of the wireline exchange carrier industry to address technical interconnection and other standards issues in the post-AT&T divestiture telecommunications environment. AT&T has traditionally performed or sponsored joint industry activities to develop and administer common technical standards; however, upon divestiture of the Bell Operating Companies (BOCs) on January 1, 1984 or thereafter, dominance over such activities by a single firm is neither likely nor desirable. Yet...there is a continuing need for common interface standards for interconnection and interoperability among the various independent providers of telecommunications services and equipment. ECSA was formed to meet this need in a prompt, efficient manner and to provide for representation of the various groups interested in the interconnection standards formulation process.

[Representatives of exchange carriers] agreed to form the ECSA as an association of the exchange carrier industry.

In summary, the positions and views of the ECSA are as follows:

The ECSA, as now constituted and organized with the proposed T1 Committee, is the most appropriate forum and organization for the needed development of voluntary technical interconnection standards by private industry;

No direct FCC regulatory involvement in the interconnection standards formulation process is necessary or desirable; and

The development of interconnection standards pursuant to ECSA/ANSI organization and procedures is fully consistent with antitrust principles and policy.[40]

8.4 The First Report on ISDN

On 30 March 1984, the FCC met at a regular open meeting, heard a presentation on the *ISDN First Report* agenda item before them by Common Carrier Bureau staff member Michael J. Slomin, and adopted it without comment. In the sections below, the many policy analyses and observations of the *Report* are largely organized by generic ISDN divisions: introduction, network aspects, user-network interfaces, services, role of the FCC, and conclusion. This is done to group the material in the manner in which the CCITT deals with ISDN issues. The tendency for the FCC to always analyze these developments in *Computer II* terms is less useful than the CCITT approach.

8.4.1 *The Introductory Summary*

One significant event had occurred between the adoption of the *First Report* and the filing of the reply comments — the Study Group XVIII annual meeting of experts at Brasilia. The event was significant enough to be mentioned in the introduction of the *First Report*, together with a brief report on the favorable responses to many of the concerns that had surfaced in this proceeding.

> [I]t might be noted that the existence of this proceeding, and the preparation of thoughtful and comprehensive comments by the parties, appears to have had a salutary effect on ISDN evolution during its pendency. For example, issues of significant concern to virtually all commenting parties involved the continued availability of dedicated leased channels, the ability to select multiple service vendors in the multiple-vendor United States telecommunications market, and the development of ISDN classifications which accommodate the basic/enhanced service dichotomy of *Computer II* (and its related structural and regulatory effects). Great strides were made in the ongoing ISDN planning efforts in Geneva, Switzerland, in Kyoto, Japan and in Brasilia, Brazil, to refine the evolving CCITT international ISDN recommendations to address these issues, in part because the United States delegations were sensitized to these issues and were adequately prepared by the comments to address them in depth.[41]

Also mentioned in the introduction of the *First Report* in a kind of "good news, bad news" format were the general character of the comments filed.

> We have received comments in this proceeding which represent a broad spectrum of interests, specifically, those of user groups, exchange and interexchange carriers, enhanced service vendors, equipment manufacturers, the data processing community, and government agencies. As will be discussed below, there are areas of broad and virtually universal consensus: that ISDN represents a natural and desirable next step in the evolution of telecommunications; that our overall national pro-competitive policies are desirable and important, and that implementation of ISDN within the United States should be consistent with these policies; that the FCC has tentatively defined an appropriate role for itself in the evolution of ISDN; and that it is important to ensure that as ISDN is implemented, the benefits of existing services, primarily dedicated leased channels, are not lost.[42]

Comments by AT&T and the Bell Operating Companies suggest that the specific *Computer II* implementations of the overall competitive framework might require refinement in an ISDN environment, but they are supportive of the overall thrust of *Computer II* to promote the competitive benefits of unregulated provision of customer-premises equipment and enhanced services.[43]

There is somewhat less consensus on specific Computer II-related issues which have arisen in the domestic and international ISDN planning processes. AT&T and the Bell Operating Companies argue for more flexibility in the application of *Computer II*, while others urge that the *Computer II* policies are appropriate and that any reconciliation with ISDN planning which may be necessary should be accomplished through the introduction of additional flexibility in the ISDN concept. [One commentor, MarTech Strategies, goes so far as to recommend that in the light of the development of ISDN, the Commission institute a "computer III" proceeding.[44]] The *Computer II* issues include: the treatment of network channel terminating equipment (NCTE) as unregulated customer-premises equipment, and the related absence of an appropriate ISDN interface to which unregulated NCTE might be connected; the treatment of protocol conversion and processing as provision of enhanced service (requiring structural separation of these activities and related facilities by AT&T and the Bell Operating Companies under Computer II); and the development of ISDN service classifications which are compatible with the basic/enhanced service dichotomy of *Computer II*.[45]

Also noted was the tendency of some parties to raise more detailed ISDN issues than the ones posed in the *NOI*.

Other rather technical ISDN issues were raised in comments because this proceeding represented an additional forum in which such issues might be raised, e.g., whether ISDN should evolve to accommodate both active and passive bus structures at the interface, whether power should be provided from the interface towards the equipment or system connected therewith, whether the specified bit rates for switched ISDN channels adequately accommodate the capabilities of digital equipment presently used in the United States, whether efficiencies promised by newer digitized voice equipment might be foreclosed, bit rate specifications, etc.[46]

8.4.2 User-Network Interface Issues

Issues associated with the basic user-network interface that arose in the proceeding fell into three categories: general comments, the D-channel usage (raised by IBM) and the U interface. The last category received the greatest attention by far, largely because of the attention focused on the matter by the *NCTE Decision*.

General Comments

Several comments argue that draft CCITT recommendations specify a user/network interface which is, in their view, needlessly complex. There are two dimensions to this concern. First, to the extent that the "interface" in this context is thought of as encompassing a requirement that functions be included within the customer-premises equipment to be connected to the loop facilities (including "NT1" and "NT2" equipments or their functions), unnecessary costs could be imposed on the customer-premises equipment to the extent that it includes functions which are not used, but which might be included in the ISDN recommendations to support a full range of ISDN services.

[Footnote 36] Comments of ICA (which urges adoption of a simple basic interface capable of accommodating both switched and non-switched services) and IBM (which argues that the ISDN interfaces have been structured with relative universality for a full range of ISDN services, with the result that they are needlessly complex and include unnecessary functions when subscribers in fact choose to utilize only a subset of the ISDN services available). IBM is concerned that a complex ISDN interface might not prove to be as well suited for transmission of data as for voice. When this concern is read against its substantive comments in favor of non-modification of our NCTE decision, it is clear that IBM is restating in an ISDN-focused manner its fundamental concern during the course of the Second Computer Inquiry that inclusion of functions in the networks which support data communications could, in some circumstances, adversely affect the efficiency of data processing unless any limitations inherent in these functions can be avoided by users (and the suppliers of the equipment they use).

This approach would be at odds with our consistent Part 68 approach to governmentally-mandated equipment standards (as opposed to voluntary ones adopted for other purposes). The Part 68 requirements (and, in some circumstances, comparable ones

contained in carrier-initiated tariffs) specify only technical limitations which prevent "harm," and not ones which address the efficiency or utility of the connection. A simple analogy will demonstrate this. Our Part 68 rules impose voice-band signal power
maximums (for other than live voice) to limit the potential for
interference with others' channels (loop and interexchange); they do
not impose signal power minimums. Obviously, if the signal power
is insufficient, communications will not occur. The marketplace, and
voluntary standardization to some extent, have ensured that terminal equipment generates sufficient signal power to be useful. If ISDN
has a range of capabilities and the user chooses only to utilize some
of them, an interface to the full range of capabilities would not be
necessary. Just as our Part 68 processes would not require the user's
equipment actually to be capable of communicating, ISDN recommendations should not be interpreted as requiring the termination
equipment to include functions which are not actually to be used
by the termination.[49]

Use of the D-channel

A second dimension to this concern relates to ISDN planning
which would limit the users to which the ISDN channels might be
put. For example ISDN includes a "D channel" primarily intended
to be used for signalling, and if this specification is viewed by carriers
as binding on their ISDN implementations or ultimate offerings to
the public, it might not be made available for alternative uses. While
the Commission would probably view this issue as a use-of-service
restriction, it might be framed as a "technical" one through the
vehicle of specification of the network interface. Furthermore, hardware and software limitations at a central office could through
technical means limit office termination of that channel were connected solely to signalling equipment.

We do not have sufficient information before use on this [use of
the D channel] to reach a judgement on the merits. Telephone loops
today have far more bandwidth than the nominal 4 kHz voiceband
transmissions that they are generally used to support, yet it has not
been argued that we should mandate that carriers make the additional bandwidth available to subscribers. To do so would engender
investment in additional facilities by carriers. Implementation of
ISDN implicitly involves complex cost/benefit tradeoffs in the
design and costs of loop plant, central office facilities and premises
equipment, and very complex considerations of how to evolve
towards ISDN when present facilities are largely 4 kHz analog ones.

It may be that use of the "D channels" for other than signalling might be relatively inexpensive; but it also may be that restrictions of these channels to signalling might promote a less costly transition from existing offerings to ISDN. This information has not been provided, and we regard this issue as one which might be pursued in the future [footnote omitted].[50]

The U Reference Point and NCTE

In June, 1983, the Commission clarified that digital NCTE is customer-premises equipment within the meaning and policies of the *Second Computer Inquiry*, and that it therefore is to be provided on a competitive unregulated basis no differently than other customer-premises equipment ...ISDN planning efforts have assumed that a device denominated to the "NT1"will be provided as part of the loop facilities, and only the interface to that device, denominated the "T" interface, will be specified. [Indeed...it has been assumed that much of the equipment which is to be connected with the termination of an ISDN loop is to be connected through additional terminating equipment, i.e., the "NT2". Some administrations have assumed that they will be providing both "NT1" and "NT2" equipment, perhaps combined in a single unit.] [In the United States,] the "NT1" equipment, if located at a customer's premises, is NCTE.

Our NCTE decision as applied to ISDN implicitly requires that an interface to the input of the "NT1" be established. Stated alternatively, our NCTE decision requires that there be established an interface to the loop, to which customer-premises equipment (including any "NT1" device or device which includes the functions of the "NT1") may be connected. At an earlier stage of the ISDN planning process such an interface was discussed (it was denominated the "U" interface), but this interface no longer appears in the CCITT ISDN planning documents.[51]

[I]t appears clear than an interface to the loop facilities (i.e., at the input to the ISDN "NT1") will be required to facilitate the provision of equipment or capabilities comparable to the "NT1" by subscribers in the United States. Since ISDN planning has been directed towards arriving at relatively uniform international recommendations governing ISDN, it may prove appropriate for the CCITT to arrive at a suitable definition of a "U" interface to facilitate this. [B]ut if the CCITT fails to do so, one or more appropriate domestic "U" interfaces could be arrived at for use in the United States, through carriers initiatives in their tariffs and technical references, through voluntary standardization activity, or, if related to protection of the facilities from "harm", through Commission rulemaking processes (i.e., our Part 68 processes). To avoid potential confusion and inconsistency of domestic implementations of ISDN with the international recommendations, it would be desirable for the international ISDN planning efforts to include sufficient flexibility as they evolve to accommodate the "U" interface concept. Therefore, we urge that this matter be pursued in the continuing ISDN planning efforts.[52]

8.4.3 Issues Related to Services

The third category of ISDN issues dealt with in the *First Report* are those related to the provision of services. Neither the comments nor the *First Report* fully exploited the full range of service issues. Instead, the focus largely revolved around two matters related to the *Computer II* basic/enhanced dichotomy (the effect on the US regulatory environment due to the manner in which the CCITT and ISO distinguish between services in their models), and dedicated private line service. The subject of private lines gave rise to greater expression of concern than any other matter. This was reflected in the inordinate number of paragraphs in the *First Report* devoted to the subject.

Use of CCITT's Basic/Teleservice Model

In the following four paragraphs, the *First Report* attempts to suggest a nexus between the CCITT's basic/teleservice distinction and the FCC's basic/enhanced, as well as an "accommodation" of the latter by the former.

It was argued in a number of comments that ISDN planning efforts had, at the time the comments were prepared, envisioned ISDN as encompassing a melange of basic and enhanced offerings which appeared largely inseparable. As we observed in the Notice, CCITT planning documents classified ISDN in two categories of offerings, the so-called "bearer" services which appeared largely to include what we would term basic services under *Computer II*, and the "telecommunications" services which included operations on protocols which we would classify as enhanced under Computer II. We sought comment on whether this bearer/telecommunications split approximated the basic/enhanced dichotomy of *Computer II*. While there is some disagreement in the comments on this point, it appears that such an approximation was not present.[53]

The requirement that underlying basic offerings continue to be available to the public is a fundamental *Computer II* policy, applicable not only to carriers subject to structural separation, but to all carriers. Therefore, it is important that the ISDN plans include sufficient flexibility to accommodate the regulatory structure of the Communications Act which, as interpreted by *Computer II*, limits Title II regulation to basic services. In this regard, the results of the recent Brasilia meeting may have created such flexibility.

At Brasilia, the previous "bearer" and "telecommunications" service classifications were modified in a manner which appears better to accommodate the basic/enhanced service dichotomy of the United States — but without in any way impeding the flexibility of other administrations to pursue different policies. [Rec. No. I.200] now establishes a single overall ISDN service category, "telecommunications", which includes two subcategories, "bearer" services and teleservices". The "bearer" services category now includes together services such as MTS, telex and private line which would be classified as basic under the *Computer II* decisions, although this category also encompasses protocol operations which might constitute some "bearer" services as enhanced. The "teleservices" category includes operations on protocols (and possibly databases) which, if provided over common carrier facilities in the United States, would classify the offerings as enhanced services.

While it appears that not all of the offerings now encompassed under the "bearer" category would be basic, the changed ISDN definitional structure at least now appears to treat together the services which we would classify as basic, minimizing potential conflict between the international ISDN efforts and domestic *Computer II* policies.[54]

Use of the ISO's OSI Model

Entwined with the definition of services issue, is the utility of using the International Organization for Standardization's Open Systems Interconnection model. This issue was extensively considered in the FCC's *Protocol Decision* which is mentioned here.

ADAPSO argues at lengththat while the Open Systems Interconnection (OSI) model may be useful as a starting point for designing an ISDN network architecture, it should be used neither to draw distinctions between basic and enhanced, nor to determine those services that must be performed as part of the network and those which may be offered separately. We reached a similar conclusion in the *Protocol Decision*.

A potential problem with use of the OSI hierarchical model was a basis for the design of ISDN communications offerings, which was raised analogously in ADAPSO's comments on the inadequacy of permanent virtual circuits as a substitute for dedicated leased circuits, is that the network processing of protocols invoked as the OSI hierarchy is traversed, may serve as a limitation on the use of the information transmission capabilities made available to users. The OSI model involves great agility at each step of its hierarchy, but to some degree, communications efficiency could be sacrificed in the achievement of this agility, by the requirement that each layer of the OSI model be traversed sequentially. It is not our function to make the design choices which are involved in a decision whether or not to utilize the OSI model as a basis for design. We note that while the OSI model has been used as a starting point for configuration of ISDN architectures, proposals that considerably modify or interpret the model have been presented for ISDN planning. To the extent that this model drives the design choices of carriers in implementing what we would classify as basic services (including the processing associated with call initiation, routing, flow control and cessation which we clarified in the *Protocol Decision* as associable with basic service), the carriers are free to make such choices. Implementation by enhanced service providers of the OSI model is their choice, since they are not regulated.

We are committed to the policy that basic services be improved through the introduction of new technology, including public switched services (which are the most prevalent basic services available to, and used by, the public). Public switched telecommunications services have efficiencies, through the sharing of common facilities. Butthere are also efficiencies associated with the use of dedicated private line services. And, if it develops that those that implement ISDN using a specific control, signalling or other model provide less efficient communications capabilities, the continued availability of unencumbered basic offerings including private line will ensure that other approaches may be used. Absent this policy, if it were to develop that implementation of the OSI or other architecture were undesirable or inappropriate, no alternatives might then be available.[55]

Provision of Dedicated Private Line Services

This subsection of the *First Report* began with a statement of the obvious — most of the commenting parties were concerned about the continued provision of dedicated private line services.

At the time the *Notice* was adopted, it was unclear whether the
ISDN planning efforts to date were directed toward a conceptualization of ISDN which would replace dedicated private line (or
leased channel) services, or whether ISDN would develop along with
traditional private line offerings. As a sub-element, ISDN included
"permanent virtual circuit" line offerings, and in the *Notice*, we
requested comment on whether permanent virtual circuits might be
an adequate substitute for dedicated private line offerings.

A dedicated private line is available at all times for its user's use,
and it does not require use of a routing protocol within the telecommunications network, or with attached terminal equipment, for
its use. In contrast, a number of alternatives are available which
appear initially to be somewhat like private line These alternativesdo
not involve the provision of dedicated circuits. They involve use of
facilities shared among a multiplicity of users.

Virtually all the comments and replies stress the importance of
maintaining the availability of dedicated private line offerings (and
in some cases, only analog ones), notwithstanding the creation of
new ISDN alternatives, for various reasons. Because this issue
proved so important to those filing comments, in this section of our
report we are specifically summarizing the points made as a preclude
to our discussion of our perception of this issue.[56]

The *First Report* then digresses to clear up an ambiguity contained in the
Notice.

[I]t is important to note that there was some conceptual confusion
in the comments, caused by the way we framed this issue and by
some ambiguity in the CCITT ISDN planning documents at the time
the comments were prepared. In more recent planning documents,
ISDN is envisioned as encompassing two groups of offerings, circuit-
switched offerings (including non-switched "permanent" or dedicated offerings) and packet-switched offerings. The circuit-switched
category has three sub-elements: immediate service (i.e., public
switched circuits switched together for the duration of a call upon
demand, much as MTS operates); reserve service (i.e., advance
reservation of a circuit-switched circuit together for the duration of
a call upon demand, much as MTS operates); reserve service (i.e.,
advance reservation of a circuit-switched circuit to ensure its availability during the prearranged time period); and permanent service
(channels which bypass circuit-switching capabilities). The last of
these is dedicated private line or leased circuit service. [S]ince it is
not clearly encompassed in the ISDN planning documents, the

fundamental question whether substitution of new alternatives to dedicated private line would adequately serve user's needs has been answered. [I]t is not contemplated that dedicated private line offerings will necessarily be discontinued as a consequence of the emergence of ISDN.[57]

The packet-switched category currently has two primary subelements: immediate service, and permanent virtual circuits. However, the distinction between these is not the same distinction as arises in the circuit-switched category, as both of these are switched services. In packet-immediate service, an initializing packet is used to inform the packet network of the ultimate destination of ensuring packets (including full destination address information), and the network returns a virtual circuit number to be [prefixed] to each ensuing packets. [This] consumes less overhead than transmission of the entire destination address. [I]n essence, the virtual circuit number is an abbreviated "dialing" code to be used for the duration of the call on a packet-by-packet basis. In packet-permanent service, the virtual circuit number is preassigned to the subscriber and an initializing packet is unnecessary. Thus, when we requested comment on the comparability of only one of the packet-switched subservices (permanent virtual circuits), we evoked comments not only on the fundamental question of whether there is a continuing need for dedicated private line services, but also on whether any packet-switched offering is comparable with private line, or whether any other "demand" leased line alternative is comparable with private line.[58]

After attempting to clear up this confusion, the comments of the parties on this subject were extensively reviewed. The *First Report* then develops a rationale based on past decisions, especially *Computer II*, for requiring the availability of private line services in the United States. This series of paragraphs ends with a rather interesting footnote (included in the fourth paragraph, below) developing and underlying legal argument to backup the policy determination.

Under the Communications Act, common carrier offerings must be generally available upon request. [T]hese offerings must be reasonable. [A]nd they must be made without unjust or unreasonable discrimination. We have consistently interpreted these statutory mandates as requiring common carrier offerings to be made available in a manner which maximizes consumer flexibility in the use of such offerings. [This has promoted] the efficiency of the many enterprises which depend directly or indirectly upon telecommuni-

cations. [C]onsumers have had the flexibility, through the use of
their own terminal equipment, communications facilities and en-
hancements, to optimize their specific uses of generally-offered
common carrier communications.

In *Computer II*, we interpreted these mandates as requiring that
basic common carrier offerings, unencumbered by protocol processing which created an enhanced service, continue to be offered
generally, so as to support a wide range of unregulated data and
information processing and terminal equipment uses.[59]

The comments on the lack of comparability of virtual circuits to
dedicated private line (or leased channel) services convince us of the
wisdom of these United States policies in favor of consumer choice
and general offerings of unencumbered basic communications capabilities. Most of the comments conclude that virtual circuitsand
other alternativesare not comparable to private line service on
technical grounds. Several comments note that network operations
on protocols are associated with virtual circuits, i.e., processing to
set up the virtual circuit as needed, and that this processing denies
some flexibility and efficiency in the usage of the virtual circuits.
Other comments urge that the technology of a digital ISDN intrinsically denies flexibility now present in the use of analog private line
services, i.e., because of the amplitude and time quantization associated with a digital transmission technology.

While AT&T, the BOCs and GTE implicitly argue that ISDN
implementations of virtual circuitsmay adequately serve many subscriber needs which are today satisfied with private line services, it
is significant that many of the users themselvesare unwilling to be
made totally dependent upon this value judgement. The users accept
the claim that ISDN may satisfy some of their needs, but they
strongly urge that dedicated private line services remain available
if ISDN implementations of alternatives in fact do not do so for
technical or economic reasons. The data processing communi-
tyargues strongly that the intrinsic limitations of virtual circuits
could unacceptably impede the efficiency of information processing,
as compared with private line. Also significant is that AT&T and
the BOCs themselves recognize that ISDN may not adequately serve
all current private line service needs.

We view these arguments as sound. It is clear that while packet-
switched service have utility for relatively low-speed "bursty" voice
or data communications, they are not as efficient as dedicated
private line services for high-speed non-"bursty" communications

because of the overheads associated with packet transmission. More broadly, our *Computer II* unbundling principle would best be served by the continued availability of dedicated private line services notwithstanding the emergence of packet-switched and circuit-switched ISDN alternatives, and we would urge the United States delegations to the CCITT to continue to make this point. [Furthermore, Section 214(a) of the Act might have applicability if there were a broad scale discontinuance or impairment of dedicated private line services, in view of the strenuous arguments of users and others that the public convenience and necessity would not be served by substitution of ISDN alternatives for private line. *See*, ITT World Communications Inc. v. New York Tel. Co., 381 F.Supp. 113 (S.D.N.Y. 1974).] In this regard, we commend the efforts of our delegations and the CCITT groups which revised the ISDN working documents more specifically to ensure the concept that dedicated private line services will coexist with and be a component of ISDN offerings.[60]

8.4.4 Network Aspects

Only two network issues were contained in the comments and considered in the *First Report* — addressing and satellite network paths.

Addressing

A very clear example of a "technical" issue with broad policy implications relates to addressing (and routing) of messages. If it is assumed that a single service provider will be providing service in a given country, it is reasonable to arrive at a message-routing numbering framework which does not have the capability of addressing multiple providers of service. This approach has been followed, for example, in the international number plan for telephone service [CCITT Rec. No. E.163] where, for the United States, there is assigned a single digit country code (0 or 1) followed by the normal ten-digit national number. Multiple providers of telephone communications from international gateways to domestic United States subscribers cannot be selected under this approach. We note, however, that for public data networks a plan had been implemented which allows for the selection of alternative domestic data service providers [CCITT Rec. No. X.121]. Currently, an assigned four-digit Data Network Identification Code (DNIC) is to precede an up-to-ten digit domestic network terminal number. In the case of the

United States, about 30 such DNIC codes have been assigned for use with important that the ISDN numbering plan not foreclose selection of multiple service providers.

We are gratified to note that it has been recognized that multiple vendor addressing is inherently required in an ISDN plan, not only to accommodate the multiple carriers and enhanced service providers of the United States market, but also to accommodate non-governmental providers of databases and local area networks in those administrations where telecommunications is otherwise a governmental PTT function. Thus, the current ISDN recommendations drafted in Brasilia set as an objective the establishment of a single worldwide ISDN numbering plan by enhancing recommendation E.163 and retaining X.121 numbering structure. The draft recommendations also provisionally limit the international ISDN number to a sequence of fifteen decimal digits. Since our current United States telephone network uses ten decimal digits (as does the TWX network), it would appear that an additional five digits (i.e., 100,000 alternative selections) could accommodate sufficient multiple suppliers even though the additional five digits must be shared on a worldwide basis.

Thus, it would appear that reasonable flexibility could be attained to ensure that the fundamental numbering plan definition does not frustrate the workings of a multiple-vendor United States market. This will require that efficient coding techniques be incorporated into the numbering plan with the five-digit constraint, so that sufficient numbers of alternative vendors are selectable. It would appear that effective United States participation in the appropriate CCITT Study Groups responsible for the development of further recommendations in this area will be essential. However, this is but the first step in movement toward implementation of ISDN in a manner which actually promotes a multiple-vendor environment. Sequential or hierarchical coding techniques will be required in the international or domestic plan (or both) to permit calls to select among multiple service providers, and to select routing.[47]

Use of Satellite Paths

[T]here are differences between satellite and terrestrial facilities, economically and technically. The former has costs which are distance-sensitive and which may support some simultaneous point-to-multipoint transmissions more economically than terrestrial transmission. But, the satellite mode also has transmission delays. If transmission is largely unidirectional, these delays may be unimportant or unnoticeable. If transmission in conversational, these delays may be significant. From our perspective, it is desirable that subscribers have the ability to make decisions between these modes on a given call or group of calls to optimize their communications, rather than for such decisions to be made for them through unnecessary technical limitations.

Thus, we endorse the comments of COMSAT and ASC that unnecessary technical limitations should not be introduced in ISDN to foreclose the possibility of multiple satellite "hops" on a given connection. When we were confronted with an analogous claim in the mid-1970s that the public would not, for conventional voice communications, accept the delays of multiple "hop" service, we concluded that to the extent that there may be differences, users should have the opportunity to choose the service attributes they require, without being foreclosed from making such a choice. Satellite Facilities for Communications Services, 61 FCC 2d 139 (1976). A similar principle should apply in the case of ISDN.[48]

8.4.5 The FCC's Role

Perhaps the most politically sensitive and complex aspect of the FCC ISDN proceeding was the role that the FCC would assert in future CCITT related forums. There were strong opposing views among both the private sector and the federal agencies. Some factions desired substantial, vigorous participation; others wanted little or none. Layered on top of this domestic dispute were international relations concerns. Some felt that substantial FCC involvement would seriously impede the flexibility of US delegations to CCITT meetings, or might lead to statements or positions that might offend PTT officials in other countries. The latter had recently occurred in the context of a 1980 *Resale and Shared Use* proceeding. The text of the *First Report* addressing this issue was carefully drafted to avoid offending anyone. The section began by describing the international and domestic ISDN "planning process."

[T]he ISDN planning process has been somewhat amorphous. Generally, the CCITT has assumed a major role in coordinating ISDN plans worldwide through the development of ISDN Recommendations. While such Recommendations are not binding on any administration in a legal sense, they have more than mere advisory status in practice, and often are treated as standards to be conformed to. A major role of CCITT Recommendations is to establish standards for the effective interworking of national networks at the point(s) of their interconnection. Absent common electrical signals, protocols and operational procedures, effective interworking is not possible. While such matters can be (and often are) worked out bilaterally between the networks to be interconnected, it has long proven desirable to arrive at suitable standards on a multilateral basis in the CCITT. Increasingly in recent years, the CCITT technical and operational standardization process has been extended beyond the point(s) of interconnection, to the services and facilities which ultimately are interconnected for international communications. Thus, in ISDN planning, Recommendations have been drafted to govern not only interconnection of national ISDNs, but seemingly to govern the design of the national ISDNs themselves.

The FCC's domestic policy on analogous issues of standardization has been generally not to adopt governmentally-mandated technical standards which are relevant to the performance of telecommunications facilities, and to limit such standards to those that directly achieve statutory purposes, in an effort to minimize regulatory impediments to innovation and design flexibility. If a new design approach arises in a manner different than existing standards contained in governmental rules, the rules themselves generally require modification before the design can be deployed, resulting in an impediment to innovation. For example, we have been moving away from standard on radio transmitting equipment which go to the use of such equipment and limiting standards on radio equipment in our rules to those that address interference. And, as noted previously, in the telephone equipment registration program we have established limits on equipment design solely to protect against "harm", without establishing standards addressing the utility or efficiency of registered terminal equipment. It has been the position of the FCC that performance standards may be desirable, but that they should be non-governmental voluntary ones adopted under the auspices of organizations such as those accredited by the American National Standards Institute (ANSI).

ISDN planning, particularly at the international level, is somewhere between these two models. As noted, while the CCITT "Recommendations" are just that, they are often treated as binding in many administrations, or by their governmental PTTs. Indeed, some administrations incorporate CCITT Recommendations in procurement and manufacturing specifications. Thus, while the United States might not pursue such a standardization model domestically, it must operate in a world community which pursues such a model internationally. Because of this, the private sector and the United

States government participated variously in CCITT deliberations in general, and its ISDN deliberations specifically.[61]

A variety of technical and other fora address ISDN planning the United States in formulating our national inputs to the CCITT, including technical organizations, voluntary standardization organizations and trade associations. However, since actual full membership in the CCITT is limited to government, the Department of State ultimately represents the United States government in that organization. [T]he Department of State has established an advisory committee (the U.S. CCITT Organization) to serve as a vehicle for seeking advice from the private sector and from other government agencies in performing its CCITT representational role. This advisory committee has served as the focal point for coordinating United States positions on ISDN to be advocated in the CCITT, through its ISDN Joint Working Party and an ISDN technical subgroup, the Technical Working Group. In the *Notice*, we tentatively concluded that telecommunications policy issues may be implicated by ISDN plans, a view which has been confirmed in the comments herein. Assuming this, we sought comment on the appropriate role of the FCC in the planning process — a role not of making or influencing decisions on the technical characteristics of facilities and services, which decisions are properly made by the private sector, but of identifying policy issues as they arise to ensure that they are adequately addressed in the technical and other judgements to be made.[62]

The Commission then sets forth five points that describe the role it expects to play in ISDN matters.

First (and foremost), it is not the function of this Commission to plan or to design carrier's and others' ISDNs.

Second, it is clear that the technical and other judgements involved in ISDN planning can and do raise policy issues, often issues relating to decisions previously reached by the FCC.

Third, given that ISDN planning may raise policy issues, we must consider how best to address such policy issues.

Fourth, our conclusion that formal FCC proceedings should not be instituted to address ISDN issues is predicated on the view that the various domestic groups involved in informal ISDN planning should employ open procedures which ensure that those with an interest in their activities have an opportunity to participate in their deliberations effectively, what might be characterized as fundamental fairness.

And *fifth*, we believe that continuation of this informal inquiry
proceeding as a vehicle for solicitation of public comment on the
ISDN policy issues which likely not be resolved in the current
CCITT plenary cycle would be desirable.[63]

Two of the footnotes in this section are rather important and worth noting.
It is not uncommon to place statements in the footnotes that significantly
expand upon or emphasize more general comment found in the main body
of the text.

Although considerable deference may be given by the Department
of State to the recommendations of the U.S. CCITT Organization
advisory committee, presidential orders bear on the FCC's role in
this process. Under these orders, "the Secretary of State shall
coordinate with other agencies as appropriate, and in particular,
shall give full consideration to the Federal Communications Commission's regulatory and policy responsibility in this area." Exec.
Order No. 12046, 43 Fed. Reg. 13349, para. 5-201 (Mar. 29, 1978),
as *amended* by Exec. Order No. 12148, 44 Fed. Reg. 43239 (July
24, 1979). Thus, this responsibility of the Department of State, and
the possibility that the FCC may advise the Department directly,
which is always present, ensures that policy concerns of the FCC
will be weighed in the deliberations of the various domestic ISDN
planning bodies.[64]

The above statement quoted from the executive order that provides *the*
basis for the FCC, Department of State, and the Department of Commerce/
NTIA sharing the responsibilities and authority in the field of international
telecommunication policy. In radio matters, the order has been used to
exercise substantial control over all ITU-related activities in the United
States. In non-radio matters, for a variety of largely historical reasons
discussed in Chapter 2,[65] this control has not been exercised. Its placement
here acts as an important reminder that the FCC does indeed have considerably more authority in the matter than it was then exercising.

The second footnote addresses what was widely viewed as one of the more
vexing attributes of the ISDN Joint Working Party's method of operation.

[A] procedure under which participants may bring to meeting for
discussion and approval, massive and complex technical documents
not previously seen by the participants, might not accord with this
concept. While flexibility should be retained to address the exigen-
cies of extraordinary circumstances, we would suggest that these
groups establish as a procedural norm that submissions of this

nature will ordinarily not be considered unless previously distributed to the participants so they may participate effectively in the discussion.[66]

8.4.6 Conclusions

The *First Report* concluded with several short paragraphs that attempted to summarize the entire proceeding to date.

[W]e view this proceeding as having served the valuable purpose of focusing the attention of the industry and of government on the policy implications of ISDN planning. Many issues raised in our *Notice* and in comments have been resolved successfully in the ISDN planning which continued during the pendency of this inquiry. Other issues have been raised which will require resolution in ISDN planning and possibly in the United States regulatory process in the future. This inquiry has served to place the affected public on notice of these, and has started the process under which these issues too may be resolved.

It is clear from the comments and our analysis that the FCC has an institutional interest in the ISDN planning process, because the results may be subject to the regulatory process in the future, and because it is possible at an early stage to seek to ensure that the planning incorporates sufficient flexibility to accommodate important United States telecommunications policies. In this report, we have emphasized the strong domestic bias in favor of voluntary standardization by the private sector, not government. However, we have acknowledged that internationally a somewhat different model is pursued. Thus, while the United States probably would not impose standards on the many technical matters now being addressed in CCITT ISDN planning, a process which by virtue of the governmental provision of telecommunications in many countries is largely a governmental one, it is important the CCITT Recommendations which are treated as binding by other administrations be consistent with important interests of the United States public in commerce, defense and foreign policy. For this reason, we conclude that the United States should participate effectively in the ISDN deliberations of the CCITT.

At the same time, we have sought to arrive at a role for the FCC in this process which promotes the statutory objectives of the

Communications Act and the public interest generally, but without
impeding the evolution of ISDN. We have concluded that the
advisory committee processes of the Department of State and the
processes of voluntary standardization organizations such as the
ECSA/T1 Committee provide an opportunity for the policy implications of largely technical ISDN planning judgements to be addressed. Through informal participation in these processes by the
FCC and its staff, we believe that these policy issues can appropriately be resolved. And finally, while we have rejected the option of
subjecting ISDN planning to the rigidities of the formal rulemaking
process, we have concluded that the informal inquiry procedure used
in this proceeding can be valuable as an additional forum for
addressing policy issues in the future — as circumscribed above —
and for that reason we are not terminating this inquiry.[67]

REFERENCES

1. *See* 5 U.S.C. sec. 554 (1976).
2. *See* Part 1 of the FCC's Rules and Regulations, 47 C.F.R. Part 1.
3. *Notice of Inquiry* [in GEN Doc. No. 83-841], FCC 83-373, 94 FCC 2d 1289 (1983) [hereafter referred to as the *ISDN NOI*] at para. 2.
4. *Id.* at 1290, para. 3.
5. *Id.* at 1294, para. 14.
6. *Id.* at 1296-97, para. 21.
7. *Id.* at 1297, para. 22.
8. *Id.* at 1297, para. 23.
9. *Id.* at 1297-98, para. 25.
10. *Id.* at 1302-3, paras. 40-42.
11. *Id.* at 1303, para. 43.
12. *Id.* at 1303-4, para. 44.
13. *Ref.* page 233, below.
14. Rec. I.130 CCITT Red Book (1985).
15. *ISDN NOI, supra,* at 1305-6, paras. 49-50.
16. *Id.* at 1306-7, paras. 54-55.
17. Although the Appendix to the *First Report* lists both the US Department of Defense (DOD) and International Telephone and Telegraph
(ITT) as commenting parties, the official docket record does not
indicate that ITT filed any comments, and characterizes the Defense
Communication Agency's submission as an "Intent to File Comments."
18. Number of pages in document. Additional number indicates the
number of pages in an appendix containing supplementary comment.

19.   The selection of comments presented here does not imply that those submitted by others are any less useful in fully understanding these issues or should be given less weight in reaching any conclusions.

20.   *ADAPSO Comments* at 2-4.

21.   *ADAPSO Comments* at 13, 15.

22.   *ADAPSO Comments* at 5-39.

23.   *CBEMA Comments* at 1-4.

24.   *IDCMA Comments* at 3-4.

25.   *AT&T Comments* at 3-4.

26.   *AT&T Comments* at 18-19.

27.   *AT&T Comments*, Appendix at 11.

28.   *AT&T Comments*, Appendix at 18-19.

29.   *BOC Comments* at 9-10.

30.   *BOC Comments* at 20-22.

31.   *IBM Comments* at 6-30.

32.   *IBM Comments* at 16-17.

33.   *IBM Comments* at 27.

34.   *GTE Comments* at 2-3.

35.   *SBS Comments* at 5.

36.   *See NTIA Comments* at 4-30.

37.   *NTIA Comments* at 30.

38.   *NTIA Reply Comments* at 3.

39.   *MarTech Strategies Comments* at 2-3.

40.   *ECSA Comments* at 2-6.

41.   *First Report*, 98 FCC 2d 249, 254, para. 10 (1984).

42.   *Id.* at 253, para. 7.

43.   *Ibid.*, at note 14.

44.   *See Id.* at 254, note 16.

45.   *Id.* at 254, para. 8.

46.   *Id.* at 254, para. 9.

47.   *Id.* at 255-57, paras. 13, 15-16.

48.   *Id.* at 257-58, paras. 17-18.

49.   *Id.* at 262-63, paras. 27, 28 and note 36.

50.   *Id.* at 263-64, paras. 29-30.

51.   *Id.* at 259-60, para. 22-23.

52.   *Id.* at 261-62, para. 26.

53.   *Id.* at 265-66, para. 35.

54.   *Id.* at 269-70, paras. 42-44.

55.   *Id.* at 271-72, paras. 45-47.

56.   *Id.* at 272, paras. 48-49a.

57.   *Id.* at 272-73, para. 50.

58.   *Id.* at 273, para. 51.

59.   *Id.* at 278, paras. 58-59.
60.   *Id.* at 278-80, paras. 60-62.
61.   *Id.* at 280-81, paras. 63-65.
62.   *Id.* at 281, para. 66.
63.   *Id.* at 284-88, paras. 75-84.
64.   *Id.* at 287, note 87.
65.   Reference page 25.
66.   *Id.* at 287, note 88.
67.   *Id.* at 289-90, paras. 87-89.

IV Future ISDN Developments

All of the issues and developments described in the preceding chapters are part of a continuum. The ISDN forums continue to grow and evolve. The CCITT Recommendations are expanded and amended as the various study groups and working teams carry on with new and old Questions through the 1985–1988 activity period. The Federal Communications Commission amends old policies and creates new ones, and, perhaps most importantly, ISDN facilities are actually brought into existance on an increasingly wide and more sophisticated scale.

In the final two chapters of this book, some of these future developments are considered, concluding with an overview on ISDN and the integrated information system environment.

CHAPTER 9 — LOOKING TO THE FUTURE

This chapter looks to ISDN's future. It is divided in somewhat the same fashion as the preceding chapters, looking at both the CCITT activity and potential FCC actions based on the public statements of the commission and commissioners in early 1985. In addition, some of the details of ISDN-like service offerings are mentioned.

Over a period of very few years, ISDN has changed from an esoteric and rarely heard subject to a household word in the telecommunication community. In 1985, it is rare to see a telecommunication trade publication that does not contain an article or advertisements concerning some ISDN development. The future for ISDN looks bright indeed, but some issues remain as vexing as ever.

9.1 CCITT 1985–1988 Activity Period

The Eighth CCITT Plenary Assembly at Malaga-Torremolinos in October 1984 took several actions that are important for future ISDN work. One of the most notable, albeit subtle, changes was the election of the former Chairman of Study Group XVIII and the veritable godfather of the ISDN concept, Theodore Irmer, to the position of Director of CCITT.

Mr. Irmer's new position is more than symbolic because the CCITT was also significantly restructured to give a number of its study groups a part of future ISDN work, as depicted in Table 1-1 in Chapter 1. The dominant function of CCITT became the study of ISDN matters. This is also reflected in Table 9-1, which lists all the ISDN related Questions for the 1985–1988 activity period. Many study groups other than Study Group XVIII now have important new ISDN issues that they will be studying.

This trend to orient the CCITT around ISDN may be furthered in the future. The Eighth Plenary Assembly established a special Study Group S for examining the possible major restructuring of the CCITT, as well as a Preparatory Committee (PC) for the 1988 World Administrative Telegraph and Telephone Conference (WATTC-88). WATTC-88 adds an important new dimension to ISDN work because of the potential for that conference to embody ISDN concepts in a treaty instrument which would govern certain telecommunication arrangements among the ITU's member nations.

Table 9-1
Questions Relating to ISDN in the 1985–88 Activity Period

Study Group COM I (Definition, operation and quality of service aspects of telegraph, data transmission and telematic services)
15/I   Definition and operational aspects of ISDN

Study Group COM II (Operation of telephone network and ISDN)
11/II   Human factors issues related to the Integrated Services Digital Network (ISDN)
17/II   Development of the World Numbering Plan for telephone and ISDN application
19/II   Evolution of the telephone routing plan in the ISDN era
31/II   Reference models for ISDN traffic engineering
40/II   Dependability of telecommunication networks

Study Group COM III (General tariff principles including accounting)
22/III   Tariff and accounting principles for the ISDN

Study Group COM IV (Transmission maintenance of international lines, circuits and chains of circuits; maintenance of automatic and semi-automatic networks)
11/IV   Transmission measuring equipment and associated maintenance test access lines
J/IV   Maintenance of digital links and maintenance of ISDN's

Study Group COM V (Protection against dangers and disturbances of electromagnetic origin)
[None]

Study Group COM VI (Outside plant)
[None]

Study Group COM VII (Data communication networks)
9/VII   Support of X-series interface DTEs in an ISDN and new interface aspects for data services in ISDNs
10/VII   General principles of interworking
13/VII   Interworking between circuit-switched public data network (CSPDN) and Integrated Services Digital Network (ISDN)
14/VII   Interworking between packet-switched public data network (PSPDN) and Integrated Services Digital Network (ISDN)
25/VII   Principles of maintenance testing in public data networks
26/VII   Maintenance and operation of international links between two public data networks
28/VII   Integration of satellite systems in data communication networks
29/VII   Quality of service in public data networks
31/VII   Numbering plan for public data networks
43/VII   Layers 1-4 of the Reference Model of Open Systems Inter-Connection for CCITT applications
46/VII   Requirements and arrangements for the provision of data services in ISDN

Study Group COM VIII (Terminal equipment for telematic services)
20/VIII   Terminal characteristics and protocols for Telematic services on ISDN
26/VIII   Teleconferencing protocols

Study Group COM IX (Telegraph networks and terminal equipment)
[None]

Study Group COM X (Languages and methods for telecommunications applications)
[None]

Study Group COM XI (ISDN and telephone network switching and signalling)
7/XI   Layer 3 of the digital access signalling system
8/XI   Data link layer of the digital access signalling system
9/XI   Switching functions and signalling information flows for implementation of basic and supplementary services
14/XI   Interworking with land, maritime and aeronautical mobile communications systems
16/XI   Signalling requirements for new transmission equipments
18/XI   Definitions for switching and signalling

Study Group COM XII (Transmission performance of telephone networks and terminals)
5/XII   Speech synthesis/recognition systems
18/XII   Transmission performance of digital systems

Study Group COM XV (Transmission systems)
3/XV   Equipment for digital transmission of television signals
11/XV   Acoustic echo control
14/XV   Equipment used in the transition period from the analogue to the digital networks
24/XV   Characteristics of digital line systems for use in local network
25/XV   Digital equipments for local broadband networks
27/XV   Characteristics of PCM multiplex, ADPCM multiplex and other terminal transmission equipments for voice frequencies.
28/XV   Characteristics of digital multiplex equipment and multiplexing arrangements for telephony and other signals
29/XV   Characteristics of 32 kbit/s ADPCM/PCM transcoding equipment
30/XV   Performance characteristics of PCM and ADPCM channels at voice frequencies
31/XV   Digital circuit multiplication equipment

Study Group COM XVII (Data transmission over the telephone network)
1/XVII   Supplement to the vocabulary for data transmission
11/XVII   Support of DTEs with V-series type interfaces on an ISDN
13/XVII   Interchange circuits
yy/XVII   Interconnection of ISDNs and/or PDNs with modem equipped terminals on the PSTN

Table 9-1
(Cont'd)

Study Group COM XVIII (Digital networks including ISDN)

1/XVIII	General question on ISDN
2/XVIII	Definition of service principles
3/XVIII	ISDN architecture functional model
4/XVIII	ISDN protocol reference model
5/XVIII	ISDN connection types
6/XVIII	ISDN-ISDN internetwork interfaces
7/XVIII	Internetworking of ISDNs and other networks
8/XVIII	Numbering and addressing principles
9/XVIII	Charging capabilities in an ISDN
10/XVIII	ISDN routing principles
11/XVIII	General aspects of user-network interfaces
12/XVIII	Layer 1 characteristics of ISDN user-network interfaces
13/XVIII	General aspects of quality of service and network performance in digital networks including ISDN
14/XVIII	Performance objectives for errors and short interruptions
15/XVIII	Performance objectives for timing and controlled slips (synchronization), jitter and wander and propagation delay
16/XVIII	Call and packet processing performance
17/XVIII	Availability performance of digital networks including ISDNs
18/XVIII	Maintenance of digital networks including ISDNs and ISDN digital subscriber lines and subscriber equipments
19/XVIII	Vocabulary for ISDN and general digital network aspects
20/XVIII	Definition of parameters at the network side of NT equipment
21/XVIII	Characteristics of digital sections
22/XVIII	Interworking between different systems based on different standards
23/XVIII	General aspects of interfaces in digital networks
24/XVIII	Network aspects of existing and new levels in the digital hierarchy
25/XVIII	32 kbit/s speech coding
26/XVIII	Wideband speech coding for 64 kbit/s digital paths
27/XVIII	16 kbit/s speech coding
28/XVIII	PCM coding laws according to Recommendation G.711
29/XVIII	Encoding for stored digitized voice
29/XVIII	Network considerations of PCM/ADPCM transcoding equipment
30/XVIII	Digital circuit multiplication (DCM)
31/XVIII	Speech analysis/synthesis techniques
32/XVIII	Speech packetization

9.1.1 Future Study Group XVIII Activity

Study Group XVIII's work in the 1985–1988 activity period will be shaped in large measure by the Questions adopted at the Plenary Assembly. (Reference Table 9-1.) Many of these are similar to those of the previous activity period, although the structure is now tied closely to that of the I-Series Recommendations. Some of the changes and additions, however, are worth noting.

One of the most significant new developments of the new activity period is reflected in Question 2 on ISDN services, which states that "broadband services are attracting increasing interest and due attention should therefore be given to their study."[1]

New Question 9 begins to confront the matter of "charging capabilities in an ISDN." In a rather remarkable understatement, Question 9 suggests "that charging information in ISDNs may be of interest to the user," and proceeds to frame three questions:

1. What characteristics and service capabilities of ISDN could have an impact on charging and tariff principles?
2. What are the network implications of the charging and tariff requirements on ISDN?

3. What network capabilities (and possible mechanisms) would be required for providing charging information to the users (where such information is to be provided)?[2]

Study Group XVIII's Question 9 is closely tied to Study Group III's Question 22, which deals with "tariff and accounting principles for the integrated services digital network."[3]

In the first of what might be considered privacy related issues, Question 10 on routing principles asks the "use to be made of information provided to the network on the services involved and on the addresses of the users."[4]

Both Questions 11 and 12 on user-network interfaces and the layer 1 characteristics refer to the possibility for and advantages of optical fiber interfaces and solicits the effect on the I-400 Series Recommendations.[5]

New Question 20 solicits "the requirements for and the desirability of the definition of parameters at the network side as seen by NT equipment?" This, of course, is the CCITT response to the contentious *NCTE Decision* in the US.[6]

New Question 23 broadly examines the subject of interfaces in ISDN and other digital networks. It points out that new interfaces for different applications may be necessary.[7]

9.1.2 The Study Group XVIII ISDN Experts Meeting, London, January 1985

The first Study Group XVIII meeting of the new activity period was held in early 1985. If it was any indication for the rest of the period, the study group will have considerable difficulty in completing its work during the scheduled meetings. Seventy-four delayed documents were tabled at the meeting. The one week scheduled for the meeting did not appear to allow for sufficient review of the material.

Because of a recent emphasis in Europe on the development of broadband ISDN systems oriented around fiber optic networks capable of transporting high definition television, many contributions were received on this subject.[8] At the meeting, the view was urgently expressed that clarification of the question was necessary. Were broadband services to fit into ISDN itself or would they constitute a separate overlay network? The majority of the delegates believed that total integration of broadband services in ISDN could be achieved.[9]

A small task group prepared a report on ISDN broadband aspects, detailing the characteristics of broadband bearer services and channel types.[10] Bit rates between several Mbit/s and 140 Mbit/s were specified, and the channel type "H4" was proposed.

WATTC-88 was also discussed, with issues relating to service definitions and tariffs earmarked for consideration in preparation for the conference.[11]

9.1.3 The Preparatory Committee/WATTC-88 Meeting, February 1985

By its resolution No. 10, the Plenipotentiary Conference of the ITU (Nairobi, 1982) decided that a World Administrative Telegraph and Telephone Conference should be convened immediately after the CCITT Plenary Assembly in 1988 to consider proposals "to establish, to the extent necessary, a broad international regulatory framework for all existing and foreseen new telecommunication services."

A large part of the move for this conference was certainly tied to the changes that had long since taken place in the CCITT itself. In the 1960s and 1970s, the CCITT had begun to assume jurisdiction over all telecommunication matters except those narrowly related to radio. It has since become the paramount ITU organ, engaging in by far the most important and greatest volume of work. At the Nairobi Plenipotentiary Conference this change was recognized by actually stating the CCITT's broad jurisdiction in the ITU's charter. Entwined with this was a desired to also replace the conceptually outdated Telegraph Regulations and Telephone Regulations with a new general treaty instrument.

The WATTCs are typically short affairs, ratifying the work that has been essentially finalized during the previous four years within the CCITT. Toward this end, the Eighth Plenary Assembly of the CCITT established a WATTC-88 Preparatory Committee (PC), which met for the first time at Geneva in February 1985.[12]

Notable contributions were made by the Nordic countries who were instrumental in calling for the conference and shaping its agenda, and by the US who submitted a complete draft set of International Public Telecommunication Regulations.[13] The US draft was carefully constructed to conform to domestic policy under which non-basic telecommunication services are not regulated. It would be very unlikely that the US would be a party to any new Regulations to the contrary.

Most countries attending the meeting seemed to share the view that applications oriented telecommunication services were so intrinsically dynamic that these services should not be defined or otherwise dealt with in the new Telecommunication Regulations.[14] The applicability of ISDN work was obvious, and described in a document prepared by the Chairman of Study Group XVIII.[15]

9.2 Potential Federal Communications Commission Actions

Chapters 7 and 8 discussed in considerable detail the many proceedings and policies of the FCC that have a bearing on ISDN developments. In early 1985, the tremors presaging a regulatory eruption on one of its major policies were experienced. During the course of making several *Computer II* related decisions, several Commissioners at the public meetings were heard to call for significant, if not fundamental, revisions to existing policy, with the staff promising a rapid response. Indeed, the items adopted reflected this sentiment.

Upon instituting the proceeding to eliminate AT&T's structural separation for the provision of CPE, discussed in Chapter 7, section 7.1, the FCC explicitly excluded the subject of enhanced services. At both the beginning and the end of the item, the FCC stated: "we are deferring until a later proceeding the issue of whether AT&T's provision of enhanced services should continue to be subject to structural separation."[16]

Four weeks later, upon granting a conditional waiver to the BOCs to provide certain protocol conversions, the FCC again stated:

> Our experience with this [Protocol Waiver] proceeding suggests the need for a different approach to treating problems of protocol conversion. We would be remiss if we did not use the record compiled here as a base to minimize or eliminate uncertainty for the future. Accordingly, in a forthcoming notice of proposed rule making we will seek to formulate general rules of future applicability to govern the treatment of protocol conversion and similar enhanced services."[17]

Nine weeks later, upon adopting a declaratory ruling on Centrex services, the FCC again stated that it would treat the North American Telecommunications Association (NATA) petition for a declaratory ruling, instead as a petition for rulemaking. The commission remarked that "[w]e will soon adopt a Notice of Proposed Rulemaking which looks toward possible changes in the treatment of enhanced services, Section 64.702(a)."[18] A footnote amplified slightly on this subject: "The forthcoming proceeding will address the kinds of enhanced services involved in the [Centrex] proceeding and will also deal with questions relating to the treatment of protocol conversion under Sec. 64.702(a)."[19]

During these public commission meetings, Commissioner Dennis R. Patrick, among others, was an ardent advocate for fundamental change in the *Computer II* doctrine. At a major trade association meeting during this period, he made a presentation outlining his views on the subject, adding some details.

We need an approach that eliminates the need to resort every five years to a new computer inquiry in which we attempt to draw a new definitional boundary between regulated and deregulated services.[20]

The Commission should protect competition where markets are naturally competitive and, where they are not, acknowledge this fact and regulate. Where regulation is necessary, we should impose only that which is essential to protect the public from abuses of market power.[21]

The BOCs still exercise monopoly control over facilities in local service areas. This justifies continued close scrutiny for potential abuses of market position.[22]

These underlying questions provide the components of the approach we seek and would include at least the following:

First, we must ask certain questions about the market for the proposed service: Is the market for this service competitive? or is it a natural monopoly? Are there inherent barriers to competition, e.g., significant economies of scale, which will tend to lead to a natural monopoly?

If — and this is a crucial condition — the carrier's cost advantages are a function of real economies and not achieved through abuse of its market position, consumer welfare will be promoted by the provision of this service within the network by the carrier. The public interest is advanced by having the service available to the maximum number of subscribers, at the lowest possible price.

Similarly, the Commission must consider whether a service will remain *unavailable* to the general public unless it can be provided within the network on an unseparated basis.

The second set of questions we must ask involves the status of the proposed service provider or "applicant": Does the applicant control facilities upon which its competitors must rely? Does the applicant provide monopoly services or control bottleneck facilities the revenues from which might be used to subsidize competitive services? More generally, does the applicant have the ability or incentive to cross subsidize?

Specifically, we must examine the potential ability to gain price advantages over competitors, not based upon real efficiencies, but upon abuse of market position.[23]

One concern is discriminatory access. Both the RBOCs and AT&T retain control over transmission facilities upon which their competitors rely. [W]e might require the carrier to establish a centralized operational group to process requests from *all* enhanced service providers for customer proprietary information or interconnection to the basic network. We might impose a reasonable delay between public release of proposed network alterations and their implementation. We might also consider requiring the carrier to act as a wholesaler of needed underlying facilities to itself and all its competitors.[24]

[T]he principles which underlie Computer II are sound. [However], we should consider replacing [the basic/enhanced definitional dichotomy] with a straightforward analysis of certain underlying questions, largely economic in nature. The answers to these questions should determine how services are regulated and by whom they are offered. In reality, I believe we are already asking these questions, then trying to frame our decision in terms of the basic/enhanced dichotomy, after the fact."[25]

It is clear that the service dichotomy and its application established under the FCC's *Computer II Decision* are likely to change significantly in the future. The reader who desires to pursue this subject is encouraged to follow the *Computer III* proceeding CC Doc. No. 85-229, initiated by *Notice of Proposed Rule Making,* FCC85-397, adopted on 25 July 1985 and released as this book was going to print.

9.3 Initial ISDN offerings

As soon as it became apparent in about 1982 that the ISDN concept would actually manifest itself in service offerings and equipment in the near future, the fires of speculation were constantly being fed by a few trade press articles and proprietary reports. Canada, France, Japan, West Germany, Sweden, the UK, and the US were all mentioned, and the variables were generally hybrid or full $2B+D$ access, for how many customers, how fast.[26] All the countries were rapidly digitizing all portions of their networks, irrespective of offering ISDN services, and estimates for introduction of initial ISDN access ranged from 1984 to 1990, depending on the country.[27]

Before the I-Series Recommendations were even formally adopted, it became clear that component and equipment manufacturers, as well as network operators, were going to rapidly proceed with ISDN prototypes. In mid-1984, ITT's *Technical Journal* carried an article discussing the detailed development of a four-VLSI-chip set to implement ISDN line termination, complementing the already well advanced development of hardware and software for the implementation of ISDN features on System

12 digital exchanges.[28] This development effort was aimed at German Bundespost's commercial introduction of ISDN to many thousands of subscribers in 1987. Looking even further into the future, and presaging the CCITT's 1985 rush toward broadband ISDN capabilities, was a companion article discussing the switching of 140 Mbit/s signals in ISDN.[29]

By early 1985, announcements of digital exchange switches that supported ISDN were made by most of the major competing manufacturers.[30] Specified 1987 availability dates were standard, although demonstration facilities would be operational almost immediately.[31]

It is interesting to compare the views of ISDN's future by two major, but somewhat institutionally disparate, network leaders: Bell Communications Research (Bellcore) in the US and the Deutsche Bundespost in the FRG. Bellcore envisions the future this way:

> The first step in the evolution to ISDN is the introduction of ISDN capabilities in a number of trial locations. Planning for ISDN technical trials is underway in several Operating Telephone Companies. These early trials are important for several reasons. First they will verify the validity of the proposed ISDN architectures. Second, they will stimulate product development of network equipment and compatible terminals, identify real costs involved in implementing ISDN, raise and resolve operations issues, stimulate network evolution planning, and provide focus to service evolution questions.
>
> Two generic types of trials are being considered. The first of these involves support ISDN basic interfaces from a digital switch in a Centrex configuration. ISDN terminals will have access to the Centrex switch through the ISDN interface with two 64 kb/s B channels for customer information and a 16 kb/s D channel for signalling and customer packet data. Technical planning support for this trial includes developing network switching and access architectures, ISDN technical service descriptions and specifications, and switching and loop systems requirements.
>
> The second type of trial implements an ISDN digital gateway from a digital central office switch to a digital PBX. The digital gateway provides primary rate ISDN access using a channel structure consisting of 23 B channels for customer information and a separate D channel for signalling.[32]
>
> Applied Research's contribution on ISDN is to look beyond current views toward broader bandwidth capabilities. The forward-looking Applied Research efforts are rooted in the near-term standards and architecture being formulated today to ensure that future wideband plans will mesh with the current direction of ISDN.[33]

And in the Federal Republic of Germany:

The Deutsche Bundespost plans to start transition from the digitalised telephone network to ISDN from 1988 onwards. For economic and operational reasons this transition will be a gradual one; that is to say it cannot be expected that complete range of services possible within ISDN will be provided on a nationwide basis right from the beginning. As users require some planning security it is pointed out that those services will be replaced by the new improved ISDN serviced in the medium term will continue to be provided during a reasonable transition period.

This allows the depreciation period of existing terminal equipment to be fully utilised. To be able to check the perfect functioning of all new ISDN components, the Deutsche Bundespost plans to carry out an ISDN pilot project in the local networks of Mannheim and Stuttgart with some 400 subscribers each. The technical equipment is planned to be installed during the second half of 1986. Trial operation will be started in 1987.

At the beginning of the next decade, when optical fibre cables and optical communication systems will be economically competitive, ISDN can be expanded to such an extent that it will be possible to integrate all narrow and broadband services (telephony, data, text and still picture communication, videophony and videoconferences) into the broadband ISDN. ISDN is an essential prerequisite for the introduction of switched broadband services, since the basic ISDN components are also suitable for future broadband communications. Moreover, broadband services basically need the same structure as ISDN. ISDN should therefore be consistently developed into an integrated broadband telecommunication network, mainly by substituting optical fibre cables for the present copper cables and by providing exchanges with the necessary broadband switching capabilities.

Finally, it will also be possible to distribute radio and television programmes over an integrated broadband telecommunication network from 1992 onwards, i.e., the broadband distribution networks, which for economic reasons will be developed separately from individual communications up to that time, could then be integrated into a common universal telecommunication network, the integrated broadband telecommunication network.[34]

The carefully charted paths of these two leaders in the field of ISDN are surprisingly similar. It is clear — *the universal, integrated information network is now being born.*

REFERENCES

1.   Questions allocated to Study Group XVIII (Digital networks including ISDN) for the 1985–1988 study period, CCITT Doc. COM XVIII-No. 1 (1984) at 20.

2.   *Id.* at 45.

3.   *See* Questions assigned to Study Group III (General Tariff and Accounting Principles) for study during the 1985–1988 period, CCITT Doc. COM III-No. 1 (1984) at 38.

4.   *Ibid.*

5.   *Id.* at 46-47.

6.   *Id.* at 115.

7.   *Id.* at 122.

8.   *See* CCITT Docs. COM XVIII-Nos. D.8, D.22, D.24, D.30, D.45, D.56, D.58, and D.71.

9.   *See* Draft Report of Working Team 1 (Services Aspects), ISDN Group of Experts, London, 21-25 Jan. 1985, Temp. Doc. 26 at 4.

10. *Id.* at Annex 4.

11. *Ibid.*

12. *See* Preparation of the World Administrative Telegraph and Telephone Conference, 1988, CCITT VIIIth Plenary Assembly Res. No. 15 (1984).

13. *See* Nordic Countries, Considerations concerning scope and structure of the new regulations to replace the existing telegraph and telephone regulations, CCITT Doc. PC/WATTC-88 No. D.5; U.S.A., Proposed international public telecommunication regulations, CCITT Doc. PC/WATTC-88 No. D.8.

14. *See* Draft Report (1st part), CCITT PC/WATTC-88 Temp. Doc. No. 9 (1985).

15. *See* Capabilities of ISDNs, CCITT PC/WATTC-88 Temp. Doc. No. 7 (1985).

16. *Memorandum Opinion and Order and Notice of Proposed Rulemaking* [in CC Doc. 85-26], FCC 85-56, __ FCC 2d __ (adopted 31 Jan. 1985) at 2, para. 1, and 17, para. 28.

17. *Memorandum Opinion and Order* [in ENF 84-15 *et al.*], FCC 85-101, __ FCC 2d __ (adopted 1 Mar. 1985) at 7, para. 10.

18. *Memorandum Opinion and Order* [in ENF 84-2], FCC 85-248, __ FCC 2d __ (adopted 9 May 1985) at 22, para. 54.

19. *Id.* at 23, n. 39.

20. The Second Computer Inquiry — Revisited, Remarks by Commissioner Dennis R. Patrick at the Communication Network Exposition (Washington DC, 29 January 1985) at 5.

21.   *Id.* at 1.
22.   *Id.* at 4.
23.   *Id.* at 6-7.
24.   *Id.* at 7.
25.   *Id.* at 9.
26.   *See, e.g.*, ISDN Developments in Europe and North America, Logica Ltd. (Sep. 1983).
27.   It is interesting to note that in 1983 Logica predicted that it would be "towards the year 2000 at the earliest...that the telephony based ISDN will be integrated with broadband switching systems." *Id.* at 4. Yet, the next year, in 1984, the German Bundespost would be establishing a 1992 target date for achieving such integration. *See* Development Strategy of the Deutsche Bundespost for the Public Telecommunications System in the Federal Republic of Germany, Federal Minister of Posts and Telecommunications, Bonn (1984).
28.   *See* Dierckx, Guebels and Six, VLSI for the ISDN Line Termination, 58 Electrical Comm. 411 (No. 4, July 1984).
29.   *See* Bottle, Switching of 140 Mbit/s Signals in Broadband Communication Systems, 58 Electrical Comm. 450 (No. 4, July 1984).
30.   *See, e.g.*, Weber, ISDN: ATT Sets Software for 5-ESS Switch in '87; Siemens Demos System, 6 MIS Week 1 (No. 22, 29 May 1985); Siemens Unit to Debut ISDN Digital CO Switch in Las Vegas, Communications Week at 22 (20 May 1985).
31.   *See, e.g.*, AT&T's ISDN Begins its Earthly Descent, 14 Data Communications 45 (No. 5, May 1985).
32.   ISDN in the Operating Telephone Companies, 1 Bell Communications Research Digest 2 (No. 8, Nov. 1984).
33.   Special Feature, 2 Bell Communications Research Digest 5 (No. 1, Apr. 1985).
34.   ISDN — The Deutsche Bundepost's Response to the Telecommunication Requirements of Tomorrow, The Federal Minister of Posts and Telecommunications, Bonn (1984) at 26.

CHAPTER 10 — CONCLUSION

In just a few years, ISDN has evolved from an esoteric concept and dream of advanced information network planners to a set of worldwide standards adopted by CCITT, and finally to the initial equipment and systems of today. This evolution occurred through a level of international and domestic work and cooperation unprecedented in the history of telecommunication.

Just as remarkable is the product — the ISDN Recommendations that represent the first blueprint for integrated information systems on a global scale.

However, this is just the beginning. The field is now clearly riding the exponential curve of change. What is remarkable and new today may well be outmoded in just a few years. For sure, future telecommunication systems will be dramatically different than they are today. Orders of magnitude increases in performance and decreases in cost are likely to continue to occur in the three most significant areas: microelectronics, photonics, and advanced applications programs.

One of the likely results is that information systems of all kinds will become ubiquitous. The intelligence and mass storage capabilities in systems will rapidly increase. At the same time, photonic links of enormous capacity will be implemented. By the end of this decade the voice cognizant, speaking system will be commonplace, clocking away at nanosecond speeds.

Integrated Services Digital Networks (ISDNs) will play a major role in this revolution. However, the nature of that role is unclear, and will certainly vary in different countries, and even within countries, among different users.

It would seem that both internationally and domestically, everyone's interests would be best served by removing many of the facades that continue to impair honest dialogue and more rational regulatory policy.

Starting with the most fundamental matter, it is clear that "telecommunication" networks have in large measure ceased to exist. The networks that exist today are in reality information networks optimized for transport services. The processing and storage capabilities located at the nodes can be shared by others within or outside the network, or they can be used by the network itself to run applications programs. The word "telecommunication" itself no longer has any particular meaning other than to conceptualize the transport of information.

The facades are both international and domestic, although at the moment the CCITT has probably the best conceptual and definitional grip on the matter. However, some of the inconsistencies and questionable material still remain imbedded in the I-Series Recommendations.

At the user-network interface, for example, a "user" is described as "a person or machine delegated by a customer to use the services and/or facilities of a telecommunication network."[1] Yet, in the sections dealing with user-network interfaces, any of the following are described as able to use these interfaces:

- a single ISDN, multiple ISDN, or non-ISDN terminal
- multiservice PBXs
- local area, private, existing telephone or dedicated networks
- specialized storage and information processing centers
- another ISDN
- service providers outside the ISDN[2]

This list clearly encompasses every kind of possible information system.

The time has come to straighten out some of the old distinctions that may have outlived their usefulness. In the new telecommunication environment, terminals can be nodes and users can be networks.

The same applies to the area of services. In the past, there was a kind of standard, very limited menu: telephone, telegraph, telex, facsimile, broadcast radio, *et cetera*. However, in an environment where all the component hardware operates under different application programs that may be swapped in and out from microsecond to microsecond in each information system, or occupy adjacent time slots in a bit stream, the notion of "services" acquires a different meaning.

The I-Series Recommendations are generally a good point of departure on the subject of services. The focus in the Recommendations is properly on a lengthy list of service attributes and generic characteristics available at the interface. This approach, as well as a substantial forbearance on restricting all but the most essential generic Recommendations for higher layer services, would seem not only a technically desirable outcome, but also a policy imperative, which will avoid impeding the potentially inexhaustible creativity of software engineers and information vendors. In the new tele-communication environment, timely and innovative applications software and information will be the stuff of national and world commerce. It is a sound approach with which WATTC-88 should find favor. The ultimate service goal for ISDN should be to enable users to access all the resources available to the network at a price that approaches their actual cost.

Network related notions such as "resale" or "value added" are simply no longer meaningful as either concepts or definitions. In the integrated information systems environment, any one information system (user or network) may instantaneously acquire information transport resources from another system that possess them. It is an intrinsic part of the reality that now exists.

On the other hand, this same reality raises significant questions about overall operational and addressing that urgently need consideration. Much of the current work has been based on the ability to place "networks" and "users," or "public" and "private," in neatly separable boxes, when today the two can be instantaneously functionally interchanged. The significant underlying questions related to making this new environment work effectively and efficiently need to be studied without the burden of outmoded categories and concepts.

The entrepreneurial opportunities for creating and distributing information will be technically unlimited. With this kind of diversity, connectivity, and interoperability, the ultimate marketplace emerges. The price charged for each discrete information attribute should be driven close to its true cost or value. Hidden cross-subsidizations become very difficult to achieve and, if desired, must be overtly created.

The regulation of information systems by government would seem unnecessary except to promote true scales of efficiency, in order to prevent inappropriate market dominance, effect national security or other important societal considerations such as the protection of privacy and intellectual property, or apply criminal sanctions for theft of service. Such societal considerations are certainly not new, only take a different form in this new information environment.

These observations may not be applicable everywhere in the world. However, where they are not, those other places and peoples will surely be affected by these developments. In the long run, everyone should benefit not only by the lower costs, but more significantly by the richer diversity of information that all of us will be able to share among our fellow inhabitants of this world.

APPENDICES

APPENDIX A — BIBLIOGRAPHY

A.1 CCITT Materials

A.2 Published Materials

1981-84 PLENARY PERIOD, REPORTS

Doc. Id.	Date	Source	Questions	Title
XVIII R1	8102	SG XVIII	-	Report on the Inter-regnum Meeting of Experts on ISDN Matters (Innisbrook 12-15 January 1981)
XVIII R2	8107	SG XVIII	1 to 19	Report on the Geneva Meeting (22 June - 1 July 1981)
XVIII R3	8102	SG XVIII	1,2,6	Report of the Meeting of Working Party XVIII/1 (ISDN)
XVIII R4	8107	SG XVIII	7,8	Report of the Meeting of Working Party XVIII/2 (Speech Processing)
XVIII R5	8107	SG XVIII	9 to 14	Report of the Meeting of Working Party XVIII/3 (Network Performance Objectives)
XVIII R6	8107	SG XVIII	3,4,5	Report of the Meeting of Working Party XVIII/4 (Switching and Signalling)
XVIII R7	8107	SG XVIII	15 to 19	Report of the Meeting of Working Party XVIII/5 (Digital Equipments)
XVIII R8	8202	SG XVIII	1 to 19	Report of the Meeting of Experts on ISDN Matters, Munich, 17-25 February 1982
XVIII R9	8206	SG XVIII	1 to 19	Report on the Geneva Meeting (10-22 June 1982)
XVIII R10	8206	SG XVIII	7,8	Report of the Meeting of Working Party XVIII/2 (Speech Processing)
XVIII R11	8206	SG XVIII	9 to 14	Report of the Meeting of Working Party XVIII/3 (Network Performance Objectives)
XVIII R12	8206	SG XVIII	3	Report of the Meeting of Working Party XVIII/4 (Switching and Signalling)
XVIII R13	8206	SG XVIII	15,19	Report of the Meeting of Working Party XVIII/5 (Digital Equipments)
XVIII R14	8211	SG XVIII	1,2,4 to 6	Report of the Meeting of Experts on Level 1 Characteristics of the Basic ISDN User/Network Interface
XVIII R15	8303	SG XVIII	1 to 19	Report of the Group of Experts on ISDN Matters (Kyoto, 14-25 February 1983)
XVIII R16	8307	SG XVIII	1	Report of Meeting (20 June - 8 July 1983)
XVIII R17	8307	SG XVIII	1	Report of Working Team 1 (Customer Access) (20 June - 8 July 1983)
XVIII R18	8307	SG XVIII	1	Report of Working Team 2 (Layer 1 Characteristics) XVIII (20 June - 8 July 1983)
XVIII R19	8307	SG XVIII	1	Report of Working Team 3 (ISDN Network Aspects) (20 June - 8 July 1983)
XVIII R20	8307	SG XVIII	1	Report of Working Team 4 (Services) (20 June - 8 July 1983)
XVIII R21	8307	SG XVIII	4	Report of Working Team 5 (Signalling) (20 June - 8 July 1983)
XVIII R22	8307	SG XVIII	5	Report of Working Team 6 (Switching for ISDN) (20 June - 8 July 1983)
XVIII R23	8307	SG XVIII	6	Report of Working Team on Vocabulary (ISDN Terms) (20 June - 8 July 1983)
XVIII R24	8307	SG XVIII	7,8	Report of Working Party XVIII/2 (Speech Processing) (20 June - 8 July 1983)
XVIII R25	8307	SG XVIII	9 to 14	Report of Working Party XVIII/3 (Network Performance Objectives) (20 June - 8 July 1983)
XVIII R26	8307	SG XVIII	3	Report of Working Party XVIII/4 (Switching and Signalling) (20 June - 8 July 1983)
XVIII R27	8307	SG XVIII	15,19	Report of Working Party XVIII/5 (Digital Equipments) (20 June - 8 July 1983)
XVIII R28	8312	SG XVIII	7	Report of the Meeting of Working Party XVIII/2 (Speech Processing) (Geneva, 21,22, & 23 Nov 1983)
XVIII R29	8407	SG XVIII	-	Final Report to the VIIth CCITT Plenary Assembly (Parts I and II)
XVIII R30	8407	SG XVIII	-	Final Report to the VIIth CCITT Plenary Assembly (Part III)
XVIII R31	8407	SG XVIII	-	Final Report to the VIIth CCITT Plenary Assembly (Part IV)
XVIII R32	8407	SG XVIII	-	Final Report to the VIIth CCITT Plenary Assembly (Part V)
XVIII R33	8407	SG XVIII	-	Final Report to the VIIth CCITT Plenary Assembly (Part VI)

1981-84 PLENARY PERIOD, CONTRIBUTIONS

Doc. Id.	Date	Source	Questions	Title
XVIII 1	8102	VIIth Plen	-	Questions allocated to SG XVIII for the period 1981-1984
XVIII 2	8012	ITT	-	Digital customer access to ISDN
XVIII 3	8101	Sweden	1,2	Customer access arrangements to the ISDN
XVIII 4	8102	Canada-BNH	1,4	Signalling principles to support access of telephone and data services
XVIII 5	8102	Canada-BNH	1,2	Location of access interfaces in an ISDN
XVIII 6	8102	SG4	3,11,12,14	Response to CCITT documents (Doc. No. 4/225)
XVIII 7	8102	Canada BNH	16	Longitudinal balance parameters for Rec. G.712
XVIII 8	8103	ATT	11	Addition to Rec. No. G.911 digital line sections on cable at 1544 kbit/s
XVIII 9	8103	EBU	11	Multiplexing and transmission of digitally encoded sound programme and television signals
XVIII 10	8103	ITT	9A	General network performance of integrated digital networks: transmission performance of digital networks
XVIII 11	8103	ATT	15	A proposed restructuring for the G.700 Series Recommendations
XVIII 12	8103	ATT	11	Addition to Rec. No. G.913 digital line sections on cable at 6312 kbit/s
XVIII 13	8103	ITT	9A	Contribution to Question 9, Part A (bit error rates)
XVIII 14	8103	SG4	3,4,8,14,15	Draft Report 707 --- Digital interface characteristics between satellite and Terrestrial Networks
XVIII 15	8103	Australia	1	Service requirements of customer access
XVIII 16	8103	SG9	9	Reply to Study Group XVIII of the CCITT
XVIII 17	8103	SG9	6,11	Comments on interconnection of digital radio sections
XVIII 18	8103	SG7	3,6	Draft Report AC/7 - performance and reliability of reference clocks

Doc. Id.	Date	Source	Questions	Title
XVIII 19	8103	Australia	9	Clarification of Rec. G.821
XVIII 20	8103	Switzerland	14	Combined communication between digital systems based on different standards
XVIII 21	8104	British Telecom	9,15,18	Jitter specification
XVIII 22	8103	British Telecom	16	Separate specification of send and receive sides of PCM channels
XVIII 23	8104	British Telecom	7	Encoding methods for higher quality speech
XVIII 24	8102	Canada–BNR	3	Synchronization method for digital networks
XVIII 25	8104	Sweden	1,2	Further consideration of ISDN customer access arrangements
XVIII 26	8104	Canada–CTCA	1	ISDN functional requirements
XVIII 27	8104	China	16C	Separated performance of send and receive sides of PCM channels at audio frequencies
XVIII 28	8104	China	11	Design for 2048/34368 kbit/s muldex
XVIII 29	8104	China	18	A Simple 2048/34368 kbit/s digital muldex
XVIII 30	8104	ATT	1	Standards and evolution towards an ISDN
XVIII 31	8104	ATT	1	Definition of integrated services digital networks (ISDN)
XVIII 32	8104	ATT	2	ISDN terminology
XVIII 33	8104	ATT	9	Impairments in digital networks
XVIII 34	8104	ATT	17	The extended framing format for equipment operating at 1544 kbit/s
XVIII 35	8104	France	7	Codecs mic D A 32 kbit/s
XVIII 36	8104	France	7	Codage a bande enlargie du signal telephonique [see Doc. No. BF for english version]
XVIII 37	8104	France	16	Choix du'un signal auxiliaire de lissage pour la mesure de la diaphonie intelligible dans un equipe
XVIII 38	8104	NTT	1,2	Network termination for customer access to the ISDN
XVIII 39	8104	NTT	1,2	Customer access rates in view of existing subscriber line transmission capabilities
XVIII 40	8104	NTT	1,3,4	Digital subscriber line signalling
XVIII 41	8104	NTT	1	Network addressing for interworking among public networks
XVIII 42	8104	NTT	3,5,18	Proposal on specifications relating to wander
XVIII 43	8104	NTT	7	Comments on the standardization of encoding methods other than PCM for speech and voice-band signals
XVIII 44	8104	NTT	19	Choice of 4th and 5th order digital hierarchical levels and digital line section at these bit rates
XVIII 45	8104	NTT	16	A generic approach to specify the performance characteristics of PCM channel measured at the 2-wire point
XVIII 46	8104	NTT	17,18	New frame structures for 1544 kbit/s and 6312 kbit/s digital paths
XVIII 47	8105	Comsat	3	Worldwide synchronous networking
XVIII 48	8105	Comsat	14	Standards conversion in a satellite TDMA network
XVIII 49	8107	Sweden	1,2	Consideration on the delta channel protocol and Ax interface
XVIII 50	8107	Canada BNR	1,2	Considerations for digital access
XVIII 51	8107	KDD	8	Comments on characteristics of digital speech interpolation systems
XVIII 52	8107	ATT	7	Evaluation of non-PCM encoding methods
XVIII 53	8107	Norway	10	An Approach to availability performance planning of telecommunication networks
XVIII 54	8107	LMEricsson	3	Proposed extension to recommendation G.822
XVIII 55	8107	FRG	16	Considerations of tolerances of signal/quantizing distortion ratio and variation of gain with input level
XVIII 56	8109	IBM Europe	1,2	User access arrangements to the ISDN
XVIII 57	8111	WP IV/5	13	Extract from Report of Meeting, COM IV-No. R6
XVIII 58	8111	LMEricsson	13	Maintenance sub-entity
XVIII 59	8111	SG XV	16,17	Extract from Report of Meeting, COM XV-No. R10
XVIII 60	8111	SG XV	19	Extract from Report of Meeting, COM XV-No. R5
XVIII 61	8111	SG XVI	9	Extract of reply to Question 1/XVI [see COM XVI-No. R1]
XVIII 62	8111	SG XVI	1	Extract of reply to Question 6/XVI [see COM XVI-No. R1]
XVIII 63	8111	SG XVI	1	Extract of reply to Question 7/XVI [see COM XVI-No. R1]
XVIII 64	8111	SG XVI	16	Extract of reply to Question 4/XVI [see COM XVI-No. R1]
XVIII 65	8111	CMBD	10	Extract of the Report CMBD-No. R1
XVIII 66	8111	FRG	9,11	Block codes-bit error patterns and probability of occurrence
XVIII 67	8111	Sweden	1,13	Digital subscriber line maintenance
XVIII 68	8112	SG III	1	Study of charging problems in ISDN [See COM III-No. R1(B)]
XVIII 69	8202	ITT	1	Handling of alarm and telemetry information on an ISDN
XVIII 70	8203	France	7	Sum. of Del. Con. COM XII-No.52 "Differential 32 kbit/s PCM : voice transmission quality & impairment units
XVIII 71	8203	France	7	60-channel PCM – ADPCM transcoder
XVIII 72	8203	France	7	Application of ADPCM to wideband speech signal encoding
XVIII 73	8203	France	16	Comparisons of smoothing signals for measuring intelligible crosstalk in PCM equipment

Doc. Id.	Date	Source	Questions	Title
XVIII 74	8203	France	16	Further measurements for separate specifications for PCM equipment
XVIII 75	8203	France	8	Digital speech interpolation equipment developed by French Admin. (CELTIC)
XVIII 76	8203	France	8	Digital speech interpolation equipment developed by French Admin. (DSI for TDMA satellite)
XVIII 77	8203	France	7	Comparison of two methods of measuring linearity
XVIII 78	8203	France	7	Differential PCM encoding at 32 kbit/s
XVIII 79	8203	France	3	Draft modification of Rec. B.822
XVIII 80	8203	France	3	Unavailability and degradation of clocks in a digital network
XVIII 81	8203	LMEricsson	12,13	Supervision of digital radio links
XVIII 82	8203	British Telecom	9	Draft for new Rec. G.82X (Control of jitter within digital networks based on 2048 kbit/s hierarchy)
XVIII 83	8203	Hungary	1,18	Proposed Modifications of some Recs. G.700 and G.900 series
XVIII 84	8203	British Telecom	3	Specification of nodal clock reliability
XVIII 85	8203	British Telecom	9	Refinement of Rec. G.822
XVIII 86	8203	British Telecom	16	Proposed amendments to G.712
XVIII 87	8203	RQ9	9	Revised text for Rec. G.821
XVIII 88	8203	WP XI/1	8,9,14	Extracts from Report of Meeting, COM XI-No. R4
XVIII 89	8203	SG XVII	1,9	Meeting of Ad Hoc Group on Question 11/XVII to draft questions to Study Group XVIII regarding ISDN
XVIII 90	8203	FRG	1,7	Use of delta modulation for "wideband speech" in the ISDN
XVIII 91	8203	FRG	9	Proposed new version of Rec. G.821
XVIII 92	8203	FRG	9	Considerations on the revision of Rec. G.821
XVIII 93	8203	FRG	15	Amendment of Rec. G.703
XVIII 94	8203	FRG	11,15	Delay of AIS emission in case of fault conditions in line terminal equipment
XVIII 95	8203	FRG	16	Performance characteristics of send and receive sides of PCM multiplexers
XVIII 96	8203	ATT	3	Comments on Para. 3 of draft Rec. G.8yy, jitter and wander in a digital network
XVIII 97	8204	Comsat	8	Digital speech interpolation characteristics
XVIII 98	8204	KDD	9	Relationship between CCIR and CCITT Recs. on error performance
XVIII 99	8204	KDD	14	PCM encoding law conversion for international digital connections
XVIII 100	8204	Intelsat	9	Error performance measures for digital satellite circuits
XVIII 101	8204	[CEPT]	1,2	Comments on the results of the ISDN experts meeting, Munich, 17-25 Feb 1982
XVIII 102	8204	CMTT	7,9	Draft Report 646-2
XVIII 103	8204	CMTT	9	Draft Report 967/CMTT
XVIII 104	8204	CMTT	1,9	Draft Report 647-2
XVIII 105	8204	CMTT	--	Draft Decision 18-3
XVIII 106	8204	SG 4	9	CCIR Doc. 4/455
XVIII 107	8204	SG 4	9	Draft Rec. 521-1
XVIII 108	8204	SG 4	9	Draft Rec. 522-1
XVIII 109	8204	SG 4	10	Draft Rec. 594/4
XVIII 110	8204	SG 4	10	Question 24-1/4, Study Prog 24A/4 & Draft Report 706-1
XVIII 111	8204	SG 4	3,14	Study Programme 2N-1/4 and Draft Report 707-1
XVIII 112	8204	SG 9	9	Draft Recommendation 594/9
XVIII 113	8204	SG 9	9	Draft Report 930
XVIII 114	8204	CCITT Sec	1	Extract from Report of Meeting, COM II-No. R4
XVIII 115	8205	Sweden	1	Services in ISDN
XVIII 116	8206	ITT	1	Alarm and telemetry services in an ISDN
XVIII 117	8206	USA	1,2,4	Multidrop configuration and interfaces
XVIII 118	8206	NTT	1,2	Proposed amendments to COM XVIII-No. R8 [Munich Report]
XVIII 119	8206	ATT	17	Bit sequence independence on 1544 kbit/s signals
XVIII 120	8206	ATT	7	32 b/s ADPCM-DLQ coding
XVIII 121	8206	NTT	7	Adaptive predictive coding with adaptive bit allocation at 16 kb/s
XVIII 122	8206	ATT	8	Characteristics of the TASI-E digital speech interpolation system
XVIII 123	8207	NTT	3	Proposed value of acceptable slip rate
XVIII 124	8207	FRG	9	Amendment of Rec. G.811 Sec. 4.2 and 5 [timing and jitter]
XVIII 125	8207	CCITT Sec	1	Extract from the report of the meeting of working party II/6 (Report COM II-R6)
XVIII 126	8207	Netherlands	12,13	Maintenance philosophy for digital and mixed networks
XVIII 127	8208	CCITT Sec	1,2,4,5	Reports of Study Group VII of interest to Study Group XVIII
XVIII 128	8208	CCITT Sec	1,2,4,5	Reports of Study Group XI of interest to Study Group XVIII

Doc. Id.	Date	Source	Questions	Title
XVIII 129	8209	AdHoc Q21/III	1A	Extracts from the report on the meeting held in Geneva on 9 June 1982 (Tariff guidelines for ISDNs)
XVIII 130	8209	USA	1	Philosophy and concept of ISDN
XVIII 131	8210	Canada	1	Proposed outline of I series recommendations
XVIII 132	8210	Draft Group	1	Report of the meeting held in Geneva (18-20 Oct 1982) [issues for further study]
XVIII 133	8210	France,BT	14	Interworking between the hierarchy based on the 2 Mbit/s level and the 1.5 Mbit/s level
XVIII 134	8210	Draft Group	1,2,4,5	Report on the Geneva meeting (20-21 Oct 1982) [structure of I-series Recs.]
XVIII 135	8211	CCITT Sec	1,9	Extract from the report of the meeting of special rapporteurs group, Tokyo, 8-14 Sep 1982
XVIII 136	8211	CCITT Sec	9	Proposal by SG II for a new recommendation on the International Telephone Routing Plan
XVIII 137	8211	SG XVI	7,16	Extract of the Report (XVI-R2) of SG XVI Meeting of 14-16 Jun 1982 on transmission impairments
XVIII 138	8211	SG XVI		Extract of the Report (XVI-R2) of SG XVI Meeting of 14-16 Jun 1982 on echo, propagation time...
XVIII 139	8211	RQ6	6	Proposals for ISDN terms and definitions
XVIII 140	8211	FRG	11,15	Clarification of the difference between w and u types of information
XVIII 141	8211	FRG	1	Inclusion in Rec. G.703, Sec. 6, of a basic frame structure
XVIII 142	8211	ISO/TC97/SC6	1C	Liaison report to CCITT SG XVIII, ISDN interfaces at Ref. Points S and T
XVIII 143	8211	IBM Europe	2	Basic access concern
XVIII 144	8211	IBM Europe	2	Functional content of network termination 1
XVIII 145	8211	IBM Europe	2	Multiple logical link control over D channel
XVIII 146	8211	HQIB,K	2	ISDN - Network issues
XVIII 147	8211	IBM Europe	2	Functions at the Common physical interface
XVIII 148	8212	Sweden	1	Digital subscriber line maintenance
XVIII 149	8212	Canada-BNR	13	Mapping of access channel information types to network connection types
XVIII 150	8212	Canada-BNR	18	Correction to CCITT Rec G.752
XVIII 151	8212	Sweden		Terms and definitions for services and choice of bearer services in ISDN
XVIII 152	8301	FRG	3,9	Designations of performance levels in Recs G.811, G.821, and G.822
XVIII 153	8302	SG IV	9	Digital path (section) performance objectives
XVIII 154	8303	SG XI	16,18	Extract from the Report of WP XI/4 (digital switching)
XVIII 155	8302	RQ8/XVII	9,11	Request to SG XVIII and SG IV concerning existing incompatibility between Recs. M.1025 and G.912
XVIII 156	8303	RQ5/VII	7	Digital encoding for voice messaging (extract from COM VII R19(B))
XVIII 157	8302	RQ8/XVII	9,11	Request to SGs XVIII & IV concerning existing incompatibility bet. Recs. M.1025 & G.912 [SG XVII-R2]
XVIII 158	8303	SG XI	3,14,15	Extract from COM XI-R19 (Report of WP XI/4 - Digital Switching)
XVIII 159	8303	SG XVII	7,8	Comments to study group XVII regarding the proposed 32 kbit/s coder and digital speech [SG XVII-R2]
XVIII 160	8302	CCIR IWP 4/2	1,6,9,10	Satellite system error performance within an international ISDN connection
XVIII 161	8302	CCIR IWP 4/2	1,6,9,10	Guidelines with respect to the application of satellites in the ISDN hypothetical reference connections
XVIII 162	8302	Hungary	1,13	Centralized maintenance of a digital transmission network, based on PCM service bits
XVIII 163	8302	LMEricsson	16	Interface characteristics for 2-wire analogue ports of PCM circuits
XVIII 164	8302	Comsat	1B,9	Hypothetical reference connections for ISDN
XVIII 165	8302	FRG	6	Comments on the output of the Paris meeting of Working Group C of JCG, April 1982
XVIII 166	8302	British Telecom	7,17	Proposal for a new draft Recommendation for 60 channel transcoder
XVIII 167	8302	British Telecom	7,17	Amalgamation of draft Recs. G.82X and G.8YY
XVIII 168	8302	British Telecom	3,9	Considerations concerning hypothetical reference circuits (HRX)
XVIII 169	8302	British Telecom	3,9	Proposals for a new draft Rec. G.81X (digital transmission models)
XVIII 170	8302	British Telecom	9	Jitter specification for the 64 kbit/s co-directional interface
XVIII 171	8303	Netherlands	9	Determination of entire block error probability curve from two points when clustering occurs
XVIII 172	8303	USA	9	Effect of clustering on the selection of error probability parameters
XVIII 173	8303	USA	9	Amendments to Recs. G.712 and G.71X
XVIII 174	8303	FRG	16	A proposal for a jitter specification for digital sections for inclusion in Rec. G.82X
XVIII 175	8303	British Telecom	9,11	Proposed amendments to Rec. G.712
XVIII 176	8303	USSR	16	Measurement method & limits for total distortion in case of sep. meas. of send & receive sides of PCM channels
XVIII 177	8303	USSR	16	Measurement of intelligible crosstalk and idle channel noise in the send side of PCM channels
XVIII 178	8303	USSR	16	Amendments to certain Recs. of Yellow Book, Volume III, Fasc. III.3
XVIII 179	8303	USSR	9	Loop testing at subscribers premises in ISDN
XVIII 180	8303	ECMA	1,13	ISDN physical interface
XVIII 181	8304	ECMA	1C	Jitter transfer characteristic from 64 kbit/s codirectional input signal to 2048 kbit/s aggregate output signal
XVIII 182	8303	Italy	9,17,18	Proposed amendments to Rec. G.712
XVIII 183	8304	Switzerland	1	Some detailed improvements in the frame alignment and definition of spare bits at the ISDN subscriber interface

Doc. Id.	Date	Source	Questions	Title
XVIII 184	8304	NTT	3	Proposed Amendments to Tie specification for a non-reference clock in Rec G.811 and wander specification in Rec. G.811
XVIII 185	8304	NTT	3	Proposed amendment to tie specification for reference clock in Rec. G.811
XVIII 186	8304	NTT	3	Proposed amendment to G.8YY for the inclusion of jitter and wander specifications at 6312 kbit/s
XVIII 187	8304	NTT	8,18	Jitter specifications for interfaces at 1544, 6312, and 32064 kbit/s
XVIII 188	8304	NTT	16	Proposed limits for crosstalk separate specifications in draft Rec. G.71X
XVIII 189	8304	NTT	19	Proposal on the addition of 4th level (97728 kbit/s) to draft Rec. G.70X
XVIII 190	8304	RQ15	1-19	Proposed framework for G.700-900 series recommendations
XVIII 191	8304	FRG	15	Return loss at the input port of the 2-, 8-, and 34- Mbit/s digital interface
XVIII 192	8304	British Telecom	9	An error apportionment strategy based on circuit quality
XVIII 193	8304	British Telecom	9	A proposed revision of Rec G.821 reflecting apportionment studies
XVIII 194	8304	British Telecom	7	64 kbit/s coding of 7 kHz bandwidth speech
XVIII 195	8304	RQ16	16	Report of rapporteur's drafting group (2-wire PCM specification)
XVIII 196	8307	ATT	18	Proposed changes to multiplex equipment jitter accommodation requirements (G.743, G.752)
XVIII 197	8307	ATT	18	Jitter accumulation in digital networks
XVIII 198	8307	ATT	8	Circuit multiplication equipment
XVIII 199	8307	USSR	1	Proposed amendments to Rec. G.721
XVIII 200	8307	British Telecom	18	An auxiliary 3rd order interface at 68736 kbit/s
XVIII 201	8312	ECMA	1,13	Fault isolation in ISDN
XVIII 202	8312	ECMA	1C	Configuration identification in draft Rec. I.431
XVIII 203	8312	ECMA	1C	Comments on Sections 5 and 6, draft Rec. I.431
XVIII 204	8312	Switzerland	7	Simultaneous wideband speech and data transmission on 64 kbit/s
XVIII 205	8312	Switzerland	1A	Specification of the non-transparent bearer services
XVIII 206	8312	ECMA	2	Comments on draft Rec. I.411 (COM XVIII-R17)
XVIII 207	8312	ECMA	2	ISDN customer access using the basic user-network interface
XVIII 208	8312	FRG	--	Proposal for new question on broadband aspects of the ISDN
XVIII 209	8312	CM WT2	1	Report of the Meeting of Working Team 2 (Layer 1 characteristics)
XVIII 210	8312	CM WT3	1	Report of the Meeting of Working Team 3 (ISDN-Network aspects)
XVIII 211	8312	CM WT4	1	Report of Working Team 4 (Services)
XVIII 212	8312	France	1B	Notes on the maintenance of digital subscriber's systems
XVIII 213	8312	USA		Loop testing on an ISDN DSL
XVIII 214	8312	FRG	1B,12	Guidelines for fault isolation (comments on App. 1 to Annex 4 of COM XVIII-R10)
XVIII 215	8312	Sweden	1B	Draft Rec. I.200 - Alternative text of paragraph 1
XVIII 216	8402	USSR	7	Evaluation of speech transmission quality of a digital system using ADPCM codecs
XVIII 217	8402	NTT	11	Draft Recommendation for digital line sections on cable at 97728 kbit/s
XVIII 218	8402	NTT	15,19	Amendments to Rec. G. 703 (inclusion of 97728 kbit/s interface)
XVIII 219	8402	NTT	18,19	Amendments to Rec. G.752
XVIII 220	8402	CMTT	1,19	Draft Rec. AA/CMTT - Digital transmission of sound-programmes - general principles
XVIII 221	8402	CMTT	1,2,19	Draft Rec. AB/CMTT - Trans. of analog high-qual. sound-prog. sig. on mixed analog & dig. cir. using 384 kbit/s
XVIII 222	8402	CMTT	9	Comments on error performance
XVIII 223	8402	CMTT	19	Note from CMTT to CCITT Study Group XVIII
XVIII 224	8402	NTT	3	Amendments to the reliability specification for clocks in Rec. G.811
XVIII 225	8403	FRG	17,19	Effects of CCITT Rec. G.821 (July 1983 version) on transmission systems
XVIII 226	8403	USSR	15	Information concerning a 15-channel PCM system at 1024 kbit/s
XVIII 227	8403	Netherlands	1,2,6	Amendments to Rec. G.703
XVIII 228	8403	CCITT Sec	1,2,4,6	I-Series of Recommendations (Brasilia Meeting, 13-24 Feb 1984) Part III of the Report
XVIII 229	8403	CCITT Sec	15,17,18	Report of the meeting of the group of experts on ISDN matters of Study Group XVIII (Brasilia, 13-24 Feb 1984)
XVIII 230	8403	RQ15	16	Draft Rec. G.70Y, 70Z and modifications to Recs. G.732, 733, 737, 738, 739, 744, and 74X
XVIII 231	8403	RQ16	16	Rapporteur's Report
XVIII 232	8403	British Telecom	16	Further proposed amendments to Recs. G.712, G.71X and G.71Y
XVIII 233	8403	British Telecom	9	Proposed revision of Rec. G.821
XVIII 234	8403	British Telecom	--	Initial thoughts on possible applications and design requirements for 16 kbit/s coding
XVIII 235	8403	RQ16	16	Report on Question 16/XVIII - Performance characteristics of PCM channels at audio frequencies
XVIII 236	8403	Chair, WP 5	15-19	Items to be discussed and recommendations to be completed at the final meeting
XVIII 237	8403	FRG	7,18	Amendment of priority list for digital access in Recs. G.737 and G.739
XVIII 238	8403	Switzerland	3	Amendments to the Recs. G.822 and G.811

Doc. Id.	Date	Source	Questions	Title
XVIII 239	8403	Switzerland	9	Proposal for a jitter specification on digital sections
XVIII 240	8403	Switzerland	3	Draft text of an annex to the question on network synchronization for the study period 1985-1988
XVIII 241	8403	NTT	9	Proposal of a new question including high-speed/broadband services for improvement of Rec. G.821
XVIII 242	8403	NTT	12,17	Study issues for PCM multiplex equipment operation at 1544 & 6312 kbit/s to offer synch. digital access options
XVIII 243	8403	NTT	3	Amendments to tie definition in Rec. G.811
XVIII 244	8403	NTT	16	Proposal for limits to total distortion including quantizing distortion
XVIII 245	8403	NTT	3	Proposals for study points on network synchronization matters
XVIII 246	8403	FRG	9,1	Proposal for a new Rec. G.82Z: Categories of transmission delay in the ISDN
XVIII 247	8403	FRG	3,9	Amendment of Rec. G.82X (G.8YY)
XVIII 248	8403	KDD	14,19	Hybrid hierarchical structures for international interworking
XVIII 249	8403	KDD	7	Continuation of Question 7/XVII (encoding of speech and voice-band signals using methods other than PCM
XVIII 250	8403	KDD	14	Proposal for Revision of Question 14/XVIII

1981-84 PLENARY PERIOD, DELAYED CONTRIBUTIONS

Doc. Id.	Date	Source	Questions	Title
XVIII A	8101	Philips	1,2	The connection of X.21 DTEs to the ISDN, interface A2
XVIII B	8101	Switzerland	1	A bit structure for a universal B-interface for ISDN access
XVIII C	8101	NTT	1,2	Customer access to the ISDN
XVIII D	8101	NTT	1,2	Use of the term "access type" and its relation to the physical implementation
XVIII E	8101	Canada-BNR	1,4	Signalling principles to support access of telephone and data services
XVIII F	8101	Canada-BNR	1,2	Location of access interfaces in an ISDN
XVIII G	8101	ATT	1,6	Definition of Integrated Services Digital Network (ISDN)
XVIII H	8101	ATT	1	General principles of Integrated Services Digital Network (ISDN)
XVIII I	8101	ATT	1	Digital subscriber line format, interface and protocol considerations
XVIII J	8101	FRG	1	Proposal for the procedure for defining possible sources and features in an ISDN
XVIII K	8101	GEC Telec	1	Customer access to the ISDN a practical approach
XVIII L	8101	Canada-CTCA	1	Comments pertaining to Question A/XVIII, point A – Service aspect
XVIII M	8101	Canada-CTCA	2	Customer/network interface to the ISDN
XVIII N	8101	Italy	1	A flexible approach to the customer access
XVIII O	8101	FRG	1	Service/terminal identification and selection in the ISDN
XVIII P	8106	Canada-BNR	16	Longitudinal balance parameters for Rec. G.712
XVIII Q	8106	USSR	15	An interface for 34368 kbit/s
XVIII R	8106	FRG	3	Proposed extension to Rec. G.822
XVIII S	8106	Canada-CTCA	1	Network addressing for interworking between the public telephone network and other public networks
XVIII T	8106	Norway	10	An approach to availability performance planning of telecommunication networks
XVIII U	8106	Norway	10	Availability predictions in digital local networks
XVIII V	8106	Norway	10	Traffic and reliability dimensioning of alternative routing networks
XVIII W	8106	France	7	32 kbit/s ADPCM Codecs
XVIII X	8106	FRG	6,15	Designations of channels and interfaces associated with digital exchanges and digital subscribers
XVIII Y	8106	FRG	16	Considerations of tolerances of signal/quantizing distortion ratio and variation of gain with input
XVIII Z	8106	British Telecom	3,9	Comments on proposed draft Rec. G.8YY
XVIII AA	8106	British Telecom	3,9	Comments on Rec. G.811
XVIII AB	8106	British Telecom	19	Standards for digital systems for the transmission of sound programme signals over long distances
XVIII AC	8106	FRG	3	Amendment of Rec. G.811
XVIII AD	8106	FRG	12	Proposal for amendment of Rec. G.704
XVIII AE	8106	FRG	16	Completion of Rec. G.712 in respect of unbalance
XVIII AF	8106	FRG	180	Problems of consistency of Recs. G. 734 and G.746 with Rec. Q.504
XVIII AG	8106	FRG	1,4	Octet structure of the information field of the ISDN delta channel
XVIII AH	8106	FRG	4	Application of the signalling system no. 7 for the ISDN
XVIII AI	8106	Italy	1	Priorities in the study of Question 1/XVIII
XVIII AJ	8106	Italy	9,12	Unavailability BER threshold for ISDN connections
XVIII AK	8106	Italy	11	Considerations concerning possible extension of Recs. G.912, G.914, G.916, and G.918 to digital radio sections
XVIII AL	8106	Italy	16	Characteristiques de qualite des voies mid aux frequencies vocales mesurees a l'extremite a deux fils
XVIII AM	8106	Sweden	1	Comments on coordination of ISDN studies
XVIII AN	8106	Sweden	1,2	Consideration of the delta channel protocol and Ax interface

Doc. Id.	Date	Source	Questions	Title
XVIII AO	8106	FRG	1	The use of the ISDN delta channel
XVIII AP	8106	FRG	1A	Implementation of services of dedicated text/data networks and analog telephone networks in the ISDN
XVIII AQ	8106	FRG	1A	Services to be taken into account in the establishment of network features of the future ISDN
XVIII AR	8106	FRG	1	Correlation matrix showing the various service requirements against the network features and capabilities
XVIII AS	8106	NTT	15,17,18	Points for discussion on the restructuring of interface and equipment recommendations
XVIII AT	8106	NTT	18	Octet-interleaved synchronous multiplexing at 6312 kbit/s
XVIII AU	8106	Canada-BNR	1,2	Considerations for digital access
XVIII AV	8106	Canada-BNR	1,2	Consolidation of proposed arrangements for customer access to the ISDN
XVIII AW	8106	Canada-CTCA	4	Telephony signalling considerations in access to an ISDN
XVIII AX	8106	Canada-CTCA	1,2	ISDN access, functional requirements
XVIII AY	8106	Canada CTCA	1,2	Factors affecting the access model
XVIII AZ	8106	Canada-CTCA	9	Bit error distributions and their impact on G.821
XVIII BA	8106	British Telecom	14	Comments on interworking
XVIII BB	8106	KDD	8	Comments on characteristics of digital speech interpolation systems
XVIII BC	8106	ATT	2	ISDN functional reference model for local digital access
XVIII BD	8106	ATT	7	Evaluation of non-PCM encoding methods
XVIII BE	8106	ATT	1,2	An example of service and implications for ISDN protocols
XVIII BF	8106	France	7	Wideband encoding of speech signals [English version of Doc. No. 36]
XVIII BG	8106	NTT	1,15	General aspects of ISDN
XVIII BH	8106	ATT	1,2	The philosophy of an ISDN
XVIII BI	8202	Canada-CTCA	1B	Functional description of ISDN
XVIII BJ	—	—	—	[Not used]
XVIII BK	8202	Canada-TCTS	1B	Utilization of 64 kbit/s connection capabilities in the ISDN
XVIII BL	8202	Canada-CTCA	1,6	Physical interpretation of access model
XVIII BM	8202	Canada	1A	Service categories and ISDN features matrix
XVIII BN	8202	FRG	1	Autonomous sub-channels (less than 64 kbit/s) in the ISDN
XVIII BO	8202	FRG	1,2	ISDN channel structures for PABX's
XVIII BP	8202	FRG	1,2	Channel structure at interfaces S (Ax), T (Bo) and U (C)
XVIII BQ	8202	FRG	1,7	Use of delta modulation for "wideband speech" in the ISDN
XVIII BR	8202	NTT	1,2	Transmission characteristics of bus structured user/network interface
XVIII BS	8202	NTT	1,2	D channel access contention resolution
XVIII BT	8202	NTT	1,2	Proposed specification items for the physical layer of basic access
XVIII BU	8202	NTT	1,2,4,5	Level 1 requirements on user/network interface for basic access
XVIII BV	8202	NTT	1,2,4,5	Definition of the hybrid access arrangements
XVIII BW	8202	NTT	1,2,4,5	Level 2 and 3 requirements on user/network interface protocol
XVIII BX	8202	NTT	1,2,4,5	Basic concepts for addressing in the ISDN
XVIII BY	8202	NTT	1A	Study approach on the standard and simple protocols
XVIII BZ	8202	FRG		ISDN definition of w-type information
XVIII CA	8202	FRG		ISDN service-analysis matrix
XVIII CB	8202	Canada-TCTS	1B	Network considerations of digital speech processing
XVIII CC	8202	Canada-CTCA		Public networks - addressing concepts and principles for interworking
XVIII CD	8202	ITT	1A	Handling of alarm and telemetry information on an ISDN
XVIII CE	8202	FRG	2,15	So: Level 1 characteristics for basic access
XVIII CF	8202	Netherlands	1,4,5	Different types of hybrid access arrangements and their objectives
XVIII CG	8202	France	1	Access at an intermediate hierarchical rate for PABX and remote multiplex or concentrator access
XVIII CH	8202	France	1	Use of the D channel for ISDN basic access
XVIII CI	8202	Switzerland	1,2	A four-wire subscriber interface (S or T)
XVIII CJ	8202	Switzerland	1,2	Contention resolution at interfaces S and T
XVIII CK	8202	NTT	1,2	Rate adaptation of lower bit rates to 64 kbit/s
XVIII CL	8202	NTT		Optimum bit rate for bi-level digital facsimile
XVIII CM	8202	ATT	1,2,4	Hybrid arrangements for subscriber access to the local exchange
XVIII CN	8202	ATT	1,2,4	Subscriber interface protocol for hybrid access to the ISDN
XVIII CO	8202	ATT	1,2	ISDN physical layer interface
XVIII CP	8202	ATT	1,2	Bit rate and channel structure for ISDN user interfaces
XVIII CQ	8202	ATT	1,2,4	Signalling and control facilities at the ISDN user/network interface

Doc. Id.	Date	Source	Questions	Title
XVIII CR	8202	ATT	1,2	The ISDN from the user's perspective
XVIII CS	8202	Sweden	1,2,4	Comments on scope of studies of ISDN network layer signalling protocols
XVIII CT	8202	Sweden	1	Comments on draft Recs. I.xxx and I.xxy
XVIII CU	8202	Canada-TCTS	1B	Intelligence requirements for the ISDN
XVIII CV	8202	British Telecom	1,2,4	Local area networks
XVIII CW	8202	British Telecom	1C,2	Channel structure of basic ISDN user interface
XVIII CX	8202	Canada-TCTS	1,6	Physical realization of the NT1
XVIII CY	8202	British Telecom	2	User-network interface access structures
XVIII CZ	8202	British Telecom	2	User to network interface - level 1 aspects
XVIII DA	8202	British Telecom	1B	Hypothetical reference connections for ISDN
XVIII DB	8202	British Telecom	1D	Interworking between ISDN and satellite systems
XVIII DC	8202	Switzerland	1,2	Generic reference configuration to be supported by LAPD
XVIII DD	8202	KDD	1A	Classification of ISDN network features based on the OSI reference model
XVIII DE	8202	KDD	1B,2	Application of OSI reference model principles to ISDN switching & signalling
XVIII DF	8202	GTE	1,2,4,5	Extended access structure for ISDN
XVIII DG	8202	GTE	1A,1E,2,7,8	Identification of an information type and set for variable bit rate and packetized voice
XVIII DH	8202	USA	1C,'2,13	Maintenance testing of ISDN access lines using loop back techniques
XVIII DI	8202	USA	1,2,4	ST configurations and interface
XVIII DJ	8202	France	1C,2	A to u-law conversion in the ISDN
XVIII DK	8202	France	1,2,4,5	CCITT Recommendations to be elaborated for ISDN
XVIII DL	8202	KDD	1B	Layered model of user/network protocol
XVIII DM	8202	Switzerland	1,2	D channel access contention resolution
XVIII DN	R202	Italy	1A	Towards a possible delineation of an ISDN "service"
XVIII DO	8206	FRG	6,11	Block codes - bit error patterns and their probability of occurrence (corr. of COM XVIII-No.66)
XVIII DP	8206	LMEricsson	16	Idle channel pattern on digital circuits containing a conversion of the PCM encoding law
XVIII DQ	8206	Switzerland	14	A flexible encoding scheme for wideband speech
XVIII DR	8206	Switzerland	7	Adaptive predictive coding with adaptive bit allocation at 16 kbit/s
XVIII DS	8206	NTT	9	Relationship between BER and % FES based on measured error performance on PCM-24B transmission system
XVIII DT	8206	NTT	16	Specifications for the performance characteristics of a PCM channel at the 2-wire point
XVIII DU	8206	NTT	16	Transmission characteristics measurement technique at analogue 2-wire ports
XVIII DV	8206	USA	1,2,4	Multidrop configurations and interfaces
XVIII DW	8206	FRG	9	Summary of contribution COM IV-No. 74 - Compatibility problems with bit error ratio measurements
XVIII DX	8206	France	8	Complements to COM XVIII-No. 76 - Speech interpolation equipments developed by the French Administration
XVIII DY	8206	Comsat	9	An experimental investigation of digital transmission chan. performance measured in a simulated satellite link
XVIII DZ	8206	GEC Telecom	1	Recommendations for the ISDN
XVIII EA	8206	Italy	9	Allocation of error performances
XVIII EB	8206	Canada-BNR	16	Transmission characteristics and limits of a PCM channel for 2-wire analogue interfaces
XVIII EC	8206	Canada-BNR	16	Proposed param. and tentative values for param. for separate specification of PCM channels at audio frequencies
XVIII ED	8206	ATT	7,8,14	Hierarchy structures for interworking between digital systems based on different standards
XVIII EE	8206	ATT	7	32 kbit/s ADPCM-DLQ coding
XVIII EF	8206	ATT	9	Error clustering on digital facilities
XVIII EG	8206	ATT	17	Bit sequence independence on 1544 kbit/s signals
XVIII EH	8206	Italy	7	Speech coding at 32 kbit/s
XVIII EI	8206	Italy	7	Subjective quality evaluation of 16 kbit/s waveform coders
XVIII EJ	8206	Italy	7	Coding of audio signals with a band larger than 4 kHz
XVIII EK	8206	NTT	1,2	Proposed amendments to COM XVIII-No. R8 - Report on the Munich Meeting of the Group of Experts on ISDN Matters
XVIII EL	8206	NTT	3	Relationship between recommendations relating to jitter and wander
XVIII EM	8206	NTT	7	Subjective evaluation results for various voiceband codecs
XVIII EN	8206	NTT	7	Encoding method for wideband speech at 64 kbit/s
XVIII EO	8206	NTT	7	An ADPCM encoding method at 32 kbit/s
XVIII EP	8206	NTT	16	Considerations on separate specifications for performance of PCM channels at audio frequencies
XVIII EQ	8206	NTT	17	New phase format for a digital path at 6312 kbit/s
XVIII ER	8206	NTT	15,19	Digital hierarchy based on the bit rates 1.5 Mbit/s - 3.3 Mbit/s, 32 Mbit/s
XVIII ET	8206	British Telecom	15	Digital interfaces

Doc. Id.	Date	Source	Questions	Title
XVIII EU	8206	NTT	3	A reference model for specifying the jitter/wander and TIE of the node with a non-reference clock
XVIII EV	8206	France	16	Performance characteristics of 2-wire PCM channels at audio frequencies
XVIII EW	8206	FRG	3	Wander in digital netowrks
XVIII EX	8206	FRG	3	Amendment of Rec. G.811, section 4.2 and 5
XVIII EY	8206	FRG	16	Amendments of Rec. G.712 and remarks on G.71x
XVIII EZ	8206	FRG	9	Revision of Rec. G.104 for application to the ISDN
XVIII FA	8206	FRG	9	Distribution of bit error ratio on hypothetical reference connection according with G.104 (amendment to G.821)
XVIII FB	8206	KDD	7	A 32 kbit/s ADPCM encoding scheme
XVIII FC	8206	FRG	9	Annex to COM XVIII - No. 92
XVIII FD	8206	Switzerland	8	Digital speech/data interpolation
XVIII FE	8206	ATT	14	Modification of coding law conversion tables 3 and 4/G.711
XVIII FF	8206	ATT	18	Proposed changes to multiplex equipment jitter accommodation requirements (G.743, G.752)
XVIII FG	8206	ATT	9	Allocation of error performance objectives
XVIII FH	8206	ATT	8	Characteristics of the TASI-E digital speech interpolation system
XVIII FI	8206	IBM Europe	7	Low bit rate encoding of speech
XVIII FJ	8206	Netherlands	9	Bit error performance measurements
XVIII FK	8206	British Telecom	9	A possible general set of call processing performance parameters
XVIII FL	8206	British Telecom	1B,9	The formulation of hypothetical reference connections
XVIII FM	8206	LMEriccsson	13	Reproduction of COM IV No. 35 - Digital access points
XVIII FN	8206	Italy	16	Comments on limits for total distortion, including quantizing distortion, and variation of gain with input level
XVIII FO	8206	Telebras-Brazil	3	Extension of contribution COM XVIII - No. 44
XVIII FP	8206	NTT	3	A comment on draft Rec. G.8yy
XVIII FQ	8206	ATT	12	New frame structure for 1544 kbit/s digital paths
XVIII FR	8206	NTT	12,13,18	Draft Recommendation dealing with modifications of fundamental parameters for 6312 kbit/s interfaces
XVIII FS	8206	NTT	16	Items to be specified for performance characteristics of a PCM channel at 2-wire ports
XVIII FT	8206	Italy	9	Allocation of error performance objectives
XVIII FU	8211	USA	1C,2	Common physical interface - Transition to ISDN
XVIII FV	8211	USA	1C	Physical interface requirements
XVIII FW	8211	USA	1C	Considerations concerning passive bus on NT1 and NT2 in ISDN
XVIII FX	8211	Switzerland	1C	Power supply and wake-up in the ISDN subscriber installation
XVIII FY	8211	Switzerland	1C	Frame-structure at S-interface for passive bus and point-to-point configurations
XVIII FZ	8211	Sweden	1C	Proposals for interface code and frame-structures at 192 kbit/s for a four wire terminal interface
XVIII GA	8211	Sweden	1C	Requirements for reach of the basic ISDN user/network interface in a point-to-point configuration
XVIII GB	8211	Sweden (CEPT)	1C	D-channel access control
XVIII GC	8211	USA	1C	Common physical interface-timing
XVIII GD	8211	USA	1C	Power transfer considerations for a common physical interface
XVIII GE	8211	USA	1C	A possible common physical interface
XVIII GF	8211	USA	1C	Consideration of flexible multiplexing structures for a common physical interface
XVIII GG	8211	USA	1C	Multiplexing interchange functions within the common physical interface for modems and PDN applications
XVIII GH	8211	NTT	1,2	Proposal for an activation procedure at the basic ISDN user/network interface
XVIII GI	8211	NTT	1,2	Basic parameters of the basic ISDN user/network interface with a passive bus arrangement
XVIII GJ	8211	NTT	1,2	Proposal for a D-Channel access contention resolution mechanism
XVIII GK	8211	FRG	1C	Evaluating scheme for comparison of frame structures of ISDN basic access at reference points S and T
XVIII GL	8211	FRG (CEPT)	1C	Layer 1 characteristics of ISDN basic access user/network interface at reference points S and T
XVIII GM	8211	ECMA	1C	Work on ISDN
XVIII GN	8211	ITT	1,2	Distribution network for ISDN and user installation
XVIII GO	8211	France	1,2	Proposal for a six wire S interface
XVIII GP	8211	Ellemtel	1	Proposals for interface code and frame structures at 256 kbit/s at the S-interface
XVIII GQ	8211	Canada-BNR	1C	Support of a passive bus at the user/network interface
XVIII GH	8211	Canada-BNR	1C	Comparison of 2 and 4 wire user/network interface based on application model
XVIII GS	8211	NTT	1,2	Comments on Common Physical interface
XVIII GT	8211	ITT	1	Procedure for activation/deactivation of network and subscriber terminals
XVIII GU	8211	British Telecom	1	A possible frame structure and interface code for the S and T interface
XVIII GV	8211	IBM Europe	1	Requirements for maintenance of complex data processing systems including distributed equipments
XVIII GW	8211	Netherlands	1,2	Proposal for frame structure and line code at 256 kbit/s

Doc. Id.	Date	Source	Questions	Title
XVIII GX	8302	FRG	1C	Intermediate channel structure at the S/T reference point
XVIII GY	8302	FRG	2	S/T interface for multiplexed access and broadband access at 2048 kb/s
XVIII GZ	8302	FRG	1B,5	Proposed reply to two questions posed by Working Party XI/4
XVIII HA	8302	FRG	1B,5	Aspects of autonomous sub-channels
XVIII HB	8302	FRG	4	Flexibility of D-channel signalling protocols for simple terminals
XVIII HC	8302	FRG	1E	ISDN customer access (layer 1) during the initial phase
XVIII HD	8302	ECMA	1C,13	Test loops at user premises for ISDN
XVIII HE	8302	FRG	1A	ISDN service/supplementary services analysis-matrix
XVIII HF	8302	FRG	1A	ISDN services and supplementary services/network functional elements analysis-matrix
XVIII HG	8302	FRG	1B,4	Requirements for end-to-end signalling message transfer
XVIII HH	8302	FRG	1B,4	Effect of p and t information on the establishment of B-channel connections
XVIII HI	8302	FRG	1B,4	Necessity of a supervisory function for the S/T reference point and specific requirements
XVIII HJ	8302	FRG	1C	Improvements in the frame structure at S or T reference points
XVIII HK	8302	Switzerland	1C	Erroneous calling by data stations
XVIII HL	8302	ISO/TC97/SC6/WG3	1C	Comments on the ISDN point R to adapt data terminals that conform with Recs. V.24, V.25, V.28, V.35
XVIII HM	8302	ISO/TC97/SC6/WG3	1C	Comments on the ISDN point S and T functional characteristics
XVIII HN	8302	ISO/TC97/SC6/WG3	1C	Comments on the ISDN point S and T physical/electrical characteristics
XVIII HO	8302	FRG	1C	Proposal for a draft recommendation: ISDN basic access user/network interface – layer one specification
XVIII HP	8302	NTT	1,2	Considerations on the octet structure preservation for low bit rate channels in the ISDN
XVIII HQ	8302	NTT	1A,1B	Compatibility checking
XVIII HR	8302	NTT	1C,2,4	Requirements on user/network interface protocol for PBX
XVIII HS	8302	NTT	1C,2	ISDN digital PBX interface at reference point T
XVIII HT	8302	NTT	1C	Alarm indication signals across the basic ISDN interface
XVIII HU	8302	NTT	1C	Considerations of loop-back test for the basic ISDN interface
XVIII HV	8302	NTT	1C	Reference configuration for powering across the basic ISDN user/network interface
XVIII HW	8302	NTT	1A,2	Proposed channel types and channel structures for channels having capacity above 64 kbit/s
XVIII HX	8302	NTT	1A,2	Clarification of framework for channel struct & access capabilities of channels having capacity above 64 kbit/s
XVIII HY	8302	France	1A	An approach for the analysis of ISDN bearer services: generating functions & executive functions
XVIII HZ	8302	France	2	Draft Recommendations I.xxx, I.xxy, I.xxw: proposed modifications
XVIII IA	8302	France	1B	Proposals for a recommendation on the functional architectural model of ISDN
XVIII IB	8302	France	1B,1E	Proposal for draft Recs. I.0040 (present G.705) – principles of ISDN & evolution from existing networks to ISDN
XVIII IC	8302	France	5	Switching aspects of ISDN
XVIII ID	8302	France	1B	Proposal for an integrated global international numbering plan
XVIII IE	8302	France	1A	Telecommunication services: ISDN communication & bearer services
XVIII IF	8302	France	1B	Considerations on intermediate channel structure
XVIII IG	8302	France	1B	Considerations about remote power feeding of ISDN terminals
XVIII IH	8302	FRG	1C	Portability and compatibility
XVIII II	8302	FRG	1B	Reference model for sub-functions of technical parameters on the ISDN user premises
XVIII IJ	8302	USA	1A	Framework for describing ISDN services
XVIII IK	8302	USA	1A,1B	Definition of 64 kb/s circuit switched capability
XVIII IL	8302	USA	1A	Definition of 64 kb/s leased circuit capability
XVIII IM	8302	USA	1A	Implementation of 64 kb/s and sub-rate leased circuit capabilities at the ISDN interfaces
XVIII IN	8302	USA	1A	On the need for packet switched capabilities in an ISDN
XVIII IO	8302	ATT	1A	The concept of multimedia calls in an ISDN
XVIII IP	8302	ATT	1C,2	The non-provision of exchange originated power to TE1 or NT2
XVIII IQ	8302	ATT	1C,2	Considerations for activation and deactivation of network termination equipment (NT1)
XVIII IR	8302	ATT	1C,2	Power activation and deactivation of customer equipment – basic access layer 1 considerations
XVIII IS	8302	ATT	2,4	Power activation and deactivation of customer equipment – basic access higher layer considerations
XVIII IT	8302	Canada-BNR	1B,1C	Network control information categories
XVIII IU	8302	Canada-BNR	1C,2	Functional requirements of the ISDN basic digital and hybrid access
XVIII IV	8302	Canada-BNR	1C,2	Considerations in support of a passive bus at the user/network interface
XVIII IW	8302	Comsat	1C,2	Characteristics of customer premises wiring topologies
XVIII IX	8302	Switzerland	1B,9	Hypothetical reference connections for ISDN
XVIII IY	8302	Switzerland	1C	Results of experiments with passive bus
XVIII IZ	8302	Switzerland	2	Reference configuration for NT2

Doc. Id.	Date	Source	Questions	Title
XVIII JA	8302	KDD	1	ISDN numbering plan
XVIII JB	8302	KDD	1	Service indication code
XVIII JC	8302	KDD	1,4,5	Digital signal processing device and its related control principles in the ISDN
XVIII JD	8302	KDD	1	ISDN hypothetical reference connection
XVIII JE	8302	Canada-BNR		Sub-addressing considerations for private network terminals
XVIII JF	8302	Canada TC	1B,1D	General principles pursuant to user selection of alternative international networks and services
XVIII JG	8302	Canada	5	B/D channel interworking for packet switched data traffic
XVIII JH	8302	Canada	5	D channel handler functional requirements
XVIII JI	8302	Canada	1A	Classification of ISDN services
XVIII JJ	8302	Canada	1B	On defining a functional architecture for the ISDN
XVIII JK	8302	Canada-TCTS	1B	Primary rate channel structure (1564 kb/s)
XVIII JL	8302	Canada-TCTS	2	Service access procedure
XVIII JM	8302	Canada-TCTS	1B	Priorities in the arbitration process
XVIII JN	8302	Canada-TCTS	1C	On-premises distribution configurations
XVIII JO	8302	Canada-TCTS	1C	Service connection models
XVIII JP	8302	Canada-TCTS	1A,2,4	Connection procedures - network responsibility
XVIII JQ	8302	Sweden	1C	Activation and deactivation procedures at reference points S and T
XVIII JR	8302	Sweden	1D	Interworking between ISDN and the analogue telephone network for data communication
XVIII JS	8302	Sweden	2,12	Maintenance philosophy for digital subscriber lines
XVIII JT	8302	Ellemtel	1C,2	Results of measurements on the 192 kbit/s frame structure
XVIII JU	8302	Switzerland	1C	C-channel recommendations
XVIII JV	8302	Switzerland	1C	Activation and deactivation procedures
XVIII JW	8302	Australia	1B,1D,1E	ISDN - Telecom Australia's proposals for network development
XVIII JX	8302	Australia	1C	Draft Rec. 1.xxy: comments and proposals for change
XVIII JY	8302	Australia	1A,1B,4,5	Change of service between voice and transparent connection
XVIII JZ	8302	Australia	1B	Low bit rate voice encoding - network implications for the ISDN
XVIII KA	8302	Australia	1B	Sub-64 kbit/s connections in the ISDN
XVIII KB	8302	Australia	1A,1B,2,4	ISDN protocol architecture
XVIII KC	8302	Australia	1A	Classification of generic telecommunication services using OSI concepts
XVIII KD	8302	Plessy	1C	ISDN user/network interface
XVIII KE	8302	Phillips	1C	Power feeding across S reference point
XVIII KF	8302	Phillips	1	Proposal for an activation/deactivation procedure
XVIII KG	8302	British Telecom	1,4	Provision for user to user signalling in D-channel protocols
XVIII KH	8302	British Telecom	1C	Practical experience of the basic access user/network interfaces
XVIII KI	8302	British Telecom	1C	User-network interface power feed considerations
XVIII KJ	8302	British Telecom	1C	ISDN interfaces in the local environment
XVIII KK	8302	Canada-TCTS	1C,2	ISDN hybrid access using the basic channel structure
XVIII KL	8302	Netherlands	1C,2	A compatible hybrid access arrangement
XVIII KM	8302	USA	1C	Comments on techniques to support several TEs
XVIII KN	8302	USA	1C	Alternatives for multiple terminal equipment connections at ISDN subscriber sites
XVIII KO	8302	USA	1C	Comparison of bus alternatives at S and T
XVIII KP	8302	USA	1C	D-channel contention mechanism for active bus interface at ISDN S and T reference points
XVIII KQ	8302	FRG	1C	Comparison of an active and passive bus in a typical customer installation
XVIII KR	8302	ATT	2	Primary rate multiplex channel structure
XVIII KS	8302	British Telecom	1C	Suggested improvements to Recs. I.xxw, I.xxx, I.xxy
XVIII KT	8302	British Telecom	1B	Network implications of change of service during an ISDN call
XVIII KU	8302	ITT	-	Comments on COM XVIII-No. 132
XVIII KV	8302	ITT	1C	Terminal portability
XVIII KW	8302	Adv Micro Dev	1C	Power availability at NT1
XVIII KX	8302	USA	1	PABX primary rate access interface
XVIII KY	8302	FRG	1C	Comparison of Florence results (s.HO) with the new USA proposals (s.KO)
XVIII KZ	8302	ISO	1C	Clarification on connection selection
XVIII LA	8302	ISO	1C	Activation and deactivation procedures at reference points S, T and possibly R
XVIII LB	8302	FRG	1C	Layer 1 activation procedure at S/T ref. point
XVIII LC	8302	France	1C	The connection of PABXs to ISDN

Doc. Id.	Date	Source	Questions	Title
XVIII LD	8302	British Telecom	1	Subscriber line maintenance – test loops
XVIII LE	8302	France	5	V interfaces
XVIII LF	8302	Switzerland	--	Activation and deactivation procedures (alternative to TD40)
XVIII LG	8306	RQ13	13,16	Proposed draft Rec. G.2X – Maintenance philosophy for analogue, digital and mixed networks
XVIII LH	8306	ATT	18	Proposed changes to multiplex equipment jitter accommodation requirements (Recs. G.743 and G.752)
XVIII LI	8306	USA	9	Fitting a two parameter block error probability curve with measured data
XVIII LJ	8306	USSR	1C,15	Usage of the relative bipulse signal at ISDN digital interfaces
XVIII LK	8306	Comsat	9	Satellite system error performance considering propagation effects
XVIII LL	8306	FRG	3	Slip control hysteresis
XVIII LM	8306	FRG	18	Proposal for amendment of Rec. G.734
XVIII LN	8306	FRG	18	Extended frame align procedures for primary rate digital signal at 2048 kbit/s, protection against false framing
XVIII LO	8306	Switzerland	3	New structure for the Recs on digital network synchronization
XVIII LP	8306	Switzerland	1B,5	Comment on draft Rec. I.320 (Numbering and addressing principles in ISDN)
XVIII LQ	8306	Switzerland	1C	Proposal for Sect. 5 of Rec. I.431
XVIII LR	8306	British Telecom	9	Derivation of error performance equipment design objectives for transmission systems on physical media
XVIII LS	8306	NTT	1C	Improvement in the frame structure at ISDN reference point S/T
XVIII LT	8306	NTT	1C	Amendments to the types of configuration
XVIII LU	8306	NTT	1C	Interchange circuit designation for the ISDN reference point S/T
XVIII LV	8306	NTT	1C	Power and depowering procedures for the basic ISDN user-network interface
XVIII LW	8306	NTT	1C	Proposal for draft Rec. I.431: basic ISDN user-network interface Layer 1 specification electrical characteristics
XVIII LX	8306	NTT	1C	Layer 1 operation mode to support a test loop within NT1 towards terminal
XVIII LY	8306	NTT	1A,2	Proposed amendments to the structure of draft Rec. I.412 (I.xxy)
XVIII LZ	8306	NTT	1A,2	Clarification of requirements for highspeed access services and proposed channel structures...at 1544/6312 kbit/s
XVIII MA	8306	NTT	1A,2	Proposed frame structures of the primary rate access at 1544 kbit/s
XVIII MB	8306	NTT	9	Error performance objectives allocation strategy for a 64 kbit/s service
XVIII MC	8306	NTT	1B,1C,4	Remote subscriber line test based on user's request
XVIII MD	8306	NTT	4	D-channel security arrangement for primary rate multiplex access
XVIII ME	8306	NTT	15	Bit sequence independent code for interface at 6312 kbit/s using coaxial pair
XVIII MF	8306	NTT	18	Proposed change to 32064 kbit/s multiplexing frame structure
XVIII MG	8306	Switzerland	2	Reference configuration for NT2
XVIII MH	8306	KDD	1B,9	Basic principles for establishing the hypothetical reference connections for ISDN
XVIII MI	8306	KDD	9	Proposal to amend CCITT Rec. G.821
XVIII MJ	8306	KDD	9	Comments on BER specification in Rec. G.821
XVIII MK	8306	KDD	3	A proposed revision of Rec. G.811
XVIII ML	8306	KDD	3	Proposal to amend para. 6 of Rec. G.811
XVIII MM	8306	Canada-CNCP	1B	Compatibility checking of telecommunication services
XVIII MN	8306	Canada-CNCP	1A,1E	An ISDN evolution scenario
XVIII MO	8306	Canada-CNCP	1D	ISDN internetworking interface to the telex networks
XVIII MP	8306	British Telecom	1,3	Comments on Rec. I.3xx
XVIII MQ	8306	British Telecom	1A	Draft Rec. I.430, I.431 – Proposed editorial revisions
XVIII MR	8306	France	1A	Telecommunication services to be supported by an ISDN
XVIII MS	8306	France	1A	ISDN bearer services
XVIII MT	8306	France	1A	Packet switching bearer service over the D channel
XVIII MU	8306	France	1A	Content, structure and use of service indication information
XVIII MV	8306	France	1B	Some general principles for definition of ISDN addressing capabilities/numbering principles
XVIII MW	8306	France	1C	Consideration on the activation/deactivation procedure
XVIII MX	8306	France	1C	Comments on the problem of reference configuration
XVIII MY	8306	France	1C	Proposal for a new distribution of the functions between levels 1 and 2
XVIII MZ	8306	France	1C	Power feeding configuration for an ISDN inpremise installation behaviour towards power source availability
XVIII NA	8306	FRG	1A,2	Broadband bearer services at the 2048 kbit/s level
XVIII NB	8306	FRG	1B	An approach to quality of service and network performance in the ISDN
XVIII NC	8306	Australia	2	High speed and primary rate channel structure
XVIII ND	8306	Australia	9	Error apportionment strategy – comments on COM XVIII-Nos. 192 and 193
XVIII NE	8306	Australia	9	Hypothetical reference connections (HRX) for the ISDN
XVIII NF	8306	Australia	1C	Suggested corrections and improvements to draft Rec. I.431

Doc. Id.	Date	Source	Questions	Title
XVIII TP	8311	NTT	1C	Layer boundary between physical and data link layers
XVIII TQ	8311	NTT	1C	Clarification of D channel access control specifications
XVIII TR	8311	NTT	1B,2	Proposal for specific values in electrical characteristics of basic access interface
XVIII TS	8311	NTT	1	Concept of connection type
XVIII TT	8311	NTT	1A	Refinement of bearer service description
XVIII TU	8311	ATT	1C	Comments on draft Rec. I.431 - Voltage and power values
XVIII TV	8311	ATT	1C	Comments on draft Rec. I.431 - Electrical characteristics
XVIII TW	8311	ATT	1C,15,17	Recommended changes to draft Rec. I.432
XVIII TX	8311	ATT	1A,1B	Establishment of connection for bearer services and network connections
XVIII TY	8311	ATT	1A,1B,6	Definition of transparent ISDN circuit - mode connection/service
XVIII TZ	8311	ATT	1B,5	Proposed signalling delay criteria for the D-channel for DSL
XVIII UA	8311	British Telecom	1B	Proposed amendment of draft Rec. I.3XX
XVIII UB	8311	British Telecom	1B	ISDN protocol reference model
XVIII UC	8311	ECMA	1C	Replace 203 - Revised comments on sections 5 and 6 of draft Rec. I.431
XVIII UD	8311	USA	1A,1B	ISDN services, protocols, and interface objectives
XVIII UE	8311	USA	1C	Physical layer activation/deactivation
XVIII UF	8311	USA	1B,1C	Loop testing on an ISDN DSL
XVIII UG	8311	Racal-Milgo	1B,1C,2	U interface
XVIII UH	8311	British Telecom	1B	Network implications of change of service during an ISDN call
XVIII UI	8311	FRG	1C	Timing requirements at S/T reference point
XVIII UJ	8311	FRG	1C	Unbalance about earth on the ISDN S interface (I.431)
XVIII UK	8311	FRG	1C	Bit phase relationship between the input and output at the So interface
XVIII UL	8311	FRG	1C	Emergency power feeding at the So interface
XVIII UM	8311	FRG	1C	Amendment to draft Rec. I.431
XVIII UN	8311	FRG	1C	Coding of signals info 1 and info 3 at the S/T reference point
XVIII UO	8311	FRG	1C	Limitations for point-to-point connections at the So interface
XVIII UP	8311	FRG	1C	Connected indication configuration in draft Rec. I.431
XVIII UQ	8311	FRG	1A,1B	Services n x 384 kbit/s and required network connection
XVIII UR	8311	FRG	1C	I.431
XVIII US	8311	FRG	1A	Proposal for new question on broadband aspects of the ISDN
XVIII UT	8311	FRG	1A,6	Terminology: definition of "transparent/non-transparent"
XVIII UU	8311	France	1B,1C	Notes on the maintenance of digital subscriber systems
XVIII UV	8311	France	1B	Amendments to I.310
XVIII UW	8311	France	1B	Proposed amendments to I.310, point B
XVIII UX	8311	France	1A	Considerations on the definition of teleservices
XVIII UY	8311	France	1A	Definition of ISDN broadband bearer services (at n x 64 kbit/s)
XVIII UZ	8311	France	1A	Leased, reserved and switched services: semi-permanent connections
XVIII VA	8311	France	1A	Multipoint services
XVIII VB	8311	France	1A	Examples of multipoint services for data applications
XVIII VC	8311	France	1A	Comments on the different types of service information in ISDN
XVIII VD	8311	FRG	1A	Quality of service parameters for ISDN
XVIII VE	8311	FRG	1A	ISDN supplementary services and facilities
XVIII VF	8311	France	1B	Comment on Rec. I.320 (addressing and numbering principles in ISDN)
XVIII VG	8311	FRG	1C	Deletion of info S6 of the activation/deactivation procedure
XVIII VH	8311	IEC/TC83	1C	Connectors for information technology equipment
XVIII VI	8311	Belgium	1B	Draft Rec. I.320
XVIII VJ	8311	Switzerland	7	Simplified transmission of wideband speech and data in 64 kbit/s
XVIII VK	8311	Switzerland	1C	A compromise proposal for activation/deactivation layer 1 procedures
XVIII VL	8311	NTT	1A	Requirement for a telecommunication service indication at level 3
XVIII VM	8311	Sweden	1C	Examples of D channel access control at layer 1
XVIII VN	8311	Sweden	1A	Draft Rec. I.200 - Alternative of paragraph 1
XVIII VO	8402	Sweden	1,2	Material for a draft recommendation for digital subscriber line maintenance (latest version)
XVIII VP	8402	FRG	1B	ISDN - numbering principles (I.320); end of address indication
XVIII VQ	8402	ECMA	1C	Detection of disconnected state
XVIII VR	8402	IEC	1C	CISPR Rec. No.___ - Data processing equip. & electr. office mach. limits of interference and measurement methods

Doc. Id.	Date	Source	Questions	Title
XVIII PJ	8306	ATT	4	Delay suffered by "s" information owing to the presence of "p" and "t" information in the D channel
XVIII PK	8306	ATT	4,5	Problems with the through-connection plan for circuit switched connections in ISDN
XVIII PL	8306	ATT	9	A proposed error free decisecond objective for a 64 kbit/s connection
XVIII PM	8306	USA	1C	Objectives for provision of emergency power to ISDN terminals
XVIII PN	8306	USA	1C	Provision for indicating to a terminal the connected state and bus versus point-to-point
XVIII PO	8306	Brazil	1C	Frame alignment procedures for TE and NT
XVIII PP	8306	Australia	6	Draft Rec. I.112 - Vocabulary of ISDN terms
XVIII PQ	8306	FRG	1C	Remote power feeding requirements
XVIII PR	8306	FRG	1C	Emergency power feeding on the S bus
XVIII PS	8306	FRG	4	On the signalling modes of the D channel
XVIII PT	8306	FRG	4	Relation between transactions and calls
XVIII PU	8306	FRG	1B	Further elaboration of draft Rec. I.3xx on ISDN network connection types
XVIII PV	8306	FRG	1C	S/T interface for the multiplex channel structure at 2048 kbit/s and for a possible broadband channel structure
XVIII PW	8306	FRG	1C	Activation/deactivation at S/T reference points
XVIII PX	8306	FRG	1C	Jitter and static deviation on the S bus
XVIII PY	8306	FRG	1D	Interworking btwn voice band facs & data term conn to ISDN & analogue teleph net & req'd ISDN cust net interfaces
XVIII PZ	8306	FRG	1C	Proposal for rcvr input char & phase relation between input & out sig of term side of ISDN subscriber interface
XVIII QA	8306	FRG	1C	Proposal for the transmitter output characteristics of the ISDN subscriber interface
XVIII QB	8306	FRG	4	End-to-end (user-to-user) signalling under the aspects of PABX-to-PABX terminal-to-terminal signalling
XVIII QC	8306	FRG	1B,4	Subaddressing principles within the ISDN
XVIII QD	8306	FRG	1A	Support of existing services in the ISDN
XVIII QE	8306	FRG	1A	Types of services supported by the ISDN
XVIII QF	8306	FRG	1C	Testing loss on the passive bus configuration
XVIII QG	8306	GTE	8	Proposed question on TASI/DSI systems for study period 81-84
XVIII QH	8306	Canada-CNCP	1B	Network identification in the ISDN numbering structure
XVIII QI	8306	Canada-TCTS	1B	ISDN addressing for interworking
XVIII QJ	8306	Canada	5	Physical interface at reference point U
XVIII QK	8306	Canada-BNH	16	Proposal for amendments to draft Rec. G.71x
XVIII QL	8306	ATT	3,9	Jitter accommodation in digital networks
XVIII QM	8306	ATT	16	Quantitative differences between noise and sinusoidal test methods for total distortion
XVIII QN	8306	ATT	9	A four grade error apportionment model
XVIII QO	8306	ATT	3	Time interval error - a tutorial discussion
XVIII QP	8306	ATT	3	Proposal for a new definition of TIE in Rec. G.811
XVIII QQ	8306	ATT	3	Proposal for amendments to the organization of Rec. G.811
XVIII QR	8306	ATT	9	Proposed clarification to draft Rec. G.821
XVIII QS	8306	USA	2	Minimum functional criteria for low cost ISDN terminals
XVIII QT	8306	China	16	Proposed limits for the send and receive sides crosstalk of PCM channels at audio frequencies
XVIII QU	8306	China	18	A proposed method for measuring jitter transfer characteristics of dig multiplexing equip't at 2 Mbit/s heirarchy
XVIII QV	8306	British Telecom	8	Circuit multiplication equipment
XVIII QW	8306	British Telecom	17	Possible improved frame structure for use at 2048 kbit/s
XVIII QX	8306	FRG	1C	Maximum line attenuation at the S interface
XVIII QY	8306	Phillips	1C	The choice of primitives supporting the activation/deactivation procedure
XVIII QZ	8306	Phillips	1C	A detailed proposal for definition of activation/deactivation on layer 1 service primitives
XVIII RA	8306	Phillips	2	On the relation between multiplexing and rate adaptation on sub-rate channels of 8, 16, and 32 kbit/s
XVIII RB	8306	USSR	1B,9	Proposed amendments to Rec. G.721
XVIII RC	8306	USSR	18	Proposed modifications to Recs. G.745, G.753, and G.754
XVIII RD	8306	NTT	16	Considerations and proposal for TBRL specification in Rec. G.71y
XVIII RE	8306	USA	16	Guidelines for electrical characteristics of basic access
XVIII RF	8306	USA	16	Proposed improvements in the basic access frame structure
XVIII RG	8306	USA	1B,9	The role of satellites in hypothetical reference connections for ISDN
XVIII RH	8306	IBM Europe	1C	Study of a two wire ISDN interface
XVIII RI	8306	Comsat	9	Statistical character of BER on satellite circuits
XVIII RJ	8306	USSR	16	Design objectives of mixed analogue digital connections
XVIII RK	8306	Switzerland	1C	Comparison between Kyoto frames and NTT frames
XVIII RL	8306	FRG	3	Amendments to Rec. G.811

Doc. Id.	Date	Source	Questions	Title
XVIII RM	8306	FRG	15	Rec. G.703, sect. 9 (interface at 139264 kbit/s)
XVIII RN	8306	FRG	16	Amendments to Recs. G.712 and G.71x
XVIII RO	8306	FRG	16	Proposed amendments to Rec. G.71y
XVIII RP	8306	FRG	1B,4	Addendum to D.C. "Qc"
XVIII RQ	8306	USSR	15	Proposed amendments to Rec. G.703
XVIII RR	8306	France	12	Proposal of signalling processing in draft Rec. G.7x2
XVIII RS	8306	British Telecom	18	An auxiliary 3rd order interface at 68736 kbit/s
XVIII RT	8306	Canada-BNR	16	Proposed amendments to draft Rec. G.71y
XVIII RU	8306	British Telecom	9	Editorial changes to Rec. G.821
XVIII RV	8306	Sweden	10	Grade of service parameter for exchanges under failure condition
XVIII RW	8306	Sweden	10	Availability performance plan
XVIII RX	8306	British Telecom	18	Error in Rec. G.737
XVIII RY	8306	British Telecom	3	Specification of slip performance
XVIII RZ	8306	NTT	1C	Modified powering/depowering procedures
XVIII SA	8306	British Telecom	14	A possible further interworking solution
XVIII SB	8311	France	7	Amendments to draft Rec. G.722
XVIII SC	8311	ISO/TC97/SC6	1C,11,13	Connector selection and pin allocations for ISDN basic access TE/NT interface
XVIII SD	8311	British Telecom	1C	Some problems with the current layer 1 frame structure and procedures
XVIII SE	8311	NTT	7	Suggestions on design requirements for wideband speech encoding at 64 kbit/s
XVIII SF	8311	NTT	7	A proposal for testing items and conditions for wideband speech encoding at 64 kbit/s
XVIII SG	8311	FRG	1A,6	The concept of ISDN services, service attributes, low-high layer functions and functional elements
XVIII SH	8311	FRG	1A,6	Definition of service attributes, supplementary services, low layer and high layer functions, functional elements
XVIII SI	8311	FRG	1A	Supplementary services based on additional low layer functions (ALLF) and additional high layer functions (ALHF)
XVIII SJ	8311	FRG	1A,1B	Possible values of service attribute & connection attribute: establishment of service, establish. of connection
XVIII SK	8311	FRG	1A,1B	Possible values of service attributes & connection attributes information transfer configuration, connection...
XVIII SL	8311	FRG	1B	Subaddressing in ISDN
XVIII SM	8311	FRG	1B	ISDN numbering
XVIII SN	8311	FRG	1H,2,15	Allocation of channels to ISDN basic access based on the frame structure of of Rec. G.734
XVIII SO	8311	FRG	1B,12	Guidelines for fault isolation (comments on appendix 1 to annex 4 of COM XVIII-R19)
XVIII SP	8311	FRG	7	Choice of a codec for 7 kHz speech (annex: 64 kbit/s coding of 7 kHz bandwidth speech)
XVIII SQ	8311	FRG	7,18	Application aspects of 7 kHz speech that may influence the choice of a codec
XVIII SR	8311	FRG	1C	Amendment of draft Rec. G.7x2
XVIII SS	8311	FRG	1C	Amendment of draft Rec. I.432
XVIII ST	8311	FRG	1C	Characteristics of cables supporting the ISDN basic access/network interface
XVIII SU	8311	FRG	1C	Limitations on the passive bus
XVIII SV	8311	FRG	1C	Testing loss and output impedance
XVIII SW	8311	FRG	1C	Remote power feeding requirements
XVIII SX	8311	FRG	1C	Pulse shape and amplitude with 500 ohm load at the So interface
XVIII SY	8311	FRG	1C	Accuracy of clocks at the So interface
XVIII SZ	8311	Sweden	1B,1C	Material for a draft Rec. for digital subscriber line maintenance (latest version)
XVIII TA	8311	British Telecom	1B	Simultaneous transmission of wideband speech and data in 64 kbit/s
XVIII TB	8311	Switzerland	1B	Addressing principles in ISDN (Rec. I.320)
XVIII TC	8311	Switzerland	7	Principles for relating identifiers to communication selection
XVIII TD	8311	France	7	Proposal for an assessment strategy for wide-band (speech) coding
XVIII TE	8311	France	7	A promising codec family to transmit wideband speech and data in audioconference and videoconference systems
XVIII TF	8311	France	7	Complements to the draft Rec. G.7x2
XVIII TG	8311	Sweden	1B	Standardization of interworking between ISDN and PSTN for data communications
XVIII TH	8311	KDD	1A	Proposal for 64 kbit/s ADPCM wideband codec
XVIII TI	8311	British Telecom	1A	Service attributes and telephone service in ISDN
XVIII TJ	8311	KDD	1B	Address/numbering principles in ISDN
XVIII TK	8311	KDD	7	Assessment of 64 kbit/s 7 kHz systems
XVIII TL	8311	Ellemtel	1C	Comments on draft Rec. I.431
XVIII TM	8311	NTT	1C,2	Proposed channel assignments for the primary rate interface structure for 1544 kbit/s
XVIII TN	8311	NTT	1C	Necessity for remote power feeding to the NT and TE using call-by-call based power/depowering process
XVIII TO	8311	NTT	1C	Reference configuration for powering/depowering

Doc. Id.	Date	Source	Questions	Title
XVIII NG	8306	Australia	1C	Star and passive bus configurations for the ISDN network/customer interface
XVIII NH	8306	Netherlands	1C,15	Channel allocation at primary rate
XVIII NI	8306	Netherlands	1C,15	Proposed answer to WP XI/4 regarding channel allocation at the V4 interface
XVIII NJ	8306	Italy	2	High speed channels up to the primary rate for the ISDN
XVIII NK	8306	Canada-CNCP	1B	Service interchange during a call
XVIII NL	8306	Canada-CNCP	1B	ISDN numbering structure
XVIII NM	8306	Canada-CNCP	1A	Redefinition of draft Rec. I.200 service classifications
XVIII NN	8306	Canada	1A,1B	Connection types
XVIII NO	8306	Canada-BNR	1A,1B	Change of connection characteristics during a call
XVIII NP	8306	Canada-BNR	1A,1B	Bearer services and connection types
XVIII NQ	8306	Canada-TCTS	1B	Applications of network connections
XVIII NR	8306	Canada-TCTS	1B	Basic and sub-attributes of connection types
XVIII NS	8306	Canada-TCTS	1B	ISDN protocol model
XVIII NT	8306	Canada-TCTS	1A	Refinement of the ISDN functional model
XVIII NU	8306	Canada-BNR	1B,1C	Basic user/network interface electrical characteristics
XVIII NV	8306	Canada-BNR	2,7	Consideration on rate adaption and sub-rate multiplexing formats in ISDN
XVIII NW	8306	Canada TCTS	1C	Improvement to basic access frame structure
XVIII NX	8306	Canada	1A,1B	Relationship between connection types, signal routing and services
XVIII NY	8306	NTT	1A,1B	Proposed amendments to draft Rec. I.120
XVIII NZ	8306	Ellemtel	7	Wideband speech encoding at 64 kbit/s
XVIII OA	8306	USA	1C	Range of attenuation of subscriber cables at the S interface
XVIII OB	8306	USA	1B,1C,4	Initiation of TEI allocation procedures
XVIII OC	8306	ATT	1C,4	Centralized call control procedures for ISDN access
XVIII OD	8306	ATT	1B,4,5	Number of primary rate access B channels that can be supported by one D channel for PABX to exchange signalling
XVIII OE	8306	USA	1B	Recommendation for signalling link delay, reliability, and error performance on primary rate access
XVIII OF	8306	USA	1B,4,5	Use of intermediate cut-through to avoid PABX voice clipping
XVIII OG	8306	USA	1B,4,5	Speech clipping and cut-through for PABX access to ISDN exchanges
XVIII OH	8306	USA	1B	Centralized control applications for station terminals in ISDN
XVIII OI	8306	ATT	1,4	Centralized control approach for simple station terminal signalling
XVIII OJ	8306	ATT	1A,1B,4	Proposal for the physical layer of the primary rate access interface
XVIII OK	8306	ATT	1B,4,5	Treatment of user to user signalling transfer similar to that of s type information
XVIII OL	8306	ATT	1,4	Strategy for providing a backup for PABX to exchange signalling link
XVIII OM	8306	ATT	1A	Maximum length of user data field for user-to-user signalling
XVIII ON	8306	IBM Europe	1C	Comments on draft Rec. I.200 on services supported by an ISDN
XVIII OO	8306	IBM Europe	1	Need for 100 meter TE to NT2 limit
XVIII OP	8306	IBM Europe	1C	ISDN "c" channel
XVIII OQ	8306	IBM Europe	1C	Maintenance loop testing in ISDN
XVIII OR	8306	IBM Europe	2	Basic ISDN interface independent of user configuration
XVIII OS	8306	IBM Europe	2	Placement of network multiplexing in ISDN reference model
XVIII OT	8306	IBM Europe	7,17	Common channel signalling system no. 7 or LAPD for primary rate access
XVIII OU	8306	France	6,7	Complements to the draft Rec. G.7X2
XVIII OV	8306	France	12	New definitions to be included in Rec. G.702
XVIII OW	8306	KDD	1B,4	Sensitivity to transmission errors of various wideband speech encoding schemes
XVIII OX	8306	KDD	2	Proposed amendments to Rec. G.704
XVIII OY	8306	USA	2	Control of ISDN network elements
XVIII OZ	8306	USA	2	A proposal for a 384 kbit/s ISDN channel
XVIII PA	8306	USA	2	Time-division multiplex structure for primary rate access interface
XVIII PB	8306	USA	2	Number of B (4 kbit/s) and H1 (384 kbit/s) channels in a primary rate multiplex interface
XVIII PC	8306	USA	1C	A proposal for a 1536 kbit/s ISDN channel
XVIII PD	8306	USA	2,4	Proposed characteristics of the primary rate multiplexed access interface
XVIII PE	8306	USA	2,4	Requirement for basic access interface D channel protocol to support low cost terminals
XVIII PF	8306	ATT	1C	Non-fixed bit-interleaved multiplexing of subrate channels
XVIII PG	8306	ATT	4	Continuous power for layer 1 to 3 functions
XVIII PH	8306	ATT	4	Packet restrictions based on signalling delay requirements
XVIII PI	8306	ATT	4	Influence of PABX attendant initial speech clipping considerations on D channel maximum packet data size

Doc. Id.	Date	Source	Questions	Title
XVIII VS	8402	British Telecom	1B	Comments on draft Rec. I.325
XVIII VT	8402	British Telecom	1B	Amendments to draft Rec. I.325 (ISDN connection types)
XVIII VU	8402	British Telecom	1B	Amendments to draft Rec. I.300 (ISDN network functional principles)
XVIII VV	8402	British Telecom	1C	Connected/disconnected indication
XVIII VW	8402	British Telecom	1B	Network implications of change service during an ISDN call
XVIII VX	8402	LMEricsson	-	Proposal for new question on general aspects of digital link maintenance in the ISDN
XVIII VY	8402	British Telecom	1C	Results of experiments on S/T interface transmitter circuit
XVIII VZ	8402	GEC Telecom	1C	Power feeding over the subscriber access
XVIII WA	8402	Canada-Teleglobe	4,5	Call characteristics in the future ISDN
XVIII WB	8402	Canada CNCP	1B	Modification to draft Rec. I.320 - called party network identification
XVIII WC	8402	Switzerland	1C	I.431 - Activation/deactivation layer 1 procedures
XVIII WD	8402	Switzerland	1C	Power feeding - specification of the value of the voltage X and its tolerance
XVIII WE	8402	Switzerland	1C	Power feeding - specification for future developments
XVIII WF	8402	Switzerland	1C	Proposal for a new question to stud the principles relating identifiers to communication selection
XVIII WG	8402	Switzerland		Specification of the type of information transferred attribute
XVIII WH	8402	Ellemtel		Round trip and differential round trip delay
XVIII WI	8402	Ellemtel		Characteristics of the reference cable
XVIII WJ	8402	France		Proposal for introducing the word "teleaction" in draft Rec. I.112
XVIII WK	8402	France		Comments and proposal on draft Rec. I.311
XVIII WL	8402	France		User to user signalling in relation with I.2xx and I.451
XVIII WM	8402	France		Proposed new coding of the "cause" information element I.451
XVIII WN	8402	France		I.451 (Q.930) - Bearer capability and low-layer capability information elements
XVIII WO	8402	France		Proposal for modification of draft Rec. I.432
XVIII WP	8402	France		Alterations to the activation procedure at terminal level
XVIII WQ	8402	France		Comments on the physical characteristics of the "S" interface
XVIII WR	8402	France		Proposal for I.325 improvements
XVIII WS	8402	FRG		Priority list of ISDN bearer services
XVIII WT	8402	FRG		Proposal for descriptions of connection attributes & their values for ISDN connection types & connection elem
XVIII WU	8402	FRG		New question /XVIII - connecting of LANS to ISDN
XVIII WV	8402	FRG		Description of ISDN bearer services
XVIII WW	8402	FRG		Priority list of ISDN connection types
XVIII WX	8402	FRG		New question /XVIII - New voice and non-voice services supported by the ISDN
XVIII WY	8402	FRG		Connection attributes: establishment of connection, connection performance and others
XVIII WZ	8402	FRG		Proposed descriptions of service attributes for ISDN bearer services
XVIII XA	8402	FRG	1C	Proposal for draft Rec. I.2xy - Tele services supported by an ISDN
XVIII XB	8402	FRG	1C	Paragraph 6.2 of draft Rec. I.431 - Timing required at the S/T reference points
XVIII XC	8402	FRG		Paragraph 6.4 of I.431 - the channel code of the B-channels
XVIII XD	8402	FRG		Alternative text of paragraph 6.3 of I.431
XVIII XE	8402	FRG		Alternative text of paragraph 5.3 of I.431
XVIII XF	8402	FRG		Pulse shape with 400 ohms load at the So-interface
XVIII XG	8402	France		Proposal for completion of Draft Rec. I.431, paragraph 8.2, 8.3, and Annex 2
XVIII XH	8402	FRG		I.431, Interconnecting media characteristics
XVIII XI	8402	FRG		I.431, paragraph 9 - power feeding
XVIII XJ	8402	FRG		I.431, paragraph 8.6.2 - Receiver input sensitivity and noise immunity
XVIII XK	8402	FRG		I.431, para. 8.6.3.2 - Allow. round trip delay of passive-bus instal. cable, influ. of add. load cap. & filters
XVIII XL	8402	FRG		I.431, paragraph 8.6.3.2 - Proposal for a method of measuring round trip delay
XVIII XM	8402	Japan	1A,2	ISDN interface taking account of home-bus
XVIII XN	8402	NTT	1B,2	Necessary information for maintenance and operations to be conveyed across the user-network interface
XVIII XO	8402	NTT	1C,2	Use of the Additional 4 kbit/s m across the primary rate interface at 1544 kbit/s & prop. amend. to I.412..
XVIII XP	8402	NTT		Proposed addition of electrical characteristics to draft Rec. I.432
XVIII XQ	8402	NTT	1A	A proposal of bearer service classification method
XVIII XR	8402	NTT	1A	Definition of rates as attributes for bearer service description
XVIII XS	8402	NTT	1C	A proposal on the values for power feeding over phantom circuit (Section 9 of I.431)
XVIII XT	8402	NTT	1C	Proposed amendments to draft Rec. I.431 electrical characteristics - 8.6.3 NT rec. input delay characteristics
XVIII XU	8402	NTT	1C	Proposed amendments to draft Rec. I.431 electrical characteristics - 8.5.5 voltage on other test loads

Doc. Id.	Date	Source	Questions	Title
XVIII XV	8402	NTT	1C	Proposed amendments to draft Rec. I.431 electrical characteristics - 8.5.6 and 8.6.4 unbalance about earth
XVIII XW	8402	NTT	1C	Proposed amendments to draft Rec. I.431 electrical characteristics - 8.5.3.2 nominal pulse amplitude
XVIII XX	8402	NTT	1C	Proposed amendments to draft Rec. I.431 electrical characteristics - 8.5.1 transmitter output impedance
XVIII XY	8402	NTT	1C	Amendment to activation/deactivation layer 1 procedure of I.431
XVIII XZ	8402	NTT	1C	A proposal on the clarification of the primitives to be defined for layer 1
XVIII YA	8402	NTT	1C	A proposal for an alternative state to the disconnected state
XVIII YB	8402	USA	2	A provision of a 1536 kbit/s H channel on a 1544 kbit/s interface
XVIII YC	8402	USA	1C,2	Flexible time-slot assignment for Ho channels on a primary rate interface
XVIII YD	8402	USA	2	Allowing a mixture of B and Ho channels on a primary rate interface
XVIII YE	8402	USA	2	The need for flexible Ho channel time-slot assignment
XVIII YF	8402	Telecom Canada	1C	Proposed amendments to draft Rec. I.431 section 8 - electrical characteristics
XVIII YG	8402	Canada-BNR	1B	ISDN connections - definitions
XVIII YH	8402	Telecom Canada	1A	New question on integrated services
XVIII YI	8402	Telecom Canada	1C	Editorial comments on draft Rec. I.31
XVIII YJ	8402	Canada-BNR	1B	Protocol model-layering perspectives for user and control planes
XVIII YK	8402	Canada-MPR	1B	Comments on draft Rec. I.300
XVIII YL	8402	Canada-MPR	1B	Proposed text for draft Rec. I.325
XVIII YM	8402	Switzerland	1A	I.200 - proposed amendments to section 2
XVIII YN	8402	Switzerland	1B	I.300 - proposed amendments to figure 1
XVIII YO	8402	Switzerland	1B	I.320 - comments on the selection
XVIII YP	8402	France	1A	I.2xx - Bearer services supported by ISDN
XVIII YQ	8402	France	1A,1B	Proposal for a global approach of the attribute method leading to draft a new Rec. I.1zz
XVIII YR	8402	British Telecom	1A,1B	Alternative voice/data circuit switched bearer services at 64 kbit/s
XVIII YS	8402	British Telecom	1A,1B	Bearer services at approximately 2 Mbit/s
XVIII YT	8402	British Telecom	1C	Recs. I.431 and I.432 comments
XVIII YU	8402	Netherlands	1,2	Proposal for a long term solution on "high layer compatibility information"
XVIII YV	8402	Switzerland	1A,9	Proposal for a new question for further analysis of the concept of supplementary services with special conside..
XVIII YW	8402	Australia	1B	New question on ISDN HRX
XVIII YX	8402	Australia	1B	Towards a unified global network addressing scheme for ISDN applications
XVIII YY	8402	Australia	1B	Comments on Draft Rec. I.311 - ISDN protocol reference model
XVIII YZ	8402	USA	1A	The need for a 56 kbit/s bearer services and connection types in ISDN
XVIII ZA	8402	USA	1C	Proposed power consumption in power down mode (section 9 of draft Rec. I.431)
XVIII ZB	8402	British Telecom	1B	Proposed new questions on ISDN connection types
XVIII ZC	8402	British Telecom	1A	Addition of both 1920 and 1536 kbit/s switched bearer services to I-series Recs.
XVIII ZD	8402	KDD	1A	Improvements on draft Rec. I.200
XVIII ZE	8402	KDD	1B,1E	Classification and clarification of definition of ISDN connection types
XVIII ZF	8402	KDD	1,14	Study points for international ISDN interworking
XVIII ZG	8402	KDD	1B	Packet type of information transfer capability on ISDN
XVIII ZH	8402	USA	1	IES coding of address information in functional address elements
XVIII ZI	8402	ATT	1B	Symmetrical call control procedures
XVIII ZJ	8402	FRG	1B	Proposed amendments to I.320
XVIII ZK	8402	USA	1C	Proposed connector for the ISDN 1544 kbit/s primary rate access
XVIII ZL	8402	KDD	1B,4	Proposed new question .../XVIII - packet information transfer capability in an ISDN & its interworking with PSDN
XVIII ZM	8402	BCR	1C	NT/TE test results
XVIII ZN	8405	British Telecom	9	Proposed new question on ISDN performance
XVIII ZO	8405	ISO/TC97/SC6/WG3	1C	Liaison statement to CCITT SG XVIII - Connector selection for ISDN TE/NT interfaces
XVIII ZP	8405	USA	1C	Changes to draft Rec. I.431
XVIII ZQ	8405	France	16	Complement to draft Rec. G.71Y
XVIII ZR	8405	France	1B	Amendments to Rec. I.330 relating to the issue of the new Rec. E.164
XVIII ZS	8405	NTT	1C	Proposed editorial changes to I-series recommendations
XVIII ZT	8405	Comsat	9	Modification of Revised draft G.821
XVIII ZU	8405	Iran	7	Introduction to the use of weighted PCM and its merits over normal PCM system
XVIII ZV	8405	Iran	1B,4	Further notes on centralized call control procedures for ISDN access
XVIII ZW	8405	ATT	7,17	Characteristics of a 48-channel transcoder
XVIII ZX	8405	ATT	10	Specification of availability for digital networks

Doc. Id.	Date	Source	Questions	Title
XVIII ZY	8405	ATT	15	G.70y treatment of bit sequence independence of 6312 kbit/s paths
XVIII ZZ	8405	British Telecom	3,9	Absolute versus relative limits for jitter and wander in G.82x
XVIII AAA	8405	LMEricsson	6,11	Symbol for two-way regenerative repeater
XVIII AAB	8405	FRG	3	Proposal for revision of Rec. G.822
XVIII AAC	8405	FRG	3	Amendment of Rec. G.811 in respect of FDM frequency comparison pilots
XVIII AAD	8405	FRG	3	Comparison between contributions of Switzerland and FRG on Rec. G.822 and G.811
XVIII AAE	8405	FRG	3	Revision of Table 2/G.811 in respect of degradation of the timing accuracy of network nodes
XVIII AAF	8405	FRC	6	Proposals for amendment of Rec. G.702
XVIII AAG	8405	FRG	9	Comments on the new draft Rec. G.81x (digital transmission models)
XVIII AAH	8405	FRG	9	Jitter tolerances of digital line sections at 2048 kbit/s
XVIII AAI	8405	Canada-BNR	2	Rate adaption into 56 kbit/s information streams
XVIII AAJ	8405	Canada	A	Proposed addition to Question A/XVIII - General question on ISDN (COM XVIII-No. 229)
XVIII AAK	8405	Canada-Teleglobe	-	Proposal for text of a new question for the 1985-1988 study period on digital circuit multiplication equipment
XVIII AAL	8405	Brazil	9	Proposal for a question on jitter specification
XVIII AAM	8405	France	11	Amendments to Recs. G.901, G.912, G.914, G.916, G.918
XVIII AAN	8405	France	18	Comments on the proposed CRC4 procedure for 2048 kbit/s frame
XVIII AAO	8405	France	7,17	Test of PCM-ADPCM transcoders
XVIII AAP	8405	NTT,Japan	15	Bit sequence independent code for interface at 6312 kbit/s using coaxial pair
XVIII AAQ	8405	NTT, Japan	3	Proposed amendment to G.811 for the inclusion of TIE specifications at 6312 kbit/s
XVIII AAR	8405	NTT,Japan	3,9	Proposed amendments to draft Rec. G.82y
XVIII AAS	8405	FRG	1,9	Proposal for a new Rec. G.82z: Categories of transmission delay in the ISDN (Rev to No. 246)
XVIII AAT	8405	FRG	15	Amendment to Rec. G.703, section 9
XVIII AAU	8405	ISO	1B	Request for comments on OSI NSAP addressing by CCITT
XVIII AAV	8405	USA	1	New question: subscriber initiated trouble isolation of ISDN
XVIII AAW	8405	USA	1	New question: definition of network side interfaces for NT
XVIII AAX	8405	Canada-BNR	16	Proposed amendments to Draft Rec. G.71y
XVIII AAY	8405	Canada-BNR	16	On limits to total distortion including quantization distortion
XVIII AAZ	8405	Canada	B,E	Comments on draft revision of Rec. G.821 prepared by the rapporteur for Question 9
XVIII BAA	8405	Canada-CNCP	B,F	Proposed amendment to Questions B and E
XVIII BAB	8405	NTT,Japan	16	Amendments to total distortion limits in Recs. G.71x and G.71y
XVIII BAC	8405	NTT,Japan	16	Comments on performance characteristics of PCM channels at audio frequencies
XVIII BAD	8405	British Telecom	9	Draft Rec. G.82x:Proposed amendments
XVIII BAE	8405	British Telecom	15	Amendments to Rec. G.703, para 9
XVIII BAF	8405	British Telecom	1B	Comments on draft Rec. I.320
XVIII BAG	8405	Switzerland	1C	Activation/deactivation - reactivation from the network side (COM XVIII No. 228 - Table 4/I.430)
XVIII BAH	8405	Switzerland	1C	Activation/deactivation - timing values (COM XVIII No. 228)
XVIII BAI	8405	Switzerland	1C	Application of electrical characteristics & frame strucyutr of I.430 to others than ISDN user-network interfaces
XVIII BAJ	8405	ATT	15	Correction to introductory section of Rec. G.70y concerning error checking bits
XVIII BAK	8405	NTT,Japan	16	Comparison of proposals made with respect to total distortion requirements in Recs. G.712, 71x and 71y
XVIII BAL	8405	ATT	7	Proposed question on transcoding equipment
XVIII BAM	8405	ATT	15,17,18	Additions to Rec. G.70y
XVIII BAN	8405	NTT,Japan	18	Proposed modifications to Rec. G.752
XVIII BAO	8405	FRG	1B	I.330 Annex A: Amendment of Section A3 for consistency with Draft Recs I.461 (X.30) and I.462 (X.31)
XVIII BAP	8405	France	1A	Categorization of ISDN bearer services in draft Rec. I.211
XVIII BAQ	8405	France	1B	Proposed modifications to the annex on question on ISDN numbering plan
XVIII BAR	8405	France	1A	Proposed amendments to draft Rec. I.211 - Bearer services supported by an ISDN
XVIII BAS	8405	France	1B	Editorial amendments to I.340
XVIII BAT	8405	France	1B,9	Draft question on charging capabilities in an ISDN: proposed amendments
XVIII BAU	8405	Sweden	10	Availability performance plan
XVIII BAV	8405	Australia	8	Amendments to proposed question on CMI
XVIII BAW	8405	Siemens	14,16	Amendment of Rec. G.711 in respect of u/A and A/u code conversion
XVIII BAX	8405	Siemens	16	Amendment of Annex A in Rec. G.712 - method of derivation of the signal-to-total distortion ration for the A-law
XVIII BAY	8405	Siemens	7,18	Clarification of some items in Rec. G.7x2
XVIII BAZ	8405	Switzerland	1A,D	Comments on draft Rec. I.211 - Bearer services supported by an ISDN - prov. of reserved comm. establishment
XVIII CAA	8405	Switzerland	2	Comments on Draft Rec. I.412 ISDN user-network interfaces - interface struc. & access capab. - prim. rate H1

Doc. Id.	Date	Source	Questions	Title
XVIII CAB	8405	ATT	1A	Modifications to alternative speech/non speech services definitions in I.211
XVIII CAC	8405	ATT	1A	Structural integrity for speech & 3.1 kHz audio services
XVIII CAD	8405	USA	1A	Introduction of alternative speech/3.1 kHz audio service in I.211
XVIII CAE	8405	USA	1A	Editorial change & clarification of restricted 64 kbit/s transfer capacity
XVIII CAF	8405	ATT	7	Proposed question on networking considerations of transcoding equipment
XVIII CAG	8405	ATT	–	Proposed question on 32 kbps encoding of speech at the customer's premises
XVIII CAH	8405	NTT,Japan	1B	Proposed editorial changes to I.330
XVIII CAI	8405	ATT	–	Proposed question on transcoding equipment for study by Study Group XV
XVIII CAJ	8405	ATT	1	Transmission of D channels over restricted 1544 kbit/s facilities
XVIII CAK	8405	ATT	1	Method for transmitting packet data on restricted 64 kbit/s transfer capabilities
XVIII CAL	8405	Switzerland	7	Modification of mode change for wide-band speech at 64 kbit/s

Doc. Id.	Date	Source	Questions	Title
1985-88 PLENARY PERIOD, REPORTS				
XVIII R1	8502	CCITT Sec	1-13,18,19	Report on the meeting of the group of experts on ISDN matters of Study Group XVIII (London, 21-25 January 1985)
1985-88 PLENARY PERIOD, CONTRIBUTIONS				
XVIII 1	8502	VIIIth Plen	—	Questions allocated to SG XVIII for the period 1985-1988
XVIII 2	8502	British Telecom	5	Proposals configurations for ISDN connection types
XVIII 3	8502	Canada-TC	1	Functional attributes of ISDN telephone terminals
XVIII 4	8502	FRG	13	An approach to quality of service and network performance in the ISDN
XVIII 5	8502	USA	2,3,4	Definition for completion of calls to busy subscriber facility provided by an ISDN
XVIII 6	8502	USA	2,3,4	Definition for user controlled add-on conference calling facility provided by an ISDN
XVIII 7	8502	USA	2,3,4	Definition for call pickup facility provided by an ISDN
XVIII 8	8502	USA	2,3,4	Definition for multi-line arrangement (key system) facility provided by an ISDN
XVIII 9	8502	Switzerland	2,5,10	Rec. 1.211, Bearer services supported by an ISDN, clarification on the attribute "reserved communication
XVIII 10	8502	France	25	Comments on the test sequences in Rec. G.721
XVIII 11	8503	Canada-BNR	15	Proposal for revision of Rec. G.824
XVIII 12	8503	ECMA	12	ISDN connector at the primary rate access
XVIII 13	8503	UK-STK	3	OSI network service and ISDN - Relays
XVIII 14	8503	UK-STK	3	OSI network service and ISDN - Architecture
XVIII 15	8503	UK-STK	4	OSI network service and ISDN - Parameter coding
XVIII 16	8503	UK-STK	8	OSI network service and ISDN - Network address
XVIII 17	8503	UK-STK	11	OSI network service and ISDN - Data transfer on B channel
XVIII 18	8503	Canada-CNCP	2	Proposal to add the telex teleservice to Rec. I.212
XVIII 19	8503	Canada-MPR	2	Inclusion of reference to X.401 in Rec. I.212
XVIII 20	8503	Canada-Teleglobe	1,33	Speech Packetization
XVIII 21	8503	Canada-Teleglobe	13	General aspects of quality of service
XVIII 22	8503	USA	2,4	Functional components of ISDN supplementary services
XVIII 23	8503	USA	1	Proposed text additions to I.211 on supplementary services
XVIII 24	8504	Canada-Teleglobe	2	Control of echo in ISDN telephone terminals
XVIII 25	8504	KDD	25	Necessity for 9600 kbit/s voiceband data transmission through 32 kbit ADPCM
XVIII 26	8504	KDD	25	Possible approach for voiceband data transmission up to 9600 kbit/s through 32 kbit/s ADPCM
XVIII 27	8504	British Telecom	23	CMI pulse mark
XVIII 28	8504	British Telecom	15	Specific phase variation
XVIII 29	8504	British Telecom	14,23	Proposal to utilize CRC processing at 2048 kbit/s
XVIII 30	8504	UK	15,22	Error performance
XVIII 31	8504	SR	13	Report of the correspondance on interworking arrangements
XVIII 32	8504	NTT	15	Performance objectives for jitter/wander in broadband services
XVIII 33	8504	NTT	17	Error performance objectives for high speed connections above 64 kbit/s
XVIII 34	8504	NTT	15	Proposed measurement method for TIWE and the amendment to TIE definition in Rec. G.811
XVIII 35	8504	NTT	15	Proposed study points on clocks at higher bit rates than second-order hierarchy
XVIII 36	8504	NTT	17	Amendment of ISDN availability performance plan decomposition
XVIII 37	8504	NTT	17	Proposal for study on ISDN teleservice performance specification
XVIII 38	8504	NTT	14	Error performance at 1.5 Mbit/s
XVIII 39	8504	NTT	28	Definition of relations between analog input signals and A/u law PCM with intermediate uniform PCM
XVIII 40	8504	NTT	27	Consideration of 16 kbit/s speech coding
1985-88 PLENARY PERIOD, DELAYED CONTRIBUTIONS				
XVIII D.1	8501	USA	1,2,5	ISDN support of services corresponding to today's special services
XVIII D.2	8501	USA	2,3,4	Call management facilities in ISDN
XVIII D.3	8501	USA	2,3,4	Definition for completion of calls to buy subscriber facility provided by an ISDN
XVIII D.4	8501	USA	2,3,4	Definition for user controlled add-on conference calling facility provided by an ISDN
XVIII D.5	8501	USA	2,3,4	Definition for call pickups facility provided by an ISDN

Doc. Id.	Date	Source	Questions	Title
XVIII D.6	8501	USA	2,3,4	Definition for multi-line arrangement (key-system) facility provided by an ISDN
XVIII D.7	8501	USA	2,4	Functional components of ISDN supplementary services
XVIII D.8	8501	USA	2,5	384 kbit/s and 1536 kbit/s demand service – modification to Rec. I.211
XVIII D.9	8501	USA	19	Proposed clarification to the definition of supplementary services in Rec. I.210 and its addition to Rec. I.112
XVIII D.10	8501	USA	8	Length of ISDN subaddress
XVIII D.11	8501	USA	8	Relation between the ISDN number and the OSI NSAP address
XVIII D.12	8501	USA	12	Electrical environment of interchange circuits – Rec. I.430
XVIII D.13	8501	USA	12	Proposed Increase in allowed input/output capacitance – Rec. I.430
XVIII D.14	8501	USA	12	Rec. I.430 – proposed specification of optional powering on TE access leads 7 & 8
XVIII D.15	8501	USA	12	Rec. I.430 – Restriction on pulse amplitude limitation
XVIII D.16	8501	ATT/Telenet	2,11	LAPD based packet mode – overview
XVIII D.17	8501	ATT/Telenet	2,11	Additions to Recs. I.211 and I.412 to cover LAPD-based packet mode
XVIII D.18	8501	Sweden	2,6,7	General consideration on ISDN-to-ISDN interfaces and interworking between the ISDN and dedicated networks
XVIII D.19	8501	Ellemtel	--	Universal access for packet and circuit oriented terminals in an ISDN
XVIII D.20	8501	Switzerland	2,5,10	Rec. I.211 – clarification on the attribute "reserved communication establishment"
XVIII D.21	8501	Switzerland	12	Power feeding at the basic ISDN user-network interfaces and interworking between ISDN and dedicated networks
XVIII D.22	8501	NTT	1,2,11	A framework for the study on mixed access interfaces containing various combinations of B- and H- channels
XVIII D.23	8501	NTT	12,18	Clarification of testing and maintenance functions in ISDN
XVIII D.24	8501	NTT	11,12	Proposal for the 1536 kbit/s H channel assignment in the primary rate user-network interface
XVIII D.25	8501	NTT	12	Electrical characteristics to be revised in Rec. I.430
XVIII D.26	8501	NTT	12	A proposal on pin assignments for ISDN basic access interface
XVIII D.27	8501	NTT	6,7	Clarification of user-to-user signalling services classes
XVIII D.28	8501	NTT	2	Framework of studies on internetwork interfaces
XVIII D.29	8501	NTT	2	Teleservices and high layer protocols
XVIII D.30	8501	NTT	1,2,11	Proposal framework for high-speed and multiplexed access having capacities of secondary and higher rates
XVIII D.31	8501	British Telecom	5	Proposals for reference configurations for ISDN connection types
XVIII D.32	8501	British Telecom	5	Proposal for additions to Rec. I.340 to take account of connection elements having differing information
XVIII D.33	8501	British Telecom	2	Proposals for the definition in Rec. I.211 of bearer services at rates lower than 64 kbit/s
XVIII D.34	8501	Telecom CAN	7,11	Interworking between ISDN and existing networks
XVIII D.35	8501	Telecom CAN	6,7	Scope, concept and principles for interworking
XVIII D.36	8501	Alcatel-Thomson	--	Maintenance: an ISDN service
XVIII D.37	8501	Alcatel-Thomson	--	Accessibility check function
XVIII D.38	8501	Alcatel-Thomson	--	A maintenance function model
XVIII D.39	8501	Alcatel-Thomson	--	ISDN virtual circuit bearer service definition
XVIII D.40	8501	Alcatel-Thomson	--	ISDN user signalling bearer service definition
XVIII D.41	8501	Alcatel-Thomson	--	ISDN reference model primitives
XVIII D.42	8501	British Telecom	5	General comments on e²eas requiring new study in Rec. I.340
XVIII D.43	8501	British Telecom	18	Proposal for an approach to the study of maintenance for customer-network interfaces
XVIII D.44	8501	Alcatel-Thomson	12	Connector at the basic rate user-network interface and primary rate user-network interfaces
XVIII D.45	8501	FRG	12	ISDN broadband bearer services definition
XVIII D.46	8501	Australia	12	Provision for alternative technologies in Layer 1 of the ISDN basic user-network interfaces
XVIII D.47	8501	Australia	11,20	Specification of V1 interface
XVIII D.48	8501	Sweden	--	Suggested scenario for ISDN-PSTN interworking
XVIII D.49	8501	Canada-Teleglobe	7	Telephony operation in an ISDN and associated interworking between ISDNs/existing telephone networks
XVIII D.50	8501	Canada-Teleglobe	1	Functional attributes of ISDN telephone terminals
XVIII D.51	8501	Switzerland	12	Layer 1 service specification – layer 1 representation as seen by the data link layer
XVIII D.52	8501	Switzerland	12	Activation/deactivation – reactivation from the network side (Table 4/I.430)
XVIII D.53	8501	Switzerland	12	Rec. I.430 – Activation/deactivation layer 1 procedures
XVIII D.54	8501	FRG	12,15	ISDN user-network interfaces for broadband services – guideline on network synchronization
XVIII D.55	8501	FRG	1,2,5,6,11,12	Requirements on digital access signalling system to assist subscribers in the user of ISDN subscriber features
XVIII D.56	8501	FRG	7	ISDN with full broadband capabilities (guidelines for design and standardisation)
XVIII D.57	8501	FRG	13	An approach to quality of service and network performance in the ISDN
XVIII D.58	8501	FRG	11	ISDN user interface: proposal for a new channel type (H4) with a bit rate in the order of magnitude of the 4th
XVIII D.59	8501	KDD	5,6,7	Significance of connection type from the view point of studies on ISDN interworking
XVIII D.60	8501	KDD	5	Application of connection types t – protocol specifications

Doc. Id.	Date	Source	Questions	Title
XVIII D.61	8501	KDD	2,5	Enhancement of connection-less packet bearer service specifications
XVIII D.62	8501	France	18	Digital subscriber line maintenance - accessibility check function
XVIII D.63	8501	France	18	Digital subscriber line maintenance - use of loop-back techniques
XVIII D.64	8501	France	18	Digital subscriber line maintenance - note on the maintenance test call
XVIII D.65	8501	France	18	Digital subscriber line maintenance - definition of test points
XVIII D.66	8501	France	12	Rec. I.430: Specification of optional powering on TE access leads 7,8
XVIII D.67	8501	France	2	Characterisation of the ISDN supplementary services
XVIII D.68	8501	France	2	General policy for the provision of connection-oriented bearer services by an ISDN
XVIII D.69	8501	ISO TC97/SC6	8	Liaison requesting comments on ISO TC 97/SC6 network layer addressing proposal
XVIII D.70	8501	ISO TC97/SC6/WG3	--	Liaison report to IEC SC48B
XVIII D.71	8501	ITT	1,2	Study programme and proposed framework of B-ISDN recommendations
XVIII D.72	8501	Belgium	4	ISDN - SS 7 packet switching interworking via the control plane
XVIII D.73	8501	Belgium	4	ISDN - SS 7 packet switching interworking via the connection plane
XVIII D.74	8501	BCMA	11	Attachment of start-stop data terminal equipment (DTE)
XVIII D.75	8501	BCMA	18	Fault isolation in ISDN
XVIII D.76	8501	Canada-BNR	7	ISDN architecture - interworking with existing DTEs
XVIII D.77	8501	Canada Telecom	7	Interworking with existing non-64 kbit/s switched networks
XVIII D.78	8501	British Telecom	---	Signalling implications of speech processing in the ISDN
XVIII D.79	8501	France	15	Deletion of time interval error curves in Recs. about syncronization
XVIII D.80	8506	LMEricsson	18	Definition of basic maintenance concepts
XVIII D.81	8506	France	25	Performance evaluation of the G.721 test sequences
XVIII D.82	8506	Comsat	25	Compatibility in ADPCM Coding and decoding
XVIII D.83	8506	NTT	18	Proposal of amendments to Rec. G.803
XVIII D.84	8506	NTT	25	Proposal of amendments to 6,312 kbit/s frame structure in Rec. G.704
XVIII D.85	8506	Switzerland	1	Rec. 1.211 "bearer services supported by an ISDN" - clarif. on attribute "reserved communication establishment"
XVIII D.86	8506	Canada-Teleglobe	1	Standard. of format/labelling for call record. in ISDNs & output inform. provided by off-line proc. of call
XVIII D.87	8506	Canada HNH	14	Method of apportioning the degraded minutes bit error objective
XVIII D.88	8506	FRG	1	Use of "information types" by SGs XVIII and XI
XVIII D.89	8506	FRG	1	Clarification of item 2.1.3. in Rec. 1.211
XVIII D.90	8506	FRG	2	Classification and applications of ISDN broadband services
XVIII D.91	8506	FRG	2,19	Broadband services proposed to be offered by the ISDN
XVIII D.92	8506	FRG	2,19	A consistent nomenclature for service attributes
XVIII D.93	8506	FRG	2	Designations of services
XVIII D.94	8506	FRG	2	Supplementary service - Abbreviated dialling
XVIII D.95	8506	FRG	2	Supplementary service - Do not disturb
XVIII D.96	8506	FRG	2	Supplementary service - Call waiting
XVIII D.97	8506	FRG	2	Supplementary service - Call completion to busy subscribers
XVIII D.98	8506	FRG	2	Supplementary service - Barring of outgoing calls
XVIII D.99	8506	FRG	2	Supplementary service - Calling number indication
XVIII D.100	8506	FRG	2	Supplementary service - Connected number indication
XVIII D.101	8506	FRG	2	Supplementary service - Advice of charge (call charging information)
XVIII D.102	8506	FRG	2	Supplementary service - Automatic alarm call service
XVIII D.103	8506	FRG	2	Supplementary service - Conference call
XVIII D.104	8506	FRG	2	Supplementary service - Three party service/hold for inquiry
XVIII D.105	8506	FRG	2	Supplementary service - Three party service/three party conference
XVIII D.106	8506	FRG	2	Supplementary service - Disconnect
XVIII D.107	8506	FRG	2	Supplementary service - Reverse charging
XVIII D.108	8506	FRG	2	Supplementary service - Registration (logging) of incoming calls
XVIII D.109	8506	FRG	2	Supplementary service - Call forwarding (immediate)
XVIII D.110	8506	FRG	2	Supplementary service - Call forwarding on no reply
XVIII D.111	8506	FRG	2	Supplementary service - Malicious call identification
XVIII D.112	8506	FRG	2	Supplementary service - Change of service during an established call
XVIII D.113	8506	FRG	2	Supplementary service - Terminal selection on the passive bus
XVIII D.114	8506	FRG	2	Supplementary service - Terminal portability
XVIII D.115	8506	FRG	2	Supplementary service - Automatic synchronization of terminals with the status of access-related facilities...

Doc. Id.	Date	Source	Questions	Title
XVIII D.116	8506	FRG	2	Supplementary service - Secret number
XVIII D.117	8506	FRG	2	Supplementary service - Change of terminal with change of service
XVIII D.118	8506	FRG	2	Direct dialling in (DDI)
XVIII D.119	8506	FRG	2	Description method of network functional components and resources used for support of supplementary services
XVIII D.120	8506	FRG	2	Possibilities and examples of user-to-user signalling
XVIII D.121	8506	FRG	2	Description of teleservices with 64 kbit/s proposed to be offered by the ISDN
XVIII D.122	8506	FRG	2	Attributes of teleservices
XVIII D.123	8506	FRG	3,11	Reference configuration for user-network interface under special consideration of broadband application
XVIII D.124	8506	FRG	3,4	Circuit switched ISDN bearer services as the basis for the OSI network layer service
XVIII D.125	8506	FRG	8	Proposal on the conveyance of dedicated data-network address information within an ISDN
XVIII D.126	8506	FRG	8	Terminal selection in a multi-point configuration
XVIII D.127	8506	FRG	11	Principles for a broadband B-channel hierarchy
XVIII D.128	8506	FRG	11	General considerations on the provision of broadband services regarding the user-network interface
XVIII D.129	8506	FRG	12	I.430, 8.2.2 and 8.2.3 test pattern for jitter and phase deviation
XVIII D.130	8506	FRG	12	I.430, 8.3.1 NT output jitter characteristics
XVIII D.131	8506	FRG	12	I.430, 8.5.1 and 8.6.1 transmitter and receiver impedances
XVIII D.132	8506	FRG	12	Transmitter output-impedance sending binary zeros (I.430, 8.5)
XVIII D.133	8506	FRG	12	Activation/deactivation procedures: timers 1 and 3
XVIII D.134	8506	FRG	12	Activation/deactivation procedures: receiving any signal in state F4 (I.430, Table 3)
XVIII D.135	8506	FRG	12	Proposed amendment for the idle channel code in I.431
XVIII D.136	8506	FRG	12	Proposal for amendment of Rec. I.431
XVIII D.137	8506	FRG	15	Amendment of Recs. G.811, G.823, and Q.502/512
XVIII D.138	8506	FRG	15	Proposal for a new Rec. G.82X: categories of transmission delay in ISDN
XVIII D.139	8506	FRG	19	Modification of the definition of "alternative mark inversion code" (Rec. G.701, definition 9004)
XVIII D.140	8506	FRG	20	Recent developments for the transmission system of the ISDN subscriber access
XVIII D.141	8506	FRG	20	On the choice of a transmission system for the ISDN subscriber access
XVIII D.142	8506	FRG	20	A transmission system for the ISDN basic access at the U-interface
XVIII D.143	8506	FRG	20	Results with laboratory test configurations at the U-interface
XVIII D.144	8506	FRG	20	Line code for the ISDN subscriber loop transmission system
XVIII D.145	8506	FRG	21	Further elaboration of Rec. G.921 in respect of error performance
XVIII D.146	8506	FRG	23	Amendment of Rec. G.735 in respect of the use of CRC4 check bits (also applicable to G.736/737)
XVIII D.147	8506	Sweden	2,4	OSI network service versus real networks
XVIII D.148	8506	Sweden	3,6,7	ISDN interworking, some concepts
XVIII D.149	8506	Microtel	7	PSTN-ISDN interworking functions
XVIII D.150	8506	BNR	22	Parity bits in 6312 kbits and 139264 kbit/s multiplexing frame structures (draft Recs. G.74X and G.75X)
XVIII D.151	8506	Canada-Telecom	7	ISDN-PSTN interworking: an approach to identifying interworking functions
XVIII D.152	8506	ITT	3,11	Reference and physical configurations for broadband ISDN (B-ISDN) user-network interfaces
XVIII D.153	8506	NTT	1,2,11	Considerations for high-speed/broadband services in ISDN
XVIII D.154	8506	NTT	2,11,12	Proposed 4 kbit/s D channel for H0 and H11 channels at 1544 kbit/s primary rate interface
XVIII D.155	8506	NTT	2,11,12	Proposed "secondary" rate user-network interface
XVIII D.156	8506	NTT	2,11,12	Proposed user-network interface, layer 1 specifications for secondary rate
XVIII D.157	8506	NTT	2,11,12	Proposed broadband channels having capacities higher than the second-order rate
XVIII D.158	8506	NTT	12	Proposed fiber-optic user-network interface
XVIII D.159	8506	NTT	2	Definition and significance of the attribute "reserved communication establishment"
XVIII D.160	8506	NTT	2	Reserved circuit switched services and its protocols
XVIII D.161	8506	NTT	2	Proposal for changing the provisional category of 64 kb/s reserved services from "essential" to "additional"
XVIII D.162	8506	NTT	2	Proposal for definition of 128 kb/s bearer service
XVIII D.163	8506	NTT	2	The provision for X.25 logical channel multiplexing on ISDN user-network interfaces
XVIII D.164	8506	NTT	2	Technical problems on layer 2 multiplexing and out of band signalling for packet mode access
XVIII D.165	8506	NTT	2,12	Network not ready indication of ISDN user-network interface
XVIII D.166	8506	NTT	7	Internetwork interface between an ISDN and a PSTN
XVIII D.167	8506	NTT	12	Proposed amendments to the pin assignment in Rec. I.430
XVIII D.168	8506	NTT	12,18	Proposals for the electrical environmental specification for interchange circuits
XVIII D.169	8506	NTT	12,18	Maintenance and testing for basic interface layer 1
XVIII D.170	8506	NTT	13,16,17	Items to be studied for the reliability/availability and traffic performance related questions in SG XVIII

Doc. Id.	Date	Source	Questions	Title
XVIII D.171	8506	NTT	18	Network operation, administration and maintenance for ISDN
XVIII D.172	8506	KDD	2,3	Study items for packet communication in an ISDN
XVIII D.173	8506	KDD	5	Proposed addition of network/inter-network attributes for definition of connection types
XVIII D.174	8506	KDD	27	Requirements of 16 kbit/s voice coding techniques and applications
XVIII D.175	8506	British Telecom	3	Comments on Rec. I.310
XVIII D.176	8506	British Telecom	3	Proposals for a draft recommendation on ISDN network architecture
XVIII D.177	8506	British Telecom	3,5	Reference configurations for ISDN connection types
XVIII D.178	8506	British Telecom	4	Comments on Rec. I.320 (ISDN protocol reference model)
XVIII D.179	8506	British Telecom	2,5,10	ISDN routing principles
XVIII D.180	8506	British Telecom	5	Amendments to Rec. I.340 (ISDN connection types)
XVIII D.181	8506	British Telecom	5	Proposed enhancement to section 3 of I.340
XVIII D.182	8506	British Telecom	8	The relationship of ISO addressing to ISDN
XVIII D.183	8506	British Telecom	8	The need for a standardised term for the sub-address field in ISDN
XVIII D.184	8506	British Telecom	8	A proposal for the definition of a simple ISDN subaddressing scheme
XVIII D.185	8506	British Telecom	12	Wiring configuration and pin allocations
XVIII D.186	8506	British Telecom	12	Layer 1 activation/deactivation procedures
XVIII D.187	8506	British Telecom	12	Requirement for the definition of connection status in Rec. I.430
XVIII D.188	8506	British Telecom	12	Changes to I.430 to formally describe indication to the management entity of connection status at the TE side
XVIII D.189	8506	British Telecom	18	Maintenance architectures
XVIII D.190	8506	British Telecom	25,31	Proposals concerning 9600 bit/s voiceband data and 32 kbit/s ADPCM systems
XVIII D.191	8506	British Telecom	15	Control of jitter/wander within digital networks which are based on 1.544 Mb/s hierarchy
XVIII D.192	8506	Sweden	2	Definition of multiservices
XVIII D.193	8506	Sweden	11	Broadband channel types and broadband interface structures
XVIII D.194	8506	Sweden	3,5-7	A possible approach to harmonization of concepts used in SG VII and SG XVIII
XVIII D.195	8506	Sweden	6,7	Interworking between ISDN and PSTN
XVIII D.196	8506	Switzerland	12	Activation/deactivation layer 1 procedures at the network side
XVIII D.197	8506	Switzerland	12	Pulse amplitude limitation in Rec. I.430
XVIII D.198	8506	ISO/TC97/SC6	4	CCITT/ISO coordination on alignment of OSI and ISDN architecture
XVIII D.199	8506	USA	3	Wideband channel structures for ISDN
XVIII D.200	8506	USA	2	Wideband services provided on an ISDN
XVIII D.201	8506	USA	2	Revisions to CCITT COM XVIII-23 for X.2 services
XVIII D.202	8506	USA	2	Definition of busy on ISDN
XVIII D.203	8506	USA	2	Proposed structure of ISDN supplementary service definitions within I.211
XVIII D.204	8506	USA	2	Consistent treatment of supplementary services for both bearer services and teleservices
XVIII D.205	8506	USA	2	Clarification of attribute names in Rec. I.211
XVIII D.206	8506	USA	2	User-to-user signalling classification, clarification and modification to I.211
XVIII D.207	8506	USA	8	Comments on E.164/X.121 interworking
XVIII D.208	8506	USA	2	Relationship between the ISDN number and the OSI NSAP address
XVIII D.209	8506	FRG	1	The Deutsche Bundespost's network evolution strategy
XVIII D.210	8506	France	2	Provision of packet switched services to ISDN users when packet handling functions are provided outside the ISDN
XVIII D.211	8506	France	2	Additional ISDN packet switched bearer services for inclusion in I.211
XVIII D.212	8506	France	2	Circuit mode N times 64 kbit/s unrestricted, 8 kHz structured bearer service (N = 2 to 30)
XVIII D.213	8506	France	2	Definition of ISDN supplementary services
XVIII D.214	8506	France	2,5	The attribute method
XVIII D.215	8506	France	2,5	Packet transfer mode for broadband services
XVIII D.216	8506	France	3	Enhancement to Rec. I.310
XVIII D.217	8506	France	5	Connection components for ISDN connection types
XVIII D.218	8506	France	11	Functional characteristics of reference point VI
XVIII D.219	8506	France	12	Considerations on the detection of a faulty terminal in a multipoint configuration
XVIII D.220	8506	France	12	Mechanism for detection of a faulty terminal in passive bus arrangement
XVIII D.221	8506	France	18	Digital subscriber line maintenance (basic access)
XVIII D.222	8506	France	18	Use of loop-back technique for fault detection
XVIII D.223	8506	France	18	Maintenance of ISDN subscriber installation
XVIII D.224	8506	USA	2,7	V-series terminal adaption to ISDN
XVIII D.225	8506	France	7	Interworking and modelling

Doc. Id.	Date	Source	Questions	Title
XVIII D.226	8506	FRG	30,31	Clarification of some items in Rec. G.761
XVIII D.227	8506	FRG	30,31	Further clarification of items in Rec. G.761
XVIII D.228	8506	FRG	30,31	Proposal for amendment of Rec. G.761, Table 8, in respect of the fault condition "transcoder failure"
XVIII D.229	8506	France	2	ISDN broadband bearer services definition
XVIII D.230	8506	Brazil	15	Proposed modification of G.742 – Second order digital multiplex equipment operating at 8448 kbit/s
XVIII D.231	8506	NTT	15	Proposal for maximum permissible jitter at 1544 kbit/s based hierarchal interfaces
XVIII D.232	8506	USA	30	Proposed 32 kbit/s ADPCM line format
XVIII D.233	8506	USA	13-17	General framework for studying quality of service/network performance in digital networks, including ISDN
XVIII D.234	8506	France	2	User signalling bearer capability
XVIII D.235	8506	France	2	User to user information in supervisory messages
XVIII D.236	8506	France	8	Address recognition by ISDN terminals
XVIII D.237	8506	France	3	Separation between call and connection control mechanisms: principles
XVIII D.238	8506	France	2,3	Needs for separation between call and connection control
XVIII D.239	8506	BNR	20	Digital transmission systems for ISDN basic access
XVIII D.240	8506	BNR	3,7	Interworking and terminal adaption
XVIII D.241	8506	BNR	8	Numbering plan interworking
XVIII D.242	8506	BNR	6,7,11	Layer 2 multiplexing
XVIII D.243	8506	BNR	29	Encoding for storage and transmission of digitized voice
XVIII D.244	8506	Sweden		Outband signalling in ISDN
XVIII D.245	8506	USA	2	Definition of functional component and method for developing functional components for supplementary services
XVIII D.246	8506	USA	12	Rec. I.430 – Assignment of interchange circuit leads at TE and NT
XVIII D.247	8506	USA	12	Rec. I.430 – Clarification of the activation/deactivation procedures and their optional status
XVIII D.248	8506	USA	12	Rec. I.430 – Section 8.8 EMI generation
XVIII D.249	8506	USA	12	Rec. I.430 – Superframe to provide spare bits for layer 1 signalling channel in TE-to-NT direction
XVIII D.250	8506	USA	12	Rec. I.430 – Clarification of the suitability of NT1 STAR configuration for point-to-multipoint applications
XVIII D.251	8506	USA	12	Rec. I.430 – Clarification of the provisions of sections 8.2 and 8.3
XVIII D.252	8506	USA	12	Rec. I.430 – Further support for an increase in the allowed input/output capacitance
XVIII D.253	8506	USA	12	Galvanic isolation for TEs
XVIII D.254	8506	USA	12	Addition to Rec. I.431 – D-channel interframe time fill
XVIII D.255	8506	USA	12	Addition to Rec. I.431 – Proposed code for idle slots and channels
XVIII D.256	8506	USA	12	Modification to Rec. I.431 – Use of error checking bits in 1544 kbit/s user interface
XVIII D.257	8506	USA	2	ISDN packet mode services and architecture
XVIII D.258	8506	USA	8	Subaddressing length and usage
XVIII D.259	8506	USA	2	Call rerouting – proposed supplementary service/supplementary functional component
XVIII D.250	8506	France	2	Proposal for the bit rate of a broadband channel on the user-network interface
XVIII D.261	8506	FRG	3,4	Refined definition of OSI-subnetwork to include both ISDN-PS and ISDN-CS
XVIII D.262	8506	STC UK	20	Standardisation of line codes at the U reference point
XVIII D.263	8506	ISO/TC97/SC6/WG3	12	Liaison report to CCITT Study Group XVIII (ISO document no. 97/6 N3636)
XVIII D.264	8506	Spain	2	Proposal for additions to the Rec. I.310 (ISDN Network Functional Principles)
XVIII D.265	8506	NTT	3	An addition to section 2 of D.162
XVIII D.266	8506	Italy	20	Subscriber interface at network side for the basic access to the ISDN
XVIII D.267	8506	USA	2	Supplementary service to provide user with tones and announcements over the B-channel
XVIII D.268	8506	France	2,5	Corrigendum to D.215 after point s, 2nd section, add the following text of III
XVIII D.269	8506	Microtel	7	Framework for PSTN-ISDN interworking

1985-88 PLENARY PERIOD, TEMPORARY DOCUMENTS

ISDN Group of Experts, London, 21-25 Jan 1985

Doc. Id.	Date	Source	Questions	Title
XVIII 1	8501	CCITTSec		Documentation for the meeting
XVIII 2	8501	WP XI/2		Report of Tokyo meeting
XVIII 3	8501	WP XI/6		Report of Munich meeting
XVIII 4	8501	WP XI/6		Objectives on 1.430 time limits
XVIII 5	8501	WT3		Report on the coordination meeting
XVIII 6	8501	C		Proposed agenda
XVIII 7	8501	SL		Liaison report from its final meeting, Todyo, 3-7 Dec 1984
XVIII 8	8501	SL		Arrangements for interworking between PDNs and ISDN
XVIII 9	8501	WP XI/6		Annex to TD3 - primitives at Layer 1
XVIII 10	8501	CCITT Sec		Report on the meeting
XVIII 11	8501	WT2		Work plan
XVIII 12	8501	WT4		Agenda for the meeting
XVIII 13	8501	WT1		Draft report of WT1 (services aspect)
XVIII 14	8501	WT1		Annex 1 to the report
XVIII 15	8501	WT3		Report of the meting
XVIII 16	8501	WT1		Continuation of TD14 (Annex 1 to the report)
XVIII 17	8501	WT4		Report of the meeting
XVIII 18	8501	WT1		Report of WT1/2
XVIII 19	8501	WT1		Report of WT1/1
XVIII 20	8501	WT3		Parts VII to X of the report.
XVIII 21	8501	WT4		Annex 4 to the report
XVIII 22	8501	WT2		Report of Working Team 2
XVIII 23	8501	WT2/3		Report of the meeting
XVIII 24	8501	WT3		Part 10 of the report
XVIII 25	8501	WT2/3		Annex to TD23
XVIII 26	8501	C WT1		Draft report of Working Team 1 (services aspects)
XVIII 27	8501	WT2		Report of the meeting
XVIII 28	8501	WT2		Numbering and addressing
XVIII 29	8501	WT4		Report on the meeting
XVIII 30	8501	WT3		Report of the meeting (TD24 + TD20)

Study Group XVIII, Geneva, 17-27 June 1985

Doc. Id.	Date	Source	Questions	Title
XVIII 1	8506	CCITT Sec		Extract from the report of the special rapporteur on interworking arrangements (COM XVIII-31)
XVIII 2	8506	WP IV/1		Extract from the report on Working Party IV/1 meeting (Geneva, 4-6 March 1985) [Report COM IV-R2]
XVIII 3	8506	WP IV/1		Extract from the report on Working Party IV/1 meeting (Geneva, 4-6 March 1985) [Report COM IV-R2]
XVIII 4	8506	SG XVII		Extract from the Report of Study Group XVII meeting (Geneva, 15-19 April 1985) [Report COM XVII-R1]
XVIII 5	8506	SG II		Extract from COM II-R4 (Report of the meeting of Working Party II/3 on numbering, routing and interworking)
XVIII 6	8506	SG II		Extract from COM II-R1 (Report on the meeting held in Geneva, 7-15 Mar 1985)
XVIII 7	8506	SG II		Extract from COM II-R2 (Report of the meeting of Working Party II/1 on operation and services)
XVIII 8	8506	SG II		Extract from COM II-R5 (Report of the meeting of WP II/4 on traffic engineering, forecasting, network planning)
XVIII 9	8506	SHQ10/VII		Request for comment rel. to Rec. 0.133: Spec for instrument to measure performance of PCM encoders and decoders.
XVIII 10	8506	SRQ10/VII		Request for comment rel. to Rec. 0.171: Spec for instrumentation to measure timing jitter on digital equipment
XVIII 11	8506	SG VII		Extract from COM VII-R7, Part VII of the Report (Report of Special Rapporteurs' (DCM)on ISDN related issues)
XVIII 12	8506	SR DCM		Report of the interregnum correspondence group on digital circuit multiplication (DCM)
XVIII 13	8506	WP VII/1		Extract from COM VII-R2 (Report of the Geneva meeting, 22 Apr - 3 May 1985), Annx 8
XVIII 14	8506	SRG		Coordination with SG XVIII on harmonization of Recs. X.200 and I.320
XVIII 15	8506	SHRG		Harmonization of OSI and ISDN architecture
XVIII 16	8506	SG VII		Extract from COM VII-R3(A) Part III: Report of WP VII/2 (Network access interfaces)
XVIII 17	8506	SG VII		Liaison statement to SG SVIII on interworking issues and Draft Rec. X.300
XVIII 18	8506	SG VII		Liaison statement to SG XVIII (extract from COM VII/R5(A) - Report of WP VII/4 (transmission and message handl..

Doc. Id.	Date	Source	Questions	Title
XVIII 19	8506	SG VII		Liaison to Q.8/XVIII on E.164/X.121 interworking abstract (app 3 to Annex 5 of COM VII-R6(A))
XVIII 20	8506	SG VII		Liaison to SG II and SG XVIII on Rec. E.164(I.331), Appendix 3 to annex 6 of COM VII-R6(A)
XVIII 21	8506	SG VII		Liaison to Questions 6,7,8,10/XVIII, 17/II and 7/XI on conclusions of SG VII on OSI network layer addressing
XVIII 22	8506	SG VII		Liaison statement to SG XVIII concerningrelationship between X.200 and ISDN - Report of WP VII/5
XVIII 23	8506	SG I		Extract from COM I-R3 - Report of WP I/2 - Message handling system services and directory services
XVIII 24	8506	SG I		Extract from COM I-R4 - Report of WP I/3 - Teletex, ISDN and teleconference
XVIII 25	8506	SG I		Extract from COM I-R5 - Report of WP I/4 - Facsimile, data and videotex services
XVIII 26	8506	CCITT Sec		Extracts from the report on the meeting of SG III (CCM III-R1)
XVIII 27	8506	SG XI		Extract from COM XI-R1 - Part II of the report
XVIII 28	8506	SG XI		Extract from COM XI-R2 (Part III - signalling system No. 7)
XVIII 29	8506	SG XI		Extract from COM XI-R3 (Part V - Digital switching)
XVIII 30	8506	HG		Draft Rec. G.72x - 7 kHz audio coding within 64 kbit's
XVIII 31	8506	CCIR Sec		Documentation for the first meeting of SG XVIII (Genava, 17-27 June 1985)
XVIII 32	8506	Coord Meet		List of proposed special rapporteurs
XVIII 33	8506	RG		Second report on the activities of the rapporteur'group on wideband speech coding
XVIII 34	8506	IWP 4/2		Extract from the report on the Montreal meeting (15-22 May 1985)
XVIII 35	8506	CCITT Sec		Chairman and vice-chairmen pigeon-holes
XVIII 36	8506	SG XVII LH		Liaison Report concerning terminal adaptation - Q11,XVII
XVIII 37	8506	SRQ23		General considerations on V-interface
XVIII 38	8506	SHQ22		Study items for Q.22/XVIII in this new study period
XVIII 39	8506	RQ		Requirements for a 16 kbit/s coding scheme for mobile radio applications
XVIII 40	8506	HQ27		Rapporteur's report on Q27/XVIII (16 kbit/s speech coding)
XVIII 41	8506	SG XII		Extract from the report, COM XII-R5, of the meeting of WP XII/4, Geneva, 6-10 June 1985 - Reply to Quest 30/XII
XVIII 42	8506	SG XII		Extract from the report, COM XII-R6, of the meeting of WP XII/4, Geneva, 6-10 June 1985 - Telephone conferencing
XVIII 43	8506	SG XII		Reply of SG XII to its Question 5/XII - speech synthesis/recognition system - Extract from the report COM XII-R5
XVIII 44	8506	SG II		Extract from COM II-R6 - Report of WP II/5 (quality of service, network management, mobile service)
XVIII 45	8506	C WP2		Agenda WP2
XVIII 46	8506	SRO7		Circuit switched aspects of interworking ISDN and existing networks, and liaison coordination
XVIII 47	8506	SG XI		Extract from COM XI-R3, Annex 7 to Part V (ref TD23)
XVIII 48	8506	SG XI		Extract from COM XI-R3 - Annex 5 to Part V (ref TD29)
XVIII 49	8506	SG XI		Extract from COM XI-R1, Part VIII
XVIII 50	8506	SHQ25		Rapporteur's Report
XVIII 51	8506	SRO7		General modelling of interworking and interworking between ISDN-PSPDN
XVIII 52	8506	SRQ3		Activities to be undertaken in order to progress work on Q.3/XVIII
XVIII 53	8506	SRQ24		Rapporteur's report
XVIII 54	8506	SHQ19		Vocabulary for ISDNs
XVIII 55	8506	C WP7		Work plan WP7
XVIII 56	8506	C WP6		Proposed agenda for meeting 20-25 June 1985
XVIII 57	8506	SRQ6		Study items and an action plan for Q.6/XVIII
XVIII 58	8506	SHQ15		Rapporteur's report on Q.15/XVIII
XVIII 59	8506	CCITT Sec		Names and addresses of special rapporteurs
XVIII 60	8506	SHQ5		Overview of documentation available for Q5/XVIII and proposals for progressing the work on the question
XVIII 61	8506	SRQ22		Request of urgent reply from Study Group XV on draft Rec. G.74x and G.75x
XVIII 62	8506	HQ30		Rapporteur's report, network considerations of PCM/ADPCM transcoding equipment
XVIII 63	8506	SRQ13		Proposed work plan for Question 13/XVIII
XVIII 64	8506	SRQ14		Interim report on Q14/XVIII: Error performance
XVIII 65	8506	Vocab G		[Agenda]
XVIII 66	8506	SRQ22		Rapporteur's report on Q.22/XVIII(part 1)
XVIII 67	8506	SRQ22		Proposed reply to SG XI on applicability of 64 kbit/s circuit with mU/A conversion to direct data
XVIII 68	8506	WP5		SG XVIII - SG III liaison on charging problems in an ISDN
XVIII 69	8506	C SWP1/1		Report of the meeting, part 1
XVIII 70	8506	RQ1		Report of WP5/1
XVIII 71	8506	C WT3/3		Report of WT 3/3 (network side of the NT; interfaces associated with the digital exchange)
XVIII 72	8506	WP 5/1		Liaison statement to SG XII relating to and urgent question on echo control in ISDN
XVIII 73	8506	SRQ3		Report of the special rapporteur's meeting on Q.3/XVIII (architecture functional model)

Doc. Id.	Date	Source	Questions	Title
XVIII 74	8506	WT2		Rapporteurs report WT2/1 (numbering and addressing) question 8/XVIII
XVIII 75	8506	SRQ4		Meeting report (June 19, Geneva) [ISDN protocol reference model]
XVIII 76	8506	SR		Report to WP5
XVIII 77	8506	C Adhoc G		Report of task group on broadband ISDN
XVIII 78	8506	C WI'3		Report of the meeting
XVIII 79	8506	RQ2		Liaison statements to SG XI
XVIII 80	8506	RQ2		Liaison statements to SG VII
XVIII 81	8506	DG WP1-1		Description material on supplementary services for bearer services and teleservices
XVIII 82	8506	RQ12		Rapporteur's report
XVIII 83	8506	RQ2		Liaison statement to SG II concerning supplementary services
XVIII 84	8506	WP8		Report of WP XVIII/8
XVIII 85	8506	C WP1		Report of first plenary meeting
XVIII 86	8506	C SWP1/1		Report of the meeting, part 2
XVIII 87	8506	C WT3/3		Part II of the report of Working Team 3/3
XVIII 88	8506	SR07		Rapporteur's report on part of Q7/XVIII
XVIII 89	8506	SRQ5		Rapporteur's report on Q5/XVIII
XVIII 90	8506			Annex to TD69, Results of analysis of some sup. service described in various documents received by SG XVIII
XVIII 91	8506	R WP1/2		Report of subworking party 1/2
XVIII 92	8506	C WP1/1DG		Report [on services]
XVIII 93	8506	C WP2		Report WP2
XVIII 94	8506	SR07		Meeting Report [modelling and interworking involving packet switching)
XVIII 95	8506	SR06		Rapporteur's report on Q.6/XVIII
XVIII 96	8506	SRQ21		Preliminary reply to question 21/XVIII characteristics of digital sections
XVIII 97	8506	SRQ24		Meeting report
XVIII 98	8506	C WI'6		Report of the meeting on performance
XVIII 99	8506	WP5		Report on the meeting
XVIII 100	8506	C WP8		Report of WP8
XVIII 101	8506	SRQ23		Report on Question 23/XVIII
XVIII 102	8506	C WI'3		Report of the meeting
XVIII 103	8506	RQ14		Preliminary reply to Q14/XVIII: error performance
XVIII 104	8506	C WI'7		Report of WP7
XVIII 105	8506	WP6AH		Report of agreements reached by the ad hoc group on principles
XVIII 106	8506	C WI'4		Report of working party 4
XVIII 107	8506	RQ17		Rapporteur's report [availability performance]
XVIII 108	8506	RQ30		Report on Q.30/XVIII: network considerations of PCM/ADPCM transcoding equipment
XVIII 109	8506	C		Draft for: liadson statement SG XVIII to SG II
XVIII 110	8506	SRQ15		Report of the discussion oin the revision of G.824
XVIII 111	8506	SRQ22		Report of the drafting group on Rec. G.74x and G.75x
XVIII 112	8506	SG XVIII		Report on the Geneva meeting (17-27 June 1985)
XVIII 113	8506	R SWP1/2		Report of sub-working party 1/2
XVIII 114	8506	AHG		Frame alignment and CRC procedures, and other aspects of CRC multiframes
XVIII 115	8506	C AHG		Report of task group on broadband aspects of ISDN
XVIII 116	8506	C SWP1/1		Report of sub-working party 1/1
XVIII 117	8506	C WP2		Report working party XVIII/2
XVIII 118	8506	DG		Proposal for text to be inserted as a new paragraph in annex to TD 117
XVIII 119	8506	SRQ21		Amendments to TD 96
XVIII 120	8506	C WP' XVIII/1		Addition to TD 85
XVIII 121	8506	SRQ19		Report of vocabulary group of SG SVIII (part of the report of WP 5/XVIII)
XVIII 122	8506	C WP' XVIII/6		Report of the meeting on performance
XVIII 123	8506	C WP2&4		Discrepancy in London report of ISDN experts group reg. treatment of SG XI temp doc concerning connection types
XVIII 124	8506	SRQ22		Report on Q.22/XVIII
XVIII 125	8506	SRQ23		Report on Q.23/XVIII
XVIII 126	8506	HQ30		Amendments to TD 108 resulting from WP7 meeting on 25 June
XVIII 127	8506	SR07		Modifications to annexes 7 and 8 of TD 117 (Working Party 2 report)
XVIII 128	8506	SGXVIII		Liaison to SG VII on interworking between ISDN-PDNs and ISDN-ISDN

PUBLISHED ARTICLES AND PAPERS ADDRESSING ISDN

Author	Title	Citation	Country
—	Special Report: Futuristic ISDN Technology Already in Advanced Planni..	4 Sat News 4 (No 33, Oct 12, 1981)	USA
—	Special Report: Futuristic ISDN Technology Already in Advanced Planni..	4 Telephon News 4 (No 22, Nov 2, 1981)	USA
—	Local Integrated Services Digital Network	Telcom Australia Rev of Act 42 (1980-81)	AUS
—	For Bell operating companies, ISDN is the future mainstay	do. at 48	
—	Beyond ISDN: Britain embarks on futuristic research	do. at 50	
—	USTA showcase features AT&T's vision of the future	Communications Week at 12 (25 Feb 1985)	
—	2 more telcos jump on ISDN bandwagon	do. at 19	
—	ISDN standards: a look inside integrated services	do. at 54	
—	AT&T's rivals work at ISDN development	do. at 56	
—	Splitting hairs: U.S. and Europe at odds over ISDN standards		
—	Fujitsu to display its ISDN system at Singapore show	Communications Week at 42 (6 May 1985)	USA
—	An introduction to Integrated Services Digital Network concepts and issues	Datapro 101 (Feb 1983)	
Abate, Cooper, et. al.	Special issue on ISDN	3 J of Telecom Networks (No 1, 1984)	USA
Abate, Rosenbberger & Yin	Switched Digital Network Synchronization	199 Telephony 33 (No 19, 10 Nov 1980)	USA
Accarino, Rossi, et. al.	Keeping the ISDN in Sync	Bell Labs Record 217 (Sept 1981)	I
Ackzell & Rassmuson	Customer Access Protocols for ISDNs	2 Comput Comm (UK) 268 (No 6, Dec 1979)	S
Alvord	ISDN — The Evolving Network Architecture	IEEE ICC 19.1.1 (Denver 1981)	USA
Altman	Creating Standards for Interconnect Systems	7 CED 31 (No 11, November 1981)	
Altman	First ISDN Customer Revealed	6 MIS Week 28 (No 17, 24 Apr 1985)	
Andrews	BOCs eager to carry data	do. at 28	
Andrews	Progress toward the ISDN	200 Telephony 27 (No 8, Feb 23, 1981)	USA
	ISDN'83	22 IEEE Comm Mag 6 (No 1, Jan 1984)	
Andrews & Smith	No 5 ESS — Overview	3 IEEE ISS 31A1 (Montreal 1981)	USA
Andry, Barbier & DePassoz	Multiservice Subscriber Connection Terminal for Local Digital Networks	4 IEEE ISS 41B5 (Montreal 1981)	
Aoyama, et. al.	Packetized Service Integration Network for Dedicated Voice/Data Subsc..	29 IEEE Trans On Com 1595 (No 11, Nov	
Artom, DeMicheli & Dogliotti	Possibility of Using the Subscriber Logs [sic] for New Services	19 Rev Fitce (BEL) 34 (No 6, Nov	I
Artom, DiPino & Dogliotti	Medium Term Prospects for New Services to the Telephone Customer	1 IEEE ICC (Denver 1981)	
Astrain	Intelsat and the digital communications refolution	7 Telecom Policy 187 (No 3, 1983)	
Barbe, DeWitt & Skelton	Software & Network:What Continental Tel Has Learned	199 Telephony 24 (No 1, Jul 7, 1980)	USA
Barbe, DeWitt & Skelton	Continental Telephone's Digital Experience	198 Telephony 24 (No 25, Jun 23, 1980)	USA
Bella & Roso	A Techno-Economical Assessment for the Introduction of New Services	3 IEEE ICC 6A.1.1 (Philadelphia 1982)	I
Bhusri	Considerations for ISDN planning and implementation	22 IEEE Comm Mag 18 (No 1, 1984)	
Bocker & Gerke	Towards a Digital Communication Network	68 Siemens Rev 10 (No 1, Jan 1981)	FRG
Bocker	Significance of ISDN Standards for Development of Future Communications	Siemens Munich Brief (Feb 1982)	FRG
Bosik	Guest Editor's Prologue	29 IEEE Trans Com 1153 (No 11, Nov 1981)	USA
Botsch	Enhanced Features and Applications f.r EWSD	2 IEEE ISS 23A4 (Montreal 1981)	FRG
Bozzomo	General Introduction to ISDN	MITRE ISDN Symp (Jan 1982)	USA
Brosio, DeJulio, et. al.	A Comparison of Digital Subscriber Line Transmion Systems	29 IEEE Trans on Com 1581 (No 11, Nov 1	
Brown and Mason	Services for the emerging ISDN	IEEE ICC 19.2.1 (June 1981)	
Burtz	CCITT Activities in the Digital Revolution	1 IEEE ICC A.2.1 (Philadelphia 1982)	
Campagno, Coudreuse & DeJean	Packet Switching for Telephone Service	Echo Rech(F) 35 (No 102, Oct 1980)	F
Cerni	The CCITT:Organization, US Participation, and Studies Toward the ISDN	NTIA Rep No 82-101 (Apr 1982)	USA
Cerni & Grey	Standards in Process: Foundations and Profiles of ISDN and OSI Studies	NTIA Rep No 84-170 (Dec 1984)	USA
Chew & Duc	International telecommunication standards: issues and implications for the 80's	NTIA Spec Pub 83-15 (Jul 1983)	
Chin & Dingle	ISDN Customer Access	IREBCON '83, Sydney, Digest 452 (1983)	AUS
Chin & Dingle	An introduction to the ISDN user part of CCITT CCSS No 7	34 Telecom J of Austral 145 (No 2 1984)	AUS
Clost, Roche & Vomscheid	An overview of the ISDN user part of the CCSS No 7	TARL, Melbourne, Rep 7701 (1984)	AUS
Collie, Kayser & Rybczynski	Perspectives of Evolution Towards the Integrated Services Digital Network	2 IEEE ICC 31.5.1 (Philadelphia 1982)	F
Cooper	Looking at the ISDN interfaces: issues and answers	12 Data Communications 125 (No 6, 1983)	USA
Cornell & Stelte	Towards a Plan for the ISDN	IEEE NTC 5.4.1 (Houston 1980)	USA
Cunningham	Progress Towards Digital Subscriber Line Services and Signaling	29 IEEE Trans Com 1589 (No 11, Nov 1981)	
Decima, Montmurro & Villani	Transport Service Standardization, issues in OS	Pacific Telecom Conf (Jan 1980)	
	Prospects for Data Communication Handling in ISDN's	XVIII Cong Int Elettron (Rome Mar 1981)	I

Author	Title	Reference	Country
Decima & Parodi	Circuit and Packet Switched Data Communication in ISDN	Proc 5th Int'l Conf Comp Com (Oct 1980)	I
Decina	CCITT Activity on Signal Processing for ISDN	Int'l Conf Sig Proc 5 (Paris, May 1982)	USA
Decina	A European View of ISDN	MITRE ISDN Symp (Jan 1982)	USA
Decina & deJulio	Progress towards user acces arrangements in ISDN	COM-30 IEEE Trans 2117 (No 9, Sep 1982)	USA
DeFerra	Performance of Integrated Digital Networks: International Standards	1 IEEE ICC 2D.1.1 (Philadelphia 1982)	I
Devault, Quinquis & Renaud	Switching in Italy: Division Switching, Activities	Keynote IEEE ISS 27 (Montreal 1981)	F
Dewitt	Asynchronous Time Division Switching, a New Concept for ISDN Nodes	4 IEEE ISS 42B5 (Montreal 1981)	USA
Dewitt	Integrated Services Digital Network	USITA Expanded Serv Bull 1-82 (Feb 1982)	USA
Doherty	ISDN Progress by North American Carriers	MITRE ISDN Symp (Jan 1982)	USA
Dorros	MacDonald's is First Customer for Illinois Bell's ISDN Field Trial	Communications Week at 17 (29 Apr 1985)	USA
Dorros	ISDN:The Telecommunications Network Architecture of the Future	5 New Jersey Bell J 38 (Summer 1982)	USA
Dorros	Challenge and opportunity of the 1980s:the ISDN	200 Telephony 43 (No 4, Jan 26, 1981)	USA
Dorros	ISDN:A Challenge and Opportunity for the 80s	19 IEEE Com Mag 16 (No 2, Mar 1981)	USA
Dorros	The ISDN - A Challenge and Opportunity for the '80s	IEEE ICC (Denver 1981)	USA
Dorros	The ISDN and the Future Telecommunications Environment	Presented at ABA annual meeting (1981)	USA
Duc	Public network's role in shaping ISDN	ISDN'83 Monteray Ca Oct 10	AUS
Duc	ISDN local networks: an overview of CCITT studies and related topics	TARl, Melbourne, Rep 7554 (Sep 1982)	AUS
Duc & Chew	ISDN customer access standardization and related developments	TARl, Melbourne, Rep 7643 (May 1984)	AUS
Duc & Chew	Evolution towards integrated services digital networks	34 Telecom J of Austral 137 (No 2 1984)	AUS
Duc & Chew	ISDN: A unified approach to telecommunications	IRBECON '83, Sydney, Digest 440 (1983)	AUS
Elias	ISDN protocol architecture	TARl, Melbourne, Paper No 60	AUS
Etesse & Prigent	Range of Services of the Deutsche Bundespost w Spec Ref to Digital	Keynote IEEE ISS 27 (Montreal 1981)	F
Eward, et. al.	Experimental Introduction of a Local Integrated Telephone and Data Ne..	3 IEEE ICC 6A.3.1 (Philadelphia 1982)	F
Falconer & Shapiro	Integrated Services Digital Networks	Tobin Fdn Meeting (Leeds, Mar 1982)	USA
Falconer & Skrzypczak	Planning for the Bell System Switched Digital Network	Telecom Net Plan Conf, Paris (1980)	USA
Falconer & Powers	The Bell System-On Its Way to a Digital Network	59 Bell Lab Rec 138 (No 5, May 1981)	USA
Fellows & Hogg	At the crossroads: planning the telecommunicatioons network	61 Bell Lab Rec 4 (No 6, 1983)	CAN
Felts, Gifford & Gratzer	An Approach to the Design of an ISDN	IEEE NTC 5.3.1, (Houston 1980)	USA
Fisher	Bell's concept of the ISDN	Telephony (25 Oct 1982) 42	USA
Fleckenstein	Integrated Digital Communications Networking	Keynote IEEE ISS 56 (Montreal 1981)	USA
Forster	Switching Technology and New Network Services	85 Telee Eng & Mgnt 68 (No 11, Jun 1981)	USA
Frank	Evolving Structure of Worldwide Telecommunications Networks	J of Telecom Networks 47 (1984)	USA
Frieden	Legal and Policy Ramifications of the Emerging [ISDN]	6 MIS Week at 20 (No 9, 27 Feb 1985)	FRG
Fuchs	Northern Telecom crows abouts its ISDN plans	15 Telecommunicat 49 (No 10, Oct 1981)	FRG
Gabler	Integrating Domestic Corporate Systems into International	1 IEEE ICC 2C.4.1 (Philadelphia 1982)	FRG
Gerke	Data and Text Communication in the Federal Republic of Germany	76 Telektronikk (NOR) 396 (No 4, 1980)	FRG
Gerke	Telecommunication Services in the Future ISDN	4th Eur Conf on Elec, Stuttga (Mar 1980)	USA
Gifford	ISDN as a Basis for Combined Telecommunication	4 IEEE ISS 42B1 (Montreal 1981)	USA
Gifford	Possibilities for the Introduction of an Integrated Services Digital ..	IEEE ICC 6A.6.1 (Philadelphia 1982)	J
Gotoh & Itoh	The User Perpsective of ISDN3	MITRE ISDN Symp (Jan 1982)	F
Guenin, Ghillebaert, et. al.	The Role of Standards in ISDN Development and Impact of New Technolo..	IEEE NTC, Houston (Dec 1980)	I
Guenin, Lucas & Montaudoin	Design Concepts of a Digital Switching System for Higher Performance	4 IEEE ISS 42C2 (Montreal 1981)	USA
Gussganger, et. al.	Satellite Systems:A Means Towards ISDN	IEEE ICC 19.5.1 (1981)	CAN
Habara	The role of satellites in achieving ISDN	Proc Int'l Zurich-Seminar A61 (197	J
Hall	Experimental System of an Integrated Communication Network with Glass..	Meeting, ITU World Plan Com (Apr 1981)	J
Handler	Strategic Planning for the ISDN	IEEE Trans Com COM-27 at 1144 (Jul 1979)	FRG
Harvey & Barry	Digital switching-forces which shape its future	3 IEEE ICC 6A.5.1 (Philadelphia 1982)	FRG
Hoberecht & Srinivas	Circuit Switched Digital Capability	IEEE ICC (Denver 1981)	USA
Iimura, Tachikawa, et. al.	Evolution and Exploitation of Bell Canada's Integrated Digital Network	GLOBCOM '82 Proc 739, Miami (Nov 1982)	CAN
Ikeda & Mori	Approaches to User Interconnection Reference Models for ISDN Communic..	IEEE NTC 521, Houston (Dec 1980)	J
Irmer	A Comprehensive Study on an ISDN in Japan	3 IEEE ISS 757 (1979)	J
Irmer	Circuit Switching System:A New Concept for Telephone and Data Integra..	NTT Int'l Symp Proc 39, Tokyo (Feb 1983)	FRG
Irmer	Worldwide trends towards the ISDN	Int Sw Symp, Montreal (Sep 1981)	FRG
	The International Approach to the ISDN-Facts and Trends	Pres at NTT Symp, Tokyo (Feb 1983)	FRG
	The International Approach to the ISDN-Facts and Trends		

Author	Title	Citation		
Irmer	The International Approach to the ISDN	49 Telecom J 411 (Jul 1982)	FRG	J
Isozaki, Matsuoka & Kitamura	Outline of Captain System and Study on Future System Utilizing Digit..	1 IEEE ICC 2		J
Ito, Kimashiro & Hasegawa	A New Approach to Integrated Service Communication Systems	IEEE NTC, Houston (Dec 1980)		F
Jacob & Nuttall	The E10B Digital Switching System:Towards the ISDN	4 IEEE ISS 14A3 (Montreal 1981)		
Johnson, Varma & Waninski	Network Operations Planning for the Bell System	1 IEEE ICC 1D.1.1 (Philadelphia 1982)	USA	
Kaczmarcyk	Illinois Bell to debut ISDN trial with AT&T 5 ESS switch	do. at 27		
Kahl	A Concept of the Digital Local Network	IEEE NTC 551, Houston (Dec 1980)	HOL	
Kano, Kitami, et. al.	ISDN User/Network Interface Protocol-Overall Architecture	D22 GLOBECOM '82, Miami (Nov 1982)	J	
Kelcourse & Siegel	Switched Digital Capability: An Overview	2 IEEE ICC 3D.1.1 (Philadelphia 1982)	USA	
Keller	Fujitsu Talking with BOCs about [ISDN] market potential in U.S.	Communications Week 2 (11 Mar 1985)		
Kelly	Trends in European Non-Voice Networks	7 Commun Int (UK) 25 (No 12, Dec 1980)	UK	
Kenedi	Plotting a Strategy for the Emergine ISDN	200 Telephony 22 (No 25, Jun 22, 1981)	CAN	
Kithara	Telecommunications in the New Decade	IEEE NTC (Houston Dec 1980)	J	
Kithara	INS — Telecommunications towards the advanced information society	Pres at NTT symp, Tokyo (Feb 1983)		
Kliem, Burmeister, et. al.	Line Concentrators for an Experimental Digital Wideband Network	4 IEEE ISS 42C1 (Montreal 1981)	FRG	
Kneisel	Goals and Strategies for Intro of Broadband Optic Syst in Bundespost Nets	3 IEEE ICC 4D.1.1 (Philadelphia 1982)	FRG	
Kobayashi	Communications and Computers: An Inevitable "Marriage"	198 Telephony 78 (Vol 4, Jan 28, 1980)	J	
Kostas	Transition to ISDN-An Overview	11	USA	
Kundig	New International Standards for Data Transmion	58 Tech Mitt PTT (SUI) 311 (No 9, 1980)	SUI	
Kundig	Data Networks-A Swiss Perspective	71 Bul Asoc Sui E1 793 (No 15, Aug 1980)	SUI	
Kundig	Strategy for Introduction of Digital IFS Communication System into Sw..	3 IEEE ICC 6A.2.1 (Philadelphia 1982)	SUI	
Langseth	Evolution of ISDN Services	MITRE ISDN Symp (Jan 1982)	USA	
Lannion	Data and Telephony Integrated Network	CNET Internal Report [undated]	F	
Latin & Slatter	Towards Multi-Service Terminal and the Digital Network	200 Telephony 72 (No 21, May 25, 1981)	USA	
Leth & Srinivas	Experimental Customer Signaling Interface for Integrated Voice & Dat..	1 IEEE ICC 2C.2.1 (Philadelphia 1982)		
Leth & White	A Level 3 Signaling Architecture for ISDN Subscriber Access	GLOBECOM '82 at 762, Miami (Nov 1982)	USA	
LeRoux & Lucas	Evolution of Subscriber Equipment in an ISDN Context	3 IEEE ICC 3I.4.2 (Philadelphia 1982)	F	
Lucas	World Developments in Electronic Switching:Report of the XIth ISS, Florence, 84	6 Commutat & Transmis (No 4, Dec 1984)		
Lueder	Communication Services and Subscriber Terminal Technology in the ISDN	3 Telcom Rep (D) 228 (No 4, Dec 1980)	FRG	
Mantelman	AT&T's ISDN begins its earthly descent	Data Communications at 45 (May 1985)		
Marsh	ISDN evolution possibilities in hte United States	J Telecommun Networks at 107 (1982)		
Martel & Fung	Protocol Evolution Towards a Multipurpose Interface	4 IEEE ISS 34B1 (Montreal 1981)	CAN	
Matsuda	A Traffic Estimation Method Reflecting Network Topology	3 IEEE ICC 4C.3.1 (Philadelphia 1982)	J	
Matt & Fussganger	Integrated Broadband Communication Using Optical Networks	29 IEEE Trans Comm 868 (No 6, Jun 1981)	FRG	
McDonald	ISDN-81:Views by Manufacturers	IEEE ICC 17.2.1 (Denver 1981)	USA	
MacDonald	issues in CCIRR Digital Studies for '984	1 IEEE ICC 1A.1.1 (Philadelphia 1982)	CAN	
Meyer & Sastry	Performance analysis of tandem burst error links with applications to ISDN	IEEE/NBS Comp Net Sym, Wash DC (Dec 1983)	USA	
Meyers	ISDN 81 Report	200 Telephony 44 (No 4, Jan 26, 1981)	POL	
Michna	Trends in Development of BIU Systems (Elec Telephone Exchanges)	53 Zegl Telekom(POL) 337 (No 10, 1980)	J	
Mijioka, et. al.	HDXIO Full-Digital Switching System:Architecture and Technology	4 IEEE ISS 13A4 (Montreal 1981)	I	
Montemurro & Villani	Integrated Text-Communication Serviced Digital Networks	Fondazione Ugo Bordoni, Rome (1980)	I	
Montemurro & Villani	Evolution Towards Local Digital Integrated Networks	28 Note Recens (I) 209 (No 2, Apr 1979)	I	
Montemurro & Villani	Integration of the Procedure of Access to a Multiple Service Integra..	29 Note Recens (I) 119 (No 3, Jul 1980)	I	
Montemurro & Villani	Implementation of a New Digital Telephone/Data Subset	3 IEEE ISS 926 (1979)	I	
Montemurro & Villani	Customer Access to ISDNs	IEEE NTC, Houston (Dec 1980)	I	
Moore, Whall	Customer Access to the ISDN Facilities	4 IEEE ISS 42B6 (Montreal 1981)	U4	
Mossotto & DiPino	ISDN Customer to Network Signaling-D-Channel Protocol Level 1 Aspects	D23 GLOBECOM '82, Miami (Nov 1982)	I	
Ohnsorge	The Role of Signalling and Protocols in the Emerging ISDN	IEEE ICC 19.3.1 (Denver 1981)	FRG	
Okada, Yusa, Okimi & Harada	Success, Goals and Limits of Very High Capacity Fibre Optic Systems	3 IEEE ICC 6D.2.1 (Philadelphia 1982)	J	
Oliver & Orbell	Evolution strategy of digital transmion network	IEEE ICC 71.2.1 (June 1981)	UK	
Parodi, DiPino & Musumeci	System Evolution-Integrated Services Networks	4 IEEE ISS 41B1 (Montreal 1981)	I	
Partridge	Evolutionary Steps Towards an Integrated Services Digital Network	4 IEEE ISS 42B2 (Montreal 1981)	UK	
Plank	UK Experience in planning and evolving towards a multi-service digit..	Int'l Stand Sem, Melbourne (May 1983)	FRG	
Robin & Grandjean	Integration of Telematique Services in a Digital Switching System	4 IEEE ISS 41A5 (Montreal 1981)	F	

APPENDIX B

SECTION 1

VOCABULARY OF TERMS FOR ISDNs*

*Unless otherwise indicated, the terms are contained in CCITT Rec. I.112 (Red Book, 1985). The terms divided into five categories: 1. General; 2. Services; 3. Networks; 4. Access; 5. Signalling. Paragraph numbers are those indicated in I.112. Those with a "G" paragraph identification are contained in the G.112 supplemental glossary. Those with an "E" are contained in the annex to Rec. I.331 (E. 164).

INDEX

1. GENERAL

101 **Communication.** The transfer of information according to agreed conventions. *Note*: In French and Spanish the corresponding terms "communication" and "communicacion" have additional specific meanings in telecommunication.

102 **Signal.** A physical phenomenon one or more of whose characteristics may vary to represent information. (1001)

103 **Analogue signal.** A signal whose characteristic quantities continuously follow the variations of another physical quantity representing information.

104 **Discretely-timed signal.** A signal composed of successive elements in time, each element having one or more characteristics which can convey information, for example, its duration, its waveform, and its amplitude. (1003)

105 **Digital signal.** A discretely-timed signal in which information is represented by a number of well-defined discrete values that one of its characteristic quantities may take in time. (2006) *Note*: The term may be qualified to indicate the digit rate, for example: "140 Mbit/s digital signal".

106 **Transmission.** The action of conveying signals from one point to one or more other points. (1004) *Note 1*: Transmission can be effected directly or indirectly, with or without intermediate storage. *Note 2*: The use of the English word "transmission" in the sense of "emission" is deprecated.

112 **Digital circuit, digital telecommunication circuit.** A combination of two digital transmission channels permitting bidirectional digital transmission of signals between two points, to support a single

channel providing the facility. *Note 2*: In a telecommunication network, use of the term "digital circuit" is generally limited to a digital telecommunication circuit directly connecting two switching devices or exchanges, together with associated terminating equipment. *Note 3*: A digital telecommunication circuit may permit transmission in both directions simultaneously (duplex) or not simultaneously (simplex). *Note 4*: A digital telecommunication circuit that permits transmission in one direction only is referred to as an unidirectional digital telecommunication circuit. A digital telecommunication circuit that permits transmission in both directions (whether simultaneously or not) is referred to as a bidirectional digital telecommunication circuit. (3003)

113 **Switching**. The process of interconnecting functional units, transmission channels or telecommunication circuits for as long as is required to convey signals.

114 **Digital switching**. Switching by means that may assume in time any one of a defined set of discrete signal states, in order to convey digital signals.

115 **Exchange**. An aggregate of traffic carrying devices, switching stages, controlling and signalling means, and other functional units at a network node that enables subscriber lines, telecommunication circuits, or other functional units to be interconnected as required by individual users.

116 **Digital exchange**. An exchange that switches digital signals by means of digital switching.

117 **Integrated digital transmission and switching**. The direct (digital) concatenation of digital transmission and digital switching, that maintains a continuous digital transmission path.

2. SERVICES

201 **Service, telecommunication service**. That which is offered by an administration or RPOA to its customers in order to satisfy a specific telecommunication requirement. *Note*: Bearer service and teleservice are types of telecommunication service. Other types of telecommunication service may be identified in the future.

202 **Bearer service**. A type of telecommunication service that provides the capability for the transmission of signals between user-network interfaces. *Note*: The ISDN connection type used to support a bearer service may be identical to that used to support other types of telecommunication service.

203   **Teleservice** [*telecommunication service*]. A type of telecommunication service that provides the complete capability, including terminal equipment functions, for communication between users according to protocols established by agreement between administrations or RPOAs.

204   **Teleaction service** *[telemetry service]*. A type of telecommunication service that uses short messages, requiring a very low transmission rate, between the user and the network. *Note*: Examples of teleaction services are: telealarm, telecommand, telealerting.

205   **Demand service, demand telecommunication service**. A type of telecommunication service in which the communication path is established almost immediately, in response to a user request effected by means of user-network signalling.

206   **Reserved circuit service, reserved circuit telecommunication service**. A type of telecommunication service in which the communication path is established at a time specified in advance by the user, in response to a user request effected by means of user-network signalling. *Note*: The duration of the communication, or the time of release of the communication path, may also be specified in advance by the user.

207   **Permanent circuit service, permanent circuit telecommunication service**. A type of telecommunication service in which the communication path is established in response to a customer request effected by means of an operational or administrative message. *Note*: Release of the communication path is effected in a similar way to its establishment.

208   **Service attribute, telecommunication service attribute**. A specified characteristic of a telecommunication service. *Note*: The value(s) assigned to one or more service attributes may be use to distinguish that telecommunication service from others.

3.   **NETWORKS**

301   **Link, transmission link**. A means of transmission with specified characteristics between two points. *Note*: The type of the transmission path or the capacity is normally indicated, e.g., radio link, coaxial link, or 2048 kbit/s link.

302   **Digital link, digital transmission link.** The whole of the means of digital transmission of specified rate between two digital distribution frames (or equivalent). *Note 1*: A digital link comprises one or more digital sections and may include multiplexing or demultiplexing, but

not switching. *Note 2*: The term may be qualified to indicate the transmission medium used, for example: "digital satellite link". *Note 3*: The term always applies to the combination of "go" and "return" directions of transmission, unless stated to otherwise. *Note 4*: The term "digital path" is sometimes used to describe one or more digital links connected in tandem, especially between equipments at which the signals of the specified rate originate and terminate. (3005)

303   **Node, switching node**. A point at which switching occurs. *Note*: The term "node" is sometimes used to refer to a point at which circuits are interconnected by means other than switching. In such a case, a suitable qualification should be used, for example: "synchronization node".

304   **Digital switching node**. A node at which digital switching occurs.

305   **Network, telecommunication network**. A set of nodes and links that provides connections between two or more defined points to facilitate telecommunication between them.

306   **Digital network, integrated digital network**. A set of digital nodes and digital links that uses integrated transmission and switching to provide digital connections between two or more defined points to facilitate telecommunication between them.

307   **Integrated services network**. A network that provides or supports a range of different telecommunication services.

308   **Integrated services digital network (ISDN)**. An integrated services network that provides digital connections between user-network interfaces.

309   **Connection**. A concatenation of transmission channels or telecommunication circuits, switching and other functional units set up to provide for the transfer of signals between two or more points in a telecommunication network, to support a single communication.

310   **Digital connection**. A concatenation of digital transmission channels or digital telecommunication circuits, switching and other functional units set up to provide for the transfer of digital signals between two or more points in a telecommunication network, to support a single communication.

311   **Switched connection**. A connection that is established by means of switching. *Note*: A switched connection may be used to support both demand and reserved circuit services.

312   **Non-switched connection**. A connection that is established without the use of switching, for example by means of hard-wired joints.

313   **Exchange connection**. A connection that is established through an exchange, between the terminations on that exchange, or two or more channels or circuits.

314   **ISDN connection**. A connection that is established through an ISDN between specified ISDN interfaces.

315   **Connection attribute, ISDN connection attribute**. A specified characteristic of an ISDN connection. *Note*: The value(s) assigned to one or more connection attributes may be used to distinguish that connection from others.

316   **Connection type, ISDN connection type**. A description of a set of ISDN connections that consists of stated values of one or more ISDN connection attributes.

317   **Connection element, ISDN connection element**. A part of an ISDN connection which part has stated values of one or more ISDN connection attributes.

318   **Switched connection element, switched ISDN connection element**. An ISDN connection element that is established by means of switching.

319   **Non-switched connection element, non-switched ISDN connection element**. An ISDN connection element that is established without switching.

320   **Point-to-point ISDN connection**. An ISDN connection that is established between two specified ISDN interfaces.

321   **Point-to-multipoint ISDN connection**. An ISDN connection that is established between a single specified ISDN interface, and more than one other specified ISDN interface. (3618)

4.   **ACCESS**

401   **User, user of a telecommunication network**. A person or machine delegated by a customer to use the services or facilities of a telecommunication network.

402   **User access, user-network access**. The means by which a user is connected to a telecommunication network in order to use the services or facilities of that network.

403   **Function**. A set of processes defined for the purpose of achieving a specified objective.

404   **Layer**. A conceptual region that embodies one or more functions between an upper and a lower logical boundary within a hierarchy of functions. *Note*: The Open Systems Interconnection (OSI) reference model has seven layers.

405   **Protocol**. A formal statement of the procedures that are adopted to ensure communication between two or more functions within the same layer of a hierarchy of functions.

406   **Access protocol**. A defined set of procedures that is adopted at an interface at a specified reference point between a user and a network to enable the user to employ the services or facilities of that network.

407   **User-user protocol**. A protocol that is adopted between two or more users in order to ensure communication between them.

408   **Interface** (1008). The common boundary between two associated systems.

409   **User-network interface**. The interface between the terminal equipment and a network termination at which interface the access protocols apply.

410   **Layer interface**. The interface between adjacent layers of a hierarchy of layers.

411   **Physical interface**. The interface between two equipments.

412   **Interface specification**. A formal statement of the type, quantity, form and order of the interconnections and interactions between two associated systems, at their interface.

413   **Physical interface specification** [*physical interface*]. A formal statement of the mechanical, electrical, electromagnetic and optical characteristics of the interconnections and the interactions between two associated equipments, at their interface.

414   **Channel (2), access channel**. A designated part, having specified characteristics, of the information transfer capability at the user-network interface. *Note 1*: The information transfer may be, and usually is, bidirectional. *Note 2*: See also term 108, transmission channel.

415   **Interface structure, ISDN user-network interface structure**. The number and type of the access channels that appear at an ISDN user-network interface.

416   **Access capability, ISDN access capability**. The number and type of the access channels at an ISDN access interface that are usually available for telecommunication purposes.

417   **Terminal equipment**. Equipment that provides the functions necessary for the operation of the access protocols by the user.

418   **Network termination**. Equipment that provides the functions necessary for the operation of the access protocols by the network. *Note*: The network termination provides essential functions for transmission purposes.

419   **Functional group** [*functional grouping*]. A set of functions that may be performed by a single equipment.

420   **Reference point**. A conceptual point at the conjunction of two nonoverlapping functional groups.

421   **Reference configuration**. A combination of functional groups and reference points that shows possible network arrangements.

422   **Multipoint access**. User access in which more than one terminal equipment is supported by a single network termination.

423   **Access contention**. A conflict between the demands made on a network termination in multipoint access.

424   **Access contention resolution**. The arbitration of conflicting demands on a network termination in multipoint access.

5.   **Signalling**

501   **Signalling**. The exchange of information specifically concerned with the establishment and control of connections, and with management, in a telecommunication network.

502   **Channel-associated signalling**. A method of signalling in which signalling information relating to the traffic carried by a single channel is transmitted in the channel itself or in a signalling channel permanently associated with it.

503   **Common channel signalling**. A method of signalling in which signalling information relating to a multiplicity of circuits or functions or for network management, is conveyed over a single channel by addressed messages.

504   **In-slot signalling**. Signalling associated with a channel and transmitted in a digit time-slot permanently (or periodically) allocated in the channel time-slot.

505   **Out-slot signalling**. Signalling associated with a channel and transmitted in one or more separate digit time-slots not within the channel time-slot.

506   **Speech digit signalling**. A type of channel-associated signalling in which digit time-slots primarily used for the transmission of encoded speech are periodically used for signalling.

SUPPLEMENTAL GLOSSARY

E   **Address** [*in network addressing*]. The information which is necessary to identify a point in the subscriber's installation (group of terminals, terminal or specific function of terminal equipment). The point unambiguously defines: 1. a port where the information flow of the connection concerned prasses in outgoing or incoming direction, or 2. the point of origin or destination for the information flow, e.g., NSAP (Rec. X.200). (*See* Rec. I.331 Annex)

E   **Address delimiter**. A coded character which indicates different parts in an address, e.g., beginning of a number of address, end of address, *et cetera*. (*See* Rec. I.331 Annex)

E   **Addressing** [*network addressing*]. The provision of the address by allocation or indication of a number and possibly one or more non-numeric characters. (*See* Rec. I.331 Annex)

G   **Addressing**. The process by which a calling user indicates the identity of the called user on a particular call. It includes a network addressing (numbering) component to identify the called user-network interface, and may also include further information (sub-address) to identify a particular terminal beyond the public network. (*See* Rec. I.330)

G   **Basic access**. A term used to describe a simple standardization combination of access channels that constitute the access arrangements for the majority of ISDN users. (*See* I.400-series Recs.)

G   **Network architecture functional model**. A representation of the functions of a network (in this case an ISDN) as seen at the user-network interface. These functions are normally characterized in terms of protocols, performance, *et cetera*. (*See* Rec. I.32x)

G   **Higher layer functions**. Functions in layers 4 to 7 of the open systems interconnection (OSI) protocol reference model. They usually relate to information storage, processing, or message facilities. Capabilities necessary to support these functions are normally provided within the user terminals, but the network may contain the physical entities necessary to provide the functions. (*See* Rec. I.320)

E   **International prefix**. The combination of digits to be dialed by a calling subscriber making a call to a subscriber in another country, to obtain access to the automatic outgoing international equipment. (*See* Rec. I.331 Annex)

E   **International number**. The number to be dialed following the international prefix to obtain a subscriber in another country. (*See* Rec. I.331 Annex)

G   **Link access protocol (LAP)**. The formal set of procedures applied at the user-network interface to convey information between the corresponding layer 2 entities of the user and of the network. These procedures are within layer 2 of the OSI model.

G   **Lower layer functions**. Functions in layers 1 to 3 of the OSI model. They are concerned mainly with the establishment, holding and release of a telecommunication path. (*See* Rec. I.320)

E   **National Destination Code (NDC)**. A code field, which combined with the Subscriber's Number (SN), will constitute the National (Significant) Number of the International ISDN Number. The NDC will have a network or Trunk Code Selection Function. The NDC can be a decimal digit or a combination of decimal digits (not including any prefix) characterizing a numbering area with a country (or group of countries included in one integrated numbering plan). The NDC has to be inserted before the called subscriber's number when the calling and called parties are located in different numbering areas, NDC assignments are a national responsibility and therefore the NDC structure varies from one country (or geographical area) to another. It may take a trunk code format in accordance with Rec. E.160, or serve for selection of a destination network. The NDC can, in some instances, provide a combination of both the above actions. (*See* Rec. I.331 Annex)

E   **National** [*significant number*]. The number to be dialed following the trunk prefix to obtain a subscriber in the same country (or group of countries, included in one integrated number plan) but outside the same local network or numbering area. (*See* Rec. I.331 Annex)

G   **Numbering**. The assignment of unique identities to a user-network interface. (*See* Rec. I.330)

G   **Open systems interconnection (OSI)**. A concept in which the relationships between a network and the services which it can support are shown by a hierarchy of protocol layers. Each layer contains one or more functions contained between an upper and a lower logical boundary. Each layer uses the services of the lower layers in conjunction with its own functions to create new services which are made available to the higher layers. The following designations are a brief summary of the layers of the model:

Layer 1 (Physical)	Includes transmission of signals and the activation and deactivation of physical connections.
Layer 2 (Link)	Includes synchronization and some control over the influence of error within the physical layer.
Layer 3 (Network)	Includes routing and switching functions.
Layer 4 (Transport)	Uses layers 1 to 3 to provide an end-to-end service with the required characteristics for the higher layer functions.
Layer 5 (Session)	Allows presentation entities to organize and synchronize their dialogue and to manage their data exchange.
Layer 6 (Presentation)	Includes data formatting and code conversion.
Layer 7 (Application)	Provides the means by which the user programs access the OSI environment and may contain part of these user programs.

G   **Protocol reference model**. A conceptual arrangement of the functions comprising protocols. The OSI model is an example of a protocol reference model. (*See* Recs. I.320, X.200)

E   **Single stage selection** [*special prefix, or national Destination Code method*]. An interworking method where the information provided includes a code indicating that conventions for the codes it precedes are other than those defined for the ISDN numbering scheme. (*See* Rec. I.331 Annex)

E   **Subaddress** [*network address extension*]. Part of an address, for example, which identifies to the subscriber's terminal equipment a point in the subscriber's installation (group of terminals, terminal or specific function of terminal equipment). The sub-address is agreed by the calling and called party and transferred by the network. However, sub-address information is not processed by the public network. (*See* Rec. I.331 Annex)

G   **Subaddressing**. An expansion of addressing to identify individual users, processes, or groups of users within a larger group of users or processes that are identified by a single network number.

E   **Subscriber number**. The number to be dialed or called to reach a subscriber in the same local network or numbering area. This number is the one usually listed in the directory against the name of the subscriber. (*See* Rec. I.331 Annex)

G   **Terminal**. An equipment, located in close proximity to the user which presents to the user the information received from the network in a form compatible with the user's requirements and performs also the complementary function from the user to the network.

G   **Test loop**. A mechanism incorporated into a terminal or into the network whereby the transmit path of a communication may be connected back upon the receive path. Such a loop may be activated either by the user or by the network, and may take the form of an electrical connection (physical loop) or the repetition of a sequence of digits (logical loop).

E   **Trunk code**. A digit or combination of digits (not including the trunk prefix) characterizing the called numbering area within a country (or group of countries, included in one integrated numbering plan). (*See* Rec. I.331 Annex)

E   **Two-stage selection**. An interworking method whereby an address in the originating ISDN network is used to access an Interworking Unit (IWO) which is a point of an exit (outlet) or an entry (inlet) to another network. A second stage of selection is then used to indicated the address in the destination network. (*See* Rec. I.331 Annex)

APPENDIX B — SECTION 2

ACRONYMS AND ABBREVIATIONS RELATED TO ISDN ISSUES AND DEVELOPMENTS

ACE	Application connection element
AHLF	Additional high layer functions
ALLF	Additional low layer functions
ANSC	American National Standards Committee
ANSI	American National Standards Institute
APP	Application connection component
ATT	American Telephone and Telegraph Company
BCC	Bearer connection component
BHLF	Basic higher layer functions
BLLF	Basic low layer functions
BNR	Bell Northern Research
BOC	Bell Operating Company
BT	British Telecom
BTI	British Telecom International
CCF	Connection control function
CCITT	International Telegraph and Telephone Consultative Committee
CCIR	International Radio Consultative Committee
CCIS	Common channel interoffice signalling
CCS	Common channel signalling
CEPT	European Conference of Post and Telecommunication Admistrations
COM	Committee
CPE	Customer premises equipment
CRF	Connection-related functions
CSU	Channel service unit
CT	Customer terminal
DBPX	Digital private branch exchange
DNIC	Data Network Identification Code
DOC	Department of Commerce (US)
DOD	Department of Defense (US)
DOJ	Department of Justice (US)
DOS	Department of State (US)
ECMA	European Computer Manufacters Association
ECSA	Exchange Carriers Standards Association
EIA	Electronics Industry Association
ET	Exchange termination interface
FAX	Facsimile
FCC	Federal Communications Commission
FRG	Federal Republic of Germany
FTSC	Federal Telecommunications Standards Committee
HLF	High layer functions
HRX	Hypothetical reference circuit
IBM	International Business Machines Corp.
ICC	International Communications Conference
IEC	International Electrotechnical Commission
IEEE	Institute of Electrical and Electronic Engineers
IFIP	International Federation on Information Processing
IRC	International Record Carrier
IRU	Indefeasible right of use
ISDN	Integrated services digital network
ISO	International Organization for Standardization
ISS	International Switching Symposium
ITU	International Telecommunication Union
IWP	Interim Working Party
JWP	Joint Working Party
k	kilo (1 000)
KDD	Kokusai Denshin Denwa Co., Ltd (Japan)

LADT	Local Area Data Transport
LAN	Local area network
LAP	Link access protocol
LATA	Local Access and Transport Area
LLF	Lower Layer Functions
LT	Line termination
M	Mega (1 000 000)
MFJ	Modified Final Judgment
MPT	Ministry of Posts and Telecommunication
MTS	Message telephone service
MUX	Multiplexing
NC	National Committee
NCTE	Network channel terminating equipment
NECA	National Exchange Carriers Association
NET	Network
NOI	Notice of Inquiry
NPRM	Notice of Proposed Rule Making
NT1	Network termination interface 1
NT2	Network termination interface 2
NTIA	National Telecommunications and Information Administration
NTT	Nippon Telegraph and Telephone
OAM	Operational, administrative and maintenance
OCC	Other common carrier
OSI	Open systems interconnection
PBX	Private branch exchange
PAD	Packet assembler/disassembler
PCM	Pulse code modulation
POTS	Plain old telephone service
PSN	Packet switched network
PSTN	Public switched telephone network
PTT	Post and Telecommunications Ministry
R&O	Report and Order
RBOC	Regional Bell Operating Company
RDI	Restricted digital information
RPOA	Recognized Private Operating Agency
SCC	Specialized common carrier
SCP	Stored program controlled
SG	Study Group
SIO	Scientific and industrial organization
SP	Signalling point
SS	Signalling system
SS7	Signalling System No. 7
STP	Signalling transfer point
TA	Terminal adaptor
TC	Technical Committee
TCC	Telephone country code
TCE	Transportation connection element
TE	Termination equipment
UDI	Unrestricted digital information
USSG	United States Study Group
VAN	Value added network
VLSI	Very large scale integration
WATS	Wide area telephone service
WATTC	World Administrative Telegraph and Telephone Conference
WP	Working Party
WT	Working Team

Note: See also Table 8-1 for a listing of acronyms associated
with US parties to the FCC's ISDN proceeding.

INDEX